Understanding Abnormal Psychology

Basic Psychology

This series offers those new to the study of psychology comprehensive, systematic and accessible introductions to the core areas of the subject. Written by specialists in their fields, they are designed to convey something of the flavour and excitement of psychological research today.

Understanding Children's Development
Third Edition
Peter K. Smith and Helen Cowie

Understanding Neuropsychology
J. Graham Beaumont

Understanding Cognition
Peter J. Hampson and Peter E. Morris

Understanding Abnormal Psychology
Neil Frude

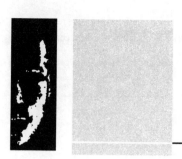

Understanding
Abnormal Psychology

Neil Frude
University of Wales, Cardiff

Clinical Research Tutor, South Wales
Clinical Psychology Training Course

Consultant Clinical Psychologist

BLACKWELL
Publishers

First published 1998
Reprinted 2000, 2002

Blackwell Publishers Ltd
108 Cowley Road
Oxford OX4 1JF
UK

Blackwell Publishers Inc.
350 Main Street
Malden, Massachusetts 02148
USA

British Library Cataloguing in Publication Data

A CIP catalogue record for this book is available from the British Library.

Library of Congress Cataloging-in-Publication Data
Frude, Neil.
   Understanding abnormal psychology / Neil Frude.
       p.   cm.– (Basic psychology)
   Includes bibliographical references and index.
   ISBN 0–631–16194–5 (alk. paper) – ISBN 0–631–16195–3 (pbk.: alk. paper)
   1. Psychology, Pathological.   I. Title.   II. Series: Basic psychology (Oxford, England)
RC454.F78   1998
616.89–dc21   97–16962
                                                                                                            CIP

Typeset in 10 on 12pt Palatino
by Best-set Typesetter Ltd, Hong Kong
Printed in Great Britain by Athenaeum Press Ltd, Gateshead, Tyne & Wear
This book is printed on acid-free paper.

Contents

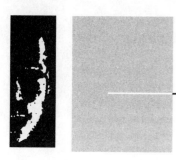

Acknowledgements

The author and publishers would like to thank Dr Gavin Phillips at the University of York for his editorial work on this volume.

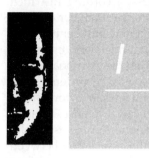

Introduction

Various forms of madness have been recognized throughout history, and in every culture, and a multitude of theories and myths have been devised to account for such conditions. Madness has been attributed to the influence of supernatural forces, the anger of the gods, the influence of the moon, an unbalanced temperament, 'bad blood' (i.e. hereditary factors) and licentiousness. And those who have exhibited flagrant signs of psychological disorder have been variously ostracized, revered, laughed at, feared and pitied.

It is possible to distinguish between three views of the nature of abnormal psychological conditions: 'the supernatural view', 'the somatogenic view' and 'the psychogenic view'. Supernatural accounts focused on the idea of possession by evil spirits, which was prevalent at various times within Chinese, Egyptian, Greek and Hebrew cultures. There are, for example, several biblical accounts of the casting out of devils as a means of curing people with 'an unclean spirit'.

The supernatural view was strongly challenged by Hippocrates, the fifth century BC Greek physician, who maintained that madness resulted from a somatic ('bodily') disturbance. His somatogenic account distinguished between several different forms of madness, including paranoia and melancholia (depression), and Hippocrates believed that they all reflected some kind of brain pathology. He suggested that the healthy functioning of the brain depended on a balance being maintained between four vital fluids (or 'humours'), namely blood, phlegm, black bile and yellow bile. An excess or deficiency in any of these fluids, Hippocrates claimed, gave rise to various types of psychological disturbance.

Supernatural explanations were almost completely supplanted by somatogenic accounts by the eighteenth century, although there had long been adherents of the psychogenic view of madness, according to which psychological disturbances are essentially reactions to traumatic or disturbing experiences. And then, towards the end of the nineteenth century, the psychogenic view was given a powerful new impetus, and a very distinctive slant, by the emergence of what is now recognized as psychoanalysis. Sigmund Freud (1856–1939) suggested that psychological disorders reflect emotional pressures resulting from the action of unconscious forces. He emphasized the importance of unconscious anxiety and defences against anxiety, and considered that an infant's early experiences were especially important in shaping personality. He also stressed the association between personality and the emergence of psychological disorders. Freud's writings inspired a movement which dominated thinking for over half a century. However, Freud had started his medical career as a neurologist and never lost sight of somatic factors. His theory assumed the existence of powerful biological drives and he often expressed the belief that the unconscious mechanisms he described would eventually be shown to have a neurobiological basis.

As psychology developed as an academic discipline, it was inevitable that contemporary thinking in the subject would influence ideas about psychological disorder. Psychoanalytic ideas were largely rejected, and the major emphasis was placed on studying behaviours which could be objectively observed and measured. Ivan Pavlov (1849–1936), the Russian physiologist, investigated the nature of reflexes, and demonstrated that it was possible to condition animals to become fearful of previously neutral objects. Later studies in learning, and particularly the influence of J.B. Watson (1878–1958) and B.F. Skinner (1904–90), contributed to the domination of behaviourist thinking in psychology, and this had a significant effect on how psychologists viewed abnormal behaviours. Over the past twenty years or so, both general psychology and abnormal psychology have paid considerably more attention to cognitive processes such as memory and judgement, and to the idea of people as active strategic agents who search for meaning and strive to cope with difficulties. There has also been an increased emphasis on the relevance of stressful experiences and social relationships. Contemporary psychogenic views of abnormal behaviours and experiences, however, generally acknowledge the importance of somatogenic factors.

◀'Normal' versus 'Abnormal' Behaviour and Experience▶▶▶

Although most people experience psychological problems from time to time, relatively few people will ever be diagnosed as suffering from a psychological disorder. While almost everyone occasionally feels 'down' or 'sad', such experiences are not usually so severe and so persistent that they would merit a clinical diagnosis of depression. And whereas 'normal' psychological symptoms are often 'understandable' and 'appropriate' reactions to life events, many psychological disorders are marked by behaviours and emotional states which appear unrelated to, or disproportionate to, environmental circumstances.

But although distinctions can be made between 'normal' and 'abnormal' behaviours and experiences, it is often impossible to tell on the basis of informal interaction with a person whether or not he or she is suffering from an abnormal psychological condition. This was demonstrated in an audacious study by Rosenhan (1973), in which he established that even mental health professionals may find it impossible, by means of normal observation and interaction, to distinguish between psychiatric patients and other people. In this classic study, eight subjects who were in good psychological health, including Rosenhan himself, presented themselves at various psychiatric hospitals and complained of hearing a voice saying the words 'empty', 'dull' and 'thud'. These 'pseudo-patients' did not report any other symptoms, but all were admitted to hospital, and seven of the eight were diagnosed as 'schizophrenic'. During their stay in the hospital the subjects behaved quite normally and began writing notes on what they observed. While some of the other patients concluded that the 'pseudo-patients' were journalists conducting a study of life in a mental hospital, several of the mental health professionals commented on the 'persistent writing' in their case reports, and interpreted this behaviour as symptomatic. On average, the pseudo-patients remained in the hospital for 19 days before they were discharged, and during that time none was detected as an 'impostor' by any member of the hospital staff. At the time of discharge, most were described as suffering from 'schizophrenia, in remission'.

Rosenhan's conclusion from his study was that once people are admitted to a mental hospital even their normal activities are likely to be viewed as abnormal, and they are not likely to be treated as capable human beings. In a further study, Rosenhan (1975) informed certain psychiatric hospitals that during the next three months one or more pseudo-patients would present themselves at the hospital. Staff at these hospitals were asked to try to 'spot the pseudo-patient' and to keep records of their suspicions. More than one-fifth of the patients admitted to these hospitals during the study period were identified as pseudo-patients by at least one staff member, and in a number of cases several health professionals agreed that a particular patient was in fact an impostor. However, all such designations were mistaken, because Rosenhan had in fact misled the hospital authorities and had not sent any pseudo-patients to any of the hospitals (Rosenhan, 1975).

◀ **What Is Abnormal Psychology?** ▶ ▶ ▶

'Psychology' can be defined as 'the study of behaviour and experience', and we might therefore expect 'abnormal psychology' to be defined simply as 'the study of abnormal behaviour and experience'. However, the field focuses on only *some* 'uncommon', 'atypical' and 'anomalous' psychological phenomena. Extreme violence, superb memory skills and extraordinary religious experiences, for example, are not central topics within the field of abnormal psychology. What, then, is the characteristic which differentiates those behaviours and experiences which are included within the field and those which are not?

The fact that abnormal psychology focuses on such disorders as depression, anxiety states and eating disorders suggests that the conditions included within the domain of abnormal psychology may all be 'distressing' to the person involved. Most of the states and conditions studied within 'abnormal psychology' are indeed very distressing, but exceptions can be found to this general rule. For example, people suffering from advanced dementia often appear contented or indifferent, while people experiencing a state of mania may feel deliriously happy. Furthermore, distressing and problematic behaviours and experiences, such as extreme violence, self-mutilation or chronic pain, are usually considered only if they occur in association with certain other abnormal psychological symptoms.

Another criterion which might be thought to characterize the conditions included within the abnormal psychology domain is that of 'disablement' (or 'impairment of functioning'). But while it is certainly the case that many people who suffer from a psychological disorder find it difficult to cope with normal life demands, this criterion also raises a number of problems. For one thing, disablement is often relative to circumstances. Thus a specific phobia may be disabling in one situation or cultural setting but not in another. A severe snake phobia would not prove disabling to someone living in a Western city, but might seriously incapacitate a person living in a tropical rainforest. Similarly, a fear of flying would not be experienced as a handicap by a person who never had any need or opportunity to fly, but would prove a severe obstacle for a person whose career progression depended on frequent international travel.

A final criterion which needs to be considered is that of organic pathology. Perhaps the defining characteristic of those states and disorders included within the realm of abnormal psychology is that they are all associated with some form of recognized biological damage or impairment. However, this criterion does not provide the demarcation we are seeking, for relatively few of the conditions studied within abnormal psychology are associated with any identifiable organic pathology.

The difficulties met in trying to identify a defining characteristic reflect the fact that abnormal psychology is a social construction which has evolved over time without a prescriptive and regulating definition. The discipline is greatly influenced by the work of practising professionals, including clinical psychologists and psychiatrists. Indeed, although the approach of abnormal psychology is different from that of the more clinically focused discipline of psychiatry, the states and conditions covered by the two disciplines are identical. Abnormal psychology 'shadows' psychiatry; the characteristic which decides whether a condition is included within abnormal psychology is simply whether it is recognized as a diagnostic category within orthodox psychiatry. Thus, in effect, abnormal psychology can be defined as the psychological study of psychiatric disorders. To map out the 'territory' of abnormal psychology, therefore, we need to consider the domain of psychiatry. This task is made easy by the fact that standard psychiatric classification systems exist.

◄Classification►►►

DSM-IV

The American Psychiatric Association's Diagnostic and Statistical Manual of Mental Disorders (DSM) was first published in 1952, and a revised version (DSM-II) appeared in 1968. This was followed by DSM-III (1980) and DSM-III-R (1987). The current version (DSM-IV) was published in 1994. The other major system currently in wide use is ICD – the International Classification of Disease, produced by the World Health Organization. The latest version of this is ICD-10 (1992). Although we will focus on the DSM system, it should be noted that, in their latest versions, the two systems have become very similar.

The earliest versions of DSM were influenced to a significant degree by psychoanalytic thinking. For example, reflecting the psychodynamic concept of a neurotic disorder, they included 'neurosis' as a major category. The early versions also defined many diagnostic categories not just in terms of descriptive features but also in terms of the supposed causes of the conditions. In later versions this causal (or 'aetiological') focus has been all but abandoned, and each condition is now defined in terms of observable signs and symptoms.

The DSM system is 'multi-axial' and allows the person's current psychological condition to be evaluated on five separate axes. Most clinical syndromes are classified on Axis I, and the personality disorders and mental retardation, which are stable long-term conditions, are diagnosed on Axis II. These first two axes allow the clinician to make a diagnosis on the basis of specific clinical information. The other three axes allow additional information to be coded. Thus, Axis III concerns relevant aspects of the person's physical health and Axis IV focuses on psychosocial and environmental problems. Axis V is used to provide a rating of the individual's global level of functioning on a 100-point scale. This extends from 1 (persistent violence, suicidal behaviour or inability to maintain minimal personal hygiene) to 100 (symptom-free, with superior functioning across a wide range of activities). Thus a person may be diagnosed as suffering from a depressive disorder (Axis I), while at the same time having an antisocial personality disorder (Axis II). The person may also be assessed as having no related physical disorder (Axis III), as having housing and occupational problems (Axis IV) and as having functioned over the past year at a general level of 30 on the global scale (Axis V).

DSM-IV includes specific criteria for the diagnosis of nearly 300 separate disorders, each being precisely defined in terms of a number of specific clinical features. The disorders are grouped in major categories such as 'the anxiety disorders' and the 'substance-related disorders', on the basis of similarities between conditions (see Box 1.1 for a listing of the major Axis I and Axis II categories). The system provides explicit criteria (often specifying, for example, how long a feature must have been present before it counts as a relevant symptom). Such information is more detailed and more precise than

Box 1.1
DSM-IV: Major Categories (Axis I and Axis II)

Axis I Disorders

- *Disorders usually first diagnosed during infancy, childhood or adolescence:* these include emotional, intellectual and behavioural disorders. Although they have an onset before adulthood, some are lifelong conditions. 'Mental retardation', although it falls within this category, is coded on Axis II.
- *Disorders of cognitive impairment:* these are caused by brain damage or deterioration and include acute conditions (such as delirium) and chronic disorders (such as dementia – widespread impairment of memory, learning and judgement).
- *Substance-related disorders:* these are conditions in which the use of alcohol or other drugs has led to substantial physical damage or psychological distress. These disorders are identified in terms of the substance involved.
- *Schizophrenia and other psychotic disorders:* the psychoses involve a loss of contact with reality. There is usually a marked impairment of emotional and social functioning, and the person may experience hallucinations and delusions.
- *Mood disorders:* these are divided into 'depressive disorders', marked by profound sadness, low self-esteem and various behavioural changes, and 'bipolar disorders', in which periods of depression alternate with periods of 'mania' (increased activity and excessive engagement in pleasurable but unhealthy activities).
- *Anxiety disorders:* these include the phobias (persistent and irrational fears of specific objects or situations), panic disorder (marked by frequently recurring attacks of panic), generalized anxiety disorder (characterized by persistent excessive worrying about a wide range of issues), post-traumatic stress disorder (a condition in which fear and other symp-

toms relate to a particular traumatic event) and obsessive–compulsive disorder (a condition marked by persistent obsessional thoughts and/or compulsive behaviours).
- *Somatoform disorders:* these are conditions in which physical symptoms or bodily preoccupations result from psychological distress. In the conversion disorders a physical complaint such as the paralysis of a limb has no medical basis. In cases of somatization disorder, the client constantly seeks treatment for imagined physical complaints.
- *Dissociative disorders:* these conditions involve disturbances of consciousness, memory (dissociative amnesia) or identity. In dissociative identity disorder (formerly known as multiple personality disorder), the person's usual identity is replaced by one or more different identities.
- *Sexual and gender identity disorders:* these include disorders of sexual functioning (disorders of sexual arousal, for example, or of orgasm) and the paraphilias. The paraphilias (which include paedophilia, voyeurism and other forms of 'sexual deviation') are conditions in which sexual gratification is gained primarily through engagement in bizarre or illicit activities. Gender identity disorder is more commonly known as 'transsexualism'.
- *Eating disorders:* these include anorexia nervosa, which involves a preoccupation with thinness and excessive weight loss, and bulimia nervosa, which is characterized by episodes of binge eating followed by self-induced vomiting and other methods of attempting to offset potential weight gain.
- *Sleep disorders:* these include chronic disturbances in the amount or quality of sleep, and various types of behavioural disturbance which occur during sleep

(including persistent sleepwalking and 'sleep terrors' – waking suddenly in a state of confusion and panic).

- *Impulse control disorders:* these include pathological gambling, fire-setting ('pyromania') and a number of other conditions. The common feature is a recurrent and irresistible urge to engage in activities which, although they may be pleasurable, are in some way harmful.
- *Adjustment disorders:* these are excessive emotional reactions following stressful events.

Axis II Disorders

- *Personality disorders:* these are stable personality traits which are maladaptive and create difficulties in the person's life. DSM-IV specifies ten personality disorders, including antisocial personality disorder (a chronic disregard of other people's rights and interests, and persistent antisocial behaviour) and obsessive–compulsive personality disorder (in which the person is preoccupied with punctuality, precision and perfection, is highly resistant to change and pays excessive attention to trivial matters). Each of the ten disorders may be diagnosed as the client's main psychological problem, or it may be diagnosed as a chronic disorder underlying a more acute disorder.
- *Mental retardation:* this is a general intellectual deficit which is present during infancy and can be assumed to be a lifelong condition. There is a subclassification in terms of severity, and criteria are provided for the diagnosis of mild, moderate, severe and profound retardation.

Box 1.2
DSM-IV: Example of Diagnostic Criteria

To illustrate the level of detail with which diagnostic criteria are specified in DSM-IV, we can consider the criteria used to diagnose 'major depressive disorder, single episode'. The disorder is defined as involving a single 'major depressive episode', which does not suggest that a diagnosis of 'schizoaffective disorder' would be more appropriate, and occurs in the absence of any of a number of psychotic conditions, including schizophrenia. This diagnosis is only given if the client has not experienced an episode of mania.

A 'major depressive episode' is diagnosed in the following way. The first criterion for recognizing such an episode is that five or more of a list of symptoms must have been present within a single two-week period. The client's symptoms must have included one or both of the first two items on the list. These symptoms are:

1 Depressed mood for most of the day, nearly every day.
2 Diminished interest or pleasure in almost all activities for most of the day, nearly every day.

Evidence of depressed mood or diminished interest or pleasure may come from the person's self-report or from others' observations of the client's behaviour. The other symptoms in the list are:

3 Significant weight gain or loss (not associated with dieting), or an increase or decrease in appetite nearly every day.
4 Difficulty sleeping, or sleepiness nearly every day.
5 Physical agitation or retardation nearly every day.
6 Fatigue or loss of energy nearly every day.

7   Feelings of worthlessness or excessive or inappropriate guilt nearly every day (delusional guilt 'counts', but guilt about being ill does not).
8   Diminished ability to think or concentrate, or indecisiveness nearly every day.
9   Recurrent thoughts of death, recurrent suicidal ideas, attempted suicide or a specific plan for committing suicide.

It is also specified that the individual symptoms should not be clearly due to delu-

sions (except guilt), hallucinations or a general medical condition. The condition does not count as a 'major depressive episode' unless it causes significant distress or impairment which affects the person's functioning in social, occupational or other areas. Neither does it count if it meets criteria for another type of episode (a 'mixed episode'), if the symptoms are caused by a physical complaint or by drugs or if the symptoms are better accounted for by bereavement.

that included in previous versions of the manual (Box 1.2 provides, as an example of the type of definition given by DSM-IV, the criteria used to diagnose 'major depressive disorder'). Unlike some earlier versions, conditions are defined without any reference to variables which are assumed to have played a causal role in the development of the disorder. Exceptions to this general rule include the 'adjustment disorders' and 'post-traumatic stress disorder', where reference is made to stressful events preceding the onset of the disorder.

DSM-IV highlights the fact that there may be considerable variation in the features associated with different cases which nevertheless merit the same diagnosis. The manual therefore identifies certain essential defining features for each condition and then indicates a number of features which, while they may aid diagnosis, are not assumed to be present in every case. The manual also contains, for each disorder, many additional details, including information about epidemiology (the prevalence of the disorder, and any differential patterning across gender, age groups etc.), predisposing factors, the clinical course of the disorder and comorbidity (other disorders frequently found in association with the condition being defined).

Although research evidence has played an increasing role in determining which conditions are included within the manual, and how they are classified, it would be unwise to imagine that an enterprise such as DSM could ever be free from the influence of strongly held views, prevailing orthodoxy and political considerations. DSM reflects an emerging consensus within a committee consisting of people who take a range of views.

The consensus among psychiatrists is subject to change, some of which reflects wider social changes. Thus, while homosexuality was included as a disorder in both DSM-I and DSM-II, only 'ego-dystonic homosexuality' (a homosexual orientation which is distressing for the individual) was included in DSM-III (1980). Later versions do not include any category making specific reference to homosexuality. The omission of homosexuality as a listed disorder followed a vote by members of the APA committee, whose judgements were undoubtedly influenced by profound changes in the social attitude towards homosexuality. Current controversies regarding the status of particular forms of female 'sexual dysfunction' might well lead to relevant changes in future revisions of the DSM system (see Chapter 7).

Criticisms of DSM

Every version of DSM (and of ICD, the other major classification system) has been subjected to a new wave of criticism. Some critics object to the whole enterprise of classification and diagnosis, and contend that categorization and labelling are essentially dehumanizing. They are unmoved by the argument that DSM classifies conditions, not people. Other critics complain that the whole DSM approach represents the inappropriate 'medicalization' of psychological distress.

More specific objections are raised by many critics who accept the value of classification and are sympathetic to the general DSM approach. Some object to the inclusion or exclusion of particular disorders. Many clinicians regret omission of particular categories which they continue to find clinically useful. Thus DSM-III abandoned a number of classificatory terms, including 'hysteria' and 'neurosis', which were still widely used. On the other hand, some object to the inclusion of 'conditions' such as 'nicotine dependence', 'stuttering' and 'mathematics disorder' in the manual. Others find it confusing that 'partner relational problems' and 'sexual abuse of a child' are included as 'conditions' (while fully accepting that such problems often contribute to the development of various psychiatric conditions). Another criticism of DSM is that it is essentially 'categorical'. Cases are assigned to categories, and no distinction is made between different levels or degrees of a particular condition.

Despite these controversies, DSM is very widely used and is generally accepted as a substantial improvement on earlier systems. The main purpose of DSM is to aid diagnosis, and it does provide a very effective means of identifying a wide range of clinical conditions (especially in its most recent version).

◀Diagnosis▶▶▶

Diagnostic systems such as DSM provide a set of templates with which the clinician can compare information relating to the condition of a particular client. The effectiveness of diagnosis can be measured in terms of two variables – reliability and validity. 'Diagnostic reliability' refers to the level of diagnostic consistency. It might be measured, for example, by assessing how far two or more clinicians agree in their diagnosis of a range of clients. 'Validity' refers to the accuracy of diagnosis. The concepts of reliability and validity are critical to the evaluation of all forms of assessment.

Reliability

The need to achieve the highest possible degree of diagnostic reliability has led to substantial efforts, over many years, to improve relevant clinical practices. The clinician's interviewing style, for example, may be improved by training. A relaxed and overtly sympathetic manner will encourage clients to feel at ease and to respond freely to questions, and clients who feel respected by the clinician are more likely to disclose information about particularly sensitive issues. Training in 'clinical insight' and flexibility of thinking may also produce similar gains.

The acquisition of diagnostically relevant information is also more consistent when clinicians use a standardized interview schedule as a means of collecting information rather than relying on a more personal, and perhaps more casual, style of conversation and observation. When a standardized examination format has been used to assess various aspects of the client's condition, the application of established, comprehensive and clear diagnostic criteria should result in a high level of agreement between clinicians about which diagnosis applies to the particular case.

Research on the use of DSM-I and DSM-II indicated that reliability levels were unacceptably low, and it then became a prime concern of those involved in developing DSM-III to provide definitions which included clearly identifiable signs and symptoms. Extensive 'field trials' are now used to investigate diagnostic reliability as each new revision is being prepared, and feedback from such trials often produces significant improvements. The field trials conducted during the development of DSM-IV involved more than 6000 clinicians, many of whom made diagnoses on the basis of sets of videotaped client interviews. Early indications suggest that the use of DSM-IV is associated with reasonably good levels of diagnostic reliability. However, as might be expected, agreement levels tend to be considerably higher for clear-cut behavioural conditions, such as substance-use disorders and psychosexual disorders, than for less 'concrete' conditions such as the personality disorders. The diagnostic reliability estimates associated with the major diagnostic categories are represented by a kappa coefficient of between 0.65 and 0.92 (kappa is a statistic which provides an estimate of the percentage agreement between judgements after chance agreement has been taken into account).

It should be appreciated that the reliability figures obtained in field trials may considerably overestimate the level of diagnostic reliability to be expected in normal clinical practice. This is because the clinicians involved in field trials make their diagnoses after they have watched videotapes of interviews with clients. Thus, precisely the same information is available to each participating clinician. In normal practice, two clinicians who interviewed a client on different occasions would witness somewhat different aspects of the client's behaviour and would ask somewhat different questions, or would, at least, phrase their questions in a different way. Thus the evidence available to them would be somewhat different, and this would tend to reduce their level of agreement about the most appropriate diagnosis.

Validity

Even perfect diagnostic reliability does not guarantee the validity of the diagnosis. Clearly, two psychiatrists who arrive at the same diagnosis might both be wrong. It is fairly common in clinical practice for additional evidence to shed new light on a case and to demonstrate that an early diagnosis was erroneous.

The provision of a diagnosis does not mean that the person's condition is fully understood. Hence, any diagnosis given at an early stage of clinical contact, especially, should be treated as a working hypothesis and should be re-examined throughout the course of clinical assessment and intervention.

Differential diagnosis and comorbidity

Many clients present with symptom patterns that immediately suggest a number of alternative diagnoses. Thus a client who appears withdrawn and inactive may be suffering from an organic disorder such as dementia or may be suffering from depression. Ambiguities can often be resolved by further investigation. The DSM system identifies potential problems with differential diagnosis, alerting the clinician to conditions which are similar in terms of their symptomatology and suggesting how it might be possible to discriminate between them.

The issue of differential diagnosis must be distinguished from another issue, that of 'comorbidity'. Many clients suffer from two or more abnormal psychological conditions at the same time. When one specific condition is commonly found in association with another specific condition there is said to be a high comorbidity between the first and the second. Thus the fact that many people who have developed the disorder known as agoraphobia also suffer from depression can be conveyed by stating that agoraphobia is marked by a high comorbidity for depression.

When it is possible to establish that one condition probably led to the development of the other condition, the condition with the earlier onset would be labelled 'primary' and the consequent condition 'secondary'. Thus clients who suffer from the eating disorder bulimia nervosa often also suffer from depression. Typically, the difficulties associated with the eating disorder produce the profound mood disturbances, so that in many cases bulimia is the primary disorder which then leads to a secondary depression.

Culture, gender and diagnosis

Some disorders are diagnosed much more frequently for females than for males, or vice versa, and some disorders are diagnosed more frequently for people from some cultural groups than for people from others. Thus women are about twice as likely as men to be diagnosed as suffering from depression, and women are around nine or ten times more likely than men to be diagnosed as suffering from the eating disorder anorexia nervosa. For some disorders, differences in diagnostic rates between different cultural and subcultural groups are equally striking. This raises the question of how far such variations in diagnosis reflect a real difference in psychopathology between the groups, and how far they might reflect certain biases in diagnostic practice.

The diagnostic framework used by the clinician is one potential source of such bias. 'Received clinical wisdom', or even a formal diagnostic system such as DSM, might include certain implicit gender-relative or culturally relative assumptions which distort clinical judgement. In a classic study, Broverman et al. (1970) found that trained clinical psychologists, psychiatrists and social workers (both male and female) judged women to be 'healthier' if they were somewhat submissive, dependent, excitable and concerned with their appearance. However, the same judges reported that men who showed these characteristics were likely to be 'unhealthy'.

Cultural influences on diagnostic practice have been demonstrated in a number of studies. For example, in the 1960s it was found that psychiatrists working in New York were about twice as likely to make a diagnosis of schizophrenia as were their counterparts working in London. Research conducted by the US/UK Diagnostic Project (Cooper et al., 1972) established that the difference in the number of people diagnosed as suffering from schizophrenia did indeed reflect diagnostic procedures rather than clinical differences in the client population. This was established by comparing the diagnoses given by British and American psychiatrists after viewing a standard set of videotapes of clinical interviews conducted with a wide range of US and UK clients.

Diagnostic practices may also change over time, and this means that it is difficult to make accurate statements about whether particular conditions are more or less prevalent now than they were in the past.

◄Contemporary Models of Mental Disorder►►►

The supernatural view of abnormal psychological conditions no longer exerts any significant influence. Contemporary views of the nature and origins of psychological disturbance reflect the somatogenic and psychogenic traditions, and many different variations on these basic themes have been elaborated over the past century. A number of different frameworks, or 'models', of mental illness contribute to contemporary thinking. Unlike theories, models are not 'right' or 'wrong' but should be judged in terms of whether they are useful or not useful. A 'good' model is one which is coherent and reasonably comprehensive, and provides a picture consistent with the established facts. Models can guide understanding and they often generate ideas which can then be translated into testable hypotheses. The fact that the various models used to explain the nature and origins of abnormal psychological conditions are based on different premises and may employ quite different concepts means that it is often difficult for proponents of different approaches to engage in a meaningful dialogue. Disagreements are likely to focus more on basic assumptions than on disputes about the facts of the matter.

In the following sections we examine a number of models which continue to exert an influence, and following this we consider how it might be possible to move towards an integration of at least some of these models.

The biological model

It has long been clear that an individual's behaviour and experience may change as a result of physical or chemical changes in the brain. It would certainly have been noted in ancient times that profound psychological disruption often followed head injury (sustained, perhaps, in an accident or in a battle), and it would also have been recognized that the ingestion of certain substances (including alcohol and hallucinogenic plant materials) led to profound changes in behaviour, sensory experience and mood. It was therefore reasonable to draw the conclusion that apparently spontaneous psychological disturbances might reflect some form of underlying brain dysfunction. In some cases it would have been possible to confirm this idea at autopsy by identifying gross anatomical abnormalities within the brain of someone who had suffered from a severe and chronic psychological disturbance.

More recently, the idea that at least some forms of psychological disturbance reflect an underlying organic pathology has been supported by a mass of research findings. For example, various disorders have been shown to be associated with disturbances in the metabolism of substances known as neurotransmitters, the chemicals responsible for the transmission of electrical impulses between brain cells. Depression has been linked to low levels of activity of the neurotransmitters serotonin (5-HT) and noradrenaline, schizophrenia has been linked to excessive dopamine activity and several of the anxiety disorders have been shown to be marked by low activity levels of gamma aminobutyric acid (GABA).

Sophisticated techniques developed to investigate brain function, including various types of 'brain scan', have also provided compelling evidence of abnormalities and dysfunctional activity patterns in the brains of people suffering from a variety of psychological conditions. Furthermore, such studies have been able to demonstrate that various indices of brain function change systematically with alterations in the client's clinical state. On a different biological theme, numerous research studies have indicated that genetic factors are often implicated in the development of psychological disorders. Studies of the familial patterns of psychological disorder have demonstrated that vulnerability to many specific forms of disorder is related to genetic make-up, and in recent years more direct studies of genetic factors have linked particular disorders to specific genes.

Further support for a biological view of psychological disorders comes from the fact that a number of drugs known to affect brain metabolism, including anti-anxiety, anti-depressant and anti-psychotic drugs, are effective in relieving behavioural, cognitive and emotional symptoms. Thus it is clear that many forms of psychological disorder are associated with significant biological irregularities, and in some cases the evidence strongly suggests that biological factors are actually responsible for the onset of the psychological condition.

At one time most mental health professionals found it useful to distinguish between psychological disorders known to reflect some biological aberration – the organic disorders – and disorders for which there was no known organic pathology (these were then assumed to stem from psychological causes and were known as 'functional disorders'). Over the years, however, this distinction has been somewhat undermined. Many disorders have been shown to result from an interaction between biological and psychological factors, and a number of disorders which once appeared to be functional have been shown to have an organic basis.

The fact that research has demonstrated the relevance of biological factors in an increasingly wide range of disorders has encouraged some people to claim that eventually every psychological disorder will be shown to be the result of some form of brain dysfunction. The implication that psychological factors play little or no causal role in the development of many psychological disorders is regarded as outrageous by those who focus their attention on social and psychological antecedents, and there are several good reasons for challenging the most extreme and extensive claims made for the significance of biological factors.

For example, it does not follow from the fact that a psychological condition is *associated* with certain biological indices that it must have been *caused* by biological factors. It needs to be recognized that, even when specific symptoms can be attributed to changes in brain chemistry, those chemical changes may be the effects of psychological processes. For example, although the distress experienced by a person following the tragic death of a child may well be reflected in disturbances in brain chemistry, the distress clearly results from the traumatic event and the psychological aftermath of the loss. Even though there are clear biological correlates of the extreme distress, it would clearly be inappropriate to regard the bereaved parent as suffering from 'a biological disorder'.

Caution also needs to be exercised when drawing inferences from the fact that psychotropic (mind-altering) drugs are often effective in relieving psychological symptoms. Such effectiveness does not prove that the primary cause of the individual's distress was a chemical disturbance. For example, anti-depressant medication might relieve the symptoms of depression even in cases in which the person has clearly become depressed as a result of occupational redundancy or bereavement. In such cases, the drug may control the symptoms by reversing, neutralizing or counterbalancing chemical changes precipitated 'naturally' (or 'intrinsically') by the impact of the disturbing life event.

Thus the evidence that biological factors are often associated with abnormal psychological conditions should not be misunderstood as demonstrating that such conditions are 'nothing more than' physiological disturbances or that some form of physiological disturbance is always 'responsible for' the onset of a condition. While it is clear that some disorders are indeed 'brain disorders' (various forms of dementia being obvious examples), there are many conditions for which there is no direct evidence of organic causes, and there are many cases in which the onset of an abnormal condition appears to have been triggered by a particularly stressful environmental situation.

Many critics of the biological model have pointed to the fact that it implies a rather passive view of people. In many biologically based accounts people are portrayed as organisms who are at the mercy of their genetic make-up and their neurochemistry. This view contrasts with that of certain other models, particularly the cognitive model, which portrays people as conscious, strategic and motivated agents who actively strive to understand situations and struggle to cope with problems and life stresses.

The biological model has many strengths, including its clarity, its openness to empirical research and its links with many well established sciences. Theories developed within this framework predict specific associations between variables, each of which is clearly and operationally defined. The explicitness and precision associated with the model, and its integration with the biological and medical sciences, make it especially powerful, particularly when contrasted with certain other models (such as the psychodynamic and humanistic-existential models), which often appear to use concepts which are somewhat vague and esoteric, and often rely on subjective evidence.

The psychodynamic model

The psychodynamic, or psychoanalytic, model originated in the work of Sigmund Freud (1856–1939). However, since Freud first wrote about his ideas at the turn of the century, psychoanalytic thinking has developed in many diverse ways. The fundamental idea shared by all psychodynamic thinkers is that human actions and experiences are strongly influenced by unconscious processes which take place within a structured and dynamic 'psyche'. Freud suggested that the personality could be considered as comprising three elements: the id, the superego and the ego. Reflecting the emphasis he placed on biologically based instincts, Freud maintained that the id drives people to satisfy their basic biological needs and to seek pleasure – the 'pleasure principle'. A person driven by unrestrained id impulses would be 'reckless, savage and lecherous'. The superego, which reflects internalized parental values, acts as a restraining force on the id and is often the source of unwelcome guilt, which may be conscious or unconscious. Freud's third personality component is the ego, which mediates between the id and the superego. The ego seeks to find ways of satisfying the basic needs of the id without violating the rules or values established by the superego and in accordance with environmental realities. Thus sexual release might be postponed and pursued in an acceptable way by engaging in courtship.

Freud suggested that an individual's personality develops through five psychosexual stages at which different needs and desires dominate. These are:

- *The oral stage* – from birth to about the age of 2 years. At this stage satisfaction is gained primarily through the ingestion of food and stimulation of the mouth area.
- *The anal stage* – around the time of toilet training. The child gains pleasure through defecation and is acutely sensitive to the parents' responses to this activity. Thus the child is affected by the parents' expressions of disgust, pleasure or anxiety, and by the degree to which they are strict or lax with regard to toileting.

- *The phallic stage* – this is the stage at which children become preoccupied with the anatomy and functioning of their genitals. Freud proposed the controversial theory that boys become sexually attracted to their mothers (the Oedipus complex), and that girls become sexually attracted to their fathers (the Electra complex). Taking the Oedipus complex as the example, the boy develops a physical desire for the mother and then regards his father as a rival for the mother's love. His resulting jealousy and fear of his father leads to a strong sense of identification with his rival, and this may lead the boy to imitate the father's behaviour and to take on his moral (superego) values.
- *The latency stage* – this is a fallow period in which developmental processes initiated in earlier stages are consolidated and some later changes are anticipated.
- *The genital stage* – finally, the person achieves sexual maturity both physically and psychologically.

Freud maintained that some people experience special difficulties in progressing through these stages, and that problems at any stage may lead to complexes and fixations which adversely affect the development of the ego. He argued that unacceptable sexual and aggressive urges which arise at the various developmental stages are forced out of consciousness (repressed) but may persist as a source of tension and eventually lead to acute anxiety. The ego attempts to deal with this anxiety by means of various 'defence mechanisms'.

If the ego is not strong enough to reconcile the different demands imposed by the id, the superego and the outside world, or if it fails in its attempts to reduce anxiety, neurotic symptoms are likely to develop. The nature of an individual's symptoms will depend upon the nature of the underlying conflict, the individual's personality and the nature of any defence mechanisms employed.

Although defence mechanisms are used to reduce anxiety, they may also precipitate neurotic problems. Each of the defence mechanisms involves some degree of reality distortion which may interfere with the person's ability to deal with the demands of everyday life, and if such distortion becomes extreme it may result in disorientation and delusional symptoms.

Psychoanalytic treatment involves the identification and modification of unconscious elements. Freud maintained that symptoms could be alleviated by bringing repressed fantasies and emotions into consciousness. This process is labelled 'catharsis'. Freud originally used hypnosis as a means of uncovering repressed memories, but he later abandoned this in favour of other methods, including free association and dream interpretation. Freud developed a complex system for interpreting the symbolism of dreams.

At a later stage of his thinking, Freud also emphasized the therapeutic relevance of a process which he labelled 'transference'. This is an unconscious and emotionally charged way of relating to other people, in which complex patterns of feelings engendered by early relationships, particularly with the parents, are transferred to interactions with other people. Freud suggested that the client's response to the psychoanalytic therapist is often marked by tension because the client unconsciously identifies the therapist with a parent figure, and engages in transference. Freud believed that an analysis of such transference could provide the therapist with significant insights into the nature of a client's psychopathology.

Other psychoanalytic theorists

Many of Freud's followers eventually objected to important elements of his theory and went on to establish psychoanalytic schools of their own.

Carl Gustav Jung (1875–1961) was a Swiss psychiatrist who collaborated closely with Freud before challenging Freud's view that the sexual drive is the primary motivating force. Jung suggested that the sexual drive is just one among many creative instincts, and he believed that neurotic conditions develop when people fail to realize their potential in any one of a range of different domains. As a therapist, Jung helped clients to recognize their potential for growth and to deal with any inner conflicts that might be blocking the realization of their potential. He made extensive use of dream interpretation and of clients' responses to visual images. Jung believed that the mind (or 'psyche') is shaped not only by the individual's personal experiences but also by the 'collective unconscious', a reservoir of the aggregated experience of the human race. He suggested that the existence of this universal component of the psyche is revealed by the fact that many icons, archetypes and narrative themes recur repeatedly across cultures and over different historical periods.

Alfred Adler (1870–1937) was another associate who eventually parted company with Freud, again following a disagreement about the significance of the sexual drive. Adler emphasized the relevance of the individual's striving for power and control. He believed that a child's relative powerlessness can lead to a lasting sense of inferiority which may distort relationships with other people. A person may overcompensate for perceived inferiority by seeking power through any means, and at any cost. A sense of inferiority may lead to callous self-centredness, bullying, a withdrawal from social relationships or any one of a number of psychological disorders. Adlerian therapy endeavours to help the client to examine values relating to power and dominance. The goal is to reduce the individual's preoccupation with power issues and to foster the development of a positive sense of fellowship and empathy with other people.

Erik Erikson (1902–94) practised as a child analyst and developed an elaborate model of developmental stages from infancy through to old age. He maintained that individuals face disparate developmental tasks at different stages and that several kinds of ego development may occur at the various stages. Erikson maintained that psychological difficulties arise when healthy ego development is blocked by social constraints or psychological obstructions. He saw the therapist's task as being that of helping the client to acquire basic trust and confidence. Erikson emphasized the importance of healthy relationships in facilitating the individual's optimum growth, and he often included members of the client's family in his therapeutic work.

The contribution of the British psychoanalyst Melanie Klein (1882–1960) has been particularly influential in Europe. Klein worked mostly with children and suggested that they had complex unconscious fantasies even within the first year of life. She maintained that anxiety often arises out of conflicts precipitated by natural destructiveness ('the death instinct'). In recent years, many British analysts of the 'object relations' school have abandoned the traditional psychoanalytic emphasis on instinct-related tension and have focused instead on individuals' relationships with 'objects' – including good and bad objects of love and loss. Another recent British contribution which has its roots in analytic thinking and which continues to have a growing influence on many areas of developmental psychology and the psychology of social relationships is John Bowlby's 'attachment theory' (Bowlby, 1980). This theory represents a significant elaboration of the traditional analytic theme of the lasting impact of early relationships, and has recently been applied to such issues as the development of romantic relationships, deficiencies in parenting and grief reactions in adults whose partners have died.

Psychoanalytic ideas and therapeutic practices have been widely criticized on a number of grounds. Some critics suggest that there is little supportive evidence for the majority of psychoanalytic ideas, that they exaggerate the importance of an individual's early experiences and that they fail to acknowledge the relevance of physiological and cognitive factors in the development of psychological disorders. Other critics maintain that there is no good evidence for the effectiveness of psychoanalytically based treatments (Eysenck, 1985), although this is hotly disputed. Psychoanalytic therapy is highly intensive and is often protracted, and even those who believe the approach to be effective recognize that it is hardly 'cost-effective' relative to other forms of therapy. Dissatisfaction with the long duration of this form of therapy has led analysts to introduce new strategies designed to abbreviate the therapeutic process. For example, some 'brief therapists' deliberately set out to provoke some degree of anxiety, the idea being that when a client's customary neurotic defences are aroused the therapist will be able to bring about beneficial changes.

The behavioural model

Whereas the psychoanalytic and biological models regard the symptoms of psychological disorders as products of some underlying physical or personality problem (intrapsychic conflict, for example, or brain dysfunction), the behavioural model regards symptoms as learned habits, or 'maladaptive learned responses'. Thus disorders are regarded merely as 'patterns of abnormal behaviours', and it follows that a modification of the abnormal behaviours will eliminate the problem. Such modification is not regarded as 'merely superficial' because it is not accepted that there is any more fundamental, or 'underlying', problem.

This view contrasts sharply with the psychoanalytic model, according to which eliminating symptoms would leave the initiating problem unresolved, and might simply lead to further symptoms by a process known as 'symptom substitution'. The fact that symptom substitution generally does not occur (for example, when a symptom is eliminated by behaviour therapy) is taken by behaviourists as evidence that there is no underlying neurosis or mental disorder.

The behavioural model explains the origins of psychological disorders in terms of the theories of learning and conditioning, which have been repeatedly explored and validated in scientific experiments. Behaviourists emphasize the key importance of classical conditioning and operant conditioning in explanations of the acquisition of maladaptive responses; for example, an anxious response to a situation which does not, in fact, present a real threat. Many experiments have been conducted to show that maladaptive responses such as anxiety or helplessness can be conditioned under laboratory conditions (studies of this type are referred to as 'experimental psychopathology'). Clearly, the creation of anxiety states and other 'abnormal' responses through conditioning procedures does provide an illustration of the processes which might be involved in the development of anxiety disorders, but such a demonstration cannot prove that this is how such disorders actually develop.

The behavioural model has certainly been highly productive in terms of the generation of new therapeutic procedures. Various 'behaviour therapy techniques', which were devised on the basis of the theoretical principles of learning, have been shown repeatedly to be remarkably effective in treating a range of disorders. However, we must remember that the power of a procedure to relieve symptoms does not necessarily carry any implications about the way in which the disorder originated.

Although it is possible to put forward a behavioural interpretation of almost any form of psychological disturbance, including schizophrenia and manic-depressive disorder, for example, the most convincing behavioural accounts focus on such conditions as the phobias, anxiety state disorder, obsessive–compulsive disorder, substance abuse, sexual disorders and abnormal expressions of aggression. Furthermore, although emphasizing observable behaviours, many behavioural therapists include cognitive elements – verbal instruction or visual imagery, for example – which play important roles in many forms of 'behaviour therapy'.

The cognitive model

According to the cognitive model, many forms of mental disorder are caused by difficulties in the effective processing of information or, at another level, from errors or biases in thinking. An emotional condition such as anxiety or depression, for example, may reflect particular false beliefs held by the client, or errors in logical inference. The person's emotional disturbance therefore follows from an erroneous conclusion.

It is clear that most, if not all, psychological disorders are accompanied by disturbances of thinking. People who are depressed, for example, have 'depressed thoughts', are pessimistic in their outlook and may draw extremely gloomy conclusions from meagre evidence about their own shortcomings, or about how other people regard them. Common-sense explanations of the relationship between depression and depressed thinking would suggest that the person's emotional state leads to distortions – a depressed mood leads to depressed thinking. However, according to the cognitive model of mental disorder, such distortions of thinking are primary rather than secondary. Pessimistic thoughts lead people to become depressed and worried thoughts lead to anxiety. Thus a person who overestimates the likelihood of catastrophe and perceives many situations as highly threatening is likely to end up in a state of extreme anxiety. Cognitive theorists do not deny that emotional disturbance can further distort thinking. For example, depression can promote a pessimistic view of things; or feelings of anxiety can lead to extreme apprehension. A reciprocal relationship (a 'vicious circle') between disturbed thoughts and disturbed feelings is therefore often proposed. But they do maintain that the cognitive distortions, rather than the emotional states, are primary.

The cognitive model implies that positive emotional changes and symptom reduction can be brought about by correcting biases in thinking and educating people out of their false beliefs. Cognitive therapy is now very well developed and has been shown in many research studies to be highly effective in reducing the symptoms of a wide variety of disorders. However, as in the case of other models, the fact that a therapy based on the model is effective does not 'prove' that the model is 'valid' in its account of the origins of the condition.

Cognitive therapists attempt to identify patterns of thinking which may have caused or which may be helping to maintain the client's condition. Clients are asked to report their thoughts when encountering a mild rebuke, for example, or when facing a mildly threatening situation. The client and therapist work together, in a therapeutic mode known as 'collaborative empiricism', to discover problematic thought patterns and beliefs. The therapist then shows the client how to avoid logical errors, and challenges any false beliefs that appear to be maintaining the condition. Although many clients have idiosyncratic false beliefs, some such beliefs are very widespread within the culture. Thus the 'just world hypothesis' is reflected in the belief that people get what they deserve and that bad things only happen to bad people. Someone who espouses such a belief may therefore conclude that because he or she has experienced a personal tragedy he or she must be 'a bad person'. A cognitive therapist helping such a client might challenge the belief that people 'only get what they deserve' by helping the client to think, for example, of instances in which innocent people had met with misfortune which was clearly 'undeserved'. Thus false beliefs may be challenged 'empirically', by quoting or demonstrating relevant facts.

Many clients are unduly pessimistic about how they would perform in a challenging situation; for example, when meeting an authority figure or when visiting the dentist. They are often convinced that they will suffer an acute breakdown or 'go to pieces'. Behavioural 'experiments' may help to convince such people that their fears are unfounded and that they actually perform reasonably well in the feared circumstances.

Thus cognitive therapy often involves behavioural elements, just as behavioural therapy often involves cognitive elements. Indeed, many people make little distinction between these perspectives and describe themselves as 'cognitive–behavioural' theorists or therapists. Cognition is frequently considered to be a kind of 'behaviour', and most behaviourists have come to acknowledge that cognitive factors play an important role in determining behaviour (a good deal of laboratory research has established that even rats and pigeons make extensive use of cognitive representations).

The cognitive model has been applied to a wide range of disorders, including depression, the anxiety disorders, the eating disorders and substance abuse. Clearly, it would be inappropriate to attempt to account for neurological disorders such as dementia in cognitive terms. However, such disorders do lead to profound disturbances of cognition, and cognitive interventions may serve a useful function as part of the rehabilitation process. Despite several early attempts to devise a cognitive model which could account for the development of schizophrenia, the view that this condition stems primarily from distorted beliefs about the world is no longer tenable. However, in recent years many studies have demonstrated that cognitive methods can be very effective in ameliorating some of the symptoms manifest in the acute phase of schizophrenia.

The humanistic-existential model

The humanistic approach to psychology reflects a fundamental belief that individuals are motivated towards personal growth and self-sufficiency. Humanistic psychologists focus on experience (that is, they take a 'phenomenological' stance) and they emphasize the importance of a positive sense of self, individual choice and individual goals. Psychological problems are said to develop when a person refuses or is unable to accept responsibility for all his or her thoughts and actions. Furthermore, any major disparity between how a person views herself ('the self-image') and what she would wish to be ('the ideal self') is likely to produce severe emotional distress (in the form of anxiety, guilt, anger or depression).

Many humanistic thinkers and practitioners are particularly vociferous in their rejection of the 'medicalization' of human suffering, and many refuse to make any reference to diagnostic categories, regarding the diagnostic process as 'dehumanizing'. Those conditions which are generally identified as psychological disorders are viewed by humanistic therapists simply as different varieties of human distress. The person who experiences such distress is regarded as a 'client', rather than a 'patient', and clients are helped to overcome their distress by means of counselling (or, simply, 'helping').

The counsellor (or 'helper') takes a non-judgemental and non-directive stance, and attempts to provide a therapeutic setting in which the client can engage in frank and deep self-exploration. As this exploration proceeds, a natural 'healing' process is said to occur in which the person moves towards self-acceptance, undergoes a process of personal growth, and gains the capacity to live 'authentically'. 'Authenticity' involves realistic awareness, a caring attitude towards oneself and others, spontaneity and an openness to new experiences. Therapy is not viewed as something which the therapist 'administers' to the client. Rather, the therapist is regarded as a person who can assist the client in self-healing and personal growth, and the process by which such assistance is provided is often described as 'client-centred' or 'person-centred' (Rogers, 1961).

The above description mainly reflects the contribution of Carl Rogers (1902–87), but several other humanistic theorists, including Abraham Maslow (1908–70) and Rollo May (1909–94), have also made highly significant contributions to the field. In his theory of motivation, Maslow suggested that human needs, and the motives or drives associated with these needs, can be depicted in the form of a hierarchy. The most basic needs relate to essential physiological requirements (for food and drink, for example), and beyond this stage the hierarchy progresses to higher levels of needs relating to safety, affiliation (including love and acceptance by others) and esteem. Maslow maintained that needs at one level must be satisfied before the individual develops any strong motivation to fulfil needs located at a higher level. When every need has been fulfilled, including those at the highest level, the individual is said to have attained the final stage of personal growth and to have become 'self-actualized'. Maslow suggested that most people manage only brief glimpses of self-actualization during what he termed 'peak experiences'.

Existential ideas have had a profound influence on many humanistic thinkers, including Rollo May and Victor Frankl (1905–). Existential philosophers emphasize the significance of the fact that human beings are aware of the limited and constrained nature of their existence ('being'). On the other hand, human beings are essentially free. Their power as agents of their own fate, and their freedom to make deliberate choices, means that people bear the responsibility for how they choose to live their life. Existential therapists focus on many of these issues. They help clients to come to terms with their mortality and the essential 'meaninglessness' of their existence, they help people to recognize the extent of their own freedom to make choices and they help people to act responsibly and to accept responsibility.

Carl Rogers, in particular, insisted that the humanistic model was not incompatible with a rigorous scientific approach, and he engaged in several major empirical studies concerned with the examination of his ideas regarding the process of counselling. However, many humanistic practitioners are hostile to the idea that their theories and practices might be 'tested' by means of 'objective' empirical research. Some go further, and maintain that a scientific approach to human affairs is bound to be subject to fundamental distortions and that orthodox psychology provides no more than a shallow, limited and biased account of the experience of being human. The anti-science views associated with this approach is one reason why the humanistic approach to abnormal psychology (and to psychology in general) has become much less influential over the past twenty or thirty years. Rogers's ideas continue to exert a major influence on mainstream counselling and psychotherapy, but several of the other forms of humanistic therapy are now generally practised by 'complementary therapists' rather by those working within the orthodox field.

The family systems model

Most models of psychopathology focus on individuals who are regarded either as 'mentally ill' or as psychologically disturbed or distressed. The family systems model, however, suggests that most problems which present in terms of individual psychopathology are actually manifestations of family disturbances. Each family is seen as a unique social system in which any alteration is bound to affect every element within the system (elements include the family members and the relationships between them). Changes reverberate through the family system so that it is often impossible to understand family processes in terms of simple cause–effect associations. Family systems have a natural propensity to 'settle down' into patterns which reduce immediate tensions, but such patterns may prove dysfunctional in the longer term. Persistent avoidance of conflict, for example, may exact long-term costs. In some cases one member of the family develops symptoms as a way of reducing a fundamental instability in the family system. Thus a child's psychosomatic aches and pains, or excessive unruliness, may function as a mutual focus of concern for parents whose relationship is in jeopardy. If the child's symptom serves to curb parental conflict, thus maintaining the marital relationship, systemic pressures may impel the child to remain unwell or unruly.

It follows from this analysis that intervention will sometimes need to be focused on the whole family. The aim of family therapy is to identify maladaptive system dynamics and to help the family to change to more adaptive ways of functioning. If a new equilibrium can be achieved, and a solution found to problems which threaten to destroy the system, the family will no longer 'need' the 'identified patient' to maintain the presenting problem.

The family systems approach has become highly influential over the past thirty years. Many variations have been developed, and the field has been well researched. The approach does not offer an account of every type of psychological disorder (although it would certainly have something to say about the impact *of* families, and *on* families, of all forms of disorder). Psychoanalytic theory was influential in the early development of family therapy, but systemic thinking employs concepts borrowed from engineering, psychology, sociology and anthropology. Recent influences include various philosophical and literary approaches (including 'constructivism' and 'postmodernism'). And, although the family systems model is radically different from the biological model, several family therapists (including a number of child psychiatrists) have made useful attempts to integrate biological evidence and family systems thinking (for example, Lask and Fosson, 1989).

Family therapy is often effective in treating families in which one or more members have been diagnosed as suffering from a psychological disorder, but the same approach is also widely used to help families with non-psychiatric problems. Because family therapy is used to help families experiencing parenting difficulties, marital conflict and violence, it can be seen that the problem domain addressed by this form of therapy overlaps only partially with the domain common to psychiatry and abnormal psychology. Furthermore, although family therapists originally focused their attention on families, the nature of the approach encouraged the application of systemic thinking to other types of social system, including schools, hospitals and industrial organizations. Experienced family therapists now work increasingly with systems other than the family, and they sometimes work with a 'wide system' such as a family, plus the group of professionals involved in helping that family.

The sociocultural model

Some theorists have attempted to characterize psychological disorders, and to account for their development, by focusing on processes occurring at the community level, or even at the societal level. Such analysts emphasize the relevance of cultural ideologies and practices, and factors such as unemployment and poverty, and suggest that psychological distress can only be appropriately understood when it is viewed in a cultural context.

Those who follow the sociocultural approach regard individual families and neighbourhoods as micro-systems which reflect the wider social environment, and they focus much of their interest on the impact of social policies. A policy which does nothing to alleviate poverty, for example, is seen as contributing to 'misery', which may then be reframed as 'depression'. The fact that the prevalence of many psychological disorders varies systematically with gender, social class and cultural background is taken by sociocultural theorists as support for the view that disorders are largely a product of social conditions. Sexism, racism and social class division are held responsible for much of the distress commonly characterized as 'psychopathology'. Thus the fact that depression affects twice as many women as men is seen as reflecting women's oppression and lack of opportunity.

Several approaches to intervention follow from this model. Some focus on the individual and attempt to help the person to cope more effectively with adverse social conditions. For example, the client might be helped to identify and make use of local resources, or to build a more effective social support network. Other forms of intervention are seen as preventive rather than therapeutic, and aim to change those aspects of the social environment which are held responsible for precipitating or maintaining distress. Some 'therapists' work as political activists, engaging directly in national or local political affairs, while others work as consultants or advisors; for example in matters relating to environmental planning and resource allocation.

Community psychologists work in schools, industrial settings, churches and clinics, and with voluntary associations and government agencies, to promote improvements in environmental and social conditions. These forms of intervention aim to reduce the levels of stress and hardship experienced by families and individuals, and to enhance community welfare and social support.

Towards Integration ▶▶▶

The value of integration

No single model can satisfactorily account for the entire range of psychological disorders and it would be unrealistic to claim that any single model is comprehensive, exhaustive and universally applicable. The biological model contributes a great deal to our understanding of the origins of conditions such as dementia and schizophrenia, but does not provide a satisfactory account of the nature and origins of the clinical phobias or of the type of depression which often develops following a tragic bereavement. The development of a phobia might be better understood by employing the behavioural model or the cognitive model, and a case of post-bereavement depression might be better understood using a model which focuses on social relationships or psychodynamic processes. However, no single model can ever provide a totally comprehensive account of a condition. Even if the initiating cause of a psychological condition is biological, for example, social and cognitive processes need to be considered if we are to understand how people suffering from the condition respond to their primary symptoms.

It is certainly possible to address different aspects of a condition in a serial fashion, focusing first on concepts and issues relevant to one model before turning to questions relating to another model. Such a serial process may produce a 'patchwork' which provides a general (but somewhat disorganized and confusing) representation of the condition. Such a process often occurs in clinical practice, with respect to individual cases. A person's current physical and psychological state may be described, and early life experiences and current relationships reported, with little attempt made to articulate possible relationships between elements from the different domains.

At a general level, it would be extremely advantageous if a comprehensive account of a particular type of abnormal psychological condition could be achieved by integrating ideas and information from different perspectives into a cohesive whole. It would clearly be impossible to achieve a 'grand integration' involving every approach which currently commands some support, because some of the assumptions made be various approaches are irreconcilable. However, a substantial degree of integration is possible, and various attempts have been made to consolidate concepts and accounts derived from at least some of the wide range of contemporary approaches.

The pressing need for integration is made clear by the fact that diverse research studies of many psychological disorders repeatedly demonstrate the relevance of variables relating to different levels of explanation and different psychopathological models. Thus studies of schizophrenia, depression, the eating disorders and many other conditions have provided strong evidence of the relevance of biological *and* psychological *and* social variables.

The fact that none of the basic models can accommodate all of the factors which have been shown to be implicated in such conditions confirms the need for an integrative framework. This need is now widely acknowledged, and some progress has already been made. In particular, major steps have been taken towards developing a 'biopsychosocial' framework which can accommodate biological and psychological and social elements and map out the possible relationships between elements from these different levels or domains (Engel, 1980).

The diathesis–stress model

For a whole range of disorders, it is quite clear that: (a) long-term predispositional factors play an important causal role; and (b) the disorder often appears to develop following a particularly disturbing environmental event. The 'diathesis–stress model' easily accommodates these two – somewhat disparate – facts, and suggests that many psychological disorders result from the impact of an environmental event (the stressor, or 'stress', factor) on a person who has a predisposing vulnerability (the 'diathesis' factor). People low in vulnerability to a particular condition ('resilient') will only develop the disorder if they are subjected to extreme stress, whereas highly vulnerable people may develop the disorder even when subjected to only a moderate degree of stress (see Figure 1.1).

For most psychological disorders, vulnerability is affected by a wide range of factors, including the individual's genetic constitution and 'biological history' (of injury and infection, for example), and many aspects of personal history, including traumatic experiences in childhood or adulthood. Thus vulnerability (and its opposite, resilience) is partly determined by 'nature' (biological factors) and partly determined by 'nurture' (environmental or experiential factors).

For some disorders (schizophrenia being a likely example), the necessary diathetic element might be represented only in a small subgroup of the population. Thus susceptibility to the disorder would be limited to those unfortunate enough to belong to the 'at-risk' subgroup. Most people would be effectively 'immune' to the condition and would never develop the disorder no matter how much stress they were to experience. For many disorders, however, most people might be susceptible to some degree, with a broad range of susceptibility levels within the population extending from 'high resilience' to 'high vulnerability'.

An individual is not simply more or less vulnerable to psychological disorders in general, but may have different levels of vulnerability for each disorder, just as individuals may be highly vulnerable to some physical diseases and immune to others. Thus each individual may be thought of as having a 'diathetic profile' across the range of psychological disorders. But, generally speaking, however high an individual's susceptibility to a particular disorder, the condition will not actually develop unless the person experiences a critical degree of stress (usually in response to adverse environmental events).

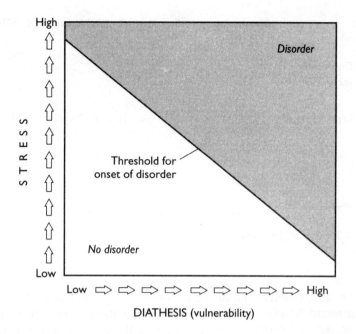

Figure 1.1 Diathesis–stress model. For a given disorder, as the level of vulnerability (diathesis) increases, the degree of stress needed to precipitate the disorder decreases

The 'stress' component of the diathesis-stress model also needs careful consideration. As well as different levels of stress there are different types of stress, and some disorders may be precipitated more readily by some types of stress than by others. Thus, whereas stress resulting from involvement in a near-fatal road accident may be particularly likely to precipitate an anxiety disorder, the type of stress experienced following a bereavement might be more likely to lead to depression.

However, the type of stress that results from an environmental 'stressor' will also reflect an individual's perception (or 'appraisal') of the situation, and different people are likely to appraise a distressing situation in different ways. An individual's general 'outlook' or 'appraisal style' will reflect his or her beliefs, values and personal circumstances. People who judge a distressing environmental event in totally disparate ways are likely to experience different levels and different types of stress. An individual's customary 'appraisal style' can be regarded as a diathetic element, but it clearly mediates the 'stress' factor. Besides this, stress is likely to have profound effects on how the individual judges further events (which will, in turn, affect the stressful impact of those events).

Causal chains

Abnormal psychological conditions result from complex causal patterns which take a variety of forms. It is useful to think of the antecedents of a

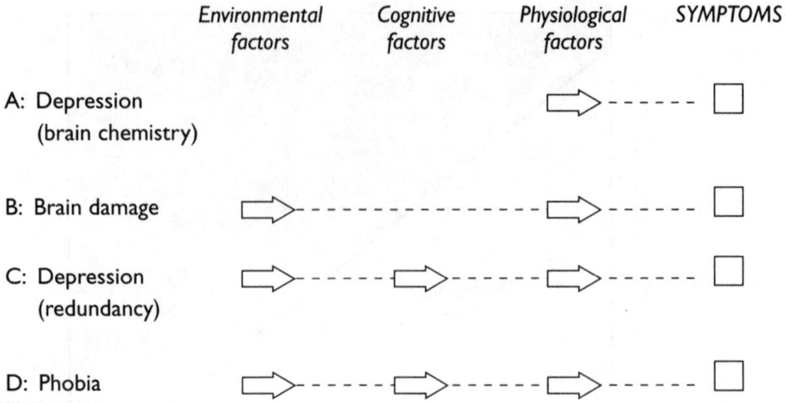

	Environmental factors	Cognitive factors	Physiological factors	SYMPTOMS

A: Depression
(brain chemistry)

B: Brain damage

C: Depression
(redundancy)

D: Phobia

Figure 1.2   Causal chain model

condition as forming a 'causal chain', and to recognize that such chains may be of different 'lengths' and may include elements of several different kinds. The *immediate* antecedent of any psychological symptom, whether the symptom is behavioural, cognitive or emotional, is always some aspect of brain physiology (simply because all experiences and responses are mediated by physiological mechanisms). In some cases a physiological process will itself be abnormal or 'faulty', but in other cases the relevant physiological reaction is a normal response to an extreme (or 'abnormal') environmental or psychological antecedent.

Disturbances at the physiological level may arise in a variety of ways. Many apparently 'spontaneous' abnormalities in brain functioning involve disturbances in the complex and delicate chemical neurotransmitter system. There are individual differences in vulnerability to such irregularities which appear to be determined, at least in part, by genetic factors. Physiological disturbances may also be the result of structural changes in brain tissue, resulting perhaps from ageing or from trauma-induced injury.

Figure 1.2 provides examples of a number of causal pathways which may lead to psychological symptoms. For every pathway, symptoms are immediately preceded by a physiological element, but this should not be taken to imply that there is always some form of physiological *disturbance*. Some conditions are essentially psychological responses to extreme environmental conditions, and others may reflect an abnormal style of psychological response to relatively innocuous events.

Pathway A in Figure 1.2 refers to a case of depression which is directly attributable to disturbances in brain chemistry; in this case the causal chain does not extend back beyond the physiological level. The relevant physiological changes can be regarded as essentially 'spontaneous' and as leading directly to the symptoms. However, in the case of traumatically induced brain damage (pathway B), the causal chain extends back to the environmental event which caused the brain damage. There is no suggestion, in Figure 1.2, that psychological processes are causally implicated in the conditions associated with pathways A and B (although the diagram might be extended to indicate that psychological responses to the primary symptoms may lead to the development of secondary symptoms).

For many disorders, however, psychological processes *do* play a vital role. Some abnormal psychological conditions are clearly responses to social changes, for example. Causal explanations which include psychological variables as principal elements are represented by pathways C and D in Figure 1.2. In pathway C, an environmental event (loss of employment) is the initiating cause of a case of depression. However, it is safe to assume that the link between the environmental situation and the person's symptoms is mediated by psychological elements such as the perception of having been rejected, pessimistic thoughts about the future and recurrent feelings of loneliness. In the case of a phobia (pathway D), one or more environmental events may lead particular types of stimuli to be experienced as threatening. Thus a person who experienced a devastating house fire might subsequently develop intense phobic fears of fire and closed spaces. In such a case, the environmental event (the fire) might be identified as the primary trigger for the phobic disorder, but any reasonable explanation of the link between the traumatic event and the persistent symptoms would need to focus on psychological processes (such as frequent recall of the original trauma and worries about another fire breaking out).

A physiological element is, as always, included as the immediate precursor to symptoms in the causal chains depicted in pathways C and D. Thus psychological responses to environmental situations are seen as leading to biological effects, which then become apparent as signs and symptoms of an abnormal condition. Furthermore, neurological (and, more specifically, neurochemical) effects may persist and may eventually play an autonomous role in generating and maintaining symptoms.

The model illustrated in Figure 1.2 helps us to understand that there may be fundamental differences in the nature of the causal pathways leading to different disorders. Indeed, as we can see from the inclusion of pathways A and C in Figure 1.2, even different cases of the same type of disorder may result from very different causal pathways. The causal path model can also help us to understand why quite different forms of treatment may be effective in treating the same condition. In general terms, a condition can be treated either by removing a factor necessary for the maintenance of the symptoms or by bringing about changes which suppress, neutralize or counterbalance the symptoms.

For example, in the case of pathway A (depression resulting directly from a disturbance in brain chemistry), the most obvious approach to treatment would involve a drug intervention to correct the chemical abnormality which precipitated (and may be maintaining) the person's depressed mood. Such an intervention might well be successful, for several relatively effective anti-depressant drugs are available. However, when a case of depression has been triggered by an environmental change (as in pathway C), intervention at a number of different levels (that is, at a number of different points along the causal pathway) might be effective in breaking the causal chain and alleviating the symptoms.

At the 'environmental' level, providing a new employment opportunity for a person who has become depressed following redundancy might be sufficient to stem the depression. Alternatively, intervention at the psychological level might help the person to 'come to terms with' the redundancy and to adopt a more realistic, and more optimistic, view of the future. This too could break the causal chain. Finally, the use of anti-depressant medication might also be effective in such a case, 'correcting' a chemical disturbance which may have arisen as a result of psychological processes such as persistent worrying.

Different strategies, operating at different points along the causal pathway, might also be used to alleviate phobic symptoms (pathway D). For example, it might be possible to change the person's estimation of the degree of threat represented by the phobic stimulus, or gradual exposure to fearful stimuli might reduce the person's phobic response. However, the fact that the pathway also includes the ubiquitous biological element suggests that some form of physical intervention (for example, the use of an anti-anxiety drug) might also prove effective in reducing the fear experienced when confronting a phobic object.

Thus although the model illustrated in Figure 1.2 is schematic, and is clearly oversimplified in many ways, it does illustrate a number of important points. It indicates that environmental events and psychological processes are key factors in the genesis of some psychological disorders but not others; that some causal chains are more extended than others; and that effective intervention may be possible at several different points along a particular causal chain.

As it stands, Figure 1.2 tells only part of the causal story, for the pathways end with the appearance of 'primary symptoms'. But such symptoms are maintained and shaped by additional factors, including the individual's active response to the symptoms, and other people's reactions. The establishment of primary symptoms may mark the end of the precipitating causal chain, but such symptoms then produce various environmental, psychological and physiological effects. For example, people who are depressed (whether the primary cause of their depression is a chemical disturbance or a major life change) tend to lose much of their customary enthusiasm and spontaneity and often find it difficult to concentrate on work tasks or to engage enthusiastically in social interactions.

If such effects are severe and prolonged, the repercussions may include dismissal from work and rejection by friends and family members. Such repercussions are bound to add to the person's difficulties and may reinforce feelings of isolation, guilt and 'personal failure'. Thus even when a person becomes depressed primarily as a result of 'spontaneous' neurochemical changes, the social and environmental consequences of the symptoms may well add to the severity and persistence of the condition. Stated somewhat differently, an initial depression resulting from neurochemical changes might produce psychological and environmental consequences which then precipitate a secondary depression.

Adverse psychological and environmental consequences of symptoms often exacerbate the person's clinical condition, so that various 'vicious circles' develop. Thus, other people's responses to the client's symptomatic behaviour may lead to further disturbances. Vicious circles also operate at the individual level. For example, a person suffering from an anxiety disorder may worry incessantly about the meaning and implications of the anxiety symptoms, and thereby increase the symptom severity. And just as people are often made anxious by their anxiety symptoms, they are often depressed by their depressive symptoms. Psychological symptoms may also lead to behavioural changes which then disrupt physiology. For example, intense and continual worrying may lead to chronic sleeplessness which then disrupts metabolic processes. Any consequent physiological symptoms may, in turn, provoke further worrying.

The 'causal chain' model sometimes conveys the erroneous impression that psychological disorders arise and are maintained in a wholly 'determined' way, and that people play little or no part as active agents. However, people are rarely passive in the face of behavioural, cognitive and mood changes. They react to their symptoms, and strive to understand and conquer them. Many people become very proficient at managing their symptoms, and develop a range of effective self-control skills. Some, however, employ strategies which are counterproductive and exacerbate the distress.

Whereas abnormal psychology usually focuses on the initiating part of the causal chain, and on the issue of what 'causes' particular disorders, most clinicians are acutely aware that the client's primary symptoms very often constitute only a minor part of the client's problems. In many cases the repercussions of the client's diagnosed disorder are more handicapping, and more debilitating, than the disorder itself. Many clinical interventions therefore focus on secondary symptoms and on other secondary effects of the client's clinical condition. Much of this work, particularly with those who are suffering from the more severe and longer-term conditions, takes the form of 'rehabilitation programmes'.

It is in the nature of a vicious circle that it can be broken at any point, and many of the adverse repercussions of abnormal psychological conditions are either psychological (commonly, these involve beliefs, appraisals and thinking styles) or social (that is, they involve the marital, family and community systems). This means that it may be extremely beneficial to provide individual psychological, or family-based, interventions even in cases in which the condition has a primary physical cause.

Thus people who suffer serious cognitive deficits as a result of head injury often develop secondary emotional symptoms. Frustrating experiences owing to impaired memory functioning, for example, may lead to recurrent bouts of intense anger and aggression. In many such cases, the client and his or her family eventually find the secondary 'personality changes' more distressing than the primary symptoms. A psychologist might be able to help in such a situation, perhaps by training the client to use special memory and recognition skills which might compensate for some of the primary cognitive problems. But the client's emotional disturbance might also be reduced as a result of counselling or psychotherapy. For optimal effectiveness, such an intervention might focus not just on the individual but on the family system. In cases of head injury, profound learning difficulties, schizophrenia, or any of a wide range of psychological and medical conditions, it is clear that much of the distress experienced by clients and their families stems from secondary problems. And these can often be alleviated through psychological interventions.

Conclusions ▶▶▶

Abnormal psychology is an academic discipline, closely related to the professions of clinical psychology and psychiatry, which is concerned with the psychological study of those conditions generally recognized as psychiatric disorders. The most influential current system of psychiatric classification – DSM-IV – was discussed and evaluated.

Many different accounts of 'madness' have been suggested throughout history, and even today there are several diverse approaches for understanding abnormal psychological conditions. The various models focus on different aspects, employ different concepts and often differ profoundly in their basic assumptions about the nature and origins of psychological disorders. It would be impossible to devise a grand synthesis involving all the contemporary models, but research has clearly demonstrated the relevance of very diverse factors to many disorders and this clearly points to a need for at least some degree of integration.

The 'biopsychosocial approach' provides the basic framework within which progress can be made. Within this general framework, the diathesis-stress model offers a means of accounting for the development of a wide range of disorders that have been shown to reflect both long-term vulnerability factors and the impact of stressful experiences. A 'causal pathway' model also provides a useful means of integrating diverse evidence. It illustrates how different conditions might arise by quite different causal routes, and can account for the fact that a range of quite different intervention methods might prove effective in treating a particular type of condition. This model also emphasizes the fact that the primary symptoms of a psychological disorder often have profound effects on social, environmental, psychological and physiological variables, which then maintain or exacerbate the condition.

Further Reading ▶▶▶

Tyrer, P. and Steinberg, D. (1993) *Models for Mental Disorder: Conceptual Models in Psychiatry*, 2nd edn. Chichester: Wiley.

Examines the different models which currently influence thinking in psychiatry and abnormal psychology, discussing the strengths and weaknesses of each.

Parker, I., Georgaca, E., Harper, D., McLaughlin, T. and Stower-Smith, M. (1995) *Deconstructing Psychopathology*. London: Routledge.

A highly challenging 'deconstructive' critique of the presuppositions and practices that underlie the study of psychopathology.

◀Discussion Points▶▶▶

1 How is the field of abnormal psychology defined, and how has the field been shaped?
2 Why is it useful to classify psychological disorders (make reference to the DSM system in your answer)?
3 What does it mean to 'diagnose' an abnormal psychological condition? Discuss some of the factors that can limit the accuracy of a diagnosis.
4 Compare and contrast the cognitive–behavioural model of psychopathology with *either* the biological model *or* the psychoanalytic model.
5 Discuss the assumptions made by the humanistic-existential, family-systems and sociocultural models of psychopathology, and consider how each of these models challenges the idea that psychological problems are 'diseases' of an individual person.
6 Research shows that, for many disorders, biological, psychological and social factors all play a role in the development of the condition. How is it possible to integrate information from these different domains to provide a comprehensive causal account?

2 Anxiety Disorders

The disorders to be discussed in this chapter are all marked by considerable emotional distress, high levels of anxiety, frequent fears and persistent worrying. Anxiety disorders account for more 'cases' of psychopathology than any other category. Recent large-scale studies in the United States have indicated that during any 12-month period as many as 7 per cent of the population will suffer from an anxiety disorder. More women than men are affected (although the sex ratio differs markedly between different disorders), and the prevalence is higher among those aged under 45 years than among older people. Many clients who develop an anxiety disorder recover quickly, but if the condition persists for more than 6 months there is a high probability that it will persist for at least another two years unless treatment is provided. Fortunately, highly effective therapeutic procedures are available for most of the anxiety disorders, and there is a high rate of success when appropriate help is provided.

◀The Clinical Picture▶▶

Each of the anxiety disorders is marked by intense anxiety and persistent avoidance behaviour (see Table 2.1).

Chronic anxiety is the most pronounced symptom of some of the conditions (especially generalized anxiety disorder), whereas others (particularly the phobias) are characterized by a fear and avoidance of particular situations. The anxiety disorders are usually highly distressing, both for the client and for his or her relatives, and they are associated with a variety of emotional, physiological, cognitive and behavioural signs and symptoms:

Table 2.1 The anxiety disorders

Simple phobia	A persistent and irrational fear of a particular type of object or situation
Social phobia	A persistent fear of social situations; the fear may be extensive or may be elicited by only a limited range of social situations
Agoraphobia	A fear of being in public places (particularly those from which escape might be difficult or embarrassing in a case of emergency)
Panic disorder	A condition marked by frequently recurring attacks of panic and terror
Generalized anxiety disorder	Persistent excessive worrying and feelings of anxiety which are not restricted to a limited range of situations or issues
Post-traumatic stress disorder	A condition in which fear and other symptoms relate to a traumatic event which occurred some weeks, months or years before onset
Obsessive–compulsive disorder	A condition marked by persistent obsessions and/or compulsions (the latter often have a ritual quality)

It should be noted that although a person is likely to receive only one of these diagnoses, many clients will meet the diagnostic criteria for two or more of the conditions.

- *Emotional aspects.* Many people who suffer from an anxiety disorder feel 'on edge', 'excitable' or 'restless', and are apprehensive about the future. Irritability and feelings of intense anger are also relatively common. In extreme cases, an anxiety disorder will restrict the person's lifestyle to such a degree that the condition amounts to a form of disablement.
- *Physiological aspects.* Physiological symptoms include cardiovascular (palpitations and pains across the chest), respiratory (constriction in the chest, breathlessness), gastrointestinal (dry mouth and difficulty in swallowing) and genito-urinary (especially a frequent need to urinate) problems. Other symptoms include dizziness, blurred vision, trembling, headaches and disturbances of sleep.
- *Cognitive aspects.* Many of those who suffer from an anxiety disorder feel distracted and confused and find it difficult to 'think straight'. An inability to focus attention on immediate concerns, and to think coherently, is likely to disturb the client's social functioning, so that he or she may find it difficult and distressing to carry on a conversation with a friend or to join in normal family activities. Thoughts of impending catastrophe will tend to promote a general sense of apprehension, and many situations are likely to be appraised as menacing. Other cognitive effects include depersonalization (a sense of altered personal identity) and derealization (a fleeting sense of the world being unreal, or a feeling of being detached from the world).
- *Behavioural aspects.* Many clients become very agitated. Some show a marked tremor or signs of increased muscle tension (which may cause them to frown and present with a 'worried look'), which may have significant detrimental effects on those perceptual-motor skills which

call for precision and fine coordination. The more pervasive conditions, such as agoraphobia and post-traumatic stress disorder, are likely to interfere with the performance of everyday activities more than the simple phobias, for example, which may be considered relatively 'dormant' until the person is confronted with a situation that arouses distinct fear. Finally, most of the clients who suffer from an obsessive–compulsive disorder engage repeatedly in certain compulsive behaviours, many of which have a ritualistic quality.

- *Social aspects.* Those who have a social phobia may strenuously avoid contact with other people, and this will have extreme effects on any established relationship. The person's difficulties may also have devastating effects on employment and participation in educational courses. When the condition has persisted for several months or years, friends may prefer to avoid contact with the client, and family members may find it increasingly difficult to remain sympathetic.

◄Phobias► ►

A phobia (the term comes from the Greek word for 'fear') is a persistent propensity to experience acute fear when confronted with a particular type of object or situation. Crucially, the fear experienced is disproportionate to any real threat presented by the situation. Phobias are specified in terms of the type of stimulus which elicits the extreme fear response, and many have alternative names derived from Greek or Latin roots. Thus spider phobia is sometimes referred to as 'arachnophobia' and a fear of closed spaces as 'claustrophobia'.

Phobias are very common. A major US study of over 18000 adults indicated that phobias which met a criterion of clinical significance were more common than either depression or alcohol-related conditions (Boyd et al., 1990). The study monitored respondents' health over a one-month period, and the prevalence rate for phobias was found to be in the region of 6 per cent, making the condition the most common psychiatric disorder in the community. The prevalence rates were significantly higher for women than for men for both simple phobia and agoraphobia (but not for social phobia).

◄The Simple Phobias► ► ►

The 'simple phobias' include animal phobias (fear of insects, reptiles or mammals), 'situational phobias' (fear of heights, open spaces, closed spaces or thunderstorms) and 'illness phobias' (fear of blood, cancer, AIDS etc.). To merit clinical attention, a phobia must be persistent and distressing, and must constitute a serious constraint on the person's lifestyle.

Epidemiology

Fewer than 1 per cent of the clients who consult clinical psychologists and psychiatrists are seeking treatment for a simple phobia. Epidemiological

Box 2.1
Simple Phobia: Case Vignettes

Snake phobia (ophidiophobia)

Marcia is afraid of snakes, and even when she sees a picture of a snake in a magazine she recoils in horror and has to turn the page quickly. She would find it impossible to remain in the same room as a real snake, even if the animal were out of sight and confined to a totally secure tank. Marcia fully recognizes that her fear is irrational.

Needle phobia (belonophobia)

Mark has a fear of needles, particularly long needles. Whenever he has had an injection he has broken out in a cold sweat and has not been able to look at the syringe, and on two such occasions he fainted. He now refuses to have an injection unless his wife is with him and has fully informed the medical personnel about his profound fear. Mark insists that he is not afraid of any pain associated with having an injection but that it is the thought and sight of the needle itself which triggers his intense reaction. He has had several nightmares involving injections,

and at home his family avoid all mention of needles.

Flying phobia (aerophobia)

Sheila, who is now aged 42, flew for the first and last time when she was 28. The occasion was her honeymoon, and she remembers her great reluctance, during the wedding preparations, to agree to the plan that the couple should fly away to a romantic destination. Friends assured her that her fear simply reflected that fact that she had never flown before and that the experience would be enjoyable. However, her anxiety immediately before and during the flight reached such a pitch than she developed intense panic symptoms and 'became hysterical' on the aeroplane. She says that that experience, and the fear associated with having to make the return flight, spoiled her honeymoon. She was prescribed a mild tranquillizer before the return trip, and this appeared to reduce the intensity of many of her symptoms. Although she accepts that flying is a safe way of travelling she has vowed that she will never make another flight, and her family have long since given up trying to persuade her to change her mind.

studies have shown consistently that more women than men are affected. The sex ratio of 2:1 is often quoted, averaged across different types of simple phobia.

Aetiology

Psychoanalytic accounts   According to classical psychoanalysis, phobias develop as a result of anxiety generated by intrapsychic conflict associated with the suppression of certain basic impulses. The phobic object is held to be a substitute for (and often the symbolic equivalent of) the 'real' object of fear. Thus in Freud's classic case of 'Little Hans' a child developed an exaggerated fear of horses following an experience in which a horse had reared up in the street. Freud considered that what appeared to be a simple animal phobia was in fact a reflection of the child's fear of his father. Freud suggested that Hans had sexual feelings for his mother, and that the intrapsychic conflict which these feelings generated had led to the phobia. Hans was said to have had an unconscious fear that his father would learn of his erotic interest in the mother and castrate him. The inadmissible nature of Hans' unconscious dread of his father, Freud claimed, led to a displacement of the fear on to a neutral and 'suitable' type of object – horses.

Behaviourist accounts   Behaviourists, in particular, have had something of a field day in taking the above Freudian analysis to task. The behaviourist critics maintain that most phobias are acquired by a simple process of conditioning, and that the case of Little Hans provides a good illustration of such a conditioning process. The child's experience of extreme fear when the horse reared in front of him, they assert, left him with a learned fear, and his subsequent avoidance of horses then served to reinforce and maintain this phobia.

When someone has a fear of one object or situation then other objects or situations which become associated with it may also acquire fear-eliciting properties. The classic demonstration of the acquisition of fear through association was reported by Watson and Rayner (1920). An infant known as Little Albert had been playing happily with a white rat for several weeks before the experimenter began a fear induction procedure in which, whenever Albert reached towards the rat, a steel bar was struck with a hammer, making a loud frightening noise. After several trials, Albert acquired a fear of the rat and would cry whenever the rat was presented. According to some accounts this fear also generalized to other objects which bore some similarity to the rat, including a rabbit and a Santa Claus mask with a white beard.

Albert's acquisition of a fear of rats can be explained in terms of classical conditioning. In classical conditioning, an initially neutral stimulus comes to elicit a conditioned response (CR) by virtue of association with an unconditioned stimulus (US). In the case of Albert's acquisition of fear, the loud noise was the US. By association, the rat eventually came to elicit the fear CR by association with the loud noise. The fact that the conditioned fear was also elicited by objects bearing some resemblance to rats (such as a rabbit) can be explained in terms of 'stimulus generalization'.

Watson and Rayner may have been fortunate in their original choice of a rat as the conditioning stimulus (CS), whereas those who later attempted to produce fear responses to such objects as opera glasses and articles of clothing may have been less fortunate. It appears that human beings are 'prepared' to acquire fears of some objects but not of others. For example, Ohman et al. (1975) paired pictures with electric shocks and found it easier to produce conditioned fear to pictures of snakes and spiders than to pictures of faces and houses. Moreover, although the subjects' conditioned fear responses to the pictures faded (or were 'extinguished') when the electric shock was no longer presented, extinction occurred less rapidly when the conditioned stimulus was a picture of a snake or a spider than when it was a picture of a face or a house.

So why does extinction not occur in phobic patients? The answer is that people usually escape or avoid situations which have become fear-eliciting. Because fear reduction acts as a positive reward, avoidance responses are reinforced and are therefore strengthened and maintained by a process of operant (or instrumental) conditioning. This account of the origins and maintenance of conditioned fear is known as the 'two-factor account' of fear and avoidance (Mowrer, 1939, 1947, 1960). Simply stated, it maintains that fears are acquired through classical conditioning and maintained as a result of the operant conditioning of avoidance behaviour.

Vicarious learning   'Vicarious learning' (also labelled 'modelling' and 'observational learning') occurs when a person learns by observing the actions and reactions of another person. Thus a child who witnesses a parent's fear whenever a spider or a wasp appears might well develop a fear of such animals. Children often have the same persistent fears as their parents and other relatives (May, 1950). Similarities in the fear profiles of those who are related by blood might conceivably reflect shared genetic characteristics, but it seems much more likely that a particular fear will be common to several relatives as a result of 'fear contagion' through the process of vicarious learning.

Cognitive accounts   Persistent, and even disabling, fears may result from misinformation and false beliefs. Thus a person may acquire a fear of an unfamiliar object or situation by reading or hearing about the dangers supposedly associated with it. Those who believe that a particular situation or object presents a real threat when it is really quite innocuous may drastically curb their activities and suffer unnecessary distress. A fear which originates from a false belief may later be maintained by conditioned response patterns which develop as a result of continual fear and avoidance. Cognitive theorists add that phobias distort people's judgements about feared situations, so that they process relevant information selectively, think about the situation in an irrational manner, and misinterpret pertinent cues (Foa and Kozak, 1986).

Treatment of simple phobias

Drug treatment   No drug can provide a 'cure' for a phobia, but anti-anxiety drugs may substantially reduce the fear experienced in response to a threatening situation. The use of medication is valuable when the person knows in advance when he or she will encounter a frightening situation. Thus a person with a flying phobia might take a mild tranquilliser a little time before a planned flight. The drug effects are merely temporary and do not lead to any reduction in the phobia itself (O'Sullivan and Marks, 1991).

Psychoanalytic treatment Psychoanalysts claim that what appears to be a straightforward fear of the phobic object often signifies some deep-seated psychological conflict which the object symbolizes in some way. Thus, the most effective way of eliminating such a phobia is to discover its real meaning and then to deal with the underlying conflict. However, there is little evidence to suggest that psychoanalysis is effective in treating phobias.

Behavioural and cognitive–behavioural treatments Exposure-based interventions can be highly effective in achieving long-term reductions in phobic fear and phobic avoidance (Marshall, 1988). The most widely used exposure method is desensitization, which involves the use of relaxation and the presentation of a graduated series ('hierarchy') of stimuli representing the phobic object or situation. Over a number of sessions there is a gradual progression through to the top of the hierarchy so that, eventually, the client is able to remain in a relaxed state even when presented with stimuli which were originally rated as likely to produce intense fear (Goldfried and Davison, 1976).

The stimulus items may take the form of words spoken by the therapist ('imaginal desensitization') or actual examples of the fear-inducing objects ('*in vivo* desensitization'). For example, a set of small and large spiders, dead and living, might be assembled to be displayed to phobic clients, and later handled by them. Both forms of desensitization are very effective in reducing simple phobias. Although the success of desensitization was initially explained in terms of counter-conditioning, more recent evaluations have tended to emphasize the role of cognitions. Changes in subjects' beliefs about whether they will experience fear in response to particular situations appear to contribute significantly to the beneficial effects that have been shown to result from desensitization programmes (Emmelkamp, 1992).

Desensitization involves unhurried incremental exposure to the feared stimulus. In sharp contrast, 'flooding' involves rapidly exposing the client to extremely fearful scenes, often within a lengthy single session (Emmelkamp et al., 1992). Clients initially experience intense anxiety, but this eventually subsides. However, if a flooding session is curtailed before the client has experienced a high level of fear, the severity of the phobia may actually increase, rather than decrease. The potential dangers, and its distressing nature, means that flooding is rarely the treatment method of choice for cases of simple phobia.

A number of the methods used to treat clients with simple phobias employ some form of 'modelling'. As the therapist models a relaxed response to a feared situation, the client will clearly focus not only on the therapist's behaviour but also on those aspects of the situation which normally elicit fear. Thus modelling involves exposure. Therapists who employ modelling techniques recognize the importance of both of the elements of exposure and observational learning, and many also emphasize the importance of changes in the client's beliefs and expectations. Clients who participate in modelling procedures are likely to experience a gradual reduction in the 'fear of fear' and may slowly come to accept that they will be able to cope when confronting a situation which previously elicited fear. Thus modelling helps clients to develop a confidence about their own responses and it may increase their sense of personal effectiveness or 'self-efficacy' (Bandura, 1977).

Some people develop an exaggerated fear not because they have been subjected to a conditioning process but because they believe the particular type of object or situation to be dangerous. In some cases the belief is simply based on misinformation. Thus a man whose fear of wasps is based on the false belief that wasp stings are often fatal might lose this fear as soon as he receives information from a credible source about the relatively innocuous nature of wasp stings. In many cases, however, the mere provision of factual information will not alter the conviction on which a fear is based. Treatment programmes based on cognitive techniques aim to inform the client about relevant facts while also changing the person's convictions.

Although the theoretical distinction between 'conditioned fears' and 'belief-based fears' may be clear, it is often difficult to make the distinction in practice. The fact that both cognitions and conditioning processes may help to maintain a phobia suggests that an optimal approach to the treatment of the simple phobias should involve both exposure methods and cognitive techniques (Marks, 1987; Warren and Zgourides, 1991). Some of the more elaborate therapeutic programmes that have been developed to treat a fear of flying employ both types of intervention. They provide instruction in the physics of flying, and also include a brief flight.

◀Social Phobia: the Clinical Picture▶▶▶

A social phobia is an exaggerated fear of at least some types of social situation. Even those who suffer from a severe social phobia are usually able to remain calm when they interact with at least some members of their own family, but when a phobic response is elicited by a wide range of social situations the condition is labelled 'generalized social phobia'. A condition in which fears are elicited by a more limited range of social situations is labelled 'non-generalized social phobia'.

As with other types of phobia, the main symptom of social phobia is emotional distress in the form of extreme anxiety or fear. The main behavioural effect is a pronounced tendency to avoid any social situation perceived as threatening. When circumstances demand social interaction, the person's acute anxiety may lead to marked difficulties in communicating and a considerable awkwardness in many aspects of non-verbal behaviour.

Many overestimate the degree to which they are the focus of other people's attention (Trower and Turland, 1984) and remain highly self-conscious, constantly monitoring and criticizing their own social performance. Oversensitivity often leads to inferred criticism where none was intended. Consequently, many clients will experience a strong urge to escape from the situation. Escape will have the immediate effect of reducing anxiety, but it is likely to make matters worse in the longer term.

Epidemiology

Even well conducted large-scale studies return markedly different estimates of the prevalence of social phobia in the adult population. Thus the Duke Epidemiological Catchment Area Study of over 3000 subjects estimated the lifetime prevalence as 3.8 per cent (Davidson et al., 1993), whereas data from the US National Comorbidity Survey suggested a lifetime prevalence of 13.3 per cent (Judd, 1994).

None the less, it is generally agreed that social phobia usually begins at some time during adolescence or early adulthood, and several studies have reported somewhat higher rates for women than for men. Although social phobia often becomes a chronic disorder, the condition can usually be treated very effectively. It is therefore disappointing that probably no more than one-quarter of those who suffer from social phobia ever seek treatment.

Aetiology

The fact that social situations can easily become threatening suggests that human beings may be 'prepared' to acquire social fears (Barlow, 1988). Laboratory experiments have demonstrated the relative ease with which fear responses can be conditioned to pictures of certain 'social' stimuli (pictures of angry faces, for example) and have established the fact that such conditioning is relatively resistant to extinction (Ohman, 1986).

Vulnerability to social phobia may be partly determined by genetic factors. Clients who suffer from social phobia obtain relatively high scores on measures of 'neuroticism' or 'trait anxiety', and it is well established that individual differences on this variable reflect the influence of genetic factors. The results of twin studies in which one or both siblings within each pair has been diagnosed as suffering from social phobia also support the idea that genetic factors may play a significant role in the aetiology of the disorder (Andrews et al., 1990; Fyer, 1993) (see Box 2.3 for a discussion of how evidence is gained of an involvement of genetic factors in the development of psychological disorders).

However, environmental influences also appear to play an important role in determining an individual's level of vulnerability. Adverse social experiences during childhood, for example, may affect social development such that in adulthood the person will be highly self-conscious and will tend to regard other people as threatening and highly critical. Many socially phobic clients have a history of parental criticism (Bruch and Heimberg, 1994), rejection or neglect during childhood, and report that their parents were highly sensitive to any criticism made by other people (Bruch, 1989).

A prominent characteristic of almost all cases of social phobia is a profound 'fear of negative evaluation'. Clients are generally preoccupied with how well they are 'coming across' to other people during social interactions. Rather than attending in a relaxed way to what other people are saying or

Box 2.2
Why Worry? Worriers' Assumptions about the Usefulness of Worrying

Borkovec (1994) conducted a series of studies to examine worriers' assessment of the benefits of worrying (they also recognized that there were 'costs'). Five of the benefits frequently reported by worriers are listed below.

1   *Superstitious avoidance of catastrophe.* Worriers sometimes imagine that worrying about a threatening event will make it less likely to happen. They acknowledge that there is little basis for such a belief, and that it is unreasonable, but they nevertheless 'feel it to be true'.
2   *Actual avoidance of catastrophe.* Some worriers believe that worrying may enable them to discover an effective strategy for avoiding or preventing catastrophe.
3   *Avoidance of deeper topics.* Some people suggest that their worries about relatively trivial topics or improbable events act as a distraction from thinking about concerns which are more deep-seated, more immediate or more upsetting.
4   *Coping preparation.* Worrying about a possible disastrous event can be seen as a way of 'steeling oneself' against the

event. Thus, if disaster struck, a person who had worried about such a possibility might be better prepared to cope than someone who had never contemplated the prospect. In addition to 'lessening the blow', worrying about an event may also involve the cognitive rehearsal of strategies which would prove useful either in avoiding or escaping from a threatening situation, or in helping the person to cope with the aftermath. Thus there are held to be advantages of worrying in terms of both 'fortifying' the individual and aiding 'planning'.
5   *Motivation enhancement.* Worry may be regarded by the worrier as positively motivating. Worrying about an issue helps to 'keep it in mind' so that the person is unlikely to forget to attend to relevant matters (worry about the possible consequences of arriving late at a meeting, for example, may prompt the person to arrive on time). Worry may also help to keep a person motivated. Worrying about possible failure in an examination, for example, may encourage the person to work conscientiously.

doing, many clients remain highly self-conscious. An overconcern with other people's opinions may lead them to become hypervigilant for any possible sign of criticism, disapproval or rejection from those they meet, and oversensitivity often leads clients to infer criticism where none was intended. Compliments may be ignored and excessive attention paid to any slightly adverse comment or gesture. Those who suffer from a social phobia also tend to engage in 'mind-reading' – making unwarranted assumptions about what other people are 'probably' thinking.

The emotional distress experienced during a social encounter is likely to be fuelled by many negative and disruptive thoughts. Clients often focus on the possible calamities that might arise in the situation, worry about other people's judgements of their performance, and imagine that their anxiety is immediately evident to others. Thus they may worry that their lack of composure will be revealed by such signs as speech hesitancies, trembling, or blushing (Barlow, 1988).

Extreme self-consciousness and self-criticism during social encounters will generate anxiety, and this is likely to have disruptive effects on the client's social performance. As the person becomes more and more anxious he or she is likely to find it increasingly difficult to interact in a natural and relaxed way. Conversation may become awkward and stilted as the person stumbles over words and phrases, and such minor mishaps are likely to generate additional self-criticism and more anxiety. Eventually the client may be in a state close to panic, and signs such as voice tremor and blushing may reveal the intensity of the person's distress.

Treatments: drugs

Although drugs are sometimes used to help clients suffering from social phobia, their usefulness is limited. The drugs most frequently prescribed are benzodiazepines (a class of anti-anxiety drugs which includes Librium, Valium and Ativan), beta blockers and monoamine oxidase inhibitors (MAOIs, a class of anti-depressant drugs). In addition, drugs which inhibit the reuptake of the neurotransmitter substance serotonin (5-hydroxy-tryptamine, or 5-HT) are sometimes prescribed.

While all these different types of drugs may be effective for some people, the benefits usually remain only for as long as the person continues to take the drug. Furthermore, each drug has a number of potential side-effects.

Psychological treatments

Exposure   Most effective treatment programmes involve some degree of exposure to the social situations which the client perceives as threatening. Initially, exposure is likely to take the form of imagined scenarios and role-plays, but *in vivo* exposure techniques will also be used. The tasks undertaken by the client will generally progress gradually from those which present relatively little challenge (for example, travelling on a bus with a friend) to those which are much more demanding (for example, asking a stranger for directions to another part of the town).

Cognitive approaches   Cognitive approaches used to treat social phobia include rational–emotive therapy (RET), self-instructional training (SIT) and anxiety management techniques (AMT). Cognitive restructuring approaches (of which RET is an example) usually involve a detailed exploration of clients' beliefs and their judgements about their own behaviour and other people's responses in social situations. Following the exploration stage, the therapist will begin to challenge erroneous or unjustified beliefs.

Cognitive restructuring is usually supplemented by training in practical strategies for changing thinking patterns during social encounters and for managing any anxiety that arises. Anxiety management may involve the use of relaxation techniques, rational self-talk and distraction. When the client is well practised, homework assignments are devised to encourage the use of the broad range of adaptive cognitive strategies (Barlow, 1992).

Social skills training (SST)   Many of those who suffer from social phobia are not seriously deficient in social skills. However, if the therapist is able to identify an area of social performance which might benefit from training, various techniques may be employed to enhance the relevant skills. The methods employed in such training are likely to include modelling, role-play and direct instruction. Reinforcement and feedback (often by means of videotape) are important elements.

Evaluation studies have demonstrated that social skills training can lead to a considerable reduction in the level of social anxiety, but a carefully graduated exposure to social situations may well produce a desensitization effect. Cognitive changes may also play an important part (Edelmann, 1992). Furthermore, any performance improvement may prompt a considerable growth in confidence. Thus the effectiveness of SST may owe at least as much to changes in beliefs and increased confidence as to any real increase in performance skills.

Comparative treatment studies   Studies which have compared the effectiveness of a number of different behavioural and cognitive approaches to the treatment of social phobia have generally found little to choose between them in terms of effectiveness. Thus, in a series of studies Emmelkamp and his colleagues (Emmelkamp et al., 1985a, b; Mersch et al., 1989) found that rational–emotive therapy, self-instructional training, *in vivo* exposure and social skills training were all of a similar high level of effectiveness. Other research, however, has suggested that there may be particular benefits of including both of the elements of exposure and cognitive restructuring (Mattick et al., 1989).

Group treatment   Although tailoring a treatment programme to the individual's specific needs may be useful, there would appear to be several advantages of conducting treatment sessions for social phobia with groups of people suffering from the condition (Heimberg et al., 1993). In addition to the fact that this mode of delivery is particularly efficient in the use of resources, the group context is useful because clients are able to meet and interact with several other people within an environment that can be perceived as relatively safe. If the atmosphere during sessions is relaxed and supportive, then the experience of participating in the group may be powerfully desensitizing. Clients may be able to learn from other people's experiences and may derive insight and self-confidence through helping others to overcome their social fears.

◀Agoraphobia▶▶

Over half of all clients who receive treatment for a phobia are suffering from agoraphobia. Literally translated, the term 'agoraphobia' means 'fear of the market place'. The condition is also sometimes described as a 'fear of open spaces'. However, both of these descriptions are misleading because they suggest that the agoraphobic client has a fear of a rather specific range of situations. In fact, many agoraphobic clients are terrified of walking along streets, visiting shops and using any form of public transport, and they may be able to bear such situations only if a friend or relative remains close by. The widespread nature of their situational fears leads many agoraphobic clients to remain confined to their home for long periods, and because the majority of those affected are mature women, the condition has been dubbed 'the housebound housewife syndrome'.

The clinical picture

Many who suffer from agoraphobia are in a chronic state of high physiological arousal (Marks, 1969). The arousal may be experienced as a general sense of restlessness and tension, but there are also likely to be specific somatic symptoms (shortness of breath, dry mouth or cardiovascular symptoms, for example). Any attempt to leave the house or to travel alone is likely to precipitate a state of acute anxiety. The cognitive effects of such anxiety may include confusion, an inability to think coherently and problems in remembering familiar routes. Worries at this time are likely to focus on the possibility of a crisis, and on the 'catastrophic' social consequences that might follow.

The main behavioural aspect of agoraphobia is avoidance of a broad range of situations and activities. Thus some clients avoid using public transport, visiting shops and walking anywhere outside the home. Others have an extreme fear of certain types of vehicle, or of such contrivances as lifts and escalators. Agoraphobia places severe restrictions on the client's range of activities, and may also have profoundly detrimental effects on the quality of life of other members of the family.

Epidemiology

The lifetime prevalence of agoraphobia is variously estimated at between 0.5 and 1.0 per cent of the population. While all the epidemiological evidence indicates that a substantial proportion of agoraphobic clients are women, the female: male ratio found in studies has ranged between 2:1 and 7:1. Several of the larger epidemiological surveys (most of which have employed DSM criteria) have returned figures nearer to 2:1.

The onset of an agoraphobic condition usually occurs when the person is between 22 and 35 years old. If the condition remains untreated it is likely to persist for many years, although the severity of the symptoms may vary considerably from month to month. Spontaneous remissions do occur; it is not unknown for a person who has been unable to leave the house for many years to lose the disabling fear suddenly. Such a dramatic transition often appears to be triggered by a major change in life circumstances.

Aetiology

Some people appear to be more vulnerable than others to the development of agoraphobia, as a result their genetic makeup. A genetically based 'neuroticism' factor may render an individual susceptible to the development of any one of the different forms of anxiety disorder, including agoraphobia. It is also likely that adverse experiences in early life may increase vulnerability to this condition. Psychoanalytic accounts of the origins of the condition often emphasize the role of childhood experiences and suggest that the disorder results from the displacement of certain types of repressed and unconscious conflict generated in the early years. However, the evidence for such psychodynamic explanations is extremely tenuous. We can be more confident about a link between vulnerability to agoraphobia and the experience of severe stress during adulthood. For example, in the major survey conducted by Thorpe and Burns (1983) many agoraphobic clients reported that their disorder began soon after a major stressful event such as a bereavement or a serious physical illness.

The evidence suggests that agoraphobia may be both a phobic response to threatening situations and a strategy for maintaining a sense of safety (Rachman, 1984), and this means that a comprehensive account of the aetiology of the condition requires consideration of both of these aspects.

Agoraphobia as a phobia

According to the behavioural account, agoraphobia is a maladaptive learned response which develops as a conditioned fear of certain situations. A radical overgeneralization of this fear might then lead to fear being elicited by all but the most familiar situations. Furthermore, fear often leads to avoidance and, according to Mowrer's 'two-factor model' (Mowrer, 1939, 1960), avoidance of feared situations will be positively reinforced by a reduction in anxiety. The relief experienced in reaching 'safety' (usually, the home) will often strengthen the avoidance response and increase the positive 'reward value' (or the 'attractiveness') of the home.

A rather similar account can be provided in terms of cognitive processes. A person who has a distressing experience in a particular location will tend to regard any similar environment as threatening. Following escape to a safe location, thoughts about the traumatic event may stimulate fantasies about future scenarios involving similar, or even more horrendous, ordeals. If judgements of threat are generalized to a wide range of situations, the person may conclude that the best strategy for avoiding adversity is to remain in the relative safety of the home.

Thus both the behavioural (conditioning) and cognitive accounts of the development of agoraphobia 'as a phobia' suggest that one or more negative experiences lead to specific fears (or appraisals of threat), which then generalize so that they are eventually provoked by a wide range of situations. Many cases of agoraphobia do appear to have developed following a particularly upsetting experience in an outside location. Thorpe and Burns (1983) found that 70 per cent of agoraphobic patients were able to identify a specific event which they held to be responsible for the onset of their condition, and Uhde et al. (1985) found that most of their clients attributed the onset of their agoraphobia to a particular panic episode.

Thus there is some empirical support for the view that agoraphobia is learned avoidance behaviour, and that the condition develops in the same way as other types of phobia. However, most phobias have a relatively restricted focus, whereas the agoraphobic client feels threatened by a wide range of situations.

Agoraphobia and safety

Rachman (1984) emphasized the fact that much of the behaviour associated with agoraphobia can be understood as an attempt to achieve and maintain a sense of safety. He pointed to the contrast between danger signals and safety signals. Danger signals, for the agoraphobic client, are likely to include symptoms of increased physiological arousal, the view of a crowded shopping centre, and the sight of a lift or escalator. Safety signals will probably include many aspects of the home environment. Rachman pointed out that most of the behavioural methods used to treat agoraphobic clients focus on reducing the power of danger signals, and suggested that adding powerful safety cues to threatening situations should be equally effective.

Factors which trigger a condition may be quite different from those which serve to maintain it. In the case of agoraphobia, while there is little evidence to support the suggestion by Goldstein and Chambless (1978) that agoraphobia may develop as the result of strong interpersonal conflict (especially if it involves the spouse), it is clear that family relationships are often crucially important in determining the course of the disorder and the client's response to treatment. Thus, while the onset of the condition may reflect the impact of a traumatic incident or a threat to the individual's sense of security, the disorder may be maintained by interpersonal factors. Other people's compassionate responses, or an exemption from unpleasant chores, may provide valuable secondary gains which help to sustain the condition.

Treatment

Drug treatment Both tricyclic antidepressants (particularly imipramine) and the MAOIs, as well as some of the benzodiazepines, are able to provide short-term symptomatic relief in a significant proportion of cases. However, many of these drugs have adverse side-effects, and the agoraphobic symptoms tend to return soon after the medication is stopped.

Psychological treatment   Behavioural and cognitive–behavioural treatments are the most effective forms of intervention for agoraphobia. A substantial reduction in fear can be achieved following gradual exposure to anxiety-provoking situations. Agoraphobia is treated more effectively by *in vivo* (real-life) treatment than by imaginal exposure (Emmelkamp et al., 1992). '*In vivo* desensitization' for agoraphobia involves encouraging the client to make more and more adventurous forays while remaining in a relaxed state. It has been shown that a few relatively long exposure sessions are more effective than a greater number of shorter sessions, and because of this most treatment programmes are fairly intensive.

Sessions with the therapist are usually complemented by 'homework assignments'. Some clients prefer to tackle their problem without the guidance of a therapist, and they may make use of a self-help programme. Several of these have now been developed and published, and most include adaptations of the exposure strategies which would normally be managed by a therapist (e.g. Mathews et al., 1981).

Cognitive therapists who offer treatment for agoraphobia generally attempt to change the client's beliefs about the likely consequences of an excursion beyond the home. A meta-analysis of outcome studies of the treatment of agoraphobia (Mattick et al., 1990) suggested that a permanent reduction in agoraphobic symptoms is best achieved by the use of cognitive behaviour therapy combined with exposure, and it is now generally agreed that cognitive interventions should be used to supplement, rather than replace, techniques involving direct exposure (Warren and Zgourides, 1991). However, others have claimed that cognitive strategies add very little to exposure treatment and that exposure alone is usually sufficient to bring about a positive and lasting change (Emmelkamp et al., 1986).

Partner involvement in treatment   Therapists treating clients with agoraphobia may invite the client's partner to become involved in the treatment programme as a 'resident therapist' or 'co-therapist' (Bennun, 1988). The results of outcome studies have also shown that, overall, the handing over of the day-to-day management of a treatment programme to the client's partner does not detract from the effectiveness of the treatment (Barlow et al., 1981; Cobb et al., 1984).

Partners may not always welcome an improvement in the client's condition. Perlmutter (1990) found that while some partners were highly supportive of the therapist, others appeared to become increasingly anxious as the treatment proceeded, and sometimes even attempted to obstruct or undermine the therapist's efforts. When a family system has adapted successfully to accommodate to the client's disorder, there may be considerable resistance to any alteration which would demand a further revision of family patterns. Overall, there is little evidence to suggest that partner-facilitated treatment is any more effective than professional-only treatment (Dewey and Hunsley, 1990).

◄Generalized Anxiety Disorder►►►

The clinical picture

People who suffer from generalized anxiety disorder (GAD) worry excessively about a wide range of issues. While they recognize that their concerns are greatly exaggerated, they find it impossible to stop worrying. GAD clients find it difficult to relax because they are chronically anxious. Because their anxiety is so extensive, and does not usually relate to the immediate environmental context, it is often described as 'pervasive anxiety' or 'free-floating anxiety'.

Although descriptions of GAD often emphasize the diffuse nature of clients' worries, it is often possible to identify particular worry themes. Thus GAD clients often worry about family, money, work and health. These are also the issues which most other people worry about, but GAD clients' worries are especially persistent and particularly intense (Sanderson and Barlow, 1990). GAD clients may experience a chronic tension and feel constantly 'on edge'. Among the physical symptoms commonly reported are shortness of breath, palpitations, sweating, difficulty swallowing and a tension in the stomach.

Box 2.3
Evidence of Genetic Involvement in Psychological Disorders

How is it possible to determine whether genetic factors contribute to the risk that an individual will develop a particular type of psychological disorder? Several different types of research may provide evidence of genetic involvement. The earliest attempts to establish such involvement took the form of painstaking examinations of the history of particular families. Later work has involved an assessment of patterns of a specific disorder within large numbers of clients' families. The finding that several people within the same family tend to suffer from the same disorder provides an indication that a vulnerability to the disorder may be

inherited in some way, particularly if there is a positive association between the genetic closeness of a relative and his or her increased likelihood of suffering from the same disorder as the client. Such a pattern has been demonstrated for schizophrenia, for example, in which there is a clear correlation between the closeness of an individual's blood relationship to a person diagnosed as schizophrenic and the risk of that individual also being diagnosed as suffering from a schizophrenic disorder (Gottesman, 1991).

The fact that a disorder occurs in several members of the same family does not prove that a genetic factor is involved. Such a familial pattern might reflect some kind of 'psychological contagion', or the fact that members of a family often experience the same stressful events. For stronger proof of genetic involvement we need to consider evidence from other types of research, including twin studies and adoption studies.

Twin studies provide a powerful way of assessing the influence of genes on the development of a psychological disorder. Monozygotic (MZ) twins result from the splitting of a single fertilized egg and are genetically identical. Fraternal, or dizygotic (DZ), twins, however, come from two different eggs and share only 50 per cent of their genes. Thus if a psychological disorder is genetically influenced, more MZ twin pairs than DZ twin pairs will be concordant for the disorder (concordance means that both twins suffer from the disorder; if only one twin suffers from the disorder the pair are said to be 'discordant').

Because twins are usually reared together, it could be argued that high concordance figures for twins reflect the effects of a shared environment, rather than a shared genetic profile. However, this objection is undermined when the concordance levels found for MZ twins are significantly higher than those found for DZ twins. Furthermore, some studies have managed to trace and assess twins who have been reared apart, and in several cases concordance rates for twins reared apart have been shown to be similar to those of twins who shared the same childhood environment.

If vulnerability to a particular disorder is in part genetically determined, the children of parents who suffer from the disorder should remain at increased risk of developing the same disorder even if they are adopted at an early age. Several studies have examined the adult offspring of clients suffering from particular psychological conditions, and several have found a high prevalence of the relevant disorder among the adopted offspring, thus supporting the hypothesis of a genetic contribution to vulnerability.

Family studies, twin studies and adoption studies may be able to establish that an individual's vulnerability to a particular disorder is linked to genetic factors, and they can even indicate the likely strength of a genetic effect. But in recent years it has become possible to conduct studies which address the genetic issue in a less circumspect way, by examining genes directly. Major advances have been made, and information about the involvement of genetic factors in a wide range of disorders is bound to increase dramatically with the completion of the Human Genome Project, which began in 1990. This is an ambitious programme to map the entire sequence of the human genome (consisting of up to 100 000 genes).

Studies which establish a genetic involvement in the vulnerability to psychological disorders need to be seen in proper perspective. While there is evidence of some genetic involvement in a wide range of disorders, rates of concordance between even close blood relatives are typically low, and even in the case of monozygotic twins, concordance usually reaches only a modest level. Thus the available evidence does not suggest that psychological disorders are genetically predetermined. The evidence does indicate the relevance of genetic factors for many abnormal psychological conditions, but the same evidence also suggests that even for these disorders other causal factors play an essential role.

Many of these signs suggest a high level of autonomic arousal, but while some studies support this view (e.g. Taylor and Arnow, 1988), recent reviews have concluded that most GAD clients show rather little autonomic variability (Borkovec, 1994). Some writers have suggested that whereas most anxiety disorders are associated with excitation of the sympathetic division of the

Box 2.4
Generalized Anxiety Disorder: Case History

Robert, a professional man in his early thirties, consulted his physician because he felt that his worrying was 'getting out of hand'. He said that he had 'always been a worrier' and that many of his relatives had 'problems with their nerves'. It seemed that as a child Robert had been excessively shy and had been heavily protected by his mother. He also had a profound fear of the dark and was too timid to join in what he considered to be the rougher school sports. During adolescence he developed a social phobia. He was troubled by certain aspects of his appearance and felt that other people were looking down on him. From an early age Robert had been labelled 'a worrier' by his parents (he was their only child), and on more than one occasion when Robert was present, they had spoken openly to their friends about his general nervousness, and about his worries concerning school, his health and his appearance. Robert was mortified by these episodes.

Although he experienced extreme anxiety during examinations, Robert did very well academically and began to study at a local college. He had been accepted at a far more prestigious institution but explained that he had preferred not to go 'too far from home'. When taking examinations at college, and later for professional qualifications, he developed stomach cramps, diarrhoea and severe headaches. Subsequently he experienced similar symptoms immediately before attending job interviews.

Since adolescence, Robert had been extremely shy in the company of young women, but eventually, through his involvement with a supportive young persons' group, he met and and fell in love with a young woman. Unfortunately, she too had fairly severe emotional problems. Most of the time they managed to steady one another, but they would sometimes work themselves into what Robert described as 'a mutual panic'. They got married some three years after they met. The couple had had little sexual contact before the marriage, principally because Robert was very apprehensive about physical intimacy. His anxieties about sex continued, and for a long time after the wedding Robert had been unable to consummate the marriage.

Robert found it difficult to settle into married life and worried excessively about his new responsibilities. He felt that he was not working well and believed that his colleagues were ridiculing him. He worried that he would have to give up his job, or that he would be dismissed, and the prospect of unemployment filled him with terror. He worried about money and about the prospect of being unable to maintain his mortgage payments. He also worried increasingly about his lack of sexual prowess. He felt that he was letting his wife down in many ways, and was very fearful that she would one day leave him.

As a result of his emotional distress, Robert began to drink excessively. He also smoked heavily to 'soothe his nerves'. He then worried about the health effects and financial costs of his drinking and smoking. When the couple first appeared at the clinic, some three years after their marriage, it appeared that Robert was on the verge of a severe breakdown. He was tearful and complained of numerous physical symptoms. It was clear that his wife was eager to help but that she was finding it extremely difficult to cope with Robert's psychological state, especially as she was, by her own admission, 'not a strong person'.

autonomic nervous system (ANS), which normally prepares the organism for 'fight or flight', GAD clients respond to threat with inhibition of the sympathetic ANS, so that, in effect, they 'freeze' (Hoehn-Saric and McLeod, 1988)

GAD can be disabling in a number of ways. Constant worrying interferes with many day-to-day tasks, and clients often cope badly when they face a real problem or threat. Their symptoms may be exacerbated when they face circumstances which are moderately demanding or challenging. A general lack of confidence means that they often avoid challenges, and are therefore likely to underachieve in academic and employment situations.

Epidemiology

The lifetime prevalence of the disorder is usually estimated at between 2 and 7 per cent of the adult population. The female: male ratio is variously estimated at between 1.2 : 1 and 2 : 1. Although GAD usually begins in early adult life, the majority of clients report that they were always of a somewhat nervous disposition (Newman and Bland, 1994). Following a gradual onset, the disorder usually follows a chronic course, although the severity of the symptoms may vary considerably over time.

Aetiology

Biological factors   Family and twin studies have provided some support for the hypothesis that there is a genetic predisposition towards GAD. However, what is inherited is a non-specific neurotic trait, rather than a specific vulnerability to generalized anxiety disorder (Woodman, 1993). Indeed, the results of one major twin study indicated that the same genetic factors might influence vulnerability to GAD and depression (Kendler et al., 1992). A number of studies have indicated that many people who suffer from GAD show disturbances in some aspects of hormonal functioning, including the secretion of adrenaline and noradrenaline. Other research has also identified a number of disturbances in brain neurotransmitters.

Psychoanalytic accounts   Freud suggested that most anxiety develops as the result of emotional conflict. This conflict arises between the 'id' (instinctive drives and impulses) and the 'superego' (the conscience). When the ego, which attempts to mediate, is in danger of being overwhelmed then anxiety becomes apparent. However, psychoanalytic accounts have not been supported by any significant body of research evidence.

Behavioural accounts   Behavioural explanations suggest that GAD is a conditioned anxiety response which has generalized to such a degree that any environmental situation is likely to include one or more of the elements which elicit anxiety.

Cognitive accounts GAD is associated with a number of disturbances in cognitive functioning. In processing simple stimulus information from the environment, for example, GAD clients are hypervigilant with regard to possible threat (Mathews and MacLeod, 1986). Worrying may be maintained through certain immediate benefits. For example, worrying about relatively trivial matters may provide a useful distraction from more substantial concerns. However, if disturbing images are constantly avoided then the person's anxieties are likely to be maintained.

Thus, cognitive factors may play a major role in maintaining GAD. However, the basic hypervigilance, and the tendency to perceive threat, may reflect a general nervousness which is both deep-seated and longstanding, and may result from a biological predisposition or from a stressful early history. Overall, cognitive accounts of GAD have attracted considerable support, but remain somewhat speculative and cannot be said to provide a comprehensive picture of the aetiology of the condition.

An integrated account Barlow (1988) suggested that neurobiological differences between people affect the ways in which they react to adverse life events, and that some people will react intensely even to relatively minor events. Such people are likely to be chronically anxious and apprehensive. The cognitive effort involved in incessant environmental scanning and self-monitoring is likely to produce a high state of arousal, and any consequent performance decrement (in social interaction, or at a work task, for example) is then likely to produce further increases in arousal.

Drug treatment

Several classes of anti-anxiety drug can bring rapid and substantial relief in the short term to at least some of those who suffer from GAD. Such drugs include the benzodiazepines, buspirone, beta blockers and tricyclic antidepressants. However, as with all of the other anxiety disorders, the long-term effectiveness of drug treatment is limited.

Psychological treatment

Psychotherapy Many different psychotherapeutic methods have been used to treat generalized anxiety disorder, including classical psychoanalysis, brief analytic therapy and person-centred counselling. However, few clients make a complete recovery, and initial gains recede over time. Most comparison studies (see below) have reported that cognitive therapy programmes are more effective than both the analytically based forms of psychotherapy and person-centred counselling.

Relaxation and anxiety management training Relaxation training can be effective in reducing the moderate levels of anxiety normally found in GAD clients (Tarrier and Main, 1986), but relaxation is more effective in combination with anxiety management training. Janoun et al. (1982) found that GAD clients derived significant benefits from anxiety management training, and that improvements were likely to be maintained for some time following the treatment.

Cognitive therapy   Clients able to identify particular worry themes may be challenged about the beliefs which underlie these worries (Beck and Emery, 1985). Butler et al. (1987) developed a treatment package which includes, as well as a number of cognitive techniques, exposure to situations that are normally avoided. Clients are also taught relaxation and distraction techniques so that they will be able to pre-empt the development of anxiety, or to maintain control when it does occur.

Treatment comparison studies   Borkovec and Costello (1993) found significant longer-term benefits of cognitive behaviour therapy (CBT) by comparison with other treatments. In another controlled trial, CBT was shown to be more effective than behaviour therapy in reducing levels of anxiety and depression and in changing cognitive patterns (Butler et al., 1991). Durham et al. (1994) compared cognitive therapy (CT), brief psychodynamic therapy and anxiety management training (AMT), and found that the CT clients showed the greatest reduction in symptoms. Moreover, CT has been shown to be more effective than the use of drugs (Warren and Zgourides, 1991).

◀Panic Disorder▶ ▶ ▶

The clinical picture

People who are having a panic attack frequently believe that they are dying or suffering an acute nervous breakdown. The attack develops suddenly and generally reaches a climax within 10 minutes, and the person may be severely anxious for many hours afterwards. After several panic episodes the person is likely to become very apprehensive about the possibility of another attack, and constant hypervigilance and the close monitoring of bodily symptoms may prove extremely debilitating.

Epidemiology

Around one-third of the adult population will suffer a panic attack within any 12-month period (Norton et al., 1986). The recent experience of a major life event appears to increase an individual's vulnerability to such an attack (Barlow and Craske, 1988), and many attacks are precipitated by an acute threatening situation such as being stuck in a lift or receiving deeply distressing news. An isolated attack may have little lasting effect, but many people remain very anxious about the possibility of a further attack. Onset can occur at any age, but is most common between late adolescence and early adulthood.

Box 2.5
Panic Disorder: Case History

Ken Dickson, a 32-year-old accountant, had experienced frequent episodes of panic since the age of 17. His first attack occurred shortly following the sudden death of his father. He was working in a library when he suddenly felt faint. He describes how it became difficult for him to breathe and how he became increasingly aware of his heart pounding. His head felt 'as if it were about to burst' and he could hear the throbbing of his heart. He felt that he was about to die and sat still in his chair, wondering whether to call for help. After about ten minutes the state subsided. However, Ken was left feeling extremely weak and worried, and he wondered whether he should seek emergency medical help. He did not do this, and neither did he inform his doctor about the attack. He also decided not to tell his mother because he feared that, coming so soon after his father's death, such news might cause her to worry unduly. Several weeks passed before he had another attack, this time when travelling on a bus. Following this second attack he did consult his physician, who suggested to Ken that he had 'probably just experienced a couple of panic attacks'. Ken was not convinced and asked for a consultation with a heart specialist. A series of medical tests soon confirmed that there was nothing physically wrong, but by now Ken had had three further attacks, each separated by a week or two. He had also begun to consult medical textbooks (reading both the sections on panic and those on heart attacks and similar medical emergencies).

Since his first severe panic episode, fifteen years ago, Ken has continued to have regular attacks, although occasionally several months have passed without a recurrence. Ken married at the age of 26, and by this time his girlfriend had been with him on a number of occasions when he was having an attack. She had tried to convince him that his long history of such episodes indicated that they did not signify any serious medical condition, but her efforts to reassure Ken had not been very successful. By the time the couple consulted a clinical psychologist for help, Ken's life had become seriously affected by the condition. He was having attacks almost daily and he avoided situations which he associated with a high risk of an attack. He would no longer use escalators or lifts, attend church ceremonies, or go to the cinema. Six months before the initial consultation, Ken had a severe attack when the couple were on holiday. They were having sexual intercourse in their hotel room at the time, and since then Ken had refused to have any sexual contact with his wife.

Ken described himself as 'totally confused' about the nature of his attacks: 'Whenever I look back on an attack, and especially when I think of all attacks I've had over the years', he said, 'I feel that they must be "just psychological". But when I'm having an attack, I'm always convinced that it is leading up to a heart attack. All kinds of images flash through my mind and I'm convinced I'm going to die right there and then.'

Aetiology: biological factors

Family and twin studies suggest a genetically transmitted predisposition to panic disorder (Crowe, 1990; Mendlewicz et al., 1993; Woodman, 1993). Over half of all clients with the disorder report that at least one of their close relatives also suffered from the condition. Genetic studies have also identified at least one gene locus which appears to be directly implicated in the aetiology of panic disorder (Crowe, 1990).

However, it is not clear how genes might affect the biological make-up of those who are vulnerable. Further, Gelder (1989) conducted a wide-ranging review of biological factors associated with panic disorder, and concluded that there was no convincing evidence of an association between panic disorder and any specific biochemical or physiological abnormality.

The hyperventilation hypothesis   The fact that panic attacks can be induced by voluntary overbreathing ('hyperventilation') led to the hypothesis that panic disorder might result from involuntary hyperventilation (Hibbert, 1984a,b). Hyperventilation also produces a substantial increase in physiological arousal, and this has led to the use of overbreathing as a technique for inducing panic attacks under laboratory conditions (see Box 2.6).

Box 2.6
The Experimental Induction of Panic Attacks

Panic attacks can be systematically induced by exposing a person to a sudden loud noise or phobic stimulus, or by administering a stimulant drug. In the laboratory, panic attacks are often induced by administering caffeine or sodium lactate, or by asking the person either to inhale a mixture of oxygen and carbon dioxide or to hyperventilate for about two minutes. Hyperventilation involves breathing rapidly so that the oxygen available exceeds normal metabolic requirements. An experimentally induced panic attack usually lasts for around five minutes, during which time there are significant psychological effects as well as substantial physiological changes. These include sharp increases in skin conductance and muscle tension and a heart rate increase of up to 40 beats per minute.

Experimentally induced panic often produces vivid imagery and thoughts of mental or physical disaster (Greenberg, 1987). Many subjects report that their thoughts 'raced' and that their normal thinking processes were disrupted. The nature of the emotional experience during such episodes depends largely on the person's knowledge and expectations. Studies of the emotional effects of hyperventilation have shown that whereas many subjects become very anxious, others experience a kind of pleasurable excitement. The variability in response depends on cognitive factors, including the person's 'set' (expectations) and recollections of previous occasions of hyperventilation. Thus subjects who have hyperventilated when feeling faint tend to experience anxiety in the experimental situation, whereas those who associate the effects of hyperventilation with an earlier gratifying drug-induced experience, or a sexual encounter, tend to experience the effects of experimental hyperventilation as pleasant (Clark and Hemsley, 1982). Some researchers have deliberately manipulated subjects' expectations, leading some to believe that the effects of hyperventilation would be pleasant and some to believe that the effects would be unpleasant. Subjects' emotional experiences during such studies often follow the expectations created by the investigators.

Aetiology: cognitive–behavioural explanations

Panic attacks usually occur when symptoms of heightened physiological arousal cause an individual to develop profound and acute health fears. These fears further increase arousal, and thus a vicious circle is established between physiological arousal and fear. To understand the process, therefore, we need to understand both the initial physiological arousal and the nature of the cognitions that provoke the intensifying fear.

The increase in physiological arousal which usually initiates a panic attack may have a physical or psychological cause. Possible physical antecedents include various medical disorders (certain cardiac conditions, for example), and excessive intake of a drug such as nicotine or caffeine. Psychological responses which may precipitate a sharp increase in physiological arousal include basic responses to strong stimuli (such as a loud noise) and responses to complex social situations which are appraised as embarrassing or threatening.

Awareness of heightened physiological arousal may or may not result in a panic attack. The cognitive model of panic (Clark, 1986, 1988; Salkovskis, 1988) suggests that attacks arise through 'catastrophic misinterpretations' of physiological cues. Bodily sensations normally associated with anxiety are misinterpreted as indicating imminent calamity. Even those who merely believe that they are in danger of fainting may become extremely distressed about the possibility of 'causing a scene' and becoming the focus of other people's concern. Such thoughts are likely to generate extreme fear and to increase still further the level of physiological arousal. Awareness of this heightened arousal will then tend to reinforce catastrophic misinterpretations, and the vicious circle between fear and increased arousal will have turned through another full cycle (Clark, 1988; Beck, 1988).

However, some people who have experienced a panic attack have no recall of any 'catastrophic thinking' at the time. Moreover, it is unclear why people who have had several panic attacks continue to make catastrophic interpretations. Their experience on past occasions should have taught them that their symptoms do not signify an imminent heart attack, for example. However, this objection may assume a degree of rationality greater than that which normally prevails during an attack. The cognitive account has also been criticized on the grounds that people sometimes wake from sleep in a state of panic. However, this objection might reflect an inaccurate view of sleep as a state of mental inactivity. It is clear that both rational thinking and the irrational thought processes and images we associate with dreaming may continue during at least some of the stages of sleep.

Treatment

Drug treatment   Benzodiazepines (which reduce anxiety) and drugs which attenuate the physiological responses that accompany panic attacks (beta blockers, for example, which reduce palpitations) have shown significant efficacy. Drugs which prevent the reuptake of the neurotransmitter serotonin, tricyclic antidepressants and the monoamine oxidase inhibitors (MAOIs) have also been found to be useful.

However, many of these drugs are associated with disagreeable side-effects, and in the case of the benzodiazepines there is a risk of addiction.

Behavioural treatments Most behavioural treatments are based on graded exposure to the physiological signs which normally accompany panic. If the client can be exposed to such symptoms without panicking, then the phobic avoidance and anticipatory anxiety which normally follow these symptoms may be eliminated. Another form of behavioural treatment involves the use of a 'safety signal' – usually in the form of a 'good luck charm' or some subtle 'safety movement' – which the client believes will protect against the possibility of a panic attack (Rachman, 1988).

Cognitive treatment Cognitive–behavioural approaches attempt to change the maladaptive thoughts which the patient has when anticipating or experiencing a panic attack. A principal focus of such techniques involves changes in the individual's understanding and beliefs about panic attacks (and, especially, about physiological symptoms). However, various behavioural strategies may also be taught. Thus the client may learn special techniques for the control of breathing, and may learn to distract attention from bodily sensations.

Mattick et al. (1990) concluded from their meta-analysis of treatment outcome studies that a cognitive approach may be the most effective of the available psychological treatment methods. Furthermore, the improvements achieved through this type of intervention are usually maintained over the longer term.

◄Obsessive–Compulsive Disorder▶ ▶ ▶

Obsessive–compulsive disorder (OCD) is a form of anxiety disorder in which the principal symptoms are obsessions and compulsions. Obsessions are intrusive and disturbing thoughts, images or impulses. Compulsions are voluntary but disagreeable repetitive motor or cognitive actions, usually performed in a ritualized way. Obsessional thinking is often related to common fears and preoccupations. Thus, obsessional thoughts may focus on aspects of death and disease, accident and injury or dirt and contamination. Religious and sexual themes are also common. The fact that the same general issues are reflected in obsessional thinking across cultures may indicate that these issues have some fundamental biological significance. Thus human beings may be 'prepared' to develop obsessions of particular kinds (de Silva et al., 1977). The following examples illustrate the wide range of content found in obsessional thinking:

- persistent fears about contracting AIDS;
- vivid imagery of an accident, including images of blood and dismembered bodies;

- vivid and sickening images of filth (slime and faeces, for example);
- a recurrent impulse to shout or yell an obscenity in a public place;
- persistent images of nuclear holocaust;
- a recurrent impulse to hit people;
- a recurrent intrusive thought, such as: 'The world is about to end';
- thoughts of having hit a pedestrian while driving (of being an unwitting 'hit and run' driver).

The following are examples of compulsive actions:

- frequent, very thorough and ritualized handwashing;
- excessive checking of gas taps, electric plugs and locks;
- inordinate and pointless counting (for example, counting books on library bookshelves, lamp-posts when travelling by car or patterns on wallpaper);
- reciting a short 'magical incantation' a set number of times before getting out of bed in the morning;
- hoarding (for example, great reluctance to part with newspapers, milk bottles, food packaging);
- collecting (for example, extreme efforts to collect every item of a 'trivial' set of items);
- insistence on symmetry (for example, constant rearranging of pictures on the wall, furniture or books on a shelf to ensure precise alignment);
- hesitancy (for example, strong hesitation and anxiety experienced when posting a letter);
- retracing (for example, retracing a driving route to seek reassurance that one has not caused an accident along the way).

For many compulsive behaviours, it is not only what is done which is important, but how it is done. Compulsive acts generally include some element of ritualized or stereotyped performance. A ritual involves a fixed sequence of steps with a clear beginning and end. Although we tend to think of compulsive rituals as physical actions, some rituals are covert. Thus some people engage in cognitive rituals such as silently reciting the alphabet before reading any book or newspaper article. In a typical case of obsessional-compulsive disorder, an initial obsessional thought will provoke a sequence of distressing thoughts. In order to alleviate the distress, the person may then engage in certain compulsive actions. Hence, those who engage in compulsive handwashing or compulsive checking do so not because the activity is inherently gratifying but because it offers relief from emotional distress.

Types of obsessional thinking

Obsessional thoughts   These are repeated and intrusive thoughts, words or phrases which are often disturbing for the client. They may take the form of single words, musical phrases or arithmetic formulae. Such thinking often focuses on future possible events and may involve violent, sexual or religious themes.

Obsessional images These are vivid images which intrude repeatedly. The images are often disturbing and may be violent or sexual in nature.

Obsessional doubts These are repeated thoughts which indicate uncertainty about actions recently performed. For example, the person may worry about whether or not he or she has turned off a gas tap or locked a door.

Obsessional impulses These are recurrent urges to perform actions which would be dangerous, aggressive or socially embarrassing. Thus a person might have a recurrent impulse to shout obscenities in church, or to strangle a child.

Obsessional phobias These are recurrent obsessional thoughts with a fearful content. For example, the person who experiences an obsessional impulse to stab someone with a knife may become highly anxious whenever he or she sees a sharp knife.

Obsessional ruminations These are intrusive streams of thought around rather general themes (often of a religious, moral or philosophical nature) which occupy the person for long periods.

Types of compulsions

Checking rituals These are repeated actions stemming from an uncertainty about whether a particular task (such as turning off a gas tap, or locking a window) has been performed. Checking rituals are most commonly associated with obsessional doubts.

Cleaning rituals These are repeated actions involving washing the body or thoroughly cleaning specific areas of the environment. The most frequent clinical example is compulsive handwashing, which usually stems from the person's obsessional belief that he or she is dirty or contaminated.

Obsessional slowness This involves a greatly exaggerated thoroughness in an activity (often dressing, or attending to some aspect of personal hygiene) so that an inordinate amount of time is taken to complete a routine task. Thus a person may spend up to two hours dressing, making sure at each stage that the clothes are finely adjusted on the body. Obsessional slowness is relatively rare, but the condition can be severely disabling and is particularly difficult to treat (Veale, 1993).

Box 2.7
Obsessive–Compulsive Disorder: Case Profiles

Mary: compulsive handwashing

Mary, aged 28, had developed many rituals in childhood. She would bathe her dolls repeatedly, then dress and undress them, arranging their clothes with excessive neatness. She also became extremely anxious when she had to use a toilet away from home. It was not until early adolescence that she was able to verbalize her anxieties. It then appeared that she was plagued with thoughts that the toilet might be dirty, that she might become locked inside and that she might leave the toilet in a dirty state. Even when she used the toilet in her own home, she would clean it thoroughly before use, flush repeatedly (sometimes up to twenty times) and then scrub it with the strongest available disinfectant. At school her problem had been noted and special arrangements had had to be made for her.

In later life her toileting problems remained intense. After defecating or urinating she would wash her hands in undiluted disinfectant. She would also sometimes scrub her fingers with a steel-wool cleansing pad, or use a scrubbing brush with scouring powder. She repeated this ritual up to twelve times every day, with the result that her skin was in a very raw and blistered condition.

Simon: calculation checking

Simon, a 32-year-old accounts clerk, had always been highly conscientiousness and methodical in his work. However, on one occasion he had made an auditing error which had cost his company a large sum of money, and since that time he had become a compulsive checker. He would spend ages checking and rechecking figures. He insisted on working out even simple calculations a number of times, and would often use several different methods to cross-check his mathematics. He was reluctant to let any figures leave his desk, even when they were urgently required. During the night his sleep would be seriously disturbed as he tried to recall and check the calculations he had made throughout the previous day. His loss of sleep probably contributed to several further errors made in calculating accounts, although these always emerged later as a result of his repeated checks.

Jenny: route retracing

Jenny, a 22-year-old office worker, had been repeatedly late for work over a number of months, and when she explained the reason to her manager, he advised her to seek psychological help. It emerged that she often experienced intense worries about whether she had been responsible for an accident when driving to work. Her conviction that she might have knocked over a cyclist or a pedestrian would lead her to retrace her route, often more than once, seeking evidence of a collision. While retracing her journey she would survey the road and the roadside for any sign of an injured accident victim. Whenever she saw something which she thought might be blood she would stop the car and carry out a close inspection. Any sight or sound of an ambulance led her to imagine that she had been responsible for an emergency. Eventually, she would terminate her search and proceed to work, often arriving late and in a highly distressed condition. In the evening she would anxiously consult the local paper for any report of an accident involving a hit and run driver. On two occasions she had telephoned the local hospital to enquire whether they had treated any victim of a road accident who had been injured in the past few days while cycling or walking along any part of her route to work.

Epidemiology

Very large-scale epidemiological studies have now established that around 2.5 per cent of people are likely to suffer from OCD at some time during their life (Robins et al., 1984). Onset generally occurs in early adult life, usually before the age of 35 years. Overall, there is very little difference in the prevalence of OCD for men and women, although some studies have reported that women are at slightly higher risk. However, there are appreciable differences between men and women for certain subtypes of the condition. Thus more women suffer from handwashing and cleaning compulsions, whereas more men suffer from conditions marked by either checking or obsessional slowness (Noshirvani et al., 1991).

Aetiology

A satisfactory aetiological account of OCD needs to address the issue of individual differences in vulnerability, and the question of why some vulnerable people, but not others, develop the disorder. Vulnerability to OCD is likely to reflect both biological and environmental factors. We will briefly consider the evidence relating to individual differences in vulnerability before examining psychoanalytic, behavioural and cognitive aetiological accounts.

Vulnerability to OCD

Genetic factors   Family studies indicate that around 6 per cent of the parents of clients presenting with an obsessive–compulsive disorder have suffered from the condition, and twin studies have indicated substantially higher concordance rates for monozygotic (MZ – identical) twins than for dizygotic (DZ – fraternal) twins. Thus Carey and Gottesman (1981) reported concordance rates for OCD of around 25 per cent in DZ twins and around 65 per cent in MZ twins. These patterns indicate that vulnerability to OCD is partly genetically determined (the twin study method of investigating the possible implication of genetic factors in the development of psychological disorders is described in Box 2.3).

Neurochemical abnormalities   Genetic factors affect behaviour via anatomical structures and physiological functioning. In the case of OCD, many studies have suggested an association between obsessive–compulsive disorder and some abnormality in the metabolism of one of the key neurotransmitter chemicals, serotonin. Drugs which inhibit the reuptake of serotonin appear to produce the specific therapeutic effect of reducing obsessional thinking (Jenike et al., 1990).

Gross organic factors   The fact that a relatively high prevalence of obsessional symptoms is found in patients suffering from encephalitis, head injury and brain tumours provided an early indication that organic factors may underlie at least some cases of obsessive–compulsive disorder. Recent studies involving brain imaging techniques have indicated that dysfunctions in the frontal lobe and in part of the structure known as the striatum are present in a relatively high proportion of OCD clients (Baxter et al., 1987). Furthermore, many neuropsychological studies have revealed specific cognitive deficits which might be expected if these areas were damaged or dysfunctional (Tallis, 1995). However, not all OCD clients may have a brain dysfunction, and some of the neurophysiological and neuropsychological patterns which have been identified might be the result of the disorder itself or of medication used to treat the condition.

Early experiences   Rachman (1977) suggested that certain compulsive behaviours might reflect a style of upbringing in which the parents placed great emphasis on unreasonably high standards. The various psychoanalytic accounts which emphasize the role of early experience tend to regard OCD as arising from an obsessional personality, but the link between this personality type and obsessive–compulsive disorder is very tenuous.

Accounting for the onset of the disorder

Stressful events   The onset of OCD often follows either a discrete stressful life event (a death in the family, for example) or a life situation marked by longer-term stress (for example, that arising from chronic marital dysfunction) (Emmelkamp, 1982; Grayson et al., 1985).

Psychoanalytic theory   Classical psychoanalysts presented a number of different aetiological accounts of obsessive–compulsive disorder. Many of these suggested that obsessional symptoms result from repressed impulses, usually of an aggressive or sexual nature. One idea was that OCD follows harsh toilet training in infancy; another idea was that obsessional symptoms occur when the individual's psychosexual development has been arrested ('fixated') at the anal stage or regresses to this stage. As is often the case with psychoanalytic thinking, the elegant theorizing has not been matched by studies designed to test the various hypotheses.

Behavioural accounts   Most behavioural explanations of the origins of OCD employ Mowrer's two-factor model, and suggest that certain unconditioned anxiety-provoking stimuli become associated, through a process of classical conditioning, with certain words, thoughts and images, which then acquire anxiety-eliciting properties. As these thoughts and images (which are now conditioned stimuli) become associated with other thoughts, the conditioning effect generalizes and these too come to elicit anxiety. Any avoidant action that produces a reduction in anxiety will be positively reinforced through a process of operant conditioning. Subsequent reinforcement will strengthen and shape the behaviour so that it may eventually become habitual and compulsive. Avoidant (compulsive) behaviours may be cognitive or physical in nature.

Cognitive accounts Salkovskis (1985) found that intrusive thoughts often trigger an automatic sequence of distressing thoughts, many of which involve judgements of self-blame or responsibility for some hurt or injury. One client treated by Salkovskis had frequent unwanted thoughts about some drawing pins he had once taken from his workplace. Whenever this thought occurred to the client, he would automatically embark on a fantasy which included the discovery of the theft, accusations made against him and eventual disgrace. Clients suffering from OCD have long been recognized as being especially prone to feelings of guilt and have sometimes been described as having a 'tender conscience' (Rachman and Hodgson, 1980).

A general overestimation of the degree of influence they have over events may lead to an exaggerated sense of responsibility (Rachman, 1993). A related feature is the excessive moral value which OCD clients (and also those with an obsessional personality) may place on such issues as tidiness, punctuality and cleanliness. Clearly, those who espouse such values are likely to feel guilty and immoral when they judge that their behaviour has fallen short of their high standards.

Some theorists have attempted to explain the phenomenon of checking in terms of specific cognitive deficits or biases. Their accounts tend to focus either on knowledge appraisal or on memory. Thus it has been suggested that OCD clients may have lost the ability to recognize when they know something (Rapoport, 1989), or that they suffer from a cognitive deficit which prevents them from verifying judgements about certain specific issues (often, those concerned with safety). The fact that an OCD client who has checked something once, or more than once, often 'needs' to check again has been attributed to difficulties with memory, but this so-called 'mnestic deficit hypothesis' (Sher et al., 1989) has found only limited empirical support (Tallis, 1995). If OCD clients do suffer from some form of amnesia this must be highly selective, because there is no evidence that they suffer from a generalized memory impairment.

Carr (1974) suggested that OCD results from an appraisal style in which there is both an overestimation of danger and an exaggerated evaluation of the likely adverse consequences of a mishap. Such distorted views of the probability and magnitude of adverse outcomes are likely to lead to a preoccupation with the supposed threat. Other theorists have also emphasized the role played by irrational beliefs in the development of OCD. Thus Foa (1979) suggested that obsessions often reflect 'over-valued ideas' which may border on the delusional, and Foa and Kozak (1986) suggested that OCD is associated with a general view of the world as a dangerous place.

An integrated account Barlow (1988) developed an aetiological model of OCD which integrates biological, behavioural and cognitive elements. He suggested that some people are constitutionally predisposed to respond in an exaggerated fashion to intrusive thoughts and images. Such people become highly physiologically aroused by these cognitions, and are likely to experience acute anxiety. However, the physiological and emotional responses will be mediated by the individual's appraisals of the environmental situations and the cognitive intrusions that are being experienced. Some people tend to judge a wide range of situations as highly threatening, and many of their judgements reflect irrational beliefs and unwarranted assumptions. As people become preoccupied with their intrusive thoughts, they may become extremely anxious (and, possibly, depressed) and such emotional disturbance is likely to generate further intrusions. Efforts to suppress the distressing cognitions may increase their frequency, and the person may then engage in various cognitive or behavioural acts in an attempt to reduce the distress. Although such actions may well provide some immediate relief, the effect is likely to be fleeting. Thus the action may need to be repeated frequently, and may eventually become compulsive.

Physical treatment

Drugs   Anti-anxiety drugs sometimes provide short-term relief from symptoms but cannot be prescribed for more than a few weeks at a time. Longer-term drug treatment usually involves the use of a drug that blocks the reuptake of serotonin. There are a number of such drugs, including the tricyclic antidepressant clomipramine (which has been widely used and appears to be highly effective), and fluoxetine (Prozac). However, some of these drugs may have unpleasant side-effects and the symptoms often return when the drug is discontinued.

Psychosurgery   When an obsessive–compulsive disorder is particularly severe and when all attempts at therapy have failed, psychosurgery may be considered. Nowadays, the procedure used is usually a 'modified leucotomy', in which an incision is made into an area near the corpus callosum (the mass of neural fibres connecting the right and left hemispheres of the brain). Although sometimes effective, this form of treatment is very much a last resort.

Psychological treatment

Psychotherapy   Supportive psychotherapy may be beneficial in helping the person to cope with OCD, but verbal methods alone appear to have little or no effect in reducing the primary symptoms.

Behaviour therapy   Behavioural treatments focus directly on the main presenting symptoms of obsessive–compulsive disorder – the obsessional thoughts and compulsive behaviours. Control over intrusive thoughts and distressing trains of thought may be gained through the technique of 'thought-stopping'. Clients are taught to interrupt their obsessional thinking as soon as they become aware of it by suddenly and deliberately engaging in a powerfully distracting thought or action.

Most behavioural programmes include some variation of a procedure labelled 'exposure and response prevention' (Rachman and Hodgson, 1980). This involves the client being faced with a situation which would normally provoke compulsive behaviour, while he or she refrains from engaging in any ritualized activity. Most of those who manage to persist quickly habituate to the procedure, and the majority soon begin to experience a substantial reduction in their symptoms.

Summarizing the findings of 18 studies of exposure and response prevention for OCD, Foa et al. (1985) concluded that only 10 per cent of clients failed to benefit from treatment, with over half being either symptom-free or much improved. The effectiveness of the exposure and response prevention procedure can be explained in terms of conditioning theory. Thus, prevention of avoidance, and prolonged exposure to the conditioned stimulus, extinguishes the conditioned emotional response. Alternatively, the procedure may work because it leads to 'beneficial reality testing'. When avoidance behaviour is prevented, clients are confronted with the fact that the omission of the compulsive act does not lead to catastrophe. Some accounts suggest that the exposure element is effective in reducing the obsessional anxiety, while the response prevention element has a direct effect in reducing the compulsion to engage in ritual behaviours (Greist, 1992).

Cognitive methods   Van Oppen and Arntz (1994) suggest that cognitive therapists working with OCD clients should address the fundamental cognitive errors made by these clients. Focusing on the risk assessment issue, they suggest ways of correcting overestimates both of the probability of danger and of the likely outcome of the perceived danger. They take a similar two-level approach to the modification of clients' judgements of their responsibility for certain occurrences. Thus they focus not only on clients' overestimations of their responsibility but also on their exaggerated views of the consequences of the events for which they feel accountable.

Comparison studies   Comparisons of drug treatments and behavioural treatments for OCD have generally found little difference in the short-term effectiveness of these methods. An optimal treatment programme might involve a combination of behaviour therapy and the use of a drug which inhibits the reuptake of serotonin (Greist, 1992).

Post-traumatic Stress Disorder

Exceptionally traumatic events, such as earthquakes, fires and air disasters, can have profound psychological effects on survivors. Some individuals appear highly resilient, but for others the initial response is one of extreme shock, and within hours some people will develop 'acute stress disorder'. Most victims slowly return to normal functioning. However, in cases of post-traumatic stress disorder (PTSD), symptoms appear for the first time some weeks or even months after the traumatic event. PTSD is a profoundly distressing condition characterized by extreme anxiety, frequent intrusive thoughts, recurrent nightmares and feelings of guilt.

Definition of post-traumatic stress disorder

PTSD is diagnosed only when the person's psychological distress can be attributed to an event 'outside the range of usual human experience'. However, it is extremely difficult to operationalize this concept. The direct victims of a disaster are not the only ones who may suffer extreme stress. Others who may be affected include witnesses, relatives of those directly involved and emergency service personnel.

The clinical picture

Post-traumatic stress disorder is marked by a persistent state of high physiological arousal, and clients often describe themselves as 'jittery' or 'constantly on edge'. Intrusive and disturbing thoughts and images are likely to occur with some frequency, both in the waking hours and in the form of nightmares. Other symptoms of PTSD include 'psychological numbing' (or 'emotional blunting'), extreme irritability and chronic insomnia. Depression is common, as are feelings of guilt, including guilt about having survived the trauma when others perished ('survivor guilt').

Epidemiology

It makes little sense to quote prevalence rates for PTSD with regard to whole populations (of a country, for example), because the major disasters which often trigger the condition are typically located within a very circumscribed area (such as the scene of an air disaster or major fire). It makes more sense to consider what proportion of a group of people subjected to a particular traumatic event eventually developed the condition.

A US Congressional study reported that around 14 per cent of the US survivors of the Vietnam War were suffering from severe PTSD. Among the survivors of the 1988 Piper Alpha North Sea oil-rig disaster (in which three-quarters of the men who worked on the oil-rig died as the result of an explosion), almost all developed a severe form of PTSD. Relatively high rates of PTSD have also been reported among those who have been tortured and those who have been raped. A survey of rape victims reported by Foa and Rothbaum (1992) suggested that most victims met the clinical criteria for PTSD one week after the assault. In another study, Kilpatrick et al. (1987) found that 16 per cent of a group of rape victims were still reporting symptoms of PTSD after an average of 17 years following the rape.

Aetiology

The biological model   A genetic influence upon vulnerability is likely. Thus, only some of those who endure a similar traumatic incident will develop PTSD: some people may be biologically predisposed to develop PTSD whereas others may be constitutionally 'hardy'. Animals exposed to extreme environmental stressors appear to suffer permanent changes in the functioning of the brain catecholamine system, and research with PTSD clients has revealed long-term changes in the functioning of a number of brain structures, including the amygdala, hypothalamus and pituitary gland (ver Ellen and van Kammen, 1990). Metabolic studies have also revealed marked changes in hormonal levels. For example, Mason et al. (1990) found that PTSD clients had low levels of cortisol and high levels of adrenaline, testosterone and thyroxine. Such changes explain many of the most conspicuous symptoms of the condition. Psychophysiological studies have also confirmed chronic autonomic overarousal in these clients, as well as heightened autonomic reactivity to stressful stimuli.

The behavioural model   Animals subjected to unpredictable and uncontrollable aversive events show a number of long-term changes in behaviour which resemble PTSD. For example, such animals respond fearfully to a wide range of stimuli, and respond in a particularly exaggerated fashion to stimuli associated with the original aversive event. Some traumatized animals show a chronic reduction in sensitivity to pain, which may be analogous to the emotional 'numbing' found in many PTSD clients (Foa et al., 1991).

Mowrer's two-factor theory can be used to explain the development of PTSD in terms of classical and operant conditioning (Keane et al., 1985). The traumatic event is the unconditioned stimulus (UCS) and the tension or fear which it generates is the unconditioned response (UCR). Neutral stimuli associated with the trauma become the conditioned stimuli (CS) and the fear and anxiety which are subsequently elicited by these stimuli are conditioned responses (CR). The CS may be subject to considerable generalization, so that, for example, any loud noise may come to elicit the response originally elicited by the sound of gunfire. Intrusive thoughts and images may act as conditioned stimuli, but avoidance of, or escape from, such cognitive stimuli are likely to obstruct extinction and will serve to maintain the fear and many other symptoms of PTSD.

Cognitive models: The 'shattered assumptions' model   Some life events are so unpredicted that they annihilate many of the person's most cherished beliefs. Janoff-Bulman (1985) suggested that traumatic events undermine three primary assumptions which are central to people's sense of well-being: (a) the assumption that the world is meaningful and understandable; (b) the assumption of personal invulnerability; and (c) a positive self-view. When these fundamental premises are shattered, Janoff-Bulman maintains, they tend to be replaced by their opposites. Thus traumatized people have a tendency to judge the world as completely unfathomable, they tend to exaggerate their own vulnerability and they often construct a very negative view of themselves.

Cognitive models: The 'loss of emotional regulation' model   Horowitz (1979, 1986) proposed that PTSD results from a loss of emotional regulation, which is in turn a consequence of cognitive overload. Experiences will normally be readily assimilated within an individual's existing cognitive structure. Those who experience an unanticipated disaster, however, are faced with a torrent of information which cannot be assimilated within their existing cognitive framework. Such people will be overwhelmed, and until cognitive adjustments occur much of the information relating to the trauma will not be able to be accommodated. Thus, memories of the traumatic event will remain near the surface of consciousness and may be experienced in the form of 'flashbacks'.

Management of victims following a disaster

Following a disaster, it is important that survivors should receive appropriate psychological support. As a general rule, emotional support provided during the immediate aftermath of a disaster is often effective in reducing the degree of acute distress and may also decrease the likelihood that PTSD will develop at a later stage (Joseph et al., 1993).

Drug treatment

Promising results have been reported of the use of the anti-anxiety drug, buspirone. Anti-depressant medication can also be effective, probably because the anti-anxiety properties of such drugs often lead to a reduction of the client's chronic overarousal. However, because continued relief is often dependent on continuing medication, drugs cannot be said to provide a 'cure' for the condition. Indeed, medication which helps the client to avoid, rather than to cope with, threatening memories, thoughts and feelings may prove counterproductive in the longer-term

Psychological treatments

Exposure   Most behavioural and cognitive programmes for treating PTSD involve direct therapeutic exposure to memories of the traumatic incident (Fairbank and Nicholson, 1987). Exposure techniques require the client to confront the feared situation (often in imagination), the purpose being to promote habituation. In desensitization, elements of the traumatic event are gradually introduced while the client is deeply relaxed. In the techniques of flooding and implosive therapy, images which provoke high levels of anxiety are presented to clients soon after the treatment begins, while they are supported and encouraged to 'work through' the extreme distress which they experience.

In the 1980s, several reports described the use of exposure methods to treat veterans of the Vietnam War who were suffering from PTSD (Fairbank et al., 1983; Peniston, 1986; Keane et al., 1989). Both flooding and desensitization methods were found to be effective in relieving many PTSD symptoms, including flashbacks, muscle tension, general anxiety and depression. Exposure methods have also been used successfully to relieve PTSD symptoms experienced by rape victims (Foa et al., 1992) and those who have survived natural disasters, transport accidents and other traumatic incidents (Thompson et al., 1995).

Anxiety management techniques   Exposure strategies are often supplemented with training in anxiety management techniques. Thus clients are taught how to control the anxiety which emerges during treatment sessions. Some anxiety management programmes emphasize the use of such physical strategies as deep muscle relaxation and special breathing techniques, some focus on distraction methods and others concentrate on the identification and modification of maladaptive thoughts.

Stress inoculation training   Stress inoculation training (SIT) was developed for the treatment of rape victims who experience long-term psychological effects of their assault (Kilpatrick et al., 1982). Clients learn about the origins of fear and are trained in coping skills. SIT programmes usually teach clients deep muscle relaxation, breathing control, thought stopping and positive self-talk. The effectiveness of SIT has been demonstrated in a number of studies with rape victims, although the results of one important comparison study indicated that the gains achieved following SIT were less durable than those achieved by the use of exposure methods (Foa et al., 1991).

Cognitive therapy   Cognitive therapy techniques help the individual to identify and to change any unreasonable beliefs which are helping to maintain the adverse effects of the traumatic experience. Cognitive therapy may be particularly helpful in reducing such symptoms as guilt, depression and feelings of unreality or alienation. The effectiveness of the cognitive approach for dealing with PTSD has been demonstrated in a number of studies (e.g. Frank and Stewart, 1984).

Group therapy   In some cases a group of survivors may be treated together as a group. Some group therapy programmes have followed highly structured therapeutic rationales, whereas others have taken the form of informal discussion groups (many of the so-called 'rap groups' attended by Vietnam veterans fall within this category).

The fact that PTSD often leads to profound disturbances of relationships suggests that there may be benefits of addressing these issues in therapy. Figley (1988) presented a rationale for the application of family therapy to traumatized clients and their families.

Box 2.8
EMDR: a controversial treatment for PTSD

A controversial treatment known as 'eye movement desensitization and reprocessing' (EMDR) has recently had a major impact on the treatment of PTSD, particularly in the United States. EMDR was developed in the late 1980s by the psychologist Francine Shapiro, and since that time over 14000 therapists have been trained to use the method (Shapiro, 1995).

EMDR involves the client focusing on a mental image (usually a memory of a particularly distressing scene) while tracking side to side finger movements made by the therapist. As the procedure progresses, the client's attention is likely to wander to other images and thoughts, which are then reported to the therapist. In some cases new memories of the traumatic incident emerge. The treatment often enables clients to develop new perspectives on the traumatic incident, and their revised understanding may result in an immediate and dramatic reduction in symptoms. In many cases it appears that substantial benefits are derived from even a single EMDR session, even in cases which have persisted for many years.

The fact that the technique is apparently so simple, and appears to be almost instantaneously effective, has led many people to voice extreme scepticism, and some have even accused EMDR practitioners of quackery. On the other hand, those who support the method claim that there is more objective evidence of the effectiveness of EMDR than of any other psychological treatment method used to treat PTSD. They cite controlled studies of victims of Vietnam combat, rape, accidents and natural disasters as proof that EMDR can produce a rapid reduction in a range of PTSD symptoms, including emotional distress, intrusive thoughts, flashbacks and nightmares (Shapiro, 1995; Silver et al., 1995).

Many have criticized at least some of the relevant studies, but the body of evidence does suggest that EMDR may be a powerful therapeutic method. Scepticism is likely to remain, however, until a convincing rationale is developed to explain why EMDR produces such dramatic effects. At this time, there is little agreement regarding the mechanism involved, although there is no lack of suggestions. Some people contend that the beneficial changes 'merely' reflect a strong expectancy, or 'placebo', effect. Proof of this hypothesis, of course, would do nothing to challenge the usefulness of the method. Others have suggested that the eye movements induced in EMDR may replicate those of sleep and may allow the individual to integrate information (it is widely believed that memories of daytime experiences are organized and 'filed' during normal sleep). Another explanation is that EMDR works because it induces flashbacks which may generate sudden adaptive neurological and psychological changes. It has also been suggested that the repeated eye movements lead to rapid switches in activity between the left and right hemispheres of the brain, and that this process might somehow facilitate beneficial neurological realignments.

EMDR has been hailed by some clinicians as a 'miracle cure', while others have condemned the procedure as a proposterous sham. Most of those who have used the method, or have evaluated the research evidence, take a position far from either of these two extremes. This approach to the treatment of PTSD will certainly remain contentious for some time to come, and it remains to be seen whether it will eventually become a mainstay of 'orthodox' psychological treatment or whether it will be seen as a footnote in the history of clinical developments in this area.

◀Conclusions▶▶▶

The anxiety disorders are marked by considerable emotional distress, high levels of anxiety, frequent fears and persistent worrying. A phobia is an acute fear experienced when the person confronts a particular type of object or situation. Behavioural and cognitive analyses offer the most convincing accounts of how phobias originate. These accounts suggest that phobias result from the association of particular stimuli with aversive events and are generally maintained by the avoidance of situations that are judged to be threatening. The development of relatively non-specific phobias such as agoraphobia is held to reflect a widespread generalization of the conditioned fear response. Desensitization therapy, in which clients are gradually exposed to increasingly intense presentations of the phobic stimulus, has proved a very effective form of treatment for many different types of phobia.

Generalized anxiety disorder (GAD) is characterized by excessive worrying about a wide range of issues, and chronic anxiety. Genetic factors which contribute to the development of a chronically anxious personality appear to underlie a predisposition to GAD. Particular cognitive techniques, including distraction, offer the most effective form of psychological treatment.

People who are having a panic attack frequently believe that they are dying or suffering an acute nervous breakdown. Genetic factors play some part in determining an individual's vulnerability to panic episodes, in which a principle feature is a cognitive mislabelling of physiological symptoms of arousal. Treatment strategies may therefore focus on training clients how to lower arousal and how to interpret arousal symptoms more realistically.

The principal symptoms of obsessive–compulsive disorder (OCD) are obsessions (persistent intrusive and disturbing thoughts, images and impulses) and compulsions (voluntary but disagreeable repetitive motor or cognitive actions). Obsessional thoughts often have a direct relevance to the performance of compulsive, and ritualized, actions. Once again there is evidence that biological factors help to determine susceptibility to the disorder, but the condition also reflects psychological and environmental factors. Cognitive treatments involving repeated response prevention are very effective in treating OCD.

Post-traumatic stress disorder (PTSD) follows the experience of an event 'beyond the normal range of human experience'. Onset is often delayed, and is marked by a persistent state of high physiological arousal with accompanying intrusive and disturbing thoughts and images. Exposure to memories of the event often proves an effective form of treatment.

◀Further Reading▶▶▶

Edelmann, R.J. (1995) *Anxiety: Theory, Research and Intervention in Clinical and Health Psychology*. Chichester: Wiley.
  Extensive review of research and clinical studies.

Beck, A.T. and Emery, G. (1985) *Anxiety Disorders and Phobias: a Cognitive Perspective*. Harmondsworth: Penguin.

A classic exposition of the cognitive approach to understanding and treating the anxiety disorders.

Heimberg, R.G., Liebowitz, M.R., Hope, D.A. and Schneier, F.R. (eds) (1995) *Social Phobia: Diagnosis, Assessment and Treatment*. New York: Guilford Press.

Encyclopaedic review of current knowledge and theories.

Emmelkamp, P.M.G. (1992) *Phobic and Obsessive–Compulsive Disorders: Theory, Research and Practice*. New York: Plenum.

Reviews theories of the origins of phobias and obsessive–compulsive disorders, with an emphasis on behavioural and cognitive explanations and a thorough account of experimental contributions. Treatment aspects are also covered in depth.

Tallis, F. (1995) *Obsessive Compulsive Disorder: a Cognitive and Neuropsychological Perspective*. Chichester: Wiley.

Reviews the nature and incidence of OCD, with a special emphasis on cognitive processes and cognitive neuropsychology. Behavioural and cognitive methods of treatment are also discussed.

Williams, J.M.G., Watts, F., MacLeod, C. and Mathews, A. (1997) *Cognitive Psychology and Emotional Disorders*. Chichester: Wiley.

Illustrates how an understanding of cognitive processing can be applied to the emotional disorders. Links experimental cognitive psychology with abnormal psychology and aspects of clinical practice.

Warren, R. and Zgourides, G.D. (1991) *Anxiety Disorders: a Rational–Emotive Perspective*. New York: Pergamon Press.

Extensive review of research and clinical material on the anxiety disorders, with a clear focus on the clinical application of cognitive (and especially rational–emotive) methods to the treatment of these problems.

◀Discussion Points▶▶▶

1 How are phobias (including social phobia) acquired?
2 What are the symptoms of panic disorder? How might this disorder develop?
3 Distinguish between an 'obsession' and a 'compulsion'. Discuss the relationship between obsessions and compulsions in cases of obsessive–compulsive disorder.
4 Describe the clinical features of 'post-traumatic stress disorder' (PTSD) and assess the role played by cognitive factors in the development of PTSD.
5 Provide an overview of the use of cognitive–behavioural methods in the treatment of the anxiety disorders.
6 How would you account for the fact that some adults appear to be more vulnerable than others to the development of anxiety disorders?

3 Eating Disorders

From the biological perspective, eating is simply the ingestion of carbohydrates, fats, proteins and minerals. However, this description tells us very little about the psychology of eating. For humans, the act of eating takes place within a social and cultural context, and it is associated with many cultural prescriptions and proscriptions. The fact that eating is determined by a large number of diverse factors immediately suggests that disturbances to normal eating patterns might reflect a wide range of possible causes. Thus eating patterns might be disrupted by a disorder of the hypothalamus or by an individual's conscious decision to go on a hunger strike as a form of political protest.

Eating has a clear biological function: all animals eat in order to ingest nutrients. Psychologically, one of the reasons why people eat is because they become hungry, and because eating alleviates the discomfort associated with hunger. People generally feel hungry when they experience stomach contractions or when their blood sugar level is low. However, any comprehensive account of the psychology of human eating needs to consider many additional reasons why people eat. Sometimes, for example, people eat even when they are not hungry because food is available which looks, or smells, delicious.

The consumption of food is also part of the social fabric. People often eat simply because it is dinner time, even though they do not feel hungry. This can partly be explained as habit and partly as compliance with other people's expectations. Eating can also bring about a sharp change in emotion. Some people cheer themselves up by eating favourite foods. These foods tend to be high-calorie snacks such as chocolate and cake.

◀Anorexia Nervosa▶▶▶

The term 'anorexia nervosa' was first used by the English physician William Withey Gull in 1868 to label 'a particular form of disease occurring mostly in young women, and characterised by extreme emaciation'. The condition was apparently rather rare until relatively recently, however, and the present high level of concern about anorexia, both by clinicians and by lay people, reflects the fact that in recent decades the prevalence of the disorder appears to have risen at an alarming rate.

The literal translation of 'anorexia nervosa' is 'nervous loss of appetite', but the term is something of a misnomer. Most anorexic people retain an appetite for food, but however hungry they feel, they deny themselves all but small quantities of low calorie foods. The typical daily calorific intake of a person suffering from anorexia is in the region of 600–800 calories, but in some cases the self-starvation is even more extreme. Anorexia is associated with a large number of physical and psychological symptoms, and in some cases the self-starvation proves fatal.

The clinical picture

Low body weight or weight loss is a necessary element for a diagnosis of anorexia, and is assessed according to a variety of different criteria. DSM-IV uses the criterion of 15 per cent or more below the normal weight for age and height. Other systems set the weight criterion at 20 or even 25 per cent below the average. In these examples the person's weight is compared with the weight distribution of a matched population.

In addition to physical weight, criteria include: an intense fear of becoming obese, avoidance of 'fattening' foods and perceptual disturbances of body weight, size or shape. In female patients, disturbances of the menstrual cycle may also be an additional criterion for diagnosis of anorexia nervosa. According to DSM-IV, a diagnosis of anorexia requires that there be an absence of periods over at least three consecutive menstrual cycles. In males, loss of sexual interest and potency may also be considered diagnostic signs.

Behavioural abnormalities   Most of the unusual and disturbed behaviours associated with anorexia are related to the pursuit of thinness (or, to put it another way, the avoidance of fatness). The principal behavioural change is a severe restriction of eating, which amounts to self-starvation. Anorexic patients also restrict the number of foods they include in their diet, and they generally avoid all high calorie foods. Despite their frequent insistence that they are not hungry, it appears that most anorexic patients do feel hunger pangs and retain an appetite for food. Their avoidance of eating is, therefore, a form of self-denial.

Anorexic patients also use various additional strategies to ensure that they will not put on weight. Many make themselves vomit after they have eaten, or abuse laxatives or diuretic drugs in a bid to bring about weight loss. A relatively high proportion engage in activities such as running or gymnastics which demand a high expenditure of energy. Exercise can become compulsive for those who suffer from an eating disorder, and some anorexic patients devote so much time and energy to certain sports (such as long-distance running) that they do particularly well in competition.

Emotional state The majority of anorexic patients are emotionally disturbed in some way. Anxiety and depression are very common, and many patients experience rapid mood-swings. Many of the mood changes appear unrelated to the external situation, but some may be identified as responses to weight gain or to attempts by family members (or health professionals) to encourage eating.

Anorexic patients have an intense fear of becoming fat and many develop strong aversions towards high calorie foods. Anxiety levels are often high, but the major emotional problem associated with anorexia is depression. It is generally found that around half of all anorexic patients meet the criteria for clinical depression. Associated with the depression are thoughts and feelings relating to insecurity, loneliness, guilt, inadequacy and helplessness. Few patients have any thoughts of, or any interest in, romantic or sexual relationships and many develop a revulsion towards sex.

Cognitive aspects A number of cognitive distortions and irrational beliefs are commonly associated with anorexia. Some of these relate to eating (the person may be constantly preoccupied with thoughts about food and calories), while others relate to health. According to the body-image distortion hypothesis (Bruch, 1962), many anorexic patients suffer from the delusion that they are fat. Many clinicians are familiar with patients who continue to insist that they are too fat even when they are, in fact, emaciated, and when relatives try to convince such people of the reality of their physical state, perhaps by pointing to the degree of weight loss or showing photographs, they often meet with a response of firm denial or of extreme hostility.

Over thirty experimental studies have now examined the way in which people who suffer from an eating disorder perceive their own body shape and size. These studies have employed a variety of size estimation and image distortion techniques. Overall, the research has confirmed that many eating disordered patients do indeed overestimate their body size. However, the studies have also shown that the degree of distortion varies considerably with contextual factors, including the precise nature of the instructions given to subjects. It appears that at least some of the reports given by patients reflect their emotional appraisal rather than their perceptual experience. In their reformulation of the body-image distortion hypothesis, Slade and Brodie (1994) suggest that those who suffer from an eating disorder are in fact uncertain about the size and shape of their own body, and that when they are compelled to make a judgement they err on the side of reporting an overestimation of their body size.

Low self-esteem Many anorexic patients have a low level of self-esteem, lack self-assurance and feel inadequate despite a high level of intelligence and a history of academic success. Their tendency towards obsessionality may show itself in 'perfectionism', and by setting themselves the highest (often unattainable) standards they may set themselves up for failure.

Effects on social behaviour Many anorexic patients withdraw from family and friends. This self-imposed isolation appears to be a response to what the patient regards as a constant 'nagging' by other people about the need to eat. In a bid to deflect unwanted concern and attention, the patient may go to great lengths to conceal her avoidance of food or to hide her true body shape. She may pretend that she often has meals away from home, for example, and take to wearing oversized baggy clothing.

Physical effects Self-starvation and weight loss eventually produce severe deleterious effects on physical health, and some harmful effects may persist even when there has been a substantial recovery of lost weight (Sharp and Freeman, 1993). Amenorrhoea is often one of the earliest physical effects of self-starvation, and after several successive menstrual periods have been missed there may be long-term disruption of the menstrual cycle. Hormonal treatment is sometimes necessary, but in rare cases even this is not effective and the cessation of menstruation appears to be permanent.

A reduction in food intake lowers the basal metabolic rate and has serious adverse effects on the functioning of the circulatory system. Low blood pressure and a low heart rate tend to give the person a pale, wizened look and may lead to dizziness and fainting. Poor circulation can lead to a general debilitation and the person is likely to feel constantly cold. Other physical changes include nausea, severe constipation, brittle nails and a dry skin which is prone to 'cracking'. The hair on the scalp may become very thin, and fine hair may start to grow, particularly on the back and face (Garfinkel and Garner, 1982).

Severe weight loss is also associated with the bone condition osteoporosis. A reduction in bone tissue (owing to oestrogen deficiency and an excess of naturally produced steroids) leads to the bones becoming excessively porous and easily fractured. It appears that even a brief period of anorexia can result in a serious loss of bone tissue and that when this has occurred there are likely to be permanent effects whatever the outcome of the eating disorder.

Several of the physical complications of anorexia nervosa can be life threatening. In some cases self-starvation leads to kidney failure. More frequently, fatalities result from the effects of starvation on the cardiovascular system. Frequent vomiting, purging or the abuse of diuretic drugs can lead to severe disturbances in the balance of electrolytes, and such imbalances can lead to cardiovascular complications that result in the death of the patient.

Epidemiology

Prevalence The prevalence of anorexia is probably around 0.1 per cent of the general population. However, in the highest risk group (young women aged between 15 and 25) the prevalence is between 0.5 and 1 per cent. In 1992, the Royal College of Psychiatrists suggested that just under 1 per cent of women aged 15 to 25 were anorexic, but that the eating habits of many more young women could be described as 'seriously disturbed'. It is generally agreed that anorexia nervosa has become more common in recent decades.

Sex Many more women than men develop anorexia. Females comprise around 90 per cent of those cases in which the age of onset is during middle-to-late adolescence, or during adulthood. Of those cases in which the onset is between the ages of 8 and 14 years, however, around a quarter of the patients are boys.

Age In most cases the onset of anorexia occurs during adolescence, although the condition can begin much later, or earlier. Some authorities have recently voiced a special concern about anorexia in older adults, and in recent years it has become more widely recognized that children may also suffer from the condition (see Box 3.1).

Social class There appears to be a higher risk of anorexia developing in middle-class women than in those from a working class background (Andersen, 1983). This social class effect cannot be explained simply as an artefact resulting from a tendency for clinicians to apply a diagnosis of anorexia more readily to those from the middle class.

Race and culture The highest rates of anorexia occur in white women within Western cultures. In recent years it appears that there has been a considerable rise in the rate of anorexia in Japan.

Intelligence and academic achievement There has long been the suggestion that anorexia is associated with high intelligence and high academic achievement. Anorexia appears to be especially prevalent in college populations, and some estimates suggest that the prevalence among female college students may be as high as 3 per cent (Halmi et al., 1981).

Occupation and sports involvement Women involved in certain occupations have higher rates of anorexia than other women of the same age. Models, dancers and professional sportswomen are all said to be at high risk (Garfinkel and Garner, 1982).

Box 3.1
Eating Disorders in Childhood

In recent years there has been increasing concern about eating disorders among young people. A few children do suffer from bulimia nervosa, but the condition appears to be very rare in childhood. Childhood-onset anorexia, however, can no longer be described as 'rare', and clinicians are now reporting a growing number of cases in which the child is between 8 and 14 years old (Lask and Bryant Waugh, 1992). A relatively large proportion of early-onset cases are male, around a quarter of the young patients being boys. The recognition of anorexia in childhood is especially important because early self-starvation can have profound effects on growth.

The clinical picture for children suffering from anorexia is broadly similar to that found in older patients. Anorexic children are preoccupied with their body weight and shape, they often feel disgusted with their own body, they have a profound fear of becoming fat and they actively engage in dieting in order to become thinner. In addition to controlling their calorie intake, some of these children also make themselves vomit or engage in excessive exercise in order to control their weight. And even in this young group the abuse of laxatives may present an additional problem. Many of these children strive towards perfection; for example, in their performance in sport or at school. Many have low self-esteem and a number show evidence of severe depression.

Lask and Bryant Waugh (1992) stress that any case of childhood eating disorder calls for a wide-ranging assessment. In addition to a physical examination, clinical interviews are held with the child and with other family members. The families of anorexic children are often dysfunctional in some way, but although family difficulties may have contrib-uted to the onset of the illness, they rarely offer a complete explanation. In many cases it appears that what began as a 'normal diet' eventually led to a total loss of control over the regulation of eating. The child may have been prompted to embark on a diet by a playground jibe about fatness, but in many cases it is also clear that the child has been influenced by the pervasive cultural pressure towards thinness.

The physical effects of early-onset eating disorder can be very serious. Cases have been reported of young patients with such severe malnutrition that extreme low blood pressure has led to gangrene in the feet, and in other cases the ovaries of anorexic girls regress to an infantile state. In many cases there are also critical effects on the development of bone tissue. Early dieting may lead to inadequate calcification, increasing the risk that osteoporosis will develop later in life. Thus the physical consequences of sustained nutritional deficiencies in the early years can be extremely serious, not only during childhood but also in the longer term.

The implementation of a suitable dietary regime is of course critical for ensuring immediate weight gain in anorexic children. Of the various treatments which attempt to address underlying issues, family therapy appears to be more successful than other approaches, including cognitive behavioural therapy (Hodes, 1993). However, early-onset cases often prove resistant to treatment and are generally associated with a poor prognosis. Around 60 per cent of children with anorexia make a reasonably good recovery, but many remain seriously underweight. And even when there is satisfactory weight gain a number of residual psychological problems may persist.

Aetiology

Many authorities are convinced that biological, psychological and social factors all play an important role in the genesis and maintenance of the condition and that no single aetiological account will apply to all cases.

Biological models

Genetic factors Twin studies suggest that around 60 per cent of MZ twins are concordant for the condition (Holland et al., 1988). Research has also indicated that other relatives may be at slightly increased risk, although this does not necessarily implicate genetic factors. Such a family link might well be explicable in terms of environmental or social interactional factors rather than the genetic similarity between blood relatives.

Norepinephrine The regulation of appetite is one of the many functions of the hypothalamus, and animal studies have established that lesions to this part of the brain can disrupt an animal's eating. This suggests that at least some cases of anorexia might be the result of a primary disturbance of hypothalamic functioning (Kaye et al., 1988). One suggestion is that anorexia might result from the effects on the hypothalamus of to a low level of the neurotransmitter substance norepinephrine (NE). Several anti-depressant drugs (including the monoamine oxidase inhibitors and the tricyclics) increase the available NE, and these drugs sometimes play a useful role in the treatment of anorexia.

Serotonin At least some of the symptoms of anorexia nervosa are also present in obsessive–compulsive disorder (OCD). One explanation for this overlap involves another neurotransmitter, serotonin. Kaye et al. (1993) suggested that disturbances of serotonin activity may lead to a cluster of symptoms, which include rigidity, anxiety, obsessions and compulsive behaviours. These symptoms are found both in obsessional-compulsive disorders patients and in those suffering from anorexia nervosa.

Zinc A number of symptoms commonly associated with anorexia nervosa (including weight loss, changes in taste and appetite, depression and amenorrhoea) are also found in people suffering from a zinc deficiency. This raises the possibility that low levels of zinc may be responsible for some cases of anorexia nervosa, or that a zinc deficiency may help to maintain the condition. The fact that a high proportion of patients are also vegetarian may support this hypothesis, for a vegetarian diet is often low in zinc. It has therefore been suggested that zinc intake should be routinely assessed in anorexic patients and that the provision of a zinc supplement may be beneficial in some cases (Bakan et al., 1993).

Physiology and the maintenance of anorexia Whether or not biological irregularities play a significant role in the genesis of a particular case of anorexia, prolonged starvation will certainly disturb many aspects of normal metabolic functioning. Thus starvation may disturb hypothalamic and endocrine functioning, destabilizing relevant control systems and producing a chronic disruption in eating patterns. But evidence that anorexic patients show metabolic irregularities cannot be taken as proof that faulty metabolism must be responsible for the onset of the disorder. Even if an eating disorder were entirely psychological in origin, starvation would produce biological changes, and these changes might then contribute to the maintenance of the condition.

Psychoanalytic models

Fear of adulthood and sexuality According to one psychoanalytic theory, anorexia stems from an unconscious confusion between eating and the sexual instinct. Some women, it is argued, avoid eating as a way of (symbolically) avoiding sex (Ross, 1977).

Oral/sexual confusion Another psychoanalytic interpretation suggests that anorexic women have fantasies of oral impregnation and confuse fatness with pregnancy. They starve themselves because, at an unconscious level, they believe that eating may lead to pregnancy.

Regression to childhood Regression to an earlier stage of psychological development has frequently been used as an explanation of anorexia. The profound weight loss in anorexia means that the person 'shrinks' in size, and this, together with the loss of menstrual periods, is interpreted by some authors as a sign of an unconscious rejection of adulthood and a wish to revert to a childhood state.

Oral fixation Some psychoanalytic accounts suggest that anorexia is the result of arrested psychosexual development. According to Freud, a child normally passes through a series of psychosexual stages before reaching the final ('genital') stage. If, however, a child becomes fixated at the early 'oral' stage (or if an older person regresses to this stage), then sexual anxieties and obsessions are likely to become evident as disturbances of eating.

The effects of cultural ideals

Many cases of anorexia originate in a conscious decision to embark on a dieting regime. Whereas most people who diet make fairly moderate adjustments to their eating, and readjust their behaviour when they reach their target weight, some go to extremes and continue to consume very little food long after they have passed any reasonable healthy target weight. Such continual self-starvation can mark the onset of anorexia.

For those who are truly overweight, moderate dieting is reasonable and advisable. But many people who limit their calorie intake have no valid

Box 3.2
The Cultural Demand for Thinness

Many eating disorders begin when a young woman who is not substantially overweight comes to believe that she 'needs' to go on a diet. Aspects of the woman's personal history undoubtedly contribute to her dissatisfaction with her body shape, but the desire to be thin is often powerfully influenced by media images and messages. The media both reflect and help to shape a strong cultural pressure towards thinness, and the rise in the incidence of eating disorders which has become evident in recent years throughout Europe, in North America and in Japan is frequently attributed to an increase in this cultural emphasis on thinness as an ideal body shape.

The cultural pressure towards thinness may have intensified in the 1960s, when many leading fashion models appeared pre-pubescent, boyish and rather emaciated. However, there had been a distinct tendency for thin women to be chosen as fashion models since at least the 1920s, and even in the Victorian period some women were persuaded to use extremely tight corsetry in order to achieve a desirable 'wasp waist'. The fact that at other times, and in other cultures, a more rounded figure has been considered ideal suggests that the current position might be open to change. Indeed, there is already evidence of a backlash, with organized groups of women challenging the prevalent view and identifying 'sizism' as an oppressive set of attitudes having direct parallels with sexism and racism.

Women are much more likely than men or children to be the target for the media propaganda that exalts thinness, but no group is immune. The representation of the ideal female as thin is apparent in the media coverage of children's fashion and also in the design of dolls, so that even very young girls are subjected to distorted models of the ideal body shape. Sanders and Bazalgette (1993) analysed the body shape of three of the most popular dolls available for young girls (Sindy, Barbie and Little Mermaid), measuring their height, hips, waist and bust. They then transformed these measurements to apply to a woman of average height and found that, relative to real women, the dolls all had tiny hips and waists, and greatly exaggerated inside leg measurements.

Distorted ideas about what is normal and acceptable mean that many children (especially girls) become dissatisfied with their own shape even though it might be well within the healthy range. Studies indicate that by the age of 12 food and eating are often regarded as moral issues and that body shape is often a major criterion in self-evaluation and the evaluation of others (Wardle and Marsland, 1990; Hill, 1993). Furthermore, many parents of young children are unhappy with their child's body shape, and many children are aware of their parents' dissatisfaction. When we consider the numerous sources of social pressure that coerce even young children towards being thin, it may seem unsurprising that as many as one-third of 9-year-old girls are dissatisfied with their body shape, and that by this age many have already started dieting.

Men, too, are now coming under pressure to conform to an 'abnormal' ideal. There is a growing emphasis on the 'worked-out' male figure, and many men feel a strong demand to 'get in shape'. A 1993 MORI survey of adult males in the United Kingdom indicated that one-third of men had been on a diet and that nearly two-thirds believed that a change in shape would make them more sexually attractive. It remains to be seen whether the growing emphasis on an ideal male shape will lead to an increase in the number of men who suffer from eating disorders.

health reason to do so. They diet for cosmetic purposes, attempting to change their shape in order to conform more closely to their personal ideal, an ideal which is influenced by social and cultural pressures. There is a considerable demand on people to be thin, at least in industrialized cultures. Simply put, the general message is that 'thin is good, and fat is bad'.

The pressure towards thinness is a social fact, and thinness is equated not just with physical attractiveness but also with success and acceptability in many spheres. Moreover, 'being on a diet' may in itself be regarded as admirable, sensible and responsible. Thus, whether it is fuelled principally by 'cosmetic' considerations or by the hope that a diet will provide the answer to certain life problems, an individual's motivation to restrict food intake may be very strong. And the process of embarking on a dietary regime is greatly facilitated by a dedicated industry that produces a wide range of special dietary products and specialist magazines which promote the cause of 'slimming'.

Thus every year millions of people embark on a diet. Many do so for no good health reason, and some are destined to go to extremes in their dieting and to persist long after they have achieved a reasonable weight loss. Those who develop serious eating disorders represent only a small proportion of those who start dieting, but as the number of people who embark on 'a serious diet' increases we may expect more people to lose control over their dieting and to meet with serious difficulties.

Psychological models: dieting as a major focus

One central focus for the analysis of the causes of anorexia is the patient's initial decision to lose weight. We need to understand what might lead to such a decision, and how the initial dieting can then develop into a life-threatening disorder.

Factors affecting a decision to lose weight   It is reasonable to assume that anyone making a decision to go on a diet is not perfectly happy with his or her present state. In many cases the dissatisfaction will be specific to weight or body shape, but many people who diet are seeking not only to lose weight but also to solve a major personal problem. Dieting may be seen as 'the answer' to loneliness, a lack of friends, relationship problems, employment problems and so on. Many of those who experience emotional distress turn to food for comfort, and any weight gain that results from their 'comfort eating' is likely to reinforce their judgement that they need to begin a diet.

People who lack self-confidence are more likely to be critical of their body shape, and they are also more likely to judge their life as problematic and unfulfilling. They will tend to compare themselves unfavourably with other people, will be particularly sensitive to other people's critical comments and are likely to be highly susceptible to cultural messages which imply that 'thin is good'. For all of these reasons, those who have low self-esteem (and also those who are depressed), might be particularly likely to view dieting as a potential solution to their problems.

Reinforcement for weight loss   In a minority of cases people who begin to diet in a conventional way will end up limiting their calorie intake to such an extent that their dieting eventually amounts to self-starvation. In order to explain how this can happen it is useful to focus on the outcomes of dieting and the patterns of reinforcement which are likely to result from weight loss and food restriction.

When people restrict their eating sufficiently and for a long enough period, many of the changes that occur can be powerfully reinforcing. The person is likely to notice that her shape is changing to become more like her ideal. The image in the mirror changes 'for the better', certain clothes that were previously impossible to wear become wearable and some people, at least, feel fitter and more energetic as a result of losing weight. The reactions of other people to the weight loss are also very influential. Even a single admiring glance or comment may greatly strengthen the person's determination to continue with a diet. In addition, a thinner figure may reduce the frequency of negative reinforcers. There are likely to be less self-disapproval (or even self-loathing) when glancing in a mirror, fewer disappointing attempts to squeeze into clothes and fewer critical comments and disdainful looks from other people.

As if all of this were not sufficient to provide a powerful reinforcement package, there is also a more 'precise' source of both positive and negative reinforcement – the weight scales. Those who are on a diet often treat the outcome of a weighing as a judgement of their worth. The result of stepping on the scales weekly, daily or even every few hours is a powerful determinant of their emotional state. If the scales display a weight below that expected the person is likely to feel triumphant. But if the weight displayed is higher than expected, the outcome may be utter despair. Disappointment at a failure to lose weight will lead some people to abandon their diet, but others will increase their determination to succeed next time. Those who might be described as 'perfectionists' are especially likely to resolve that they will not be beaten. They endeavour to gain control of their weight at all costs, and redouble their efforts to eat less.

The pattern of reinforcement (which mainly consists of self-reinforcement) may greatly increase the frequency of such behaviours as stepping on to weight scales, looking in a mirror or wearing particular clothes. In some cases the resulting behaviour patterns become so extreme that they seriously disrupt the person's life (for example, if the person engages in compulsive self-weighing). However, what is ultimately being reinforced is not weight change but eating restriction.

Reinforcement for the restriction of food intake   If, overall, the reinforcement obtained as a result of being on a diet is positive, and the benefits outweigh the costs (the principal costs being hunger pangs and a loss of the pleasure obtained from eating), then the person is likely to continue with the diet. However, when the target weight has been reached, the reinforcement obtained from further weight loss may be only slight, or may even be negative. In some cases the end of a diet marks an instant return to a former unhealthy eating pattern, which is certainly undesirable. This pattern of 'yo-yo dieting' may prove highly dangerous.

When reinforcement depends on changes in weight or perceived body shape, it is relatively unlikely that a diet will 'get out of hand'. However, when self-reinforcement is based on food intake, there may be a much higher risk that the person will starve herself and develop a severe and persistent eating disorder. The calorific content of foods can be estimated very precisely, and the dietary information that is now widely available allows a person to calculate with some precision the calorific value of any meal, and of his or her daily intake. For some dieters the results of such calculations become the fluctuating measure of self-worth. The lower the sum calculated, the 'better' the person feels herself to be. And since it is possible to gain complete control over calorie intake, those who adopt this criterion have discovered a 'perfect' way of measuring and controlling their own 'worth' or 'value'.

Some people become absorbed in a game of calorie target beating, and the target may become ever lower. Those who are mildly obsessional may easily become engrossed in calculating their daily intake, and those who have a competitive and perfectionist streak may strive for ever lower targets.

The starvation value system For any day on which the calorie count reaches a figure higher than the current target, the person may feel angry with herself, or stupid, or 'immoral'. Thus some self-starvation can be attributed to particular patterns of self-reinforcement or, using another level of description, to extreme personal values concerning eating. Eating may become a crucial moral issue. 'Overeating' (which some anorexic people would regard as having a daily intake of more that 600–700 calories) might be seen as 'sinful', and any daily consumption in excess of 1000 calories might be regarded as a clear indication of greed, self-indulgence and the total absence of self-control. Such values, and corresponding patterns of self-reinforcement, may well help to explain why some people become trapped in a dangerous pattern of self-starvation.

Dieting as an end in itself Many people begin to diet not simply to lose weight but in order to gain certain benefits which they hope will come with weight loss. In some cases, however, the process of dieting itself proves beneficial. If the purpose of losing weight is to gain attention, to become appreciated or to develop a sense of self-control or self-worth, the person may discover that the desired benefits come as a direct result of dieting. Refusal of food may bring reinforcing attention from other people, in the form of anxious concern, or it may provide a sense of purpose and a goal in life. Thus whereas the diet may be initiated as the means to an end, dieting may take on a significance of its own and become an end in itself.

Secondary gain As extreme dieting persists, and as it becomes apparent that the weight loss is excessive, other people (especially family members) may become very disturbed by the person's constant refusal to eat. The emotional responses elicited by such refusals may include anger, anxiety and despair, and friends and relatives may engage in various responses (persuading, cajoling, pleading, hostility) in a bid to encourage the person to resume a normal eating pattern. These responses may occasionally have the desired effect, but such attention and concern can also be positively reinforcing. Continual self-starvation may also become a way of controlling or even 'punishing' other people (the parents, for example). In some cases, the dramatic weight loss will mean that the person is treated more as a child than as an adult, and certain expectations (about relationships, or academic success) may be suspended. The disorder may therefore offer a means of escape from certain unbearable pressures. Thus, as well as the many costs involved in suffering from anorexia, there may also be certain benefits. The advantages that emerge when a person is suffering from a psychological disorder (and which partially offset the more obvious disadvantages) are generally labelled 'secondary gain'.

Control

Some psychological models of anorexia suggest that the major issue in the genesis and maintenance of the condition concerns the exercise of self-control. It is clear that those who are suffering from anorexia are, in one way, exercising complete control over their eating. Some undoubtedly feel that there is little else in their life that they can control. Explanations which emphasize control may be somewhat different in emphasis from the reinforcement account given above, but they may share the view that the anorexic person adopts a 'moral' stance regarding eating.

Family-based models

Many explanations of anorexia identify difficulties within the patient's family as a likely source of the disorder.

Child-rearing patterns and a poor sense of autonomy   According to Hilde Bruch (1978), a great pioneer in the field of eating disorders, anorexia reflects a poor sense of autonomy and control, together with certain perceptual and cognitive disturbances which are often the result of ineffective parenting, especially by the mother. A parent who fails to judge accurately when her child is hungry, for example, will feed the child according to her own needs and emotional state, and this may lead the child to become confused about the relationship between hunger and eating. Such children may then become uncertain about the validity of their own needs and wishes, and this can lead to a high level of dependency. Children who lack all sense of personal effectiveness may follow parental rules and guidance in a bid to please their parents. A girl who is dutiful and unfailingly respectful may be seen as a 'model daughter', and may strive to maintain her 'perfect' image.

During adolescence, it is suggested, the increasing demand for autonomy will conflict with the daughter's well established pattern of obedience and dependency, and the inner conflict that results may prompt her to search for some sphere in which she can 'safely' exert her independence and gain control. Eating may eventually be recognized as a suitable domain in which such strength and autonomy can be exercised.

Parental preoccupation with thinness   Some families of anorexic patients are chronically preoccupied with physical appearance and with dieting (Garfinkel and Garner, 1982). Family members may initially provoke and support a dietary regime, reinforcing a child for dietary restraint and weight loss, until an abnormal eating pattern becomes so well established that it is very difficult to reverse.

Parental pressure towards high achievement and conformity   A variation of Bruch's model suggests that anorexia may be related to the emphasis by parents on a child's achievement in some sphere – in academic work, for example, or in sport or ballet. High parental expectations of the child, and the child's desire to meet these expectations, may lead to severe pressures, and any performance which is less than perfect may result in harsh self-criticism. An adolescent who feels helpless and ineffective may become passive and depressed until she finds that dietary control and weight loss are areas in which she can meet and even surpass the targets she sets for herself. Thus she develops a talent for self-starvation at which she is able to excel.

Dysfunctional family systems   Family therapists suggest that although anorexia directly affects one family member (the identified patient), the condition actually reflects a wider family pathology (Palazzoli, 1974; Palazzoli et al., 1988). Characteristics of 'anorexic families' include enmeshment (the over-involvement of family members with one another), over-protectiveness, rigidity and stringent avoidance of conflict (Minuchin et al., 1978). Adolescence is seen as posing a special threat to such families because it threatens to expose an apparent closeness as a mere facade. The development of anorexia nervosa may serve to prevent total dissension within the family and may in fact hold the family together, providing a focus for concern which unites members who would otherwise be highly antagonistic towards one another.

Intrafamilial sexual abuse   A number of studies have suggested that a relatively high proportion of women suffering from anorexia have been sexually abused (Waller, 1991). Furthermore, it has been claimed that in many cases the perpetrator of the abuse is a family member (often the father or stepfather). One explanation for the association between sexual abuse and anorexia is that the abuse may lead a girl to abhor her own femininity so that she becomes overconcerned about her body shape and size, especially around the time of puberty (Oppenheimer et al., 1985).

The blame factor   The considerable emphasis on family factors in explanations of the genesis of the eating disorders is perhaps unfortunate, because relatives of people suffering from these disorders may feel, often inappropriately, that they are 'to blame' for the patient's condition. In some cases family factors will have played little or no part, and in other cases the whole family may be judged as 'victims' of unfortunate circumstances or of a regrettable dynamic that has arisen within the family system.

It should be emphasized that family members are usually highly distressed by the patient's condition, and that most are tireless in their attempts to help. Many families readily participate in therapeutic endeavours to help the patient to regain weight. In some cases the condition will eventually prove fatal, and it is particularly important that bereaved family members do not blame themselves for the patient's death.

The management and treatment of anorexia

Attempts by anorexic patients to treat themselves are rarely successful, and because the condition is easier to treat in the early stages, it is essential that professional treatment be obtained as soon as possible. Treatment involves both medical and psychological help, with the implementation of a reasonable eating pattern as the central focus. If the patient's weight is very low, and the weight loss is continuing, it will be necessary to achieve a substantial weight gain within the shortest possible time. When this issue has been addressed then more fundamental aspects of the patient's psychological condition can be considered. These include general attitudes to food, eating and body shape, and any identifiable features of the patient's personality or personal history that may have helped to precipitate the disorder.

The promotion of rapid weight gain

For less serious cases, treatment is generally provided on an outpatient basis, but for those whose state of health is perilous, the immediate need for weight restoration will generally require inpatient treatment. Hospitalization means that a strict dietary regime can be implemented. High calorie foods are prescribed (the recommended daily intake for someone who urgently needs to gain weight would usually be around 4000 calories). However, many anorexic patients are very reluctant to comply with dietary programmes and need close supervision.

Behavioural methods Various behavioural methods have been used in a bid to encourage dietary compliance. For example, a target weight may be set and a reward given whenever the patient reaches a step towards the target. It is preferable to reinforce weight gain rather than a specified calorie intake so that patients will not consume the food presented to them, receive their reward and then make themselves vomit in the privacy of the bathroom.

Early optimism regarding behavioural methods has waned in recent years (Wardle, 1994). Any initial success is often followed by relapse, especially when the patient's fundamental beliefs and attitudes have remained unchanged. Their limited effectiveness over the longer term, and ethical problems which may arise when delivering behavioural programmes to patients who are dangerously underweight, has led to such programmes being used much less frequently in recent years.

Ethical problems in the promotion of rapid weight gain   Clinical procedures used to promote rapid weight gain raise a number of very serious ethical dilemmas. When the patient's medical condition is critical, it might seem that the use of any procedure likely to reduce the danger to life would be justified. However, many people feel that every patient has a right to refuse any treatment which she or he finds objectionable. Thus major issues surround the use of force feeding, intravenous feeding and the use of drugs. When behavioural interventions are used, one ethical problem concerns the nature of the reinforcers to be included within the programme. In some early treatment programmes, patients were initially deprived of certain 'privileges' (such as television viewing and telephone calls), which were then systematically restored as successive weight goals were achieved. However, many people feel that the use of the telephone and access to the media are rights rather than privileges and that therapists who restrict access to such amenities are infringing patients' civil rights. Most current programmes therefore include as reinforcers only those payoffs which are clearly additional to basic needs and which do not involve any form of deprivation.

Cognitive behaviour therapy   Any programme that involves a dietary regime is also likely to include an intensive (though perhaps informal) educational component, in which the patient is acquainted with the dangers of self-starvation and encouraged to discuss dietary health issues, eating habits and attitudes to food. Various cognitive therapy programmes have been developed with a view to challenging anorexic patients' unrealistic beliefs about body shape, food and eating.

The eating disorders are commonly described as problems in which eating (or dieting) is 'out of control', and a detailed exploration of issues of control is often central to cognitive therapy programmes used to treat these patients. If excessive weight loss is regarded as resulting from an inordinate degree of self-control over eating, therapy can be viewed as an attempt to establish appropriate self-control. There is a danger that programmes which implement a strict externally controlled dietary regime might actually undermine a patient's attempts to exercise appropriate self-control.

The control issue is addressed directly in Freeman's (1992) model for the outpatient treatment of patients with severe anorexia. His programme aims to promote autonomy and to encourage patients to gain the necessary control over their eating. Daily outpatient group sessions provide an opportunity for patients to discuss eating-related issues and other problems, and to express their feelings. Evaluation studies have demonstrated that this approach to treatment is often at least as effective as the traditional form of inpatient treatment for such patients.

Physical treatment methods   There is no pharmacological 'cure' for anorexia, but various drugs may have a place in treatment. In conjunction with a strict dietary regime and psychotherapeutic interventions, anti-depressant drugs often prove useful. Tranquillizers may also be prescribed if there is a high level of anxiety (for example, during mealtimes). Hormones, and drugs which stimulate the production of certain hormones, may also be used to aid the re-establishment of menstruation if this does not occur naturally after a reasonable weight gain has been achieved.

Dealing with underlying issues

Individual psychotherapy   Those who suffer from anorexia are often reluctant patients. Most forms of psychotherapy, however, emphasize the need for a good relationship between therapist and client. The therapist who works with anorexic patients needs to be especially skilled in forging a good relationship so that patients will disclose their thoughts and feelings and work enthusiastically towards therapeutic success. If a good therapeutic relationship can be established then various forms of counselling and psychotherapy may prove effective, although many authorities recommend a directive rather than a client-centred approach.

Psychotherapy focuses on the patient's current problems and attitudes and on aspects of her personal history. Most psychotherapists strive to encourage healthy eating patterns and to reinforce weight gain, and in some sessions the conversation may chiefly relate to eating and body shape. However, in many cases the principal focus will be on other issues. The patient will certainly be encouraged to explore and express her feelings towards a wide spectrum of concerns. Themes commonly explored include family relationships, attitudes to success and failure, sexual feelings and issues relating to control. In many cases it will become apparent that the patient has very low self-esteem, and the therapist may work towards increasing the patient's self-confidence and positive self-evaluation.

Crisp et al. (1991) conducted a controlled study in which anorexic patients who received psychotherapy were compared to those in a control group (these patients were referred back to primary care services). There were three treatment groups. One group of patients received therapy while they were hospitalized. Another received individual psychotherapy on an outpatient basis, and the third received group psychotherapy (again on an outpatient basis). Patients in all the treatment groups increased in weight significantly more than patients in the control group, and there were no significant differences between any of the treatment groups.

Cognitive therapy   Early on in a treatment programme, cognitive therapy is often used as a means of encouraging the patient to resume a reasonable eating pattern. At that stage the therapist will usually examine, explore, challenge and restructure cognitions that relate directly to food and to eating. The focus of cognitive therapy used at a later stage in treatment is likely to be more fundamental beliefs about the self, about control and about personal attractiveness (or acceptability) in the eyes of others. At this stage the cognitive programme may be less 'behavioural' in style and more 'psychotherapeutic' (the terms 'cognitive psychotherapy' and 'cognitive counselling' are often used). Thus a cognitive approach may be used to encourage the patient to end her self-starvation and then to modify beliefs which may have played a part in establishing the anorexic condition and which might, if unchanged, precipitate a further relapse.

Family-based approaches The relatives of an anorexic patient are rarely bystanders who simply wait for professionals to treat their ailing family member. Most are actively involved in persuading, cajoling, threatening, bribing and encouraging the patient to eat. Some of the relatives' efforts may be useful, but some will be counterproductive. It is clear that professionals, whatever their approach, should involve relatives in the treatment enterprise, so that, at the very least, their 'amateur' efforts at inducing the patient to eat do not undermine the formal treatment programme.

Family therapists suggest that anorexia should be understood as a condition generated and maintained within the family system. They point to enmeshment, over-protectiveness, rigidity and the avoidance of conflict as characteristics of anorexic families, and emphasize the threat to the family façade which may arise when a girl reaches adolescence. Anorexia is seen as the family's solution to a critical whole-family situation, and family therapists therefore seek to address the underlying dysfunction so that the anorexia is no longer 'needed' by the family and can therefore be 'safely' discontinued (Palazzoli, 1974; Minuchin et al., 1978).

Crisp (1980) suggested that anorexia arises out of a failed adolescence. When puberty is experienced as very frightening, anorexia may be a phobic avoidance response to adulthood. According to this formulation, anorexic patients need to become re-engaged in the maturation process at the point where they pulled out. Thus the patient may need to spend up to six years 'catching up' on the missed adolescence, and because psychological development during adolescence is intimately bound up with family change, the whole family should be the focus for intervention.

The effectiveness of family therapy as a treatment for anorexia has been the subject of a series of studies based at the Maudsley Hospital in London (Dare et al., 1995). All these studies have taken the form of controlled trials in which families have been assigned at random to one of a number of treatment conditions. To control for variation between therapists, the same therapists administer the different treatments. Following admission to hospital for weight restoration, patients are assigned to a particular form of psychotherapy. The first trial involved a comparison of conjoint family therapy (in which all family members are seen together) and supportive individual psychotherapy. Family therapy was shown to be the more effective form of treatment, particularly when the anorexia had an early onset (before the age of 19) and when the condition was of relatively short duration (less than three years). After five years, 90 per cent of the patients treated with family therapy were judged to be well, whereas half of those who had received the individual therapy were still suffering from an eating disorder.

In the second trial, family therapy was compared to individual supportive therapy and individual psychoanalytic therapy. Again, family therapy was shown to have greater therapeutic effect than either of the comparison treatments. In a third trial, conjoint family therapy was compared with 'family counselling', in which the therapist worked separately with the parents and with the adolescent patient. Overall, these two forms of treatment proved equally effective, with around two-thirds of patients either 'well' or 'considerably improved' one year after treatment commenced. This series of well designed studies has provided powerful evidence that family intervention can be an effective second-stage therapy for anorexia. However, the third study in the series also suggests that such interventions need not take the form of 'whole family work' prescribed originally by the family therapists who worked with this condition.

Where intrafamilial sexual abuse emerges as a possible antecedent of the anorexia, or is suspected, then help may be offered in the form of individual psychotherapy, participation in a therapeutic group or (in some cases) confronting the whole family with the problem and engaging in family therapy. In many, but not all, cases it will be judged necessary for the patient (or, preferably, the perpetrator of the abuse) to live away from the family until the initial stages of treatment have been successfully completed. The issue of whole family treatment following intrafamilial abuse is highly controversial but has been explored with sensitivity and insight by Trepper and Barrett (1989).

Outcome

The longer-term outcome for anorexia nervosa is highly variable. Some people with a history of anorexia are eventually able to maintain a safe and relatively stable weight. Some follow an oscillating pathway of recovery and relapse. And up to a half go on to develop bulimia (Kreipe et al., 1989). The prognosis is very poor for those who remain untreated and for those who are identified only after their weight has dropped to a dangerous level. The outcome for those who receive treatment at a reasonably early stage in their illness is sometimes said to conform to a 'rule of thirds' – one-third make a good recovery, one-third recover to some extent and the remaining third show little improvement and remain chronically ill.

Certain factors have been identified as predictive of a relatively good outcome. These include the anorexia being relatively 'mild' (a short-term illness with comparatively little weight loss), good social relationships during childhood and adolescence (especially within the family), the absence of self-induced vomiting and purging and the ability to eat in front of other people without undue anxiety. It also seems that the outcome may be more favourable for female anorexic patients than for males. The relationship between prognosis and the age of onset appears to be rather complex. While late onset cases (starting after the age of 20 years) and very early onset cases (starting, say, before the age of 13) have a poor prognosis, patients whose condition became apparent during middle to late adolescence appear to fare relatively well in the longer term.

Most estimates suggest that between 5 and 10 per cent of those suffering from severe anorexia will eventually die as a result of some effect of the disorder. Crisp et al. (1992) followed up two groups of anorexic patients for an average of 30 years and found that by this time 4 per cent of one sample and 15 per cent of the other sample had died. The most frequent causes of death were physical complications arising from the anorexia, and suicide.

◀Bulimia Nervosa▶ ▶ ▶

It is only since the late 1970s that bulimia nervosa (which, literally translated, means 'eating like an ox through nervousness') has been accepted as a diagnostic category. Many patients who present with bulimia have an earlier history of anorexia, and the two disorders are similar in many ways. Both involve a preoccupation with body shape and a morbid fear of becoming fat, and both involve the use of extreme measures to avoid weight gain. Many bulimic patients (as well as some anorexic patients) engage in prolonged fasting, self-induced purging, the abuse of laxatives and excessive exercise.

The major difference between the two conditions is that whereas extreme low weight is always a principal feature of anorexia, most bulimic patients maintain a weight around the average for their height. Bulimia is also characterized by bouts of 'binge-eating' in which huge amounts of food are eaten within a very short time. Such episodes are usually followed by purging, often in the form of self-induced vomiting.

Like anorexia, bulimia is found much more frequently among women than among men, and it often arises when a woman who is attempting to diet loses control over her eating behaviour. The onset of bulimia may occur when a self-initiated dieting regime leads to intense feelings of hunger. The desperate craving for food then triggers a 'binge' during which huge amounts of 'forbidden' foods are rapidly eaten. The binge is usually followed by extreme remorse and an acute fear of gaining weight, and the woman may seek to reverse the effects by purging. Although self-induced vomiting may appear a convenient way of controlling weight gain, this 'solution' to weight control is in fact very dangerous.

The clinical picture

Self-starvation Bulimic patients are typically dissatisfied with their own body shape. They are often preoccupied with the idea that they are overweight and that particular parts of their body are grotesque and unattractive. Fear of fatness and aversion to certain parts of the body may lead to frequent weighing, to continual mirror-gazing or to an avoidance of mirrors. Most patients idealize a thin body shape and feel their own body to be heavy and repulsive (Cooper and Fairburn, 1993). Many bulimic patients have a history of 'comfort eating', and the use of food to reduce unhappiness and anxiety may lead to a gain in weight which adds to the person's misery until the decision is taken to embark on a dietary regime.

Binge eating   When the hunger resulting from a period of near starvation proves overpowering, the person may suddenly break the fast and embark on a 'binge' in which vast quantities of high calorie foods are rapidly ingested. Such a session usually involves the consumption of high-calorie foods which have been totally avoided during the diet, including bread, butter, biscuits, cakes, chocolate, cheese, nuts and chips. A binge will generally take place only when the person is alone, and the food eaten during a single episode may amount to several times the normal daily calorific intake. A binge usually lasts for about an hour and several binges may occur during a single day. Following the binge, the person may experience acute remorse, feelings of guilt and depression, and a profound fear of gaining weight.

Purging   There are usually vigorous attempts to offset the effects of a binge by purging. Self-induced vomiting is one the behaviours most commonly associated with bulimia, but several other methods of purging are also frequently employed, including the abuse of laxatives, diuretics and enemas. Purging may follow each binge, and may also occur between binges. Vomiting typically brings immediate feelings of relief (because it reduces the fear of putting on weight), but afterwards there may be feelings of guilt and shame. In one patient sample (Fairburn and Cooper, 1984), half of the bulimic patients engaged in self-induced vomiting at least twice a day. All vomited in secret and some had been inducing vomiting for as long as four or five years.

Depression and low self-esteem   Many of those who suffer from bulimia show a number of other psychological disturbances, some of which may have played a causal role in the development of the bulimia, and others of which may have developed as a consequence of the disorder. Many bulimic patients have low self-esteem, for example, and many are depressed. Bulimic women frequently describe themselves as worthless and often regard their situation as helpless and hopeless. The issue of whether depression is primary and leads to bulimia, or whether depression generally arises as a consequence of the eating disorder, has been the subject of considerable debate. It is likely that the picture differs somewhat from case to case, but a number of studies suggest that depression often emerges as a consequence of bulimia (Cooper, 1985).

Other psychological symptoms associated with bulimia include anxiety, obsessional problems, and various kinds of dysfunctional impulsive behaviour (Fairburn et al., 1985). The social anxiety experienced by many bulimic patients may become especially acute when, for example, they are expected to eat in the company of other people. Some patients become very anxious whenever they think about their body shape, and some experience panic attacks. Bulimia is also associated with various obsessional tendencies and, as a group, these patients obtain high scores on measures of obsessiveness and compulsivity (Bulik et al., 1992a).

Box 3.3
Bingeing and Purging: One Woman's Experience

A number of people who have suffered from bulimia have written graphically about their experience. In her book *Glutton for Punishment* (1984), a recovered bulimic, Louise Roche, describes some of the excesses of her bingeing and purging. At one point in her account she describes how, after having starved herself for three weeks, she arose one morning and immediately rushed to the supermarket and purchased 'One large bar of chocolate, one large box of Maltesers, one thickly sliced loaf. One pound of butter. One packet of cream biscuits. Two yoghurts. Four currant buns. One fruit malt loaf.'

Having left the supermarket she then went to a pharmacist and bought a large box of laxatives: 'As soon as I get out of sight of the shop I open the biscuits and put handfuls into both pockets ... I don't even taste them, I just put them into my mouth, bite them into small enough pieces to swallow and then gulp them down. It takes me literally five minutes to devour the whole packet. Without a moment's rest I rip open the bread, take out two slices, fold them in two and take a bite ... By the time I reach the bottom of the road I have eaten half a loaf.'

Upon reaching home she made toast – six slices at a time – and laid thick wedges of butter on each slice before eating it. She then ate the large bar of chocolate and stuffed handfuls of Maltesers into her mouth, so that within half an hour of leaving the shop she had eaten everything.

The next stage involved drinking two glasses of water and then putting her fingers into her throat to make herself vomit: 'I press down again and the food begins to come. Sticky bread, lumps of butter, bits of chocolate, halves of biscuits. I count how many times I vomit and after ten I stop and examine the regurgitated mess that is lying at the bottom of the sink. I press it down the plughole, pick up pieces, squash them between my fingers, take handfuls and watch it squirm out between the gaps of my clenched fist ... I then turn back to the sink and start the whole process again'.

When she returned to her room, she opened the box of laxatives and swallowed them 'by the handful'. At the same time she examined her body, pulling at her flesh in disgust: 'I start to pull at the fat parts of my body, kneading them like dough and prodding them until they feel sore and tingle. I would love to be able just to tear it off and start again.'

Impulse disorders   A relatively high proportion of those who engage in regular binge–purge activities show other marked disturbances of behaviour. In particular, they are likely to engage in unhealthy, impulsive, self-gratificatory acts. Some classificatory systems distinguish between bulimic patients whose impulsive actions are restricted to eating behaviour ('single impulse disorder') and those who engage in a wider range of impulsive actions. Such 'multiple impulse disordered' patients not only binge and purge but also engage in the abuse of alcohol or drugs, sexual promiscuity, stealing or self-mutilation (Andersen, 1985). Some patients, indeed, can be described as 'universally impulsive' and appear to engage in most of these behaviours. The various types of impulsive action share certain features. They tend to be triggered by negative thoughts or environmental cues, they bring temporary relief from emotional discomfort and they later give rise to feelings of guilt and demoralization.

A relatively high proportion of bulimic women smoke (some report that smoking helps to decrease their appetite for food), drink large quantities of alcohol and use illicit drugs (Bulik et al., 1992b). Lacey (1993) examined the prevalence of self-damaging and addictive behaviour in 112 normal-weight bulimic women (aged 16–40 years), and found that around 20 per cent regularly abused alcohol and a similar proportion frequently used illegal drugs. Many of the women also reported indulging in some form of self-multilating behaviour, including cutting, burning or scratching. Self-mutilation may be targeted at a particular part of the body which a woman feels to be unattractive or disgusting, although the reasons for self-mutilation are highly variable (see Box 3.4).

Denial Although many people who suffer from bulimia are loath to admit to other people that they have a problem with their eating (and although they may go to great lengths to conceal their purging), bulimia is often marked by less subjective denial than anorexia. However, even when a woman suffering from bulimia acknowledges that her eating is out of control, feelings of shame and helplessness often prevent her from seeking help.

Social isolation and relationship problems Bulimic patients often withdraw from relationships and become socially isolated. Typically, they have few friends and those who do manage to maintain relationships often report high levels of conflict with their friends and partners. Many appear to crave social approval, and some are hypersensitive to criticism.

Physical consequences

Self-starvation, bingeing and purging can all lead to serious medical problems. The nutritional deficiencies and hormonal changes associated with bulimia often lead to disturbances in the menstrual cycle, for example, although amenorrhoea is not a typical feature of bulimia, as it is of anorexia.

The various forms of purging are not harmless, as many bulimic patients assume, but can prove highly dangerous. Repeated vomiting and laxative abuse can lead to abdominal pain, digestive problems, dehydration, constipation, dizziness, muscle cramping and general fatigue. The lining of the oesophagus or stomach may be damaged, and the regurgitated stomach contents, which are highly acidic, may permanently erode tooth enamel. Induced vomiting can also produce broken blood vessels in the face and eyes (thus 'bloodshot' eyes can be a sign of purging). Swollen salivary glands may lead to a facial 'puffiness', and in some cases vomiting will precipitate an epileptic seizure. One of the most serious consequences of frequent vomiting, however, is a disturbance of the normal electrolyte balance (potassium and sodium levels are frequently affected), which may then cause renal damage and cardiac arrhythmias (either of which may eventually prove fatal).

Box 3.4
Self-mutilation

Self-mutilation takes many forms, some much more serious than others. This type of behaviour is associated with a number of different psychological conditions, including mental retardation, psychosis and bulimia. Self-mutilation by people who have a severe intellectual deficit tends to take the form of head-banging or hair-pulling. Such behaviour may be motivated by a strong need for stimulation and may also reflect a relative insensitivity to pain. A lack of understanding of the dangers involved in such actions as cutting oneself with a knife may also explain why people who have profound learning difficulties often injure themselves.

When self-mutilation occurs in the context of an acute psychotic condition, it may take such extreme forms as castration, eye enucleation or the amputation of toes or fingers. Such actions are invariably the result of delusional thinking. The psychotic person may engage in self-mutilation as an act of penance, using this form of self-punishment to atone for imagined sins, or may mutilate the genitals in the hope of suppressing lustful thoughts or actions. The delusional systems which give rise to such extreme behaviours are almost always religious or sexual in nature.

Self-mutilation by non-psychotic people is rarely this extreme. In most cases it will involve a minor act of cutting, burning, hair-pulling or scratching. The motives for such actions vary widely. Some mutilating actions are little more than 'habits', and occur with little thought or intention. A broad range of other self-mutilating behaviours may be described as 'parasuicidal'. These include making scratches on the skin (an action often diagnosed as 'attention seeking') and seriously injurious behaviours which might well endanger life. Some people mutilate themselves as an act of bravado, to demonstrate their strength or courage, and some even appear to derive sensual pleasure from inflicting pain on themselves. Cases which fit this latter category may be described as 'masochistic'.

Many acts of self-mutilation stem from self-loathing. Some people express their anger in an act of aggression in which they are both the aggressor and the victim, and some injure themselves because they feel disgusted with their body. Disgust appears to be the motive which drives many bulimic women towards acts of self-mutilation, although the highly impulsive nature of so many of these women is also relevant. A woman's profound loathing of her body may be apparent from the type of damage she inflicts upon herself, and the parts of the body which are attacked (punched, scratched or cut) are likely to be those which she most despises (often the stomach, thighs and buttocks).

It needs to be emphasized that not everyone who engages in self-mutilation is suffering from a recognized psychiatric condition. Many adolescents experiment briefly with self-mutilation, for example, but discontinue the practice after some weeks or months.

Favazza and Conterio (1989) examined the clinical records of 300 patients who had engaged in self-mutilation over a number of years. They found that most patients explained their self-mutilation as an attempt to relieve some kind of emotional distress. It appeared that the self-infliction of harm was sometimes effective in relieving anxiety, although the relief was rarely long-lasting. Some patients in this sample also maintained that they derived a degree of physical pleasure from their self-mutilation, and some even acknowledged that they liked the taste of their own blood.

(Further reading: Favazza, A.R. and Favazza, B. (1987) *Bodies Under Siege: Self-mutilation in Culture and Psychiatry.* Baltimore, MD: Johns Hopkins University Press.)

Epidemiology

Most authorities agree that bulimia now has a higher prevalence than anorexia. Using criteria for the formal psychiatric diagnosis of bulimia, the
disorder affects between 1 and 2 per cent of young women in the USA and
the UK (Fairburn and Beglin, 1990). The condition occurs much less frequently in men, the female : male ratio normally quoted being in the order of
10 : 1. Prevalence estimates have risen sharply in recent years, but this may
be partly explained by the fact that a higher proportion of cases now come to
the attention of clinicians (Fairburn, 1993; Hoek, 1993).

Many people who do not meet the diagnostic criteria for bulimia nevertheless show a number of related symptoms. In one American college study
(Hawkins and Clement, 1980), 80 per cent of females and 50 per cent of males
reported occasional bingeing and purging. In a study of women attending a
family planning clinic (Cooper and Fairburn, 1983), 20 per cent had experienced at least one bulimic (uncontrolled overeating) episode, and 3 per cent
had attempted to use self-induced vomiting as a means of weight control.

Bulimia usually begins during the early adult years, and it is estimated
that around a quarter of bulimic patients are married. A relatively high
proportion come from middle and higher social class groups, and bulimia
appears to be particularly common among students and professional
women. The prevalence of bulimia in non-white populations appears to be
relatively low, although estimates may be affected by referral biases and
prejudicial diagnosis (Dolan, 1991).

Effects of publicity about the condition

On the basis of a series of interviews conducted with bulimic patients,
Habermas (1992) was able to address a number of questions concerning the
effects of publicity on bulimic behaviours and self-referral. He concluded
that the high profile of the disorder had indeed facilitated the seeking of
professional and non-professional help. He also suggested that the spread
of information about bingeing and self-induced vomiting as symptoms of
bulimia had substantially reduced the degree of guilt and self-blame experienced by those who engage in these activities.

A more disturbing conclusion was that the dissemination of information
about the purging methods used by bulimic patients may have led some
people to imitate such forms of 'weight control'. However, other people
may have been alerted to the dangers of binge eating and purging, for
example, by media coverage. Thus the media might have helped to foster a
more cautious attitude to dietary control among some of those who might
otherwise have developed an eating disorder.

Differences between anorexia and bulimia

Many people who suffer from anorexia eventually become bulimic (and a
smaller number of those who suffer from bulimia eventually become

anorexic). Both conditions involve a preoccupation with eating, an idealiza-
tion of thinness and a fear of becoming fat. The onset of bulimia typically
occurs while the person is in her late teens or early twenties, which is
somewhat later than anorexia. The major difference between the two conditions is that anorexia is marked by extreme weight whereas bulimia is not.

Compared with anorexic patients, those who suffer from bulimia are:

- more likely to experience extreme hunger;
- more likely to engage in self-induced vomiting;
- more likely to abuse diuretics and laxatives;
- more likely to have been overweight in the past;
- more likely to be sexually active;
- more likely to engage in deliberate self-harm;
- more likely to engage in drug or alcohol abuse.

Both conditions are resistant to treatment, and post-treatment improvements
are often followed by a relapse. Either condition may lead to physical damage which ultimately proves fatal, and both conditions are associated with a
relatively high suicide risk.

Aetiology

The considerable overlap between bulimia and anorexia in terms of
symptomatology, and the fact that the same person will often develop both
forms of disorder at different times, suggest that the two conditions are likely
to be similar in terms of their aetiology.

Biological factors   Although it would be remarkable if biological factors
played no part at all in an individual's predisposition to develop bulimia,
there is little evidence to suggest that such factors play a major role. The rate
of concordance for the condition is higher in monozygotic female twins than
in dizygotic female twins, but the concordance is rather low in both cases
(Kendler et al., 1991). Relatives of bulimic patients have been found to have
increased rates of a number of psychiatric problems including depression
and alcohol abuse, but such family patterns might reflect social interaction
effects rather than genetic similarity (Schmidt et al., 1993).

Certain studies have suggested that the onset of some cases of bulimia
may be predated by physiological abnormalities, but these findings have not
been widely replicated and have had relatively little impact on thinking
about the aetiology of the disorder. One early report, for example, suggested
that bulimic patients have abnormal electroencephalograms (EEGs) indica-
tive of a hypothalamic disorder (Rau and Green, 1975), and more recently it
has been proposed that bulimia may relate to a deficiency in a hormone,
cholecystokinin, which normally leads to a feeling of fullness after a meal.
Further evidence may produce additional support for these ideas, but as yet
there is no convincing biological account of bulimia nervosa, and the biological differences found between bulimic patients and others appear to be
effects (rather than causes) of the condition.

Psychological accounts   In the absence of any convincing biological account of the origins of bulimia, the field has been wide open to psychological explanations. Many of the factors implicated in psychological accounts are the same as those involved in accounts of the aetiology of anorexia and thus call for little re-examination here. Cultural ideas and images of 'the perfect body shape' or of 'an acceptable body shape', for example, are known to affect the attitudes which bulimic patients have towards their own bodies. There is evidence of disruption in the family backgrounds of many bulimic patients, and it appears that relationship difficulties often contribute to the low self-esteem which may precipitate the bulimic patient's initial decision to diet. As with anorexia, the most convincing aetiological accounts are those which emphasize dietary motivation and the reinforcement conditions which contribute to a loss of control over eating.

Dietary control   Those who develop bulimia often feel themselves to be unattractive and have an intense fear of becoming fat. In some cases the condition appears to be linked to the person's experiences early on in life. Many bulimic patients were overweight in childhood or during early adolescence (Cooper, 1985), and some authorities suggest that bulimia may be linked to general unhappiness or distress during childhood. Experience of child sexual abuse has often been cited as a factor which increases vulnerability to bulimia (Miller et al., 1993), but the evidence on this issue is somewhat unclear. The relevant studies are beset with methodological difficulties, and one comprehensive review concluded that most well controlled studies have failed to find a significantly higher prevalence of childhood sexual abuse among bulimic patients than among control groups (Pope and Hudson, 1992). Studies of patients with a particularly severe eating disorder, however, have generally indicated a high rate of sexual abuse during childhood (DeGroot et al., 1992; Waller, 1992).

Early parental rejection or a lack of parental interest may lead to personality disturbances which can jeopardize relationships during adulthood. There is certainly evidence that many bulimic patients experience severe difficulties in their adult relationships and that conflict and abandonment are often important factors in the onset and maintenance of the condition. Grisset and Norvell (1992) found that, compared with control subjects, bulimic women reported less support from friends and family, described high levels of conflict in their relationships and often appeared deficient in social skills. There is also evidence that a high proportion of bulimic women are victims of marital assault, and such victimization appears to contribute to the high levels of self-blame and the low levels of self-esteem commonly found among those suffering from bulimia (Kaner et al., 1993).

Schmidt et al. (1993) found that the onset of bulimia was often immediately preceded by a important life event such as the break-up of a serious relationship. These authors suggested that the onset of bulimia may follow a traumatic event, and that such a consequence is particularly likely in the case of a young woman who is already somewhat depressed and has long-term personality difficulties, poor social support and inadequate coping skills. Lacey (1992) reported that the majority of women who suffer from bulimia link the onset of the disorder to a crisis in a particularly important emotional or sexual relationship. He also found that many women attributed the relationship crisis to their own unattractiveness or unshapeliness. Similarly, women who feel themselves to be unpopular or unsuccessful in relationships may explain their difficulties as reflecting the fact that they are not 'attractively slim'. Thus, some patients appear to have a 'therapeutic' motive for dieting, and seem to believe that a diet will solve their current relationship problems or assure success in a future relationship.

Although the weight loss that commonly follows the initiation of a restrictive diet is highly reinforcing, the woman may find it difficult to endure the physical discomfort of hunger pangs. This discomfort, together with the anticipation of immediate emotional relief associated with particular foods, may lead to a craving which becomes difficult to control. The temptation may eventually become so powerful that restraint is lost and the woman succumbs.

Bingeing and purging   After struggling with a craving for food over many days or weeks, many people who are 'on a diet' suffer a minor lapse and consume a modest 'illicit' snack. In some cases, however, the breaking of a diet is much more dramatic. The effect is rather like the bursting of a dam, and a mass of highly calorific (and 'forbidden') food is consumed in a virtual frenzy. Such an extreme response is particularly to be expected of those who are impulsive and those for whom eating is strongly associated with relief from emotional distress.

For a person who has an abiding fear of becoming fat, such a binge is likely to produce panic and intense regret at having negated the effects of prolonged dieting. Vomiting may then appear to be an effective means of reversing the effects of the binge. The act of vomiting is immediately reinforced by the relief from anxiety (about becoming fat) and also, perhaps, by the relief of unpleasant sensations associated with the stomach being exceptionally full. A woman who is unfamiliar with the dangers associated with vomiting, or who chooses to ignore the risks, may believe that she has discovered a method of maintaining her weight without having to forgo the pleasures of eating and having to experience unpleasant hunger pangs. If, on balance, her feelings about the binge–purge routine are positive rather than negative the behaviour is likely to be maintained.

Management and treatment

Treatment for bulimia involves a two-phase approach. There is an immediate need to address the dangerous practices of bingeing and purging, and following this there is likely to be an attempt to address the underlying issues which may have led to the bulimia (for example, low self-esteem and relationship difficulties). Because many patients have similar problems with regard to the binge–purge cycle, the first phase of treatment may be conducted with a group of patients working together. But different issues of personality and personal history will need to be addressed with different patients in the second treatment phase, so that individual treatment may then be preferable.

Physical treatment methods Drugs which may be prescribed as part of a treatment programme for bulimia include anti-convulsants, appetite suppressants and anti-depressants. However, pharmacological intervention usually plays only a minor role in treatment, the major contribution coming from some form of psychotherapy. Although anti-depressant medication frequently leads to a short-term improvement, withdrawal from the drug is often followed by relapse and many people consider it inadvisable to maintain such medication over the longer term.

Psychological treatment methods Many forms of psychological treatment have been used to modify the eating and purging behaviours of bulimic patients and to address longer-term personal issues which are thought to contribute to the development of the condition. Efforts to help the person control bingeing and purging usually involve behavioural or cognitive–behavioural methods, and issues relating to longer-term factors such as low self-esteem and relationship problems are often addressed by means of cognitive therapy or some other form of psychotherapy.

Behavioural methods A thorough assessment of problematic behaviour is an initial part of any behavioural intervention programme. Thus a bulimic client will be asked to keep a careful record of eating and purging in order to establish baselines. Such self-monitoring can be beneficial in itself, because it provides valuable feedback to the client about the levels, timing and patterning of problem behaviours. Increased awareness of such aspects sometimes leads to greater self-control. The main purpose of the assessment, however, is to provide a baseline against which future changes can be measured.

'Exposure and response prevention' is a behavioural strategy widely used in the treatment of bulimia. Clients are exposed to situations in which they would normally be expected to binge, or to purge, but are prevented from responding in the usual way (often simply because the therapist is present). The aim is to break down the association between certain stimulus conditions (the presence of particular foods, for example, or the sensation of a full stomach) and the undesirable behaviours which normally follow. Thus a client may be gradually exposed to highly tempting foods while the therapist engages her in conversation, thus preventing her from indulging in a binge. In some cases clients are encouraged to eat modest amounts of high calorie foods while being deterred from over-indulging. If vomiting is the response to be prevented, the patient may be encouraged to eat until she feels the need to vomit, whereupon she is helped to resist this urge.

Exposure and response prevention is one of the elements involved in the 'group meal' which is a feature of many group therapy programmes (Franko, 1993). A group of clients plan and eat a meal, together with the therapist, while discussing their thoughts and feelings. During the meal clients eat a variety of foods, including some which are high in calories, and they may be encouraged to eat until they feel 'full'. Situational constraints – particularly the 'social' and 'therapeutic' context of the meal – act as powerful inhibitors against bingeing and purging. The group meal also provides a good opportunity for clients to express their attitudes and worries. Participation in such a meal often invokes memories of past family meals, and clients may recall times at which they experienced shame, guilt or anger related to their eating.

Cognitive behaviour therapy   Cognitive behaviour therapy is often used to change the erroneous beliefs and problematic attitudes of bulimic patients regarding body shape, eating and purging. A psychoeducational programme may inform clients about such matters as the effects of calorie intake on body weight and shape, the calorie content of various foods and the dangers of purging. It is especially important for the client to understand the links between food deprivation, hunger, craving for food and bingeing. She needs to appreciate that the regular intake of a reasonable amount of food will not lead her to become fat and will help to prevent craving for food.

Many bulimic patients are distressed because they feel fat, and are preoccupied with their weight. The cognitive therapist will help the client to identify any irrational thoughts that are helping to maintain the problem, and will challenge false beliefs. The aim is that the client herself will eventually be able to replace anxiety-inducing and self-critical thoughts with positive images and positive self-statements.

Fairburn (1985) described a cognitive–behavioural programme intended to 'hand control back to the patient'. The treatment programme consisted of three stages. During the first stage, patients were asked to monitor carefully their own eating and purging behaviour. A regular eating pattern was prescribed and clients were informed of the adverse consequences of self-induced vomiting. The second 'cognitive training' stage involved further education about body weight and eating. False beliefs and dysfunctional attitudes were challenged, and training was provided in the use of a number of strategies for solving problems (especially the type of problem which might previously have triggered a binge). The final stage consisted of progress monitoring and a further instalment of cognitive training. Fairburn (1985) showed that the programme significantly reduced the frequency of self-induced vomiting (from an average of 24 times a month to just once a month) in the majority (nine out of eleven) of the women treated.

Psychotherapy   Various forms of psychotherapy have been used to address issues which may contribute to the onset and maintenance of bulimia. Such issues may concern early family relationships, difficulties during adolescence, relationships in adulthood and low self-esteem. Clients are usually treated individually, but treatment may take place in a group setting. Lacey (1983), for example, described the use of 'insight-oriented' therapy with both individuals and groups. In addition, some therapists have worked with couples and whole families. Levine (1988) treated 'bulimic couples' (defined as 'couples in which marital conflict promotes bulimic symptoms in the wife') and found an unusually high degree of secrecy between the partners in such relationships. He suggested that it was useful for a therapist to focus on changing the balance of power in the marriage and helping the patient to deal with issues of dependency and autonomy.

A number of treatment programmes have involved members of the patient's family of origin. Schwartz et al. (1985) evaluated the use of family therapy with thirty bulimic women whose eating, bingeing and purging were said to be 'out of control'. Two-thirds of the clients were judged to be in control of their eating following treatment. Dodge et al. (1995) used family therapy to treat a number of young bulimic women (average age 16 years) and found substantial changes in their eating attitudes and significant reductions in their bingeing, vomiting and abuse of laxatives.

Comparison studies In recent years a number of studies have directly compared the effectiveness of different forms of treatment for bulimia. Approaches which have been assessed in these studies include drug treatment (anti-depressants), behaviour therapy, cognitive behaviour therapy and interpersonal therapy. In many cases patients have been given at least two of these forms of therapy at the same time.

Agras et al. (1992) assigned bulimic women to groups in which they were given anti-depressant medication, cognitive behaviour therapy or both. After 16 weeks of treatment, considerable improvement was evident for the two groups that had received cognitive behaviour therapy, but at 32 weeks the patients who had received the combined treatment appeared to be faring somewhat better. They were less preoccupied with dietary issues and experienced less hunger. The results of this study also suggested that cognitive behaviour therapy might be useful in preventing relapse when patients are withdrawn from medication.

Abbott and Mitchell (1993) investigated the impact of cognitive behaviour therapy, intensive behavioural psychotherapy, anti-depressant medication and combinations of medication and psychotherapy. Intensive psychotherapy was found to be the most effective form of treatment, although good results were also found when less intensive psychotherapy was combined with medication.

Fairburn and Hay (1992) compared anti-depressant drug treatment, cognitive behaviour therapy and a behavioural treatment strategy ('exposure with response prevention'). The behavioural treatment did not add significantly to the effectiveness of cognitive behaviour therapy, which appeared to be the most effective form of treatment. Most of the patients who received this form of treatment appeared to benefit significantly, and their improvements were well maintained.

In a further study, Fairburn et al. (1993) assigned 75 women suffering from bulimia to one of three groups. All the patients were treated for 18 weeks. One group received behaviour therapy, another cognitive behaviour therapy and the third interpersonal psychotherapy. Each patient was followed up for a year after treatment, regular assessments being made of eating habits and attitudes to eating, body shape and weight. The patient's level of social functioning was also evaluated, as was her general psychiatric condition. Cognitive behaviour therapy appeared more effective than behaviour therapy, and although interpersonal therapy did not provide as much

Box 3.5
How to Help a Friend Who May Have an Eating Disorder

Eating disorders are relatively common among young adults, especially women, and they are particularly widespread among college students. Those who suffer from these conditions often deny that they have a problem, even to themselves, and rarely seek treatment on their own initiative.

If you are aware that you yourself have a problem in this area, do contact a physician or counselling service for help. The earlier that treatment is initiated, the more likely it is to be successful.

The following guidelines offer some suggestions of what you might do if you believe that a relative, friend or acquaintance may be suffering from an eating disorder.

1 Read about the eating disorders so that you are well informed about both anorexia and bulimia.

2 If you feel that your friend's condition may be life-threatening (either because her weight has fallen dramatically, or because she may be feeling suicidal), seek help immediately. Contact a counselling service or crisis line for help, and consider the advisability of contacting the person's relatives.

3 Don't spy on your friend. She is already likely to be be self-conscious about her eating habits, and if she feels that she is being watched then her discomfort may increase and she may become even more secretive.

4 Confront your friend, but do this sensitively. Don't patronize her or assail her with criticism. Any defensiveness on her part is more likely to diminish if your approach indicates a genuine concern and a willingness to help.

5 Rather than focusing immediately on eating issues or weight loss, you might begin by mentioning to your friend that she sometimes appears unhappy or anxious. An indirect approach such as this is less likely to make her feel threatened or criticized.

6 Understand that your friend is probably feeling isolated and may be ashamed of her problem. Avoid adding to her predicament, and try not to alienate her.

7 Remember that denial is common. Your friend may deny that she has any difficulties (and you should appreciate that you may in fact be worried for no good reason). If she denies the problem, back off, while letting her know that you would be available to listen if she ever needed help.

8 If your friend agrees that she has a problem, suggest that she contact a professional or a self-help group 'to talk things over'.

9 Find out what counselling services and self-help groups are available locally. Compile a list of contact telephone numbers or addresses. If it seems appropriate, offer to accompany your friend on an initial visit to a counsellor.

10 Recognize that you should not be alone with your anxieties. Share your concern and information (with trusted friends, for example, or with a counsellor). A counsellor will help you to cope and may offer constructive ideas about how you can help your friend.

11 And, finally, remember that ultimately the responsibility for your friend's well-being does not rest with you.

improvement as cognitive behaviour therapy immediately after treatment, differences between these two groups disappeared at follow-up. The authors conclude that although cognitive behaviour therapy and interpersonal psychotherapy operate in different ways, they may be equally effective in the treatment of bulimia nervosa.

Outcome

Some bulimic patients, including some who do not receive treatment, recover completely, but others continue with their bingeing and purging for many years. Keller et al. (1992) reported low rates of recovery and very high rates of chronicity, relapse, recurrence and further psychological problems. Almost one-third of their patients retained severe bulimic symptoms three years after they were first seen. Of those who at some stage were judged to have recovered, two-thirds had relapsed within 18 months.

The fact that bulimia is highly resistant to treatment was noted by Russell (1979) in his original description of the condition. Although recent reports tend to provide a more optimistic picture of treatment outcome (Fairburn, 1993), many describe the situation only in the first weeks or months following a programme of therapy. Unfortunately, early improvement is often followed by a later relapse. Treatment failures are often attributable to the highly impulsive personality of many bulimic patients and to their somewhat ambivalent approach to treatment. Treatment failure and relapse appear to be more likely if the client lacks social support (Keller et al., 1992) and remains within a disturbed family or marital relationship (Norre and Vandereycken, 1991). A favourable outcome is associated with several pretreatment factors, including a low level of depression, relatively infrequent self-induced vomiting and the maintenance of a normal body weight during adulthood.

If a bulimic condition continues over several years, there is a high risk that serious physical complications will develop, and in some cases these will eventually prove fatal. In addition, bulimia is associated with a relatively high risk of suicide.

◀Conclusions▶ ▶ ▶

The two principal eating disorders are anorexia nervosa and bulimia nervosa, and the prevalence of both of these conditions is particularly high among young women. Anorexia is characterized by a substantial loss of body weight, an intense fear of becoming obese, avoidance of 'fattening' foods and disturbed perceptions and evaluations of weight, size and shape. Eventually, the self-starvation and weight loss will have serious consequences for physical health, and in a proportion of cases these prove fatal. Even when treatment is successful, and there is a significant restoration of weight, some of the harmful physical effects may persist.

Many different factors are included in the various accounts of the aetiology of the condition. Individual differences in vulnerability to anorexia may reflect genetic predisposition and the impact of both family and cultural influences. Whatever the predisposing factors, anorexia often develops following a deliberate attempt at dieting. There are several different motives for dieting, some of which reflect enduring psychological difficulties, and dieting becomes particularly dangerous when the extreme restriction of calorie intake becomes the primary and 'autonomous' goal. The biological, psychological and social factors that serve to maintain the disorder may be different from those that contributed to the development of the condition.

If a client's weight loss has reached a critical point, the primary goal must be an immediate weight gain. Various behavioural strategies may be used to aid the refeeding process. A number of psychotherapeutic approaches have been used for the long-term treatment of anorexia, but few have attained more than a modest degree of success. Many of those who suffer from anorexia make reluctant patients. Cognitive–behavioural methods, which are among the most effective treatment strategies, first encourage the client to end her self-starvation and then attempt to modify any more fundamental beliefs and attitudes which may be identified as relevant to the development and maintenance of the condition.

Like anorexia, bulimia is particularly prevalent among young women and can have very serious long-term effects on health. Unlike those who suffer from anorexia, however, most bulimic women maintain a weight around the average for their height. Symptoms of bulimia include a loathing of particular parts of the body and extreme concern about becoming fat. Many bulimic women engage in self-starvation, but periods of self-starvation are likely to end in a 'binge', in which vast quantities of food are eaten within a very short time. A binge is often followed by self-induced vomiting. Cultural pressures undoubtedly play a role in the development of bulimia, but the condition may also be related to relationship difficulties and impulsivity. Cognitive therapy can be an effective form of treatment, but resistance to treatment is common, and relapse rates are relatively high.

Neither of the major eating disorders can be said to be well understood. There is evidence that the prevalence of both is increasing, and the fact that the outcome can be very serious signifies an urgent need to improve on the limited effectiveness of current treatment methods.

◄Further Reading►►►

Hsu, L.K.G. (1990) *Eating Disorders*. New York: Guilford Press.

Comprehensive account, covering all aspects of the eating disorders.

Lask, B. and Bryant-Waugh, R. (1993) *Childhood Onset Anorexia Nervosa and Related Disorders*. London, Erlbaum.

Balanced description of early onset cases of anorexia nervosa, dealing with epidemiology, aetiology, treatment methods, and long-term outcome. Written by a child psychiatrist and clinical psychologist who are part of the eating disorders team at the Hospital for Sick Children, Great Ormond Street, London.

Fairburn, C.G. and Wilson, G.T. (eds) (1993) *Binge Eating: Nature, Assessment and Treatment*. New York: Guilford Press.

Definitive account of bulimia and its treatment.

Cooper, P.J. (1993) *Bulimia Nervosa: a Guide to Recovery*. London: Robinson.

A self-help manual for those who suffer from bulimia, written by one of the foremost clinicians in the field. Employs the cognitive–behavioural approach.

◄Discussion Points►►►

1 Give an account of the behavioural and cognitive disturbances associated with anorexia nervosa.
2 Why do some people who start out on a diet to reduce their weight lose control over their eating and dieting?
3 How are cultural influences relevant to the development of the eating disorders?
4 Why do people suffering from bulimia indulge in binges, and why do they purge?
5 How important are family factors in the onset, maintenance and treatment of anorexia and bulimia?
6 Review various approaches used to treat *either* anorexia nervosa *or* bulimia nervosa.

4 Affective Disorders

The term 'affective' is used by psychologists to refer to emotional states. Affective disorders are those in which the most predominant symptoms are profound disturbances of emotion or mood. Other clinical features include disturbances of thinking and behaviour. By far the most prevalent of the affective disorders is depression. Less common, but also clinically very important, is a disorder in which elation and melancholy alternate. This was formerly labelled 'manic-depressive disorder', but the term 'bipolar depression' is now used. By contrast, depression without manic phases is often referred to as 'unipolar depression'.

The term 'depression' refers to both a mood and a psychopathological syndrome. If a low threshold is set for labelling people as 'depressed', then a substantial proportion of the general population might be classified as suffering from depression at any one time. Large random population surveys commonly report that between 10 and 15 per cent of adults describe themselves as currently feeling at least 'somewhat depressed'. Because negative affective states are so prevalent, depression is sometimes referred to as 'the common cold of psychopathology'. If the threshold for applying the label 'depression' is raised to include only severe emotional disturbances, then the number of cases decreases dramatically, but even major depression is relatively common, affecting about 15 per cent of people at some time in their life (Charney and Weissman, 1988). During the 1980s depression accounted for about one-quarter of all psychiatric hospital admissions in the UK (Department of Health, 1990).

It has long been recognized that different cases of clinical (unipolar) depression originate from different causes. Depression is sometimes described as a 'spectrum disorder' and is said to be 'aetiologically heterogeneous'. Whereas some cases appear to be primarily biological in origin, others appear to be triggered by an adverse social or environmental change. In the majority of cases, however, the development and course of the disorder will reflect complex interactions between several biological and psychological factors. There is now clear evidence that changes in levels of certain key neurochemicals can precipitate a depressive episode, and it is equally clear that many cases of clinical depression are triggered by negative events in the person's life. Family bereavement, divorce, an accident and redundancy from work, for example, all render the individual susceptible to clinical depression. In other cases the depression appears to be a response not to a particular event but to long-term circumstances which are a continuing source of stress and disappointment.

Despite the general association between stress and depression, many people who are subjected to high stress do not develop a depressive disorder. Some become highly anxious, others develop a variety of behavioural symptoms and some show little or no evidence of psychological distress. There are important individual differences in vulnerability, and the risk of becoming depressed is related to a number of biological factors, to the individual's personality and early history, to cognitive style and coping skills and to the level of available social support.

◀Unipolar Depression▶▶▶

Sub-classification

It is possible to classify cases of unipolar depression in a number of different ways. Traditionally, there were two major sub-classificatory models, one which distinguished cases on the basis of the severity and 'quality' of the clinical symptoms, and one which distinguished cases on the basis of the presumed causes ('aetiology') of the condition.

'Sub-classification by symptomatology', which is rarely used nowadays, distinguished between neurotic depression and psychotic depression. Neurotic depression was diagnosed when mood levels tended to fluctuate, and when anxiety was a prominent feature. Psychotic depression was diagnosed when the symptoms were more persistent and more severe, and when there was evidence of 'reality distortion', which might include hallucinations and complex delusions. The distinction between neurotic and psychotic depression was the subject of considerable controversy for many years. The 'continuity hypothesis' maintained that the two forms of depression were only quantitatively different, the psychotic form being an exaggerated form of neurotic depression. The opposing view was that psychotic and neurotic depression were qualitatively different disorders.

'Sub-classification by aetiology' is still widely used in clinical practice, but is no longer included in the DSM system, which now avoids aetiological criteria as a basis for classification and diagnosis. The aetiological sub-classification differentiates cases in which depression is a response to an environmental precipitating event (such as a bereavement) and those in which the disorder is not associated with such an event (and is therefore

Table 4.1 Endogenous and reactive depression

	Endogenous depression	**Reactive depression**
Hallucinations	May be present	Not present
Delusions	May be present	Not present
Mood	Continuous depression	Fluctuating depression
Psychomotor retardation	Marked	Slight or none
Appetite/weight	Often severe loss	Less pronounced
Energy	Markedly reduced	May be reduced
Early morning waking	Often present	Not present
Diurnal changes in mood	Symptoms worse in the morning	Symptoms worse in the evening

assumed to result from internal – perhaps biological – processes). Cases attributed to adverse events or life circumstances are identified as cases of 'reactive (or 'exogenous') depression', and cases attributed to internal causes are identified as cases of 'endogenous depression'.

In fact, both the symptomological and aetiological forms of sub-classification tend to result in a rather similar division of cases. Most 'reactive' cases would be classified as 'neurotic' and many 'endogenous' cases might be classified as 'psychotic'. Thus different symptom patterns are associated with cases of reactive and endogenous depression, as is shown in Table 4.1.

It is now accepted that in the majority of cases both endogenous and exogenous factors play a significant aetiological role. Many people who are depressed are physically run-down, perform poorly on cognitive tasks, are pessimistic and have relationship problems. It is often very difficult to distinguish between the causes of the depression and the effects of the disorder. An endogenous depression may well produce adverse life changes (such as difficulties with a relationship or problems at work) which then help to maintain the depression. On the other hand, a depression that has arisen primarily as a reaction to life circumstances may produce physiological changes which serve to maintain the depression. The existence of such causal relationships between biological and environmental factors reinforces the view that it is often inappropriate to try to make a sharp differentiation between endogenous and reactive depression.

Before we leave the issue of the sub-classification of unipolar depression, a number of more specific categories should be mentioned. The term 'involutional depression' (or 'involutional melancholia') was applied for many years to cases of depression which emerged during the so-called 'involutional' years (usually, 40–55 in women and 50–65 in men). The symptoms of this condition were said to include anxiety, agitation, hypochondriasis and various somatic symptoms. Early aetiological accounts emphasized the importance of physiological changes occurring in the middle and late years, but such explanations gradually gave way to those which emphasized reduction in social contact and social status, a loss of external goals and rewards, and stresses induced by physical illness, infirmity and financial insecurity. Most

Box 4.1
Post-partum Depression

Three types of psychological disorder have been identified as associated with the period immediately after the birth of a child (the 'post-partum period'): the 'maternity blues' (or 'baby blues'), which is a common and short-term disorder; post-partum psychosis, which is very rare; and post-partum depression.

The 'baby blues' involves acute mood changes, high anxiety, fatigue and periods of prolonged crying (for a review of the evidence relating to this condition, see Kennerly and Gath, 1986). This condition is experienced by between 50 and 80 per cent of women who give birth (those who have just given birth to their first baby appear to be more at risk). Although it may last for more than a week, the disorder usually persists for just one or two days and is often at its peak on the third or fourth day after the birth. The extreme emotional lability may well reflect the pronounced changes in hormone levels following labour and delivery, although social and environmental stresses also appear relevant. The condition disappears, without treatment, after just a few days.

Post-partum depression usually has an onset some two days after the birth of the child and then persists for between six weeks and a year. Reflecting very different criteria used to define and diagnose the condition, it is variously said to affect between 3 and 30 per cent of women giving birth. The symptoms may include profound feelings of sadness and pessimism, tiredness, intense feelings of inadequacy and inability to cope, social withdrawal, anorexia and a loss of interest in normal pursuits. Many women suffering from post-partum depression have

thoughts of suicide, and they may feel intensely aggressive towards themselves and other people, including the baby. In a number of tragic cases this has led to infanticide (Toufexis, 1988). The seriousness of the condition, and the dangers associated with it, mean that a period of hospitalization may be advisable.

The aetiology of post-partum depression remains unclear, but there appears to be a complex interplay of physiological, psychological and social factors. The onset of the condition may well be triggered by the massive hormonal changes that take place after the birth of a child (this is consistent with the fact that women who suffer from the pre-menstrual syndrome are more at risk of post-partum depression). Certain aspects of the woman's personality may also increase her susceptibility, and those who have previously experienced one or more depressive episodes are more likely to develop post-partum depression than those who have no such history.

Various studies have also suggested that post-partum depression is related to personal conflicts associated with the pregnancy and motherhood, medical complications during pregnancy, characteristics of the baby, difficulties in establishing the initial infant–mother relationship, stressful events in the perinatal period and poor social support (Affonso and Domino, 1984; Hopkins et al., 1984). Treatment may involve various forms of psychological intervention (including supportive psychotherapy) as well as anti-depressant medication. In some cases it is useful to reduce stress by providing practical help with housework and baby-care.

modern diagnostic systems do not include involutional depression as a separate entity and there is now a general consensus that there is no justification on grounds of symptom patterns or causal history to distinguish between depression which has its onset during middle to old age and depression which has an earlier onset.

Box 4.2
Seasonal Affective Disorder: SAD

Many people experience a mild 'winter blues', but some regularly become deeply depressed when winter sets in. The DSM classification system now recognizes 'seasonal affective disorder' (SAD). The symptoms associated with this condition include low mood, extreme lethargy and sleepiness, and an increased appetite for food. Women are especially vulnerable, the ratio of women to men diagnosed as suffering from SAD being in the region of 4:1.

One aetiological hypothesis suggests that the seasonal depression is owing to high levels of the hormone melatonin, which is secreted by the pineal gland, a structure situated at the base of the brain. Environmental light suppresses the secretion of the hormone, but in the winter, it is suggested, the relatively low level of natural light permits the level of melatonin to build up, lead-

ing to drowsiness and lethargy (Rosenthal et al., 1984).

The light-deprivation hypothesis is supported by the fact that most people diagnosed as suffering from SAD show a substantial improvement following several days of 'light therapy', in which they remain for a number of hours each day in artificial daylight. In some cases, at least, this appears to restore the person's energy and to bring about a significant increase in emotional well-being. When the light therapy is discontinued, however, there may be a sudden relapse (Lewy et al., 1987). Recent evidence also suggests that SAD symptoms change in predictable ways when patients travel to places with more or less sunlight. Transfer to a place with less light tends to deepen the depression, whereas moving to a sunnier location tends to lift the depression (Rosenthal et al., 1986).

There is a similar dispute over whether it is appropriate to maintain a separate classification category for cases in which depression develops shortly after the birth of a child, although the label 'post-partum depression' is still widely used (this form of depression is examined in box 4.1).

During the 1980s it was recognized that some people regularly develop symptoms of depression during the winter months. The results of a number of clinical research studies then strengthened the case for introducing a new diagnostic category: 'seasonal affective disorder' (this condition is described in box 4.2).

Case profile: unipolar depression

Karen S., 35, was hospitalized because of overwhelming feelings of depression. On admission she had a very sad appearance, sat in a hunched position, and moved very slowly. She avoided eye contact and replied to questions with a soft monotonous murmur. Karen continually clasped her hands together. She complained of feeling 'totally wretched' and frequently spoke of 'the pointlessness of it all'. She tended to wake very early in the morning and would then be unable to sleep again. Her family reported that she often wept and rarely ate. Karen maintained on several occasions that she would be 'better off dead', but although she made frequent references to suicide there was no evidence that she had made any attempt to end her life. She said that she felt worthless and 'no good to anybody', although her marriage had apparently been a happy one and she had been successful in raising her two daughters before the onset of her depression.

Unipolar depression: symptoms

The principal symptoms of depression are sadness, pessimism and self-dislike, along with loss of interest and motivation. There may be psychomotor retardation, or agitation, or both. Somatic complaints also feature in many cases, and these may include aches and pains, loss of appetite and weight, poor sleep, menstrual changes and loss of libido. The depressed person may also think a lot about suicide and may make suicidal threats or attempts.

The principal symptoms of depression will be examined under the following headings: affective, cognitive, behavioural, somatic (i.e. 'bodily') and social symptoms.

Affective symptoms   Although sadness is the central symptom of depression, other affective symptoms may also be present, including anger and anxiety. Depression is also marked by a sharp loss of interest and enthusiasm across a very broad range of concerns. Some indication of the mixture of emotions experienced during a depressive episode is provided by the following autobiographical fragment, an account by an anonymous psychotherapist of a depressive episode in his or her life:

> During most of the period I was depressed life seemed hopeless and futile. Whilst I never again felt suicidal following my admission to hospital, most of the time I was very tired and weary and felt that it would be a great relief if life came to an end. I frequently sought escape in sleep and would stay in bed until mid-day as often as possible. At times panic and anxiety would come upon me powerfully for no apparent reason, often resulting in irrational fears as the feelings attached themselves to whatever circumstances I was in at the time. (Rippere and Williams, 1985, p. 156)

Cognitive symptoms   Those who are severely depressed often find it very difficult to concentrate. They may find it impossible to get their thoughts together, so that they easily become confused. Attempting to maintain an interest in a topic for any length of time may demand a strenuous effort. People who are suffering from profound depression often spend a considerable proportion of their time dwelling on unpleasant thoughts and memories. They are likely to adopt extremely negative attitudes towards themselves, the world and the future. Their general pessimism may be accompanied by a severe loss of self-esteem and feelings of unworthiness. Pervasive self-doubt may coincide with extensive self-blame and guilt. In particularly severe cases the guilt will take on delusional qualities. For example, the person may feel personally responsible for a national disaster or for some catastrophic historical event.

Other delusions may involve unrealistic assumptions and inferences that promote feelings of persecution or jealousy. Disturbed reality processing may also lead the person to experience hallucinations. These will typically be auditory, and may take the form of voices accusing the person of sinful deeds, suggesting participation in dangerous or illegal activities, or advising suicide.

Behavioural symptoms   Clinically depressed people often look profoundly sad. They may have a woeful facial expression and a hunched posture, and they may weep frequently. They often lose all interest in self-presentation and self-care and pay little attention to their dress and other aspects of their appearance. Those who are severely depressed generally lose their appetite for food and lose all sexual desire. Their sleep patterns are usually disturbed, and self-destructive behaviour may include self-mutilation and attempts at suicide.

The activity levels of people who are depressed tend to conform to one or other of two distinct patterns. Those who are said to be suffering from 'retarded depression' usually make only a few sluggish movements, and their speech tends to be slow and monotonous. By contrast, those who are said to be suffering from 'agitated depression' often speak in short fast bursts and find it difficult to keep still. Some pace the room for hours on end, perhaps wringing their hands or engaging in other stereotyped movements.

Somatic symptoms   People suffering from a severe depressive disorder are often physically very 'run down'. Friends may describe them as 'in need of a tonic'. They often lose weight, frequently feel physically tired and suffer from a variety of aches and pains. Because depression reduces the effectiveness of the immune system, they also run a relatively high risk of developing infections (Schleifer et al., 1984).

Depressed people are often disturbed by their physical symptoms, and may visit a physician complaining of tiredness, fatigue, weight loss, headaches or some other pain or physical discomfort. Many of these patients fail to recognize that their symptoms stem from an emotional disturbance, and they often believe that their physical complaints signal the presence of some serious physical disorder. Thus a person who loses weight due to a lack of appetite may become more depressed as the result of the pessimistic assumption that the weight loss signifies cancer. A somatic symptom of depression may therefore maintain or deepen the negative mood. In some cases the primary affective nature of the person's condition is not easily apparent even to the physician (such patients are sometimes said to be suffering from 'masked depression').

Social symptoms   Many depressed people avoid the company of others, including close friends and relatives. They may feel unattractive, unloved and unlovable, and they may have lost interest in conversation and social activities. When they are with other people they may experience a strong desire to escape. On the other hand, some depressed people actively seek the support of particular friends or relatives and become highly dependent on others.

Relatives and work colleagues may eventually find it very wearing to be with the depressed individual for any length of time. Initial sympathy may fade, and they may eventually try to avoid contact with the person. It is easy to see how a vicious circle can develop. When depressed people have little contact with other people they lose much of the support and interest which other people can provide. Feelings of isolation and abandonment may then deepen the depression.

Diurnal variation Many people who are depressed show a pronounced variation in the severity of their symptoms through the day. In some cases (particularly those identified as 'endogenous') the symptoms are worse very early in the morning (often immediately upon waking in the early hours), whereas in other cases (particularly those identified as 'reactive') the person's symptoms tend to become more severe as the day progresses.

Course and prognosis

The majority of cases of clinical depression have a sudden onset, and the condition may then gradually become more severe. A deep depression may be maintained for several days, weeks or even months before the person experiences any substantial elevation in mood. Even without treatment, the great majority of depressed people will eventually recover.

Complete recovery from a first episode of depression occurs in more than 90 per cent of cases. While in a state of deep depression, however, people often become convinced that the condition will be permanent and that there is 'no hope' of recovery. This belief often leads to the conclusion that suicide is the only way out of the depression. It is therefore crucially important to try to convince people who are severely depressed that there is every chance of a good recovery.

Half of those who suffer a major depressive episode never experience another such episode. The other half do suffer one or more further severe episodes later in their life. In a small minority of cases, however, the first severe depressive episode does mark the beginning of a chronic illness.

Following their extensive review of the evidence relating to patterns of relapse after recovery from unipolar depression, Belsher and Costello (1988) concluded that the risk of relapse diminishes as the time since the last severe episode becomes longer. Risk of relapse is higher if the patient has a history of several depressive episodes and if there is an underlying metabolic disturbance. In many cases, a relapse is obviously triggered by a stressful event. On the other hand, high levels of social support are associated with continued recovery (Cohen and Wills, 1985). Neither gender nor social class are significant predictors of relapse.

Epidemiology

General population studies suggest that at any one time up to 15 per cent of the adult population may be suffering from mild depression, although the figures vary considerably with age, sex and a number of other variables. A classic study of 400 women from the Camberwell district of London revealed that 15 per cent had been clinically depressed at some time over the previous year, and when borderline cases were also included, the proportion rose to over one-third (Brown and Harris, 1978). Studies of patients attending general practitioners show that up to 20 per cent are suffering from a depressive illness (Meakin, 1992), and in the UK around 9 million prescriptions are written each year for anti-depressant medication.

Various studies in the UK, the USA and a number of European countries suggest that the lifetime prevalence for one or more major depressive episodes is 15 per cent (10 per cent for males and 20 per cent for females). This contrasts with a substantially lower lifetime prevalence for bipolar depression (around 1 per cent). A number of demographic factors are associated with the level of risk for clinical depression, including sex, age, marital status and social class.

Sex Approximately twice as many women as men are depressed. The same ratio applies to people in the general population who describe themselves as 'feeling low at the moment', to those attending their general practitioner complaining of feeling depressed and to those who are hospitalized for severe (unipolar) depression. Furthermore, the female:male ratio of 2:1 has been reflected in research conducted in over thirty countries over half a century.

The higher rate of depression among women than among men has been explained in a number of different ways. For example, it has been suggested that women may be less reluctant than men to recognize or to disclose feelings of depression. Another suggestion is that healthcare professionals may apply a diagnosis of depression more readily to women than to men. However, there is little evidence to support these propositions, and several large and well conducted epidemiological studies have confirmed that women do have a substantially higher rate of depression than men.

A number of biological and psychosocial explanations have been put forward to account for the gender difference. Biological explanations tend to focus on hormonal differences between men and women and receive some support from the fact that major changes in women's hormonal levels (especially following the birth of a child, and during the menopausal phase) coincide with increased risk of the onset of depression.

Psychosocial explanations focus on women's social status and social roles. It is claimed that more women than men become depressed because women have relatively little power and may experience higher levels of stress. A somewhat different explanation suggests that men and women respond to stress in different ways. In the face of hardship and unfavourable life events, it is argued, women are more likely to respond in a passive and 'helpless' way whereas men are more likely to respond with outward-directed anger and aggression. This explanation could account for major sex differences in uncontrolled aggression as well as depression. A development of this hypothesis suggests that men and women respond to threatening circumstances in different ways because of major differences in the ways in which boys and girls are socialized.

One explanation which has been subjected to a considerable amount of research is that whereas men who are in danger of becoming depressed are likely to engage in distracting behaviours which help them to avoid depression, women who face a similar threat are more likely to amplify their negative mood by ruminating about their condition and its possible causes (Nolen-Hoeksema, 1987). At this point it would be premature to draw any firm conclusion about why more women than men are depressed. It is likely that a number of factors jointly contribute to the substantial gender difference in prevalence.

Age It is very rare for a child under 5 years old to suffer from a major depressive disorder, although such cases are sometimes reported. As many as 2 per cent of school-age children may be severely depressed at any one time, and the rate for adolescents appears to be around 4 per cent (Ryan, 1989). The symptoms found in childhood depression are similar to those found in adult depression, but somatic complaints and hallucinations may be more common among the very young (Ryan et al., 1987). Many cases of childhood depression are related to stressful life events such as the onset of a serious physical illness, the death of a parent or sibling and bullying at school.

The risk of depression appears to increase between early adulthood and middle age, and those in the older age group are likely to be particularly vulnerable to depression. The risk of suicide is particularly high among older adults, and approximately one-quarter of all suicides involve people over 65 years of age.

Marital status Community studies and studies of psychiatric populations indicate that married people are less at risk of developing a depressive disorder than those who are widowed or divorced (Bloom et al., 1979). Those who have a partner are also less likely to contemplate suicide (Cargan and Melko, 1982). Various explanations for the association between marital status and the prevalence of depression have been suggested (Frude, 1991). The absence of a partner may make it especially difficult for a person to cope with stress, because such coping is greatly enhanced by the availability of a confidante and by a high level of social support. People who are divorced or bereaved may be at greater risk of depression because they have been stressed by the loss of their partner, because they are socially isolated and because they experience persistent loneliness.

All of these explanations suggest that a continuing marital relationship may reduce the risk of depression (although it must be remembered that this is an average effect; a precarious, conflictual and stressful marital relationship might well increase the risk of depression). However, when we consider the nature of the association between depression and divorce we must also bear in mind the fact that long-term depression in one or both partners often has a disastrous effect on the marital relationship. A depressive illness can place such a severe strain on a couple that it contributes to the breakdown of their relationship and increases the chances that they will get divorced.

Social class   The results of several large-scale studies have suggested that the prevalence of depression is roughly the same for people from each social class. However, some research (for example, that reported by Brown and Harris, 1978) has indicated that those from lower socioeconomic groups may be substantially more vulnerable to depression than those from the middle-class population.

Historical change   Several epidemiologists have now produced evidence to show that rates of depression in the community have increased over recent decades. It is possible that people are now more willing to admit that they are depressed, and diagnostic criteria and practices might have changed. However, even when reasonable allowances are made for such spurious factors, a significant increase is still apparent. It seems that there really has been a fairly substantial rise in the rates of both mild and medium depression (Hagnell et al., 1982; Klerman et al., 1984). Rates of severe depression have increased less dramatically, and some would claim that they have not increased at all.

How can we account for the increase in the prevalence of depression over recent decades? Explanations reflect general ideas about the aetiology of depression which will be discussed later in this chapter. Briefly, and using the diathesis–stress model as a framework, an individual's vulnerability to depression can be seen to reflect genetic, cognitive and social factors, while the stressors most closely associated with depression appear to be major life events, particularly those relating to loss or failure.

Because the interval over which the prevalence of depression has been found to have increased is too short to have witnessed a significant change in the human gene pool, the increase is unlikely to reflect an increment in the genetic diathesis for depression. The increase may, however, reflect significant changes in other factors associated with vulnerability, including cognitive style (for example, people may have become more pessimistic in their thinking) and social elements (for example, there may have been a significant reduction in social support). Thus social and psychological changes might have made people more vulnerable to depression than they were some decades ago. But, in addition, people may now experience more stress, perhaps as a result of an increased rate of relationship disturbances and breakdowns. Indeed, a number of relevant factors may all have changed in an alarming way, and the historical increase in depression may reflect their combined effects. With further research it may be possible to account for the increased rate of depression more precisely, and perhaps to suggest preventive strategies, but at this stage we can only speculate about why we are living in what some have labelled 'an age of depression'.

◄Mania► ► ►

Mania is a highly agitated state of mind, often experienced by the individual as euphoria. It is accompanied by hyperactivity, verbosity and sleeplessness. In many respects the symptoms of mania are the reverse of those associated with depression. Thus the manic person may display elevated self-confidence, may lack all sense of guilt or responsibility, and may find it difficult to stop laughing and giggling. Other symptoms, including delusions and disturbances in sleep patterns, overlap with those of depression, although they usually take very different forms in the two affective states.

It is rare for someone to experience manic episodes without also experiencing alternating depressive episodes, but cases of 'pure mania' do occur. Such cases might be labelled 'unipolar mania', but in practice (for example, when applying the DSM system of classification) the general label 'bipolar affective disorder' is used. This is justified on the grounds that there is little difference between cases of persistent mania and those of the alternating state disorder in terms of their course and response to treatment. Thus there is now a preference for regarding cases of both types as examples of a single condition (Spitzer et al., 1981). In the following sections we present a case description of 'pure' mania and an account of the principal symptoms associated with manic episodes before examining the more common, alternating, form of bipolar disorder.

Case profile: mania

F.H., a single man in his mid-twenties, was brought to the hospital by his parents. They reported that he had not slept more than a few hours in the past week, that he had been singing loudly in the middle of the night and that on the previous day he had spent all the money he had saved over several years on exotic clothes and perfumes. They also complained that his behaviour was embarrassing (his father described it as 'over the top') and hinted that he had made obscene remarks to several neighbours. F.H. could see no reason for his parents' concern. He claimed that he merely felt happy, that he 'knew the secret of the universe' and that he would soon become world famous. He spoke very quickly and in short bursts. He could not sit still, but paced around, constantly flapping his hands. When admitted to a hospital ward, he discarded his clothes and attempted to engage nurses and patients in embarrassing conversations about his sexual prowess and interests. At one time he reported hearing women's voices 'begging me to tend to their erotic needs'.

Mania: symptoms

Typically, manic episodes have a sudden onset, and they may then continue for days, weeks or months. Among the various features of the manic state are the following.

- *Elevated mood.* Typically, manic people see the world as a wonderful place; they have boundless optimism and enthusiasm, and may regard other people as boring and miserable. They may ignore aches and pains, taking a pride in their 'complete health' and 'total fitness'.
- *Hyperactivity.* Most manic people are very restless and many work and play furiously, although they may find it impossible to concentrate on one topic for more than a few moments. They may also become 'hypersexual', with increases in sexual appetite and in the rate of sexual activity.
- *Sleeplessness.* When in a manic phase, people generally need little sleep. They may sleep for just a few hours before rising joyfully and energetically.
- *Delusions.* Mania is always marked by a number of distorted ideas and values, and in many cases elaborate and systematic delusions are maintained over several days or weeks. Manic delusions may take the form of ridiculously inflated ideas concerning personal wealth, attractiveness, or physical or mental powers. The manic person may claim to be famous, to know famous people or to have an insight into political conspiracies or religious truths.
- *Talkativeness and flight of ideas.* Individuals who are suffering from mania tend to speak very quickly and they may laugh at their own weak jokes. Their speech often includes many puns and may be full of innuendo. Their thoughts 'race' and they are likely to flit from one topic to another so that other people find it impossible to hold a coherent conversation with them. They are also extremely distractible.
- *Inflated self-esteem.* Those who are manic often regard themselves and their various projects and activities in an unrealistically favourable light. In some cases their delusions may take the form of 'delusions of grandeur'.
- *Reckless behaviour.* People who are suffering from mania are likely to exhibit an extreme lack of inhibition and care. They may spend money recklessly, run up enormous credit card bills, drive fast and dangerously, and engage in frequent sexual indiscretions.
- *Susceptibility to frustration.* When they are in a manic state, people are often disappointed that their attempts at 'great feats' are blocked or that other people do not share their manic delusions. Some respond with frustrated tears, whereas others become very aggressive when they are disbelieved, discredited or obstructed.
- *Abuse of alcohol and other drugs.* People who are feeling manic often indulge in an excessive use of alcohol or other non-prescribed drugs. Seeking new experiences, they may experiment with a variety of dangerous substances. As with other aspects of their behaviour, manic patients find it difficult to 'draw the line' appropriately and to behave in a moderate or controlled way.

Bipolar Disorder ▶ ▶ ▶

It has long been recognized that some people are prone to alternating episodes of extreme elation and severe depression. The term 'manic-depressive disorder' was formerly used as a label for this condition, but patients who exhibit such extreme fluctuations in mood are now said to be suffering from 'bipolar disorder'. The depression associated with this condition is indistinguishable from that found in cases of unipolar depression. The distinction between the unipolar and bipolar forms of affective disorder therefore rests on the occurrence or non-occurrence of manic episodes. In the bipolar disorder, depressed and manic states may follow one another immediately, or they may be separated by periods of normal functioning. In rare cases, both manic and depressed features are present at the same time.

Case profile: bipolar disorder

Mark R., 28, was admitted to hospital in a state of wild excitement. He announced that he had solved 'the riddle of the universe' and that he would be 'rich beyond riches'. His speech was rapid and confused, and he would sometimes stop in mid-sentence, apparently wrapped up in his thoughts, until he resumed his rapid talk. His wife reported that he had been in this state for two days, during which he had not slept more than a few hours. However, his current state had apparently been preceded by a 'deep depression' that had lasted for several weeks. During this period he had refused all offers of help and had evidently been preoccupied with failure at work, the private lives of his colleagues and the belief that his neighbours were spying on him.

Bipolar disorder: symptoms

Symptoms of bipolar depression usually include, in different phases of the disorder, at least some of the symptoms associated with unipolar depression, and some of the symptoms associated with mania.

Course and prognosis

The first episode of bipolar depression often occurs when the person is aged between 20 and 30, and the condition then tends to reappear several times throughout the person's life. Each episode may last for weeks, months or even years. The severity of the disorder tends to increase with successive episodes, although after ten years or so there may be a marked diminution in the seriousness of the symptoms.

Epidemiology

Bipolar depression is much less common than unipolar depression, having a lifetime prevalence of around 1 per cent. Women are at greater risk than men, but the sex ratio is not as pronounced as in the case of unipolar depression.

◀Aetiology of Affective Disorders▶▶▶

Unipolar depression

Some cases of severe depression clearly result from overwhelming personal adversity. The death of a close family member, the ending of the marital relationship or public disgrace, for example, may cause a person to become profoundly depressed. When personal tragedy or loss are identified as precipitating the affective disorder it may be labelled 'exogenous depression'. In many cases, however, depression is not preceded by any identifiable environmental stressor. The condition may have its onset at a time when personal circumstances are equable and when the person appears to be generally content with life. In such cases it may be assumed that the depression reflects certain intrinsic (probably biological) factors, and the condition may then be labelled 'endogenous depression'. Thus, it is clear that any comprehensive account of the causes of depression must include a consideration of biological, environmental and psychological factors.

Biological accounts: genetic evidence

A disproportionate number of the relatives of patients suffering from unipolar depression have a history of depression themselves. Such a pattern does not necessarily demonstrate genetic involvement, for the presence of one depressed person within a family might cause others to become depressed. However, when Nurnberger and Gershon (1982) reviewed the results of seven twin studies they found that the concordance rate for unipolar depression was consistently higher for MZ (identical) twins than for DZ (fraternal) twins, thus supporting the hypothesis that genetic factors might predispose people to depression. Averaged across the seven studies reviewed, the average concordance rate for MZ twins was 65 per cent, whereas for DZ twins it was only 14 per cent.

However, the fact that the concordance rate for MZ twins is far below 100 per cent indicates that depression is not 'genetically pre-programmed'. The evidence from genetic studies does nothing to contradict the view that environmental events and acquired psychological characteristics play a crucial aetiological role. Neither does the genetic evidence indicate the nature of any anatomical or physiological differences between those who are highly vulnerable to unipolar depression and those who have a low level of vulnerability. Current evidence suggests that the crucial biological differences relate to the activity of certain biochemical substances in the brain.

Biological accounts: biochemical theories

Much of the current research interest focuses on the idea that depression reflects abnormalities in 'biogenic amine metabolism'. The transmission of electrical impulses between neurons is facilitated by 'neurotransmitters', some of these neurochemicals being 'biogenic amines'. Simply put, the biogenic amine model suggests that a deficiency in certain neurotransmitters leads to depression, whereas high levels of neurotransmitter substances lead to the symptoms of mania.

Particular attention is now focused on two biogenic amines, the catecholamine norepinephrine (NE, also referred to as noradrenaline) and the indoleamine serotonin (5-HT). Low levels of these substances could account for many of the symptoms commonly associated with depression. Brain functioning is profoundly affected by neurochemical changes, some of which arise 'spontaneously' as the result of an endogenous biological process, some of which follow the administration of drugs and some of which arise in response to psychological events. A number of animal studies, for example, have shown that intense stress reduces levels of norepinephrine (Weiss et al., 1970; Stone, 1975).

Drug effects on neurotransmitter levels Drugs that are known to decrease the level of available NE tend to produce depressive symptoms in non-depressed people. A dramatic demonstration of the effect of such drugs on mood is provided when experimental subjects take a substance called physostigmine. Within minutes they are likely to become profoundly depressed and may experience suicidal wishes and feelings of self-hate (Janowsky et al., 1972).

The fact that a depressed mood can be 'artificially' induced by administering certain drugs suggests that some cases of 'natural' depression might stem from a disturbance of normal metabolic processes. Furthermore, drugs that increase the available NE tend to be effective in reducing the symptoms of people suffering from depression (such drugs include those from two major groups of anti-depressants – the monoamine oxidase inhibitors and the tricyclics). Following a similar pattern, drugs which increase catecholamine levels tend to produce manic symptoms in normal people (such drugs include amphetamine and cocaine), whereas those that reduce catecholamine levels tend to relieve the symptoms of mania.

Neurotransmitter metabolite studies Although neurotransmitter levels cannot be assessed directly in the living organism, biochemicals related to these substances (their 'metabolites') can be measured in urine and cerebrospinal fluid. One metabolite of NE – MHPG – has been the subject of a number of studies. Levels of MHPG have been found to be lower in depressed patients than in control subjects, and MHPG levels increase as patients recover from their depression. However, these relationships appear to hold only for some depressed people, and it appears that in some cases changes in levels of 5-HT, rather than of NE, may be responsible for changes in mood.

Summary A considerable body of evidence implicates biological factors (and, in particular, low levels of certain neurotransmitters) in at least some cases of depression. Such a view receives further support from the fact that some chemicals known to modulate neurotransmitters are effective in the treatment of depression. It therefore seems likely that 'spontaneous' metabolic disturbances are sometimes responsible for the onset of depression. In other cases, in which the onset of depression is triggered, for example, by environmental stressors and subsequent cognitive responses, we might also expect some disturbance of neurotransmitter activity. But in such a case the chemical state would not be regarded as the primary cause of the affective disorder.

Psychological accounts

Loss and rejection   Freud put forward a number of theories of depression, the most influential being that first published in his 1917 paper 'Mourning and melancholia'. In this he explored the similarity between depression and mourning. The two states are often triggered by loss, and they often involve a degree of ambivalence towards the lost object or person. Other common features include anger, resentment at having been 'deserted' and self-blame. The major difference between the two states, Freud suggested, is that, unlike those in mourning, depressed people experience what would now be labelled 'a loss of self-esteem'.

Freud suggested that adult vulnerability to depression has its roots in early childhood experiences, and most especially in early experiences of real or imagined loss. The idea that childhood experiences of separation and loss may leave, as a legacy, a lifetime vulnerability to sadness, anger and anxiety has remained influential. In his theory of attachment, for example, John Bowlby places great emphasis on the relevance of loss and rejection in the early years (Bowlby, 1980). In an early study conducted to investigate the issue, Beck (1967) assessed depression in a mixed group of 300 psychiatric patients. He found that whereas 27 per cent of those who were highly depressed had lost a parent before the age of 16, a similar loss had occurred for only 12 per cent of those who were not significantly depressed. Childhood loss also emerged as an important vulnerability factor in a major study of the social origins of depression in women (Brown and Harris, 1978).

Whereas early loss may leave an individual vulnerable to depression in the longer term, recent loss (and other adverse life events) may trigger the onset of a depressive illness at a particular time. In an early study, Paykel (1974) compared the recent life events experienced by 185 depressed people and 185 controls. The groups differed significantly in terms of their experience of events relating to employment, health and family relationships. Those who were depressed had experienced more disruptive events, many of which involved some form of loss. However, it was found that the experience of stress was not sufficient to precipitate a depressive episode and that depression only occurred if certain 'vulnerability factors' were already present.

Reinforcement   Behaviours which are not positively rewarded by a reinforcer, such as food, money, social attention or social approval, tend to drop out of the person's 'behaviour repertoire' and are said to be 'extin-guished'. Skinner (1953) suggested that the behavioural patterns found in depression might be the result of the 'extinction' of positive behavioural sequences, owing to a lack of positive reinforcement. Later conditioning models of depression placed a special emphasis on the roles played by self-reinforcement and social reinforcement (Ferster, 1973; Lewinsohn, 1974). Social reinforcement may lift the recipient's mood, making the person feel valued and respected, and those who lack such reinforcement are liable to feel ignored, ostracized and unloved. Withdrawal from social contact will further reduce the opportunity for receiving social reinforcement, and a vicious circle might therefore develop.

Another learning theory explanation suggests that depression is main-tained precisely because it is positively reinforced. Thus, someone who feels ignored by others most of the time, but finds that depressed behaviour brings attention, concern and sympathy, is likely to continue to behave in a depressed way. Although some people undoubtedly gain attention and sym-pathy from their depressed behaviour, it would be wrong to overemphasize the importance of such an effect, because in most cases the social costs of depression greatly outweigh any transient benefits.

Learned helplessness theory   According to Martin Seligman's 'learned helplessness' theory (Seligman, 1975), people are likely to give up trying to exert an influence on the physical and social environment when they find that important aspects of their lives are uncontrollable. And when people feel helpless, they are likely to be drained of motivation and to become depressed.

The phenomenon of 'learned helplessness' was first demonstrated in a series of experiments involving dogs. The animals were placed in a harness, and then presented repeatedly with a 'warning signal' followed by a mild electric shock. For the first few trials most of the animals struggled when the warning signal was sounded, but many soon desisted from attempting to escape and appeared to 'give up'. When the dogs were then removed from the harness and placed in a different environment in which avoidance or escape from a signalled shock was possible, most of them failed to learn the new adaptive behavioural response. Thus the passive response generalized from the harness situation to situations in which escape was possible. The animals had learned to be helpless.

A number of studies have demonstrated an analogous effect in humans. Thus Hiroto and Seligman (1975) asked students to complete a cognitive task in an individual booth in which there was a noisy fan. Half of the subjects were told that they could switch the fan off if they wished to, but were encouraged to leave it on for ventilation purposes. The other half were told that the fan could not be switched off. In fact none of the students in either group attempted to switch the fan off, but those who had been told that the fan was not controllable performed significantly worse on the cognitive tasks than those who believed that they had the power to control the fan.

Animals (including humans) who have been rendered 'helpless' as the result of some experimental manipulation share with depressed patients a number of 'symptoms', including passivity, lack of motivation, loss of appetite and disruption of learning. Dogs subjected to the learned helplessness procedure appeared to have little interest in what was going on around them, they lost their appetite, lacked vigour and vitality, and appeared 'sad' and 'withdrawn'. Following the induction of a mild form of helplessness, human experimental subjects, like depressed patients, show a number of cognitive and affective changes. Their problem-solving ability is impaired, their self-esteem is lowered for a short while and they experience negative mood changes.

Weiss et al. (1976) showed that rats made helpless in an experimental setting suffer a depletion of the neurotransmitter norepinephrine. This illustrates the general phenomenon whereby environmentally induced psychological effects are shadowed by changes in brain metabolism, and it clearly echoes biological accounts of the aetiology of depression which implicate 'naturally occurring' reductions in NE levels. The close relationship between the behavioural changes induced by learned helplessness and biochemical changes is also demonstrated by the fact that learned helplessness effects in animals are attenuated by a number of interventions that are effective in treating clinical depression, including the use of 'electroconvulsive therapy' and anti-depressant drugs (Rosenhan and Seligman, 1989).

Although the learned helplessness model provides a useful account of exogenous depression, it does not provide an explanation for all the clinical features associated with this condition. In particular, it fails to account for the chronicity of depressive disorders, for the marked individual differences in vulnerability and for the major loss of self-esteem which is often a prominent feature of the condition. In response to various shortcomings of the original learned helplessness formulation, Seligman collaborated with a number of colleagues to provide an extensive revision of the model. This employs a number of concepts from the field of social cognition, especially those associated with 'attribution theory'. The revised learned helplessness model emphasizes the way in which people perceive and interpret unfavourable events (Abramson et al., 1978).

Revised learned helplessness theory   Like the original helplessness formulation, the revised helplessness account focuses on the experience of uncontrollability. However, it recognizes that the way in which people respond to unfavourable events will depend crucially on their interpretation of the origin, meaning and implications of those events. Those who generally interpret events in a negative and pessimistic way are likely to become depressed. Thus a person's explanatory ('attributional') style will affect the risk that an unfavourable event or life circumstance will lead to depression.

The reformulation of the learned helplessness model identifies a number of dimensions of causal judgement which are especially relevant to the emotional impact of the event. Thus a person may judge that an unfavourable event has an 'internal' cause ('it was my fault that my brother died') or an 'external' cause ('my brother died from cancer'). On another dimension, an event may be judged as reflecting 'stable' causes ('my examination failure reflects my poor academic ability'), or 'unstable' causes ('I failed the examination because I was sick on the day'). Finally, a causal attribution may be 'global' ('my wife wants a divorce because I am a worthless man') or 'specific' ('my wife wants a divorce because she discovered I had an affair').

The revised helplessness model suggests that people who tend to make internal, stable and global attributions about unfavourable events are at relatively high risk of depression. However, those who tend to make internal, stable and global attributions about favourable events are generally at low risk of depression (an example of such an explanation is: 'I won the race through my own efforts, and I am likely to continue winning many events because I have developed myself into a good all-round athlete').

The attributional model remedies a number of the criticisms levelled against the earlier learned helplessness model. The tendency to explain unfavourable events by making internal attributions ('It is my fault that the relationship failed') could explain why depression is associated with a loss of self-esteem. Stable attributions about negative events ('The boss's remark indicates what he and his colleagues have long felt about me') could explain why depressive episodes tend to persist for a long time. And the tendency to make global attributions ('My failed marriage proves that I am a worthless person') could explain the pervasive nature of depression.

An 'Attributional Style Questionnaire' (ASQ) was developed to measure relevant aspects of an individual's social cognition, and the fact that scores on this test are reliable over time suggests that what is being measured is a relatively stable individual characteristic (Peterson and Seligman, 1984). A major review (in the form of a 'meta-analytic' study) of the relationship between depression and measures of attributional style was conducted by Sweeney et al. (1986). Their summary analysis of over one hundred studies involving nearly 15000 subjects indicated that the tendency to attribute negative events to internal, stable and global causes is reliably predictive of depression. The relationship between attributional style and depressed mood was demonstrated by both studies involving college students and studies involving clinical subjects.

In one study, people who were clinically depressed were shown to have significantly higher internal, stable and global scores than both schizophrenic and medical patients. The study also found that the scores of depressed patients' on the 'stable–unstable' dimension were related to the length of their depressive episode, those with higher stability scores tending to experience longer illness episodes (Raps et al., 1982).

Although the tendency to make depressive attributions is generally fairly stable, there is some fluctuation over time. A person suffering from severe depression is likely to maintain an extreme 'depressive attributional style' for as long as the episode continues, but may judge events in a less negative way during and following recovery. Various forms of cognitive therapy involve direct attempts to modify those elements of attributional style which are believed to be responsible for the origin and/or maintenance of the depressed mood. Other psychotherapeutic approaches, although they focus less directly on cognitive aspects, may also produce a favourable change in attributional style.

Box 4.3
Learned Optimism and the Prevention of Depression

Martin Seligman has recently been involved in attempts to change people's attributional styles as a means of preventing depression. In one study of 'learned optimism', first-year university students completed an attributional questionnaire and those who were identified as being among the most pessimistic were invited to participate in the study. These people were randomly assigned either to the control group or to the experimental group. Those in the experimental group attended 16 hours of workshop activity in which they learned to dispute chronic negative thoughts and acquired a number of social and work skills which might be useful in averting depression. At a follow-up evaluation, some 18 months later, 22 per cent of the workshop participants were found to have suffered moderate or severe depression, compared to 32 per cent of the controls – a highly significant difference. A school-based study also demonstrated that children can be taught to become more optimistic, and that those who acquire high levels of optimism skills are more self-reliant, more likely to perform well on academic tasks and less likely to become depressed (Seligman, 1996).

Other cognitive accounts   It has long been recognized that people who feel depressed tend to think depressed thoughts. It is commonly assumed that the depressed mood is primary, and somehow leads to the cognitive symptoms. Cognitive theories of depression, however, suggest that depressed cognitions are primary and produce the disturbances of mood. The revised learned helplessness model is one of several cognitive models of depression, and whereas this model emphasizes the importance of the perceived uncontrollability of events, other cognitive models emphasize the role of cognitive distortions and irrational beliefs.

The earliest well formulated cognitive account of the origins of the emotional disorders was provided by Albert Ellis (1962). His basic premise is that psychological disturbances often stem from irrational and illogical thinking. On the basis of dubious evidence or faulty inferences about the meaning of an event, people may draw false conclusions which then lead to feelings of anger, anxiety or depression. Ellis contends that irrational beliefs (such as 'I must be competent in everything I do'), together with certain observations ('I have not performed well on this task'), can easily lead to disheartening conclusions ('Therefore I am stupid and worthless'). His belief in the emotionally damaging consequences of illogical internalized statements led him to develop a particular approach to therapy ('rational–emotive therapy', recently renamed 'rational–emotive behaviour therapy'), in which he teaches clients to distinguish between rational and irrational beliefs, and to avoid reiterating negative, unrealistic, illogical self-defeating thoughts and self-statements.

Table 4.2 Beck's cognitive errors

Overgeneralizing	'She rejected me, so I'll never find anyone to love me.'
Selective abstraction	'I failed one of my ten tests, and I can't stop thinking about that failure.'
Excessive responsibility	'Whenever anything goes wrong, it's always my fault.'
Self-reference	'My failures must be uppermost in other people's thoughts.'
'Catastrophizing'	'My argument with my wife is a clear sign that my whole life is falling apart.'
Dichotomous thinking	'Unless I totally succeed in this, I will have failed completely.'

A somewhat different cognitive account of the origins of depression has been proposed by Aaron Beck (1967). Beck's 'cognitive distortion theory' asserts that people are at risk of developing a depressive disorder if they regularly engage in certain types of maladaptive thinking. He suggests that depressive thoughts can be seen as a 'cognitive triad' consisting of (a) thoughts about oneself (for example, 'I am inadequate and worthless'); (b) thoughts about the current situation (focusing on negatives, and systematically misinterpreting evidence); and (c) thoughts about the future (for example, 'there is no hope for the future; things will never improve'). Beck has identified a number of specific types of 'cognitive error' that may contribute to the development of depression (see Table 4.2).

Research evidence has confirmed a close association between negative cognitions and depression. Many people who suffer from depression do have irrational beliefs of the type described by Ellis (Ellis and Whiteley, 1979) and they do exhibit cognitive biases towards self-critical and pessimistic evaluations (Krantz and Hammen, 1979). A number of other disturbances of thought process and content are also manifested by people experiencing a severe depressive episode (Blackburn, 1988). Cognitive accounts of the aetiology of depression have also received some empirical support from a number of prospective studies of the outcome of a 'depressive thinking style', although the evidence from such studies has been somewhat confusing.

Whether unipolar depression originates in maladaptive thinking or whether negative thought patterns are merely symptomatic of depression, it is clear that negative thoughts may help to maintain depression. This is very significant, for whether we assign a 'causal' or a 'maintenance' role to maladaptive cognitions, it is clear that replacing such cognitions with more positive modes of thinking should help to improve the patient's condition.

Social interaction accounts Many of the aetiological models discussed above, including the psychoanalytic model and the reinforcement model, assign an important role to interpersonal relationships. Several other models focus more specifically on the role of personal relationships in the development and maintenance of depression. Some suggest that problems in childhood (such as abandonment, emotional neglect or abuse) may leave an individual particularly vulnerable to depression. In this way these theories

Box 4.4
Mood and Memory

The development and maintenance of a depressive episode may be related to an interesting phenomenon which has been extensively investigated by experimental psychologists. It appears that memories associated with a particular mood are especially likely to be recalled when that person is again in that mood state (Bower, 1981). Thus someone who is feeling unhappy may recall many negative experiences. One explanation for this phenomenon is that each emotional state is associated with a particular unit of memory which acts as a kind of repository for memories related to the emotion (for example, 'sad memories'). When the person is in a specific mood state the relevant memory unit becomes activated and the memories within it become easily available (this account is based on the semantic-network theory of long-term memory put forward by Collins and Loftus, 1975). The implication is that those who are depressed may recall many 'depressing' memories which might then maintain or deepen their negative mood.

In the laboratory, the 'mood and memory' phenomenon has been explored by inducing particular mood states in experimental subjects. This has been achieved in a variety of ways: for example, by asking the subject to read a series of self-statements ('I feel great', 'I feel very happy'; or 'I feel fairly miserable right now', 'I am very sad'), through the use of hypnotic suggestion, by asking people to recall sad or happy events in their lives or by playing musical extracts that are generally experienced as joyful or mournful. (Incidentally, there is evidence that even reading about the symptoms of depression can make people feel somewhat depressed (Rholes et al., 1987), something to bear in mind when reading a book on abnormal psychology!)

In a typical mood and memory study, experimental subjects undergo a mood induction procedure, and when the appropriate mood has been successfully induced ('happy' or 'sad', for example), they are asked to learn a list of words, to remember a number of facts or to read an affectively neutral passage from a book. At a later stage, they are again subjected to mood induction (the mood induced may be the same as that originally instigated, or may be different) and they are then asked to recall as much of the learned material as possible. Recall is found to be better when material is learned and recalled in the same mood state than when it is learned in one mood state and recalled in another.

Many laboratory studies have confirmed the effects of mood on memory (it is a 'robust phenomenon') and a number of related studies have been conducted using psychiatric patients as subjects. In one such study, Clark and Teasdale (1982) asked patients who were consistently depressed either in the morning or in the evening to relate past events in their lives. It was found that the patients remembered more negative events and fewer positive events when they were depressed than when they were not depressed. It is easy to see how recalling adverse experiences might make people feel more negative (i.e. recollections of past failures and disappointments would tend to 'bring them down'). Thus a person who is feeling somewhat 'under the weather' may be gradually drawn into a depressed state as the result of a vicious circle involving negative mood and negative memories (Teasdale, 1983).

Box 4.5
The Depressive Realism Hypothesis

Cognitive theories of depression generally assume that those who are depressed have an over-pessimistic and unrealistically gloomy view of themselves, their lives and their future. However, recent evidence suggests that non-depressed people might be somewhat over-optimistic in their perceptions and judgements, and that mildly depressed people may actually be more realistic in their judgements of themselves, their abilities and their social standing.

The 'depressive realism hypothesis' (Dobson and Franche, 1989) suggests that depressed people may be more accurate in evaluating, for example, how favourably or unfavourably others judge them, compared with those who are not depressed. 'Normal' people tend to overestimate the extent to which other people's judgements are favourable. Those who are depressed may therefore be 'sadder but wiser'. Similarly, in experimental tasks on which the person's degree of control can be manipulated, people who are depressed tend to be more accurate than non-depressed people in their judgements of how much control they have. In this situation, non-depressed people tend to develop an 'illusion of control', overestimating their influence when they are doing well and underestimating their influence when they are doing badly (Alloy and Abramson, 1979).

In line with the depressive realism hypothesis, as depressed people progress through therapy, their self-perceptions, and their judgements of the effects they are having on other people, may become less accurate (Lewinsohn et al., 1980). Thus, following successful treatment the formerly depressed person may be subject to the same positive fallacies as those who have not been depressed.

In her book *Positive Illusions: Creative Self-deception and the Healthy Mind* (1989), Shelley Taylor explores the benefits of normal favourable distortions. She suggests that 'positive illusions' (slight overoptimism, for example, or an exaggeration of self-competence) foster self-confidence and high self-esteem and help to buffer people against misfortune and distress. Lacking such self-protective distortions, people who are depressed may have a heightened awareness of unfortunate truths.

address the 'diathesis' element of the 'diathesis–stress' model. But many relationship theories also focus on the 'stress' element and suggest that relationship problems (especially those involving loss, loneliness and conflict) often precipitate the onset of a depressive disorder. The findings of an impressive and highly influential study of the social origins of depression were published by George Brown and Tirril Harris in 1978 (see Box 4.6).

Many of the social models of depression emphasize circular causal patterns. Social relationships are held to play an important role in determining the onset of a depressive episode, and depression is then seen to have a major impact on social interaction (Teichman and Teichman, 1990). The interpersonal approach developed by Klerman et al. (1984) maintains that depression reflects past, ongoing or long-term problems between the person and significant others, and emphasizes the role of interpersonal stress both in the development and in the maintenance of depression. Klerman and his associates recommend that treatment should be focused on relationship problems.

Box 4.6
The Social Origins of Depression

In a classic study, reported in their book *The Social Origins of Depression* (1978), George Brown and Tirril Harris examined the relationship between social factors and depression in a group of women from Camberwell in London. They studied women who had received hospital treatment for depression and women who had visited their physician seeking help for depression. They also studied a general population sample of 458 women aged between 18 and 65 years.

The women in the community (general population) sample were examined by a psychiatrist and asked in detail about their emotional health over the past year. It was estimated that 15 per cent of the women had suffered a depressive episode within the previous 12 months. All those in the sample were also interviewed about important events in their recent and early life, and about their current lifestyle and relationships. Information on recent severe life events showed that these had occurred four times as frequently in the group of women who had been depressed within the past year as in the group of women who had not been depressed. Such life events generally preceded the onset of the depression, and events relating to a major loss or disappointment were especially prevalent in the depressed group. Similarly, of the sample of women who had received hospital treatment for depression, 80 per cent had experienced a recent loss. It appeared that a single severe disappointment or loss was often sufficient to trigger depression, although women who had experienced more than one severe stressful event were at even higher risk. Thus the findings from this study support the view that highly stressful events are additive in their effect.

Careful examination of the data indicated that the onset of depression usually followed within weeks of a serious stressful event, and it was possible to show that the event actually triggered the depression rather than simply bringing forward the onset of a disorder that was already developing. The critical importance of severe life events and longstanding 'severe difficulties' in the aetiology of depression has been confirmed by the results of nine subsequent studies which have attempted, with various adaptations, to replicate the original research of Brown and Harris. These studies show that, on average, 82 per cent of those who become depressed have recently experienced at least one severe life event or major difficulty, compared to only 33 per cent of those in non-depressed comparison groups (Brown and Harris, 1989).

The original Brown and Harris study found evidence of a pronounced social class effect, at least for married women. Twenty-three per cent of the working class women in the general population sample had been depressed within the past year, compared with only 3 per cent of middle-class women. Among the working-class women, those who had one or more young children were at higher risk of becoming depressed than those who were childless or whose children were older. Women who were currently caring for three young children were particularly likely to have experienced a recent depressive episode. There was also a strong association between risk and marital status, which held across all social classes. Women who were widowed, divorced or separated had relatively high rates of depression.

Although there was a strong overall association between depression and the experience of one or more severe life events, only a minority (about 20 per cent) of the women who had experienced severe events and difficulties (which the authors label 'provoking agents') became seriously depressed. This suggested that people differed in their vulnerability, and a number of 'vulnerability factors' were identified in the study, including the lack of a confidante, the early loss of the mother (before the age of 11) and not being in employment. In addition, certain 'protective factors' were recognized, one of the most important of these being the presence of a partner.

On the basis of the evidence gained from their extensive study, Brown and Harris constructed a descriptive model of the social causes of depression. This model is presented in a simplified form below:

Vulnerability factors + Provoking agents (in the absence of protective factors) ⇨ Depression

For example:

Early loss of mother + A recent family death (no partner) ⇨ Depression

The original Brown and Harris study, and similar studies that have followed it, have made a very significant contribution to our understanding of the aetiology of depression. Not only has this research firmly established that social stress plays a decisive role in triggering many depressive episodes, but it has also demonstrated the fact that social factors may increase an individual's vulnerability to depression. Furthermore, it confirms that social support may offer protection against the effects of potentially stressful events.

This work cannot be said to provide an exhaustive account of the origins of depression, and the findings need to be viewed in the context of other evidence. This research emphasizes the importance of individual differences in vulnerability and identifies some of the social factors that increase the likelihood of a woman becoming depressed. But it does not challenge the view that other factors, including genetic characteristics, may also play an important role in determining vulnerability. The account given by Brown and Harris applies to cases of reactive depression, rather than endogenous depression. They do not deny that there may be 'pure' cases of endogenous depression, although their evidence does indicate that social factors are implicated in a large proportion of cases of clinical depression.

Although the work described here focuses on objective social events and lifestyle characteristics, it is clear that the affective impact of life events is mediated by cognitions (including the person's appraisal of events) and by the ways in which the individual attempts to cope with stress. A cognitive account may help to explain how the various vulnerability factors identified in this research actually operate to increase the risk of depression. Thus the early loss of the mother might engender a general pessimism, so that a stressful event occurring later in life will be perceived as highly threatening. Alternatively, a bereavement or separation later in life may revive past thoughts and feelings of loss, guilt or inadequacy.

Coyne's 'interactional systems model' (Coyne, 1984) suggests that the distress conveyed by those who are depressed elicits supportive behaviours from other people, reduces the demands that others make and inhibits overt hostility. Other people (especially family members) attempt to reduce the depressed person's aversive displays of distress by ostensibly complying with his or her wishes and making allowances for his or her behaviour. However, such responses may disguise hostility, impatience and withdrawal, and despite their attempts at concealing their negative feelings towards the depressed person, it is likely that other people will eventually convey their antagonism and aversion through subtle cues. The depressed person may then respond to signs of rejection by expressing further distress, which is likely to instigate further rejection, so establishing a vicious circle.

A number of empirical studies have supported the view that interactional patterns between depressed people and their families can sometimes perpetuate the depression (e.g. Hops et al., 1987). Furthermore, family hostility and criticism may precipitate a relapse following recovery from an earlier depressive episode (Hooley and Teasdale, 1989).

Integrating aetiological evidence

It is likely that some cases of depression are predominantly biological in origin, while others are primarily psychogenic (corresponding to the traditional endogenous/exogenous distinction). But different biological and psychological factors and mechanisms might be implicated in different cases. Thus, whereas one person's endogenous depression might be the result of a dysfunction in the metabolism of noradrenaline, for example, another case of endogenous depression might be best accounted for in terms of some other biological irregularity. And whereas one person's exogenous depression might be a 'reasonable' response to a devastating tragedy, in another exogenous case the disorder may result from irrational judgements of a minor relationship conflict. It is likely that in most cases the true aetiological picture is highly complex and involves many different factors from within both the biological and psychosocial domains.

The diathesis-stress model can be a useful tool for integrating the evidence. Factors that appear to affect vulnerability to depression include biological predisposing factors, cognitive style, personality characteristics and personal history. The stressors which precipitate depression may be rather specific. Critical events involving loss and long-term problems that involve threat or severe constraints on the individual's lifestyle seem to be particularly implicated. And while a succession of major adverse events can progressively increase the risk of depression, there is no evidence to suggest that the condition may be triggered by the additive effect of a large number of minor stressors ('hassles').

Bipolar disorder

Early psychological explanations of 'manic-depressive disorder' were adaptations of psychoanalytic explanations of depression. Manic symptoms were said to result from the individual's hapless attempt at a 'flight from depression'. Several other psychological accounts were formulated, but the case for a psychogenic aetiology was never strong, and most authorities are now convinced that the primary causes of bipolar disorder are biological (Winters and Neale, 1985). Psychological explanations can hardly account for rapid mood changes that have no obvious connection with changing environmental circumstances. Furthermore, attempts at treating the disorder with psychological methods have generally met with little success. By contrast, pharmacological treatment (particularly the use of lithium salts) is highly effective in many cases of bipolar disorder.

Bipolar disorder: biological accounts

The examination of factors associated with the aetiology of unipolar depression, earlier in this chapter, revealed that depression is often associated with particularly low levels of certain neurotransmitter substances. Drugs known to increase neurotransmitter levels (including amphetamine and MDMA – 'Ecstasy') tend to produce manic symptoms in normal people. The pattern of evidence therefore suggests that those who suffer from alternating episodes of mania and depression may be subject to wild fluctuations in neurotransmitter production, or that their neuronal sensitivity to one or more neurotransmitters may change erratically. This suggestion is supported by the results of studies that have monitored levels of MHPG (a metabolite of NE) in patients as they change between depressed and manic phases of a bipolar illness. Such research has found that the level of MHPG decreases in the few days before a period of deep depression and increases in the few days before an episode of mania (Muscettola et al., 1984).

People who suffer from bipolar depression are especially likely to have one or more relatives who have a history of bipolar disorder. The few twin studies and adoptee studies in the area indicate that at least part of the familial pattern for bipolar disorder is genetic in nature. Indeed, the genetic factor appears to be substantially stronger for bipolar disorder than for unipolar depression. In a review of twin studies of affective disorders, Allen (1976) reported concordance rates for bipolar depression of 72 per cent for identical twins and 14 per cent for fraternal twins; the comparable figures for unipolar depression were 40 per cent for identical twins and 11 per cent for fraternal twins.

Thus there is good evidence to suggest that most, if not all, cases of bipolar depression develop as the result of biological irregularities. However, the effects of this disorder are often extreme, and the condition can place an enormous strain on the person's education, career and personal relationships. Thus, although psychotherapy cannot offer much help for the primary symptoms of the disorder, it may be useful as a means of addressing secondary symptoms and other problems that have resulted from the bipolar depression.

◀Affective Disorders: Effects and Treatment▶▶▶

Depression: the personal and social effects

Personal responses to depression   How do people respond when they become depressed? Some personal reactions may help to shorten the depressive episode, whereas others may prolong the condition and add to the suffering. Many depressed people become so demoralized by their state that, in effect, they become depressed about being depressed. Preoccupation with the disturbed emotional state may prolong a depressive episode, so that excessive 'self-focusing' or 'self-directed attention' usually constitutes a maladaptive response (Musson and Alloy, 1988).

Those who suffer from depression often struggle to understand why they feel so low. Some of their explanations may make the depression easier to bear, but some are highly self-critical and are likely to make things worse. In general, it seems that those who decide that their depression has a specific cause (for example, 'I am feeling "down" because my father died'; or 'my depression is due to hormonal changes') find it easier to cope with a depressive episode (Schwarz and Clore, 1983).

Nolen-Hoeksema (1991) distinguishes between two contrasting styles of response to depression: rumination and distraction. 'Rumination' means focusing attention on the negative mood state and on other symptoms of the disorder. Those who endlessly engage in such activity are likely to remain depressed for longer than those who indulge in pleasurable and engrossing activities. In general, rumination is maladaptive, whereas distraction is adaptive. Distraction strategies include engaging in social activities, pursuing a hobby or persevering with work activities. Nolen-Hoeksema suggests that one reason why women experience depression more frequently than men is because they have a pronounced tendency to engage in ruminative thinking. This may reflect different patterns in the socialization of boys and girls, for whereas boys are often encouraged to be active, to solve problems and to develop mastery skills, girls may be encouraged to be more emotional, self-questioning and reflective.

A number of research studies have explored people's accounts of what they do in order to relieve feelings of sadness and depression. Similar tactics appear to be employed by people who merely suffer from the occasional 'low' mood state and those who sometimes experience very severe depression. Many people from both these groups maintain that they derive considerable benefits from their self-help practices (see Box 4.7)

How depressed people affect others Depression has profound effects on social interaction and the resulting disruption in personal relationships may prolong a depressive episode. Depressed people often believe that other people are avoiding them, and there is good reason to accept that they are sometimes accurate in this judgement.

Many of those who are suffering from a depression avoid meeting new people or avoid social interaction altogether. They may be unresponsive to other people's remarks and questions, and when they do make the occasional comment their speech may be slow and lacking in intonation. But although depression generally leads to a social withdrawal, it can also lead to high dependence on other people (Coyne, 1982). In a study designed to investigate the effects of communication with people suffering from depression, Coyne (1976) arranged for non-clinical subjects to hold telephone conversations with a person from either a 'depressed' group or a 'non-clinical' group. Immediately after the telephone call, each subject was asked to describe the person with whom he or she had been conversing, to rate his or her own current mood and to indicate his or her level of enthusiasm for renewing the telephone acquaintanceship. The telephone callers perceived the

Box 4.7
Self-control of Sadness and Depression

Studies with groups of depressed patients and non-clinical subjects have explored the strategies that people use to alleviate sadness or depression. Rippere and Williams (1985) noted that most of the autobiographical accounts they collected from mental health professionals who had experienced severe depression mentioned various attempts at self-help. These included: short-term strategies aimed at improving mood, 'keeping going' or reducing disability; medium-term strategies used to work through emotional problems; and long-term strategies used to alter circumstances that may have helped to provoke the depression.

Short-term strategies included distraction methods, constructive activities, reading, the use of reminder lists and the continuation of normal working patterns. Medium-term strategies included reading philosophical texts and watching heart-rending films. Longer-term strategies included changing employment and enrolling on training courses. The majority of respondents found at least some of these techniques helpful.

General population studies show that most people have clear ideas about what might alleviate a depressed mood. Thus Caro et al. (1983) reported a number of strategies which people had identified as likely to be of value in lifting a depressed mood. These included:

- attributing the depression to a particular cause;
- attempting to rectify the problem seen as responsible for the depression;
- finding social and moral support;
- engaging in diverting and distracting recreations;
- keeping busy;
- focusing attention on aspects other than the depression or depressing circumstances;
- changing thoughts about particular events in order to minimize their significance;
- engaging in self-care and self-maintenance activities;
- venting emotions;
- taking prescribed or non-prescribed medication;
- finding compensations in other aspects of life and boosting self-esteem through engagement in purposeful activity;
- taking comfort in religion.

Although there is a general consensus regarding the value of self-help strategies, people differ considerably in the strategies they consider to be most useful. For example, some find relief in passive distraction, by engaging in an activity such as watching television or reading a novel, while others find it more beneficial to participate in social events, to bury themselves in work, or to pray.

depressed patients as making little effort to be friendly and were disinclined to renew the contact. It also appeared that during their conversation with someone who was depressed, the callers themselves had become somewhat anxious and hostile, and moderately depressed.

The fact that such responses are produced even after very brief contact with a depressed individual gives some indication of the possible effects of days, weeks or even months of close interaction with such a person. There is abundant evidence that depression has a extremely detrimental effect on marital relationships and on family life (Kahn et al., 1985).

Treatments for unipolar depression: drugs

Anti-depressant medication accounts for a substantial proportion of the drug prescriptions written in the primary care setting. In the UK the annual rate of such prescriptions is around 9 million. The first effective anti-depressant drugs were introduced into clinical practice in the 1950s, and since that time many new drugs have been developed. There are three classes of effective anti-depressants: the tricyclics, monoamine oxidase inhibitors and serotonin reuptake inhibitors.

The tricyclics   The tricyclic group of anti-depressant drugs, including imipramine ('Tofranil') and amitryptyline ('Elavil') have been used for treating depression since the late 1950s. They reduce the reuptake of the neurotransmitters NE and 5-HT, thus increasing the concentration of these neurochemicals in the synaptic gap.

   The tricyclics have been shown in a number of controlled studies to be highly effective in relieving symptoms in many cases of depression. However, these drugs are lethal in overdose, and therefore present grave dangers to suicidal patients. Another problem is that the beneficial effects of the tricyclics are not apparent until the patient has been using the drug for between two to three weeks. This delay in effectiveness, and possible side-effects (especially weight gain), means that it can be difficult to persuade a patient to continue taking drugs of this class.

Monoamine oxidase inhibitors   NE is broken down by the enzyme monoamine oxidase (MAO), but the action of this enzyme can be inhibited by a group of drugs known as the monoamine oxidase inhibitors (MAOIs), which are generally effective in relieving depression. However, their use may have side-effects which can be so severe that they may prove fatal. The side-effects include elevated blood pressure if the patient ingests particular foods (including cheese, paté, yeast extract and wine) or certain other drugs (including decongestants and tricyclic antidepressants). The dangers associated with the use of the MAOIs means that they are rarely the first choice in antidepressant medication.

Selective serotonin reuptake inhibitors   A relatively new group of drugs, which include sertraline, fluvoxamine and fluoxetine ('Prozac') are now widely used for treating depression. They work by specifically blocking the reabsorption of serotonin. They have been shown to be highly effective and relatively safe, although side-effects may include nausea and vomiting. Prozac is now the most commonly prescribed anti-depressant.

Do drugs 'cure' depression?   Although drug treatment for depression is highly effective, it is not successful in all cases. For example, up to a third of patients treated with tricyclic compounds do not improve. Where symptoms are relieved it is often unclear whether the improvement should best be seen as a cure (as antibiotics may cure infection), as a treatment (as certain drugs reduce blood pressure, for as long as they are taken) or as a symptomatic treatment (as aspirin masks the symptoms of the common cold, until the illness has run its natural course). It is possible that in some cases the drug does cure the condition, whereas in others it may provide only a treatment effect or symptomatic relief.

Treatments for unipolar depression: electroconvulsive therapy

Although its use has long been controversial, electroconvulsive therapy (ECT or 'shock therapy') is still used as a treatment for depression. In the modern procedure, the patient is given a strong sedative and a muscle relaxant, and electrodes are then placed on the scalp. A current of around 100 volts is passed between the electrodes for between 0.1 and 1.0 seconds. This immediately produces a convulsion lasting up to a minute, and a few minutes later the patient regains consciousness. A course of ECT treatment may involve up to twenty such sessions, although substantial improvement is often found after five or six sessions. The results of over twenty controlled trials indicate that ECT does have substantial beneficial effects (Janicak et al., 1985), although these seem to be restricted to patients suffering from endogenous depression.

If the electrodes used in ECT are placed 'bilaterally' (one on the left side of the scalp and one on the right) there is often some loss of memory for events that occurred immediately prior to the treatment ('retrograde amnesia'). However, 'unilateral placement' (both electrodes placed on the non-dominant – usually the right-hand – side of the scalp) limits the passage of the current, resulting in little or no memory loss without any reduction in the rate or degree of symptomatic improvement (Horne et al., 1985). Despite its proven effectiveness, ECT is probably used less nowadays than in previous decades. This is partly because other forms of effective treatment have been developed, but it also reflects the fact that, for many people, ECT retains a highly disagreeable and frightening image.

Psychological treatment methods

Psychodynamic approaches   Psychodynamic therapists usually work with the depressed person to try to identify the meaning of the current depression in the context of the individual's personal history. Memories of childhood may be revived so that the person is able to work through early experiences of loss or rejection. A major part of the therapeutic effort may focus on the emotional relationship that develops between the therapist and the client. The goals of dynamic therapy are accomplished when the individual is free from depression, has gained self-assurance and has become less dependent on tokens of love and admiration from others.

Early studies suggested that dynamic treatment was often effective, but the absence of control groups permitted the alternative interpretation that improvement might simply be due to 'spontaneous remission' (depression tends to 'burn out' in time, and psychoanalytic treatments often extend over several years). Recent developments in the field have focused on short-term dynamic therapy in which the therapist is more active and directive than in traditional psychoanalysis. Contemporary approaches tend to be less concerned with the patient's early history and more with current relationships and recent events. A number of well controlled studies of innovative psychodynamic approaches have demonstrated that they may well have a beneficial impact on depression (e.g. Weissman et al., 1979).

Behavioural approaches Behavioural accounts of the origins of depression focus on the detrimental effects of low levels of positive reinforcement. Therapeutic interventions based on this approach generally aim to increase the availability of response-contingent reinforcers, often by helping the person to become more active and to perform actions that will evoke positive responses from other people. However, in some cases the depressed person will no longer value or appreciate the social responses that usually function as rewards. Thus the therapist may devise strategies to help the person to regain an appetite for social contact (such a process has been labelled 'systematic resensitization'). Despite some early success (e.g. Fuchs and Rehm, 1977), behavioural intervention programmes of the type described are rarely used today.

Cognitive therapy Cognitive approaches to therapy for depression aim to change the negative cognitive 'sets' or 'styles' that have led the person to develop an unfavourable self-image and a pessimistic outlook. Negative cognitions and irrational beliefs that invoke depressed feelings are identified, and an attempt is then made to replace these with more positive, more rational and less distorted cognitions. The aim is to make the new, adaptive, thinking styles 'natural' and 'automatic' for the person.

Albert Ellis was the first person to develop a systematic cognitive approach to the treatment of depression. His 'rational–emotive therapy' aims to demonstrate to clients that their depression is the result of implicit and inappropriate self-statements. Such statements are invariably based, according to Ellis, on irrational beliefs and/or faulty logic. The solution is to replace these statements with others that are based on 'reasonable' assumptions and on rational thinking. Once the irrational beliefs or the faulty deductions have been identified, the therapist challenges the client, disputing erroneous beliefs and exposing any logical errors in thinking.

Aaron Beck devised a somewhat different cognitive treatment for depression although, like Ellis, he is concerned to challenge the cognitive errors and irrational beliefs that are held to underlie the development of depression. Beck first trains clients to detect the automatic thoughts that lead to feelings of depression, and encourages clients to subject these thoughts to 'reality testing' (Hollon and Beck, 1979). Following this, the client is helped to modify dysfunctional attribution patterns, and is taught to explore alternative interpretations of situations which might be seen as futile or threatening. Finally, troublesome fundamental suppositions are challenged, such as 'In order to be happy, I must be successful in everything I do.' Dobson (1989) reviewed 28 studies that had evaluated Beck's approach to the treatment of depression and concluded that the evidence clearly pointed to a high level of effectiveness of this form of therapy.

Interpersonal therapy   Some approaches to the treatment of depression focus on the interpersonal system of which the individual is part. The treatment unit might be the couple or the whole family. Such therapy involves an exploration of interaction patterns that maintain depressive behaviour (Gotlib and Colby, 1987). The couple or family may be asked to act out important interactional sequences ('enactment'), so that maladaptive patterns of responding can be identified and changed. In some ('enmeshed') families, members are so closely involved with one another that it is difficult for anyone to experience his or her identity as a separate person, and therapeutic efforts may be made to help loosen relationships which appear to place overbearing constraints on individuals. The effectiveness of couple-based and family-based therapy for depression has been demonstrated in a number of evaluation studies, including those by Friedman (1975) and Beach and O'Leary (1986).

Which is the most effective form of therapy?

Depressed people benefit considerably from most types of psychological treatment (Robinson et al., 1989). In one of the most extensive studies in the field, Elkin et al. (1989) randomly assigned 250 depressed people to one of four conditions: (a) interpersonal psychotherapy; (b) cognitive behavioural therapy; (c) tricyclic drug therapy (using imipramine); or (d) a placebo drug condition. All the active treatments were found to be effective for patients suffering from relatively mild forms of depression. Patients who were more severely depressed, however, appeared to derive most benefit from drug therapy.

   Different forms of therapy may have different patterns of effects, and some may be more appropriate for some types of depression than others. The results of some studies suggest that whereas psychological therapies have more pronounced effects on the patient's social functioning, drug treatments have more effect on mood (Klerman and Schechter, 1982). The most effective treatment programmes may be those which combine drug therapy and psychological therapy. If drugs are able to reduce some of the more severe symptoms, the person may become more receptive to psychological treatment strategies, including those which aim to prevent relapse by altering the person's cognitive style. Indeed, evidence from a number of studies suggests that cognitive therapies may be more effective than drug treatments in preventing relapse (Williams, 1992).

The treatment of bipolar depression

Psychological methods are rarely used to treat bipolar depression. The principal form of treatment is pharmacological and involves the drug lithium carbonate. Although the precise mechanism is not fully understood, lithium carbonate appears to stabilize either neurotransmitter availability or neuronal sensitivity. When the patient is maintained on the appropriate dosage, the side-effects of lithium are minimal. However, the patient may become very thirsty, and an increased intake of fluids may result in frequent urination. Impairments in memory and concentration may also become apparent, and an excess of the drug may result in tremors and dizziness. Despite the effectiveness of the treatment, there may be serious problems with patient compliance. Patients may discontinue the treatment because they feel that their symptoms have abated and they no longer need medication, because they wish to avoid the side-effects or because they miss the 'high' associated with manic episodes.

The affective disorders: some notes on case management

Although the danger of suicide is relatively high for people suffering from many other types of psychological disorder, the risk of suicide is very pronounced indeed in cases of depression. A conservative estimate suggests that those suffering from severe depression are over 100 times more likely to commit suicide than those who are not currently suffering from depression. The first priority in managing such patients is to remove all obvious dangers and temptations to suicide. For example, the person's partner may be asked to take care of any dangerous drugs that have been prescribed. Every attempt should then be made to provide intensive treatment as soon as possible, and to encourage the depressed person to comply with any treatment regime.

Relatives, friends and colleagues should also be helped to understand the nature of the condition, and should be encouraged to do whatever they can to minimize the adverse impact of the illness on the person's lifestyle. Severe depression often jeopardizes important relationships and may seriously affect employment or education. Thus a person who recovers from an affective disorder may find that his or her life has become more difficult and more stressful as a result of the condition. Relatives, friends, employers and colleagues can do a great deal to reduce the potentially devastating and long-term effects of the depression.

◀Conclusions▶ ▶ ▶

Affective disorders are those in which the most predominant symptoms are profound disturbances of emotion or mood. Other clinical features include disturbances of thinking and behaviour. The principal symptoms of unipolar depression are sadness, pessimism and self-dislike, along with loss of interest and motivation. Some 'reactive' cases of unipolar depression are precipitated by the person's experience of an adverse event. The impact of such an event appears to depend crucially on how it is perceived by the individual. Those who have a pessimistic appraisal style, who make certain systematic errors in their judgements, or who hold particular irrational beliefs, are more likely to become depressed following a misfortune than those who are optimistic, balanced in their judgement, and rational in their beliefs.

'Endogenous' cases of unipolar depression appear to result from disruptions in the metabolism of certain neurotransmitter chemicals, susceptibility to such disruption probably being largely determined by genetic factors. In bipolar affective disorder, depressed and manic states tend to alternate, although they may be separated by periods of normal functioning. The principal causes of bipolar disorder appear to be biological, and genetic factors have been demonstrated to play an important part.

Cognitive psychotherapy and anti-depressant medication are both highly effective in treating people suffering from unipolar depression, although treatment often needs to be carefully tailored to the individual case.

Psychological interventions are generally not effective for bipolar depression, which is best treated by means of lithium salts.

Thus different cases of affective disorder may have quite different underlying causes, and may benefit from different forms of treatment intervention. These disorders often have devastating effects on the individual and the family which outlive the clinical condition, and help may be needed to minimize such effects.

◄Further Reading►►►

Gilbert, P. (1984) *Depression: from Psychology to Brain State*. London: Lawrence Erlbaum Associates.

Gilbert, P. (1992) *Depression: the Evolution of Powerlessness*. London: Lawrence Erlbaum Associates/New York: Guilford Press.

Both of these books by Paul Gilbert are impressive attempts to integrate information from many different sources into a coherent picture of the development of depression. The later book, in particular, takes a strong social evolutionary line.

Brown, G.W. and Harris, T.O. (1978) *Social Origins of Depression*. London: Tavistock.

Account of the classic community-based Camberwell study. Examines vulnerability and stress factors associated with the development of depression in women.

Gotlib, I.A. and Colby, C.A. (1995) *Psychological Aspects of Depression: towards a Cognitive–Interpersonal Integration*. Chichester: Wiley.

Review of the psychological literature on depression, combining a focus on cognitive functioning with an emphasis on the relevance of the social context (including early social experience, social support, and marital functioning) and interpersonal treatment methods.

Teasdale, J.D. and Barnard, P.J. (1993) *Affect, Cognition and Change: Remodelling Depressive Thought*. Hove: Erlbaum.

Provides a comprehensive cognitive account of depression, integrating clinical information and research with a general model of cognitive functioning. Describes a new approach to understanding depressive thinking.

Rippere, V. and Williams, R. (1985) *Wounded Healers: Mental Health Workers' Experiences of Depression*. Chichester: Wiley.

A collection of personal experiences of depression, all written by mental health workers. Provides an insight into the phenomenology of the affective disorders.

◄Discussion Points► ► ►

1   What are the differences between unipolar depression and bipolar depression?
2   Is it useful to distinguish between endogenous and reactive depression?
3   How would you account for the fact that twice as many women as men become depressed?
4   How are thoughts and feelings associated in unipolar depression?
5   How do social relationships affect depression, and how does depression affect social relationships?
6   Outline the various forms of therapy used to treat unipolar depression. Is it possible to say that a particular approach is the most effective?

5 Schizophrenia

A 'psychosis' is a severe psychological condition in which the symptoms are qualitatively different from normal experience (such experiences may include elaborate delusions and hallucinations). During a psychotic episode, the person loses contact with consensus reality, has little insight into the nature of his or her condition, and suffers what is sometimes described as a disintegration of the personality. By far the most common form of psychotic condition is schizophrenia.

In the 1980s, schizophrenia accounted for about one fifth of all UK psychiatric hospital admissions; about one in 100 people will be diagnosed as schizophrenic at some time during their lives. It is estimated that there are up to 300 000 schizophrenic people in the UK and 1.5 million in the USA. All of this adds up to enormous human cost, both to the patients themselves and to their relatives. The financial burden to society is also enormous. In 1990, the total cost of mental illness to the UK National Health Service was £2 billion, and around one third of this was consumed by services provided to people suffering from schizophrenic disorders. A 1991 study of the cost of mental illness in the USA conducted by the National Institute of Mental Health (NIMH) estimated a total annual cost of $129 billion, with schizophrenia alone responsible for $50 billion.

Schizophrenia is a disorder of adulthood, with the first episode often occurring in the late teens or twenties. In the acute schizophrenic state the person loses touch with reality and is likely to withdraw from contact with other people. Delusions and hallucinations are common and the person may engage in bizarre forms of behaviour. In many cases the initial acute phase of a schizophrenic illness will be followed by at least a partial recovery. Only in a minority of cases does the condition become chronic. However, a person who has experienced one schizophrenic breakdown is likely to suffer further acute episodes at some time. The 'schizophrenic career' is usually marked by a number of relapses and remissions. A person who has suffered one or more episodes of the disorder will generally retain the diagnostic 'schizophrenia' label even if he or she is currently free from any conspicuous symptoms.

In this chapter we will describe the clinical picture associated with schizophrenia, the epidemiology and the course of the disorder, before considering the various factors which appear to play some part in the complex (and poorly understood) aetiology of the condition. Finally, we will consider issues relating to the treatment and management of people suffering from schizophrenia.

◀Classification of Schizophrenia▶ ▶ ▶

Various forms of 'madness' and 'lunacy' have been described throughout history, and with hindsight we can recognize in various historical case descriptions many of the signs and symptoms we now recognize as characteristic of schizophrenia. However, the disorder (or, more accurately, this group of disorders) was first recognized as a discrete category in the late nineteenth century by the German psychiatrist Emil Kraepelin. He labelled the disorder 'dementia praecox' (adolescent dementia), reflecting a belief that this was an organically based mental deterioration of the young and was essentially irreversible. The term 'schizophrenia' (literally 'schizo' = split and 'phreno' = mind) was introduced by another psychiatrist, Eugen Bleuler, in 1911. It is often thought, mistakenly, that 'schizophrenia' refers to a 'multiple (or split) personality', but in choosing the term 'schizophrenia' Bleuler wished to convey a profound disruption of mind. Schizophrenia has been said to involve a split between the elements of thought and feeling; other people describe it as a 'shattering of the personality'; and others speak of a 'confusion between inner and outer worlds'. Bleuler suggested that there were four key symptoms of schizophrenia: disturbances of affect; irrational mental associations; ambivalence of feelings and attitudes; and autism (self-absorption and social withdrawal).

There are various ways of sub-classifying schizophrenia, based on criteria relating to the prognosis (the probable course and outcome) associated with the disorder, responsiveness to treatment, supposed aetiology and the type of symptoms that predominate. A sub-classification system that relates directly to prognosis leads to patients being diagnosed as suffering from either 'process schizophrenia' or 'reactive schizophrenia'. In reactive schizophrenia, emotional symptoms predominate and the episode appears to have been precipitated by an identifiable life crisis (the acute illness episode therefore constituting a 'reaction' to the crisis). Reactive schizophrenia tends to occur in younger people. There is relatively little disturbance of thought processes, and the individual's pre-morbid personality will have been stable and marked by reasonably good relationships with peers and family members. In such a case the prognosis would be favourable. By contrast, 'process schizophrenia' develops gradually in a person with an early history of instability and difficult social relationships, and the prognosis is relatively poor.

Another sub-classification system differentiates between positive symptom (or type I) schizophrenia and negative symptom (or type II) schizophrenia, depending on whether the symptoms are predominantly 'additions' to normal experience and behaviour (such as delusions, hallucinations and agitated behaviour), or whether they are mainly losses of normal functioning (such symptoms include flattened affect and social withdrawal). Type I schizophrenia is said to have an acute onset and a good response to drug treatment. In many respects the type I diagnostic criteria overlap with those for reactive schizophrenia, whereas the criteria used to diagnose type II schizophrenia (lack of emotional responsiveness, insidious onset etc.) overlap with those of process schizophrenia.

Such attempts at distinguishing between different types of schizophrenia have stimulated a good deal of research, and many clinicians find the distinctions useful. However, there is a lack of consensus regarding the validity and meaningfulness of such distinctions, and most clinicians (and the two major diagnostic systems, DSM and ICD) employ a classificatory system which is little different from that originally suggested by Emil Kraepelin 100 years ago. This system distinguishes between four types of schizophrenia: paranoid, disorganized (labelled 'hebephrenic' by Kraepelin), catatonic and simple schizophrenia.

Paranoid schizophrenia

Patients suffering from paranoid schizophrenia are usually thought-disordered and may experience auditory hallucinations. They frequently hold highly complex and systematic delusions which may involve ideas of persecution or grandeur. The person may show disturbances of volition (will) and abnormal movements. Paranoid schizophrenia is often not diagnosed until the fourth or fifth decade.

Case profile At the age of 35 Mrs M.G. developed angry feelings about her neighbours, claiming that they were spying on her and 'plotting to kill me by stealth'. She accused her family of conspiring with the neighbours, and of planting evil ideas in her mind. She said repeatedly that she did not belong to the family and complained of voices telling her to leave and return to her true life in an underground kingdom. Her description of this underground kingdom was at times highly detailed.

When a doctor was called she accused him of being 'the devil's agent', and she had to be forcibly removed to hospital. There she claimed that she knew all about the nurses' private lives, she accused visitors of being spies and she identified patients as famous film stars and historical characters.

Disorganized schizophrenia

The patient suffering from disorganized schizophrenia tends to engage in grossly inappropriate behaviour, often described as 'regressive' or 'silly', and may show sudden fluctuations of emotion. Hallucinations and delusions may be present, but these are generally not well organized. Disorganized schizophrenia has an earlier onset than the paranoid form, and is often diagnosed first when the person is aged between 17 and 26 years old.

Case profile   Mr P.D., an 18-year-old student, had made few social contacts since entering university. He dressed in a somewhat strange way and made comments in tutorials which were regarded by other students, and his tutors, as bizarre. One day he disrupted a lecture by laughing repeatedly in a manic and rather threatening fashion. When asked to leave the lecture he shouted odd disconnected phrases and seemed to hold a disjointed conversation with hallucinated voices. He was hospitalized, and after receiving major tranquillizers his disturbed behaviour ceased. He sat in a trance-like state, constantly intertwining his fingers, and smiled for long periods. Occasionally he would start crying or would burst out laughing.

Catatonic schizophrenia

The most prominent symptoms of catatonic schizophrenia are disturbances of movement. Periods of apparent stupor may alternate with periods of wild excitement. The patient may seem oblivious to the world, or may respond to requests with a consistent negativism. In the stuporose state the catatonic patient may adopt stereotyped 'frozen' postures, although such statuesque posturing is rarely seen today because of the availability of effective anti-psychotic drugs. Catatonic schizophrenia often has a very sudden onset.

Case profile   Ms Y.F., a 24-year-old hairdresser, was admitted to hospital, having been found at home in a state of 'rigidity', and resisting all attempts to rouse her. This state had persisted for several hours. In hospital, and after medication, she alternated between a catatonic state and a highly active state in which she ran about and performed exercise-like movements until collapsing back into a statue-like pose. She spoke rarely, and when asked a question she would repeat it rather than providing an answer. At a later stage she did the precise opposite of everything she was asked to do.

Simple schizophrenia

This is a diagnosis given when a person has developed odd behaviour over a number of weeks or months, with marked social withdrawal, progressive apathy and a blunting of emotional responses. Gross delusions and hallucinations are usually not present. Because of the absence of clear distinguishing features, diagnoses of simple schizophrenia may be especially unreliable.

Case profile   J.G., a 24-year-old man, had lived alone for a number of years, apparently with very little social contact. He was caught stealing from a shop, and the policeman who interviewed him noticed a strangeness which made him wonder whether J. was mentally ill. A psychiatrist who later examined J. found him to be extremely apathetic, to have very little knowledge of the world around him and to be obsessed with a science fiction world of his own creation. It was difficult to establish the degree to which J. actually believed in the strange things he described. He recounted things in a dreamy way and often seemed to inhabit a world of his own.

◀Course and Prognosis▶ ▶ ▶

Schizophrenia may appear at any age from the late teens onwards. In some cases the onset is gradual and it would be difficult to pinpoint a particular week, month or even year in which the person might be said to have 'developed schizophrenia'. In other cases the onset is much more acute. For many episodes it is possible to distinguish three phases: prodromal, active and residual (American Psychiatric Association, 1987). The prodromal phase occurs before there are any florid schizophrenic symptoms. The person may become listless and apathetic, withdraw from social contacts, display emotional blunting and engage in behaviours which indicate an absorbing interest in strange and fantastic ideas. In some cases the person develops a bizarre and highly personal philosophy. Transition to the active phase is sometimes triggered by a life event that the person finds particularly significant, although the significance may reflect a totally idiosyncratic perception. At this stage more florid symptoms such as auditory, visual and somatic hallucinations and delusions of persecution may become apparent. This phase may last for a few days or several years, but it is usually succeeded by a residual phase, in which the florid symptoms recede, leaving the person in an impaired state, showing little emotional responsiveness or motivation and demonstrating a pronounced disinclination to interact with other people.

Most of those who have received a diagnosis of schizophrenia continue to show at least some degree of impairment thereafter, but only a minority remain in such a poor state of functioning that they can be said to be suffering from 'chronic schizophrenia'. Thus a deterioration of functioning over time is not inevitable, and a review of all of the available studies (Eaton, 1991) indicated that no more than 20 per cent of cases become 'chronic'. About one-quarter of the people who receive a diagnosis of schizophrenia suffer just one acute episode during their lifetime. Three-quarters experience one or more further episodes. During the intervals between periods of acute illness their symptoms will be in partial or total remission. Factors that predict a positive long-term outcome for the condition include a predominance of 'positive', or type I, symptoms (see Classification of schizophrenia, above) and evidence of a well adjusted pre-illness ('pre-morbid') personality. A more comprehensive list of factors associated with a favourable prognosis is:

- acute onset of the illness;
- late onset of the first episode (i.e. at older age);
- identifiable stressor as trigger to the episode;

- positive symptoms predominate;
- stable premorbid (pre-illness) personality;
- positive long-term social relationships;
- no family history of schizophrenia.

The risk of a schizophrenic episode recurring following a period of symptom remission has been shown to be greatly reduced if the patient continues to take appropriate medication and lives in a supportive (but not overbearing or overwhelming) social environment. Such matters are discussed below.

◄Psychological Disturbances in Schizophrenia ► ►

Symptom patterns differ between the various sub-categories of schizophrenia, and between individuals. No patient will exhibit all the signs, or experience all the symptoms, associated with the condition. However, certain symptoms are commonly found in the acute phase of a schizophrenic disorder, and these are listed in Table 5.1.

The symptoms of schizophrenia can be classified in terms of the psychological functions affected, i.e. as disorders of cognition (thought processes and thought content), perception, emotion, volition (will) and motility.

Disorders of cognition: thought processes

Disturbances of both thought processes and thought content are often evident in patients' overt behaviour and, especially, in their use of language.

Thought disorder   The speech of schizophrenic patients often lacks coherence, and in conversation they may jump from one topic to another, appearing not to follow any particular theme. Disconnectedness within the speech results in what is sometimes labelled a 'word salad', often containing made-up words ('neologisms') and rhyming elements ('clang associations'). For example: 'Wonderful it was, full of wonder, like thunder sometimes, and never out to meet anyone. Son of a gun. All the time in bed and never got out. Never heard the thunder. Clatapole, maypole, maple-leaf. Bright and scrawny. Owl like. Big big eyes.'

Sometimes the speech and writing of schizophrenic patients seems very poetic, or very clever, especially when the loose associations, or the neologisms, conjure up an appealing image or hit upon a meaningful pun. A patient once made an observation on my surname:

Patient: 'Frude – fried foods – Frude is Fride. Your name is Fride'.
I protested: 'But it's spelled with a U!'
He replied: 'But U and I are one'.

Table 5.1 Acute schizophrenia: the most frequent symptoms

Symptom	Frequency (%)
Lack of insight	97
Auditory hallucinations	74
Ideas of reference	70
Flattened affect	66
Suspiciousness	66
Delusions of persecution	64
Thought alienation	52

Source: World Health Organization (1973).

There is often a special difficulty with abstract thought. This may be evident in the fact that many schizophrenic patients tend to interpret proverbs literally. For example, when asked to explain the meaning of the sentence: 'A stitch in time saves nine', a patient might respond by talking about sewing rather than addressing the general issue of timeliness.

Thought blocking   Schizophrenic patients often 'lose track' of their thoughts and are unable to get to the end of a sentence. Most people experience such difficulties from time to time, but during an acute psychotic phase the phenomenon may completely disrupt the patient's efforts to think coherently or to communicate clearly. One patient described his experience of thought blocking by explaining that: 'Thoughts are often snatched out of my brain just as I'm going to use them.'

Thought control   Some people who suffer from schizophrenia experience delusions in which they feel that other people are controlling their thoughts, or are able to read their thoughts. This may prove very threatening and disruptive, and may cause thought blocking. Some patients have described the experience as that of having thoughts 'sucked out of my mind'. Others complain that thoughts are inserted into their mind. Patients may feel that other people are tuned into their thinking, or that their thoughts are being broadcast on radio or television. In a variation of this type of symptom, some patient are convinced that they have special powers which enable them to read other people's minds or to influence other people's thoughts, feelings and actions.

Disorders of cognition: thought content

Many patients become preoccupied with certain themes. Their thinking may be influenced by a heavy symbolism, and they may develop strong and obsessional interests in particular subjects. In some types of schizophrenia (particularly the paranoid form), the person will evolve a system of confused beliefs and develop extravagant delusions which, although they are held with absolute conviction, may be totally bizarre (Garety, 1985). In earlier times, delusions often had a religious content (see Box 5.1), but these days many delusional systems reflect ideas from science fiction and high technology and employ concepts associated with television, radio, 'bugging' and computers.

Delusional ideas tend to follow certain themes, particularly those of grandeur, jealousy, persecution and control.

Delusions of grandeur   People who have delusions of grandeur are convinced that they are famous, or very rich, or very powerful or talented. The patient may believe that he or she is the world's greatest artist or a historical, aristocratic or religious figure. Sometimes the delusion involves a belief in a special relationship with a famous person. A few years ago a student disclosed to me that she had been secretly married to an international rock star during his recent visit to the local stadium. She was able to describe the ceremony in detail, and 'proved' what she was saying by producing a handkerchief that she maintained had been given to her by the star. She also produced over a hundred pages of a 'metaphysical thesis' that she had written the previous evening, explaining how God was present in the computer network system of the psychology department. She was admitted to the local psychiatric hospital and there received a diagnosis of schizophrenia.

Delusions of jealousy   It is quite common for schizophrenic patients to believe that a partner has been unfaithful, or that a romantic link has been formed between, for example, the partner and one of the professionals involved in the patient's care. Thus a delusion of conspiracy may be linked to a delusion of jealousy.

Delusions of persecution   In paranoid schizophrenia, especially, thoughts often revolve around persecution. For example, a patient may feel at risk of being murdered by secret agents from a major world power. Food may be regarded with suspicion, the assumption being that it may have been poisoned. Hallucinations may take the form of overheard whispers accusing the patient of having committed some sin, or encouraging extreme acts of aggression. Some delusions take on a highly complex and organized form. The patient may provide extensive notes about the minutiae of recent events, for example, and quote extracts as evidence of a supposed conspiracy.

Delusions of control   Patients may believe that they are able to control other people, or world events, or they may believe that they themselves are being manipulated by the thoughts of others. Thus some schizophrenic patients regard themselves as 'puppets' or 'machines' and deny that they are responsible for their own thoughts and actions.

Delusions of reference   When someone nearby is laughing in what appears to be an unfriendly or critical fashion, we may pause to wonder whether they

Box 5.1
The Diary of Vaslav Nijinsky

Vaslav Nijinsky was born in Kiev in 1889. His extraordinary dancing talent became evident at an early age and he became principal dancer with the Russian ballet. In many productions he collaborated with the famous impresario Diaghilev, and he won acclaim in many European capitals. He was undoubtedly the most famous ballet dancer of all time and his genius revolutionized many aspects of dance, but his career was brief, for at the age of 28 he suffered from a disabling psychotic disorder which overshadowed him for the rest of his life. In the early stage of his illness he kept a diary, often writing feverishly for hours on end. The following brief extracts illustrate something of the torment of his condition, and his preoccupation with bizarre and grandiose ideas. Nijinsky died in London in 1950.

'My wife thinks I am mad – she has this idea because she thinks too much. I think little and therefore understand everything I feel. I am feeling through the flesh and not through the intellect. I am the flesh. I am the feeling. I am God in flesh and feeling. I am man and not God . . . I am God in man. I feel what Christ felt. I am like Buddha. I am the Buddhist God and every kind of God. I know each of them. I have met them all. I pretend to be mad on purpose, for my own aims. I know that if everyone thinks I am a harmless madman they will not be afraid of me. I do not like people who think that I am a dangerous lunatic. I am a madman who loves mankind. My madness is my love towards mankind . . . Once I went for a walk and it seemed to me that I saw some blood on the snow. I followed the traces of the blood and sensed that somebody who was still alive had been killed . . . On the way back I saw the traces of blood, but no longer believed in their existence. God had shown me these in order that I should feel him. I felt his presence and returned. He told me to lie down in the snow. I did so. He made me lie there for a long time. My hands began to get cold, to freeze. I took my hand off the snow and said that this could not be God's wish, as my hand was hurting. God was pleased, but after I had taken a few steps He ordered me to go back and lie down near a tree' (Extracts from *The Diary of Vaslav Nijinsky*, edited by Romola Nijinsky. London: Panther, 1966).

are laughing at us – whether their laughter, in fact, *refers* to us. People suffering from schizophrenia tend to overestimate dramatically the number of remarks, glances and gestures which make reference to them. Thus they may even believe that television news broadcasts are constantly making disguised references to them, and they may assume that they are the people being referred to in any indeterminate messages (for example, 'A man is wanted for questioning by the police'). Such delusions are extreme forms of what are labelled 'ideas of reference'.

Disorders of perception and attention

Schizophrenic patients often seem to be overwhelmed even by quite ordinary environmental conditions. Stimulation may bombard them even in a quiet, plainly furnished room. They may be unable to discriminate relevant and irrelevant situational cues and thus find it difficult to 'read' situations or to make sense of what is going on. These difficulties partly reflect their inability to make use of contextual cues. In addition, they are easily distracted by 'ambient' stimulation. They may find it difficult to discriminate between novel and familiar stimuli, so that everything constantly appears new and strange. Such effects have been demonstrated experimentally in a large number of psychological studies (see the section on aetiology below). Pioneering research in this field was conducted by McGhie and Chapman (1961), who also reported first-person accounts by schizophrenic patients of how it felt to be constantly 'bombarded' by stimulation:

> The sounds are coming through to me, but I feel my mind cannot cope with everything. It's difficult to concentrate on any one sound. It's like trying to do two or three different things at the same time . . .
> The trouble is that I've got too many thoughts. You might think about something, let's say that ashtray and just think, oh! yes, that's for putting my cigarette in, but I would think of it and then I would think of a dozen things connected with it at the same time. (McGhie and Chapman, 1961, pp. 104, 108)

The most striking disorders of perception in schizophrenia are hallucinations. These are mostly auditory but some hallucinations take the form of visual images, olfactory sensations (i.e. smell or taste) or somatic ('bodily') sensations. Many hallucinations are distortions of real perceptual cues present in the environment. Thus noises in a heating system may be heard as whispers, or as musical instruments. Aspects of the form and content of hallucinations are discussed in Box 5.2.

Disorders of emotion

Many people who suffer from schizophrenia are also depressed. The depression may be closely linked to particular delusional beliefs, but in some cases it appears that the depression is associated with a degree of insight into the severity of the condition and the various repercussions it may be having, both personally and for friends and family members.

Another, classic, affective symptom of schizophrenia is a generalized lack of emotional responsiveness (sometimes referred to as 'flattening of affect' or 'bluntness of affect'). However, the degree of emotional responsiveness varies considerably from patient to patient, and may also change with different phases of the illness. Early stages may be marked by anxiety or euphoria. Later, pronounced anger or fear may result from other people's attempts to 'normalize' the person's behaviour, from delusional inferences or from the specific content of hallucinations. Another affective feature, the display of inappropriate emotion, may be one of the most disturbing aspects of a schizophrenic patient's behaviour, especially for relatives. Thus, on hearing that a serious accident has befallen a family member, the schizophrenic may burst into fits of laughter.

Box 5.2
Hallucinations: Where Do the Voices Come from?

Because hallucinations are essentially private experiences, we have to rely on people's reports of the form and content of the sounds they hear and the visions they see. Many such reports have been analysed, and a number of experimental studies have been conducted, so that a considerable amount is now known about the patterns and origins of hallucinatory experiences.

There is evidence that when some patients experience hallucinatory voices they are in fact 'hearing' their own subvocal speech. Most people 'speak to themselves' from time to time, and in a psychotic state such subvocalizations might be 'heard' as if someone else were speaking. A number of studies have shown that when schizophrenic patients 'hear voices', muscles in their throat and lips move in subtle ways. Patients can sometimes be heard to whisper during hallucinating phases and their whispers often correspond to the hallucinatory messages they report.

So why do some schizophrenic patients experience hallucinations while others do not? To some extent the tendency to hallucinate depends on the phase and nature of the illness. Hallucinations are more common in the acute phases of the disorder and are most commonly experienced by those patients who are said to be suffering from 'paranoid' or 'disorganized' schizophrenia. It has also been suggested that patients who hallucinate may have a more vivid imagination, that they may have special difficulties in structuring stimulus information or that they may be affected by neurophysiological dysfunctions in the areas of the brain that control speech perception and speech production.

Even within an acute phase of the illness, a patient will experience hallucinations more at some times than at others. Such variation might reflect short-term changes in mood, or brain biochemistry, but it also appears to be associated with more general physiological variables and with social and environmental conditions. Thus hallucinations increase in frequency and vividness when the person is under stress and becomes physiologically aroused.

The frequency and intensity of hallucinations may also vary with environmental conditions. For example, when ambient noise is loud and complex, the person may hear messages within the general clamour. On the other hand, very low levels of sensory stimulation can also elicit striking visual and auditory hallucinations (indeed, normal subjects often experience hallucinations when they are subjected to prolonged and extreme sensory deprivation). Hallucinatory experiences may also be elicited by aspects of the social environment, such as the sight of people pointing or whispering. There also seems to be a contextual learning effect, so that if a person returns to a location in which auditory or visual hallucinations have previously been experienced, there is a tendency for such symptoms to recur.

The specific nature and content of hallucinations often reflect personal interests and beliefs (including delusions) and environmental cues. Thus a schizophrenic patient who has delusions of a religious nature may hear voices which are recognized as those of saints or deities, whereas those who have paranoid obsessions involving espionage may 'hear' secret messages being passed through hidden electronic devices. In some cases a particular interest or hobby will take on an obsessional character during an acute phase of the disorder, and this may then shape the character and content of any hallucinatory experiences. The environmental context may also have a similar effect. A person who is experiencing hallucinations in a church, synagogue or mosque, for example, is likely to experience apparitions and voices that have a clear relevance to the particular religion.

Disorders of volition

In many cases, one of the early signs of the onset of a schizophrenic illness is a marked decrease of energy and initiative, together with a withdrawal of interest in almost every aspect of life and a profound reduction in motivation. The person may lack drive to such a degree that he or she automatically complies with any suggestion or request that may be made. On the other hand, some patients develop a profound negativism.

Disorders of motility

Schizophrenic patients may be physically over- or underactive, and their activity levels may change suddenly. In catatonic schizophrenia, posturing and 'waxy flexibility' may alternate with frenzied movement. Some schizophrenic patients constantly make facial grimaces, while others move their limbs in eccentric ways. Some mimic other people's behaviour, and many engage in stereotyped movements, constantly intertwining their fingers, for example, or stroking their hair.

Disorders of social interaction

One of the classic symptoms of schizophrenia is social withdrawal or 'autism'. Signs of social dysfunction may have been apparent long before the first schizophrenic breakdown, and many people whose condition is eventually recognized as schizophrenia appear never to have had much success in forming and maintaining relationships. Retrospective research into the early life of schizophrenic patients has revealed that even during their childhood many were identified as 'loners'.

During the illness phase, all social contact may be avoided. The person may wish to lie in bed for long periods with no stimulation and no social contact. Those who attempt to interact with the person may find the encounter frustrating and perplexing. Many schizophrenic patients shy away from even the most friendly of approaches, and even if they can be persuaded to enter into a conversation, other people may find it very difficult to follow their train of thought. At times the person's remarks may be highly metaphorical and abstract, while at other times they may be very precise and very concrete. However, if such problems lead to mutual avoidance, the patient's condition might become worse, because lack of social contact may increase the patient's potential for paranoia. Schizophrenic patients are often suspicious of those around them and may accuse people of spying or interfering with their thoughts. Because they rarely have any insight into their condition they may deny that they are ill, and they may therefore respond with bitter resentment when other family members insist that professional help is needed.

Psychological disturbances: cause and effect

Listing the clinical characteristics of schizophrenia in serial fashion, as above, may convey the impression that symptoms are relatively independent of one another, and that any combination of symptoms may be experienced by an individual who suffers from the condition. However, many symptoms are systematically linked together: one specific type of symptom may be closely associated with another because they arise from a common dysfunction; or one symptom may provoke another, secondary, symptom.

Bleuler maintained that primary symptoms are the direct result of an organic disorder, and that secondary symptoms reflect the person's attempts to adapt to the primary symptoms. Thus a person may attempt to cope with a problem in maintaining attention (a primary problem) by withdrawing from social interaction. Similarly, delusions may be secondary symptoms generated by conscious or unconscious attempts to make sense of complex and confusing situations.

Thus one integrative model of schizophrenic symptomatology suggests that difficulties in coping with the level of ambient stimulation produce disorientation, confusion and thought disorder. As these effects become obvious in the person's speech, other people may avoid social contact with the person. Such avoidance might increase the potential for paranoid delusions. Any attempts by other people to normalize the person's behaviour may be regarded with suspicion, and may result in accusations of harassment and interference. Thus a whole compendium of difficulties might arise from a single primary attention deficit.

Epidemiology

Data from a World Health Organization study (Sartorius et al., 1986), together with data from other studies, show very similar rates of schizophrenia across widely differing cultural contexts. For almost all of the cultures studied, the lifetime risk is very close to 1 per cent of the population. Eaton (1991) comments on this 'remarkable stability of incidence', suggesting that 'If the rate of schizophrenia is as stable across all societies and cultures as these data suggest, it is a very unusual disorder since variation of the disease rates across cultures is so common in epidemiology.'

Sex differences

Overall, there is no appreciable sex difference in the incidence of schizophrenia, in marked contrast to many other disorders (for example, the eating disorders and depression, both of which affect many more women than men). However, there is a substantial difference in the age at which men and women experience a first episode of schizophrenia, with the median age at onset being five or six years older for females than for males. To some extent this reflects sex differences in the type of schizophrenia diagnosed. More men suffer from disorganized schizophrenia, which tends to have an onset before the mid-twenties, whereas more women suffer from paranoid schizophrenia, which tends to develop from the mid-thirties onwards.

Age

The incidence of schizophrenia varies somewhat with age. The first episode generally occurs when the person is aged between 20 and 40 years. Men tend to be at highest risk in their twenties, whereas women are at highest risk in their late twenties or early thirties. Following the initial episode there is usually a period when the symptoms abate, but this remission period is often followed by another acute episode, and a pattern of relapses and remissions may continue throughout the person's life.

Social class

Schizophrenia appears to be somewhat more common in lower socioeconomic groups. At one time it was thought that this might reflect the stress of poverty and deprivation, but it now appears that the causal link is in the other direction (the disorder affects social class, rather than social class increasing vulnerability to the disorder). Thus the effects of schizophrenia are likely to lead a person to 'drift' down the social scale (Goldberg and Morrison, 1963; Silverton and Mednick, 1984). Clearly, such a debilitating disorder is likely to have major negative effects on employment, career and higher education prospects, and will thus affect socioeconomic status. Some degree of drift may occur even before the person develops clear signs of schizophrenia (Dauncey et al., 1993), probably reflecting the fact that many people who eventually develop a schizophrenic illness have personality and social problems before the onset of the disorder. In addition to the effects of the disorder on an individual's social status ('intragenerational drift'), there may also be a similar drift across different generations of the same family ('intergenerational drift'; Turner and Wagenfield, 1967), reflecting the fact that genetic factors are implicated in the aetiology of schizophrenia.

Place of residence

Relatively high rates of schizophrenia are found in inner city areas. A relatively high proportion of people who 'sleep rough' are suffering from schizophrenia, though only some of them will ever have had the condition diagnosed. Many people who suffer from the condition live in extreme poverty, not only because they are unable to work in paid employment, but also because they find it impossible to struggle over the social and bureaucratic hurdles necessary to gain state benefits. In seeking an environment in which they can live alone and undisturbed, they are often attracted to areas of dense population. Such locations, paradoxically, make it relatively easy for the person to remain anonymous, and may offer hostel accommodation as well as opportunities for squatting or sleeping rough.

Marital status

Those who suffer from schizophrenia are less likely that other people to form intimate and stable relationships, particularly if the condition had an early onset. Consequently, relatively few get married or have long-term cohabiting relationships. This is particularly true of men who suffer from the condition, reflecting the fact that they tend to experience the first acute episode at an earlier age than women. Thus, while, for some other kinds of psychological disorder, single (as well as divorced and widowed) status appears to contribute to an individual's vulnerability to the disorder, in the case of schizophrenia it appears that the illness, and the pre-morbid personality of those who eventually develop schizophrenia, reduce the likelihood that the person will get married. Many schizophrenic patients are regarded from an early age as 'odd' and 'different', and many fail to maintain a circle of friends. Such isolation, and a certain lack of social motivation, will diminish the opportunities for the formation of a stable romantic relationship.

In conclusion, the epidemiological evidence reveals little variation in vulnerability across different cultural populations. There is only a minor variation with gender, and social class and marital status patterns appear to reflect the effects of the condition, rather than possible contributory causes. Thus, in contrast to many other disorders, there is very little in the epidemiological evidence relating to schizophrenia that might provide clues regarding the aetiology of the disorder.

◂Aetiology▸ ▸ ▸

Preliminary overview

Although there is no generally accepted account of what causes schizophrenia, there is an enormous amount of evidence relating to the issue. And, as for other conditions, the evidence comes from highly disparate sources and encompasses an abundance of heterogeneous factors. It is not an easy matter to understand how such diversity might be accommodated so that the evidence can be brought together into a consolidated account. Before considering the various research findings, we will 'take a step back' and consider how it might eventually be possible to formulate an integrated account of the aetiology of the condition.

Vulnerability to schizophrenia must be determined by genetic factors or environmental factors (or both). The case for the involvement of genetic factors is now well established. Environmental factors suggested as possibly affecting vulnerability include physical trauma (especially in the perinatal stage of development), infections, toxins and various psychological stressors (including many associated with the person's family environment). The psychotic condition might develop when a vulnerable person is subjected to an environmental stressor or a 'spontaneous' biological change.

This outline adopts the basic 'vulnerability-stress' (or 'diathesis-stress') framework. Alternatively, an integrated account might be formulated by employing the 'causal pathway' device. Such an account would take the form of a narrative description of a causal chain leading from primary causes, through various mediating causes, to the primary, and later the secondary, symptoms of schizophrenia. To illustrate the style of such a narrative, we will sketch a *hypothetical* causal pathway model of the aetiology of schizophrenia. And to add a dash of realism, we will anticipate some of the evidence to be discussed later in this chapter. The model to be described is illustrated in Figure 5.1.

In this hypothetical model, the primary causes of schizophrenia are presumed to be a combination of genetic and environmental factors (both 'vulnerability' and 'stressor' factors). These produce aberrations in brain metabolism ('biochemical dysfunction') which, perhaps in addition to generating some symptoms directly, lead to disturbances in both peripheral (autonomic) arousal and central (cortical and subcortical) arousal. Disruption to the central arousal system generates a 'basic cognitive impairment' (or 'attention deficit') which then leads to a range of specific cognitive symptoms (including problems of language and communication). Various other symptoms are likely to have been generated along the way (for example, as a result of the disturbed functioning of the autonomic nervous system). And the narrative does not end there, because psychological and social reactions to the primary symptoms then produce a range of further – secondary – symptoms. For example, communication problems may lead to interpersonal conflict and exacerbate paranoia and withdrawal from social contact.

This model provides a rather crude illustration of how variables of many different kinds (biological, psychological and social) might be accommodated within a single, complex, aetiological formulation. We could easily add to the complexity of the model by adding several feedback loops (for example, interpersonal difficulties might increase physiological arousal, and affective symptoms might produce further cognitive disturbances).

So much for the hypothetical excursion! At least it demonstrated how information from different domains *might* be integrated. However, almost any model of this type will be 'too linear' and, despite its narrative form, 'too static'. A model would probably convey the dynamic interplay between factors more effectively if it were presented as a hanging mobile, with links between almost every pair of elements, rather than as a fixed two-dimensional representation.

We now need to consider the evidence pertinent to claims that particular biological, psychological and social factors play some role in generating and shaping schizophrenic symptomatology. We begin by considering a range of factors that have been suggested as possible primary causes.

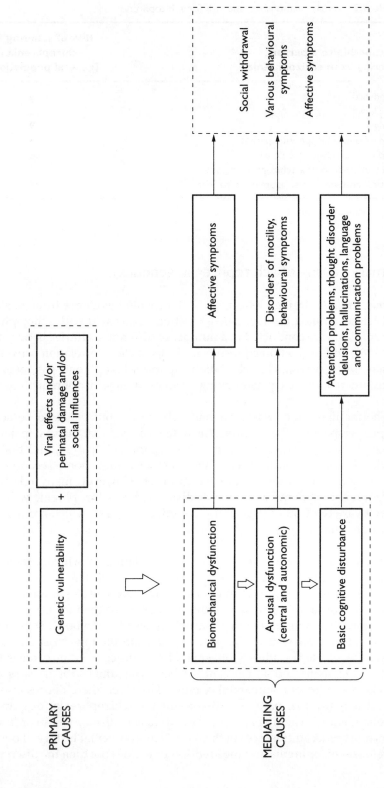

PRIMARY CAUSES

PRIMARY SYMPTOMS

SECONDARY SYMPTOMS

Genetic vulnerability   +   Viral effects and/or perinatal damage and/or social influences

MEDIATING CAUSES

Biomechanical dysfunction

Arousal dysfunction (central and autonomic)

Basic cognitive disturbance

Affective symptoms

Disorders of motility, behavioural symptoms

Attention problems, thought disorder delusions, hallucinations, language and communication problems

Social withdrawal

Various behavioural symptoms

Affective symptoms

Figure 5.1   Aetiology of schizophrenia: hypothetical 'causal chain' model from primary causes through mediating mechanisms to symptoms

Table 5.2 Family relationships and risk for schizophrenia

Relationship to a person suffering from schizophrenia	Risk of suffering from schizophrenia (%) (general population 1%)
Grandchild	5
Half-sibling	6
Sibling	9
Child of one schizophrenic parent	13
Child of two schizophrenic parents	46
Fraternal co-twin of a schizophrenic patient	17
Identical co-twin of a schizophrenic patient	48

Source: Gottesman (1991).

Primary causes of schizophrenia: genetics

Family studies   Irving Gottesman (1991) collated evidence from 40 studies that had examined the familial risk pattern associated with schizophrenia. The studies were conducted in a number of different countries between 1920 and 1987, and the combined results indicated a clear correlation between the closeness of a person's blood relationship to a schizophrenic patient and the increased risk of that person being diagnosed as schizophrenic (see Table 5.2).

The familial effect was clear and substantial, but needs to be seen in proper perspective. For example, the data indicated that the vast majority of schizophrenic patients do not have a schizophrenic parent, and that two-thirds of schizophrenic patients have neither a first- nor a second-degree relative who has suffered from the disorder. However, many relatives of schizophrenic patients who are not diagnosed as schizophrenic will suffer from a variety of other psychiatric disorders, some of which are related to schizophrenia.

Twin studies   Over a dozen twin studies relating to schizophrenia have been conducted over the past forty years, in many different countries, and their results have produced an overwhelming consensus – there is a much higher concordance for schizophrenia for MZ twins than for DZ twins (one of the early twin studies of schizophrenia is described in Box 5.3). According to Gottesman's analysis of the pooled data from the four most recent (and most sophisticated) studies (Gottesman, 1991), the concordance rate is 17 per cent for DZ twins and 48 per cent for MZ twins, thus strongly supporting the claim of a genetic vulnerability effect. However, these figures also indicate that many MZ pairs are discordant for schizophrenia, despite their genetic identity. The disparity in the psychiatric history of discordant MZ pairs must reflect differences in the twins' environmental history. If one twin develops schizophrenia and the identical twin does not then the discrepancy

Box 5.3
Schizophrenia and Genetics: a Classic Study

For 16 years, from 1948 to 1964, every one of the 45000 patients admitted to the Maudsley Hospital in London was asked whether he or she had a twin. Those who were diagnosed as suffering from schizophrenia, and had a twin brother or sister, were asked to participate in a study. Eventually, 57 twin pairs were examined in a study of the genetic basis of schizophrenia. Each case involved the patient and a traceable living twin who had agreed to cooperate.

The research workers, Irving Gottesman and James Shields (1972), then identified each pair (on the basis of blood tests, physical examination etc.) as either monozygotic ('identical') twins or dizygotic ('fraternal') twins. They found that the sample consisted of 24 monozygotic pairs and 33 dizygotic pairs. Where concordance could not be established on the basis of the co-twin's psychiatric history or from a psychiatric examination, the co-twin was followed up for between three and sixteen years. The level of concordance was eventually found to be 42 per cent in the case of MZ twins and 9 per cent in the case of DZ twins. For those cases in which a patient who was one of an MZ pair was judged to be severely ill (as assessed by the length of hospitalization), the concordance figure was considerably higher. In those cases in which the patient had been hospitalized for more than two years the concordance rate was 77 per cent, whereas for patients who had been hospitalized for less than two years, the concordance rate was only 27 per cent.

might be due, for example, to differences in the twins' exposure to pre-natal or post-natal stressors, to their different histories of infection, exposure to toxins or physical trauma, to differences in diet or to differences in their social history. Gottesman (1991) reported that of 14 known pairs of MZ twins who were reared apart, no fewer than nine were concordant for schizophrenia.

Powerful confirmation of genetic involvement comes from studies of the offspring of twins discordant for schizophrenia. Because MZ twins have identical gene complements, the risk of either twin 'passing on' any genes relevant to the development of schizophrenia will be the same whether or not they have themselves developed the illness. Thus if genetic factors are important, the offspring of both a schizophrenic twin and the genetically identical non-schizophrenic co-twin will be at a relatively high risk of developing schizophrenia.

In a study designed to explore this issue, Gottesman and Bertelson (1989) examined the rate of psychiatric illness ('morbidity') in the offspring of an established Danish twin sample. In each case the twins were discordant for schizophrenia – i.e. one had developed the disorder and the other had not. One hundred and twenty-four individuals of the parent generation were involved in the study (21 MZ twin pairs and 41 DZ twin pairs). Not surprisingly, many more children had been born to those who had not developed schizophrenia than to those who had developed the illness. But the *proportion* of offspring who developed schizophrenia was the same in both cases. The

Box 5.4
The Genain Quadruplets

The birth of quadruplets is extremely rare. Much rarer still are cases of identical quads in which all four babies survive. As can easily be imagined, cases in which one or more of a set of surviving identical quads eventually develops a schizophrenic illness are exceedingly rare (such an occurrence, it has been estimated, would occur naturally less than once in every 1.5 billion births). Identical quads are the product of the four-way splitting of a single fertilized ovum, and they are therefore, essentially, 'genetic photocopies' of one another.

There is one celebrated and well documented case in which identical quadruplets were all diagnosed as suffering from a schizophrenic illness. To protect their identity, in the published case reports the family was given the name 'Genain' and the daughters were given the names Nora, Iris, Myra and Hester (their initials correspond to those of the National Institute of Mental Health – NIMH – the centre where the family was studied and where the daughters were treated).

Mrs Genain gave birth to the four identical girls in the early 1930s. They were subjected to a good deal of publicity early in their lives, and at one time the parents actually charged admission for the public to view the babies at home. A few years later the parents also encouraged their girls to perform together as a singing and dancing troupe. Apart from such pubic appearances, the family led a somewhat isolated life, and the father, in particular, was very protective and over-involved with his daughters (it also appears that he sexually abused at least two of the girls). This over-protection continued throughout the girls' adolescence and into early adulthood.

At the age of 18 one of the young women, Hester, became highly aggressive and destructive, and dropped out of school. She then remained at home in a somewhat disturbed state. The other three finished their schooling and found office work, until, at the age of 20, Nora also became disturbed. She developed a wide range of physical and psychological symptoms which persisted over the next two years, at which time she was admitted to a psychiatric hospital and diagnosed as suffering from a schizophrenic disorder. Some months later another of the sisters, Iris, reported hearing voices and became extremely agitated. She, too, was soon hospitalized as a schizophrenic patient.

The fourth sister, Myra, had a breakdown two years later, when the women were 24 years old. She was later found to have disordered thinking patterns and poor contact with the real world and, like her sisters, she showed a range of physical signs, including insomnia and vomiting. As with her sisters, her condition was identified as schizophrenia. At this stage the family was taken to the Clinical Center of the NIMH, where they were all studied intensively by David Rosenthal and his colleagues. The sisters were treated at the NIMH for three years, but with limited success, and at the end of this period three of them were transferred to a state hospital. A later report on the quads' condition (Rosenthal, 1963) indicated that Myra was in regular employment, was married and had made good progress. Nora was out of hospital and making some limited progress. Iris had had a number of relapses and remissions, and Hester remained in a severe psychotic state and had continued to need hospital care. Twenty years later it was reported that Myra had remained relatively well and now had two children (DeLisi et al., 1984). The other three sisters were living at home with their mother, and exhibited psychotic symptoms to varying degrees. All four of the quads were maintained on medication.

The fact that all of the sisters developed a schizophrenic illness is clearly in line with the view that genetic factors are involved in the aetiology of schizophrenia. However, despite their 'photocopy' genetics, the four sisters developed somewhat different forms of psychotic illness, and experienced their first episode at slightly different ages. Thus there were significant differences, as well as striking similarities, in the course and long-term outcome of the four sisters' schizophrenic disorders. The disparities must reflect environmental differences. The intrauterine environment may have been somewhat different for each of the children; there may well have been differences in the degree to which obstetric complications affected the infants; and in infancy through to adolescence the children would have had different experiences and would have been treated in somewhat different ways by parents, peers and others. There is some evidence from the family history that Iris and, particularly, Hester, were less favoured by their parents than the other two sisters, and they seem to have had the poorest outcome. Myra was something of a favourite, and her illness appears to have been considerably less severe than those of her sisters. It is therefore possible that differential treatment by the parents, early in the girls' lives, may have had a significant effect on the severity and chronicity of the illnesses they developed in early adulthood.

morbidity rate was 17 per cent for the offspring of the MZ twins who had developed schizophrenia, and was also 17 per cent for the offspring of those who had not suffered from the disorder. A different pattern emerged for the DZ twins, however. In this case, the morbidity rate was 17 per cent for the offspring of parents who had developed schizophrenia but only 2 per cent for the offspring of those who had remained well. Thus the data indicate that having a parent who is genetically vulnerable to schizophrenia is a significant risk factor, and that it makes no difference whether the parent actually does or does not develop the disorder.

The famous case of the Genain quadruplets underlines the important role of genetic factors in schizophrenia, and the interplay between genes and environment (Box 5.4).

Adoption studies   In a classic study, Heston (1966) examined 47 adult children of schizophrenic mothers. The children had been removed from their hospitalized mothers and were reared either by relatives or in institutions. A control group consisted of other institution-reared children. Five of the offspring of schizophrenic mothers but none of the control group were diagnosed as schizophrenic. Similarly, Kety et al. (1968) examined the psychiatric history of the parents of adopted children who were diagnosed in adulthood as schizophrenic, using Danish national records of all adoptions between 1924 and 1947. The rate of schizophrenia in the natural relatives, but not the adoptive relatives, was significantly higher than that of the general population.

Gene studies   Family risk patterns indicate that the tendency to develop schizophrenia is not 'inherited' according to simple Mendelian patterns. Sherrington et al. (1988) reported data that appeared to show an association between schizophrenia and an aberration on a particular chromosome; later studies failed to confirm this. It is likely that several different genes may together determine vulnerability to schizophrenia, and one genetic model favoured by many analysts (the 'polygenic threshold model') suggests that the risk for schizophrenia may reflect the additive effects of abnormalities at several different positions on a number of genes.

Primary causes of schizophrenia: environmental factors

The fact that some people develop schizophrenia, while their MZ co-twins who have the same genetic composition do not, indicates that, unless chance alone is responsible, environmental influences must play a role in determining whether someone who is vulnerable to schizophrenia will actually develop the disorder. A wide range of physical and social factors have been suggested as possible influences, including perinatal trauma, viruses, aspects of family interaction and specific psychological stressors.

Perinatal stress　McNeil and Kaij (1978) reviewed the evidence for a perinatal stress factor, and concluded that 'obstetric complications seem to interact with a genetic influence towards schizophrenia'. Studies of the birth records of MZ twins suggest that, if the twins are discordant for schizophrenia, the twin whose birth was marked by the most obstetrical complications is likely to be the one who develops the disorder. Furthermore, if both twins develop schizophrenia, the twin whose birth was most hazardous tends to develop more pronounced symptoms and to have a less favourable prognosis.

The viral hypothesis　Various lines of research have suggested that vulnerability to schizophrenia may be increased if an infant develops a viral infection in the perinatal period (King and Cooper, 1989). In an elaboration of the viral hypothesis, Knight (1982) suggested that certain pathways in the brain (those which carry dopamine) may be damaged as the result of an autoimmune response to a viral infection during foetal development. This is sometimes offered as an explanation for the 'season of birth effect'. Several studies have shown that more schizophrenic patients were born in the winter months (in both the northern and the southern hemispheres), and it has been suggested that an increased susceptibility of winter-born infants to viral infection might be responsible for this pattern. Several recent studies have also shown an increased risk of schizophrenia in people born some months after an epidemic of influenza, suggesting that a pre-natal infection might affect the brain tissue of the developing foetus and thus predispose the person to develop schizophrenia some twenty or thirty years later (Sham et al., 1993).

The incidence of schizophrenia has declined over recent decades, and Eagles (1991) has suggested that this decrease might be due to the introduction of mass child immunization against diseases such as measles and polio several decades ago. Finally, more direct evidence of possible viral involvement comes from several studies that have reported increased numbers of viral antibodies in the cerebrospinal fluid of schizophrenic patients. How-ever, post-mortem studies have as yet failed to find abnormal viral content in the brain tissue people who suffered from schizophrenia.

Environmental factors in schizophrenia: family factors

Schizophrenia was once widely believed to be a psychogenic disorder. Various theories suggested that sufferers were 'driven mad' by stress, by existential fears or by other people (particularly family members). The main reason for the substantial decline in the status of psychogenic theories of schizophrenia was the notable failure of empirical studies to substantiate the theorists' major predictions. Nevertheless, over the past twenty years or so an impressive body of research has shown that family atmosphere is a very important determinant at least of the course of a schizophrenic illness, and psychosocial interventions based on this work have been used increasingly to bring about and maintain recovery. Before we examine the current state of play, we will briefly consider some of the original family-based formulations.

Early psychoanalytic thinking Although Freud was of the opinion that psychoanalysis was largely ineffective in the treatment of schizophrenia, he did suggest that the disorder stemmed, like the neuroses, from a conflict between the individual's basic self-gratificatory impulses and the constraints of the real world. He suggested that as a result of this conflict (which was often fuelled by an infant's oppressive family relationships), schizo-phrenic patients regress to their earliest stage in psychological development, before the ego has been properly formed and before they have developed a realistic awareness of the external world. Thus schizophrenia was seen by Freud as an infantile state, with some symptoms (such as delusions of grandeur) reflecting this primitive condition and other symptoms (such as auditory hallucinations) reflecting the person's attempts to re-establish ego control.

Faulty learning Some behaviourists attempted to characterize the symp-toms of schizophrenia as consequences of faulty learning. According to Ullman and Krasner (1975), when a child receives little or no social reinforce-ment early on in life (perhaps because the parents are disinterested, or lack essential parenting skills), then instead of focusing on social stimuli in the normal way, he or she will attend instead to inappropriate and irrelevant environmental cues. As a result, these authors suggested, the child's verbal and other behavioural responses will appear somewhat bizarre, and those who observe the child's unorthodox conduct will either avoid the child or respond erratically. Faced with such unfathomable responses, the child may exhibit more and more eccentric behaviour until eventually, usually in early adulthood, he or she will deteriorate into a psychotic state. Although such a view may be coherent in itself, it was never substantiated by a body of supportive evidence. Thus there is no justification for the idea that the parents of those who suffer from schizophrenia lacked interest in their children or were in any way eccentric in their parenting behaviour.

'Schizophrenogenic mothers'   The psychoanalyst Frieda Fromm-Reichman (1948) suggested that schizophrenia is the outcome of being reared by a mother who, while appearing warm and self-sacrificing, is actually self-centred, cold and domineering. Fromm-Reichman suggested that the responses of these 'schizophrenogenic mothers', which are replete with contradictions and ambiguities, prove confusing for the child and render the world (especially the world of personal relationships) incomprehensible. However, studies of the parents of schizophrenic patients have resolutely failed to confirm that mothers of schizophrenic patients have any of the 'schizophrenogenic' characteristics which Fromm-Reichman described. It is greatly to be regretted that her ideas once had a profound influence on clinicians, for this account essentially blamed mothers for their sons' and daughters' suffering.

The double-bind hypothesis   A somewhat similar, but less blame-oriented, account of the development of schizophrenia – the 'double-bind hypothesis' – maintains that children become conceptually and emotionally confused (and vulnerable to the subsequent development of a psychotic condition) when their parents habitually present them with contradictory messages (Bateson et al., 1956). For example, although the statement 'I really do love you' has a literal positive meaning, it may be spoken in such a way, or in such a context, that it conveys a very different sentiment. Other double-bind communications simultaneously request or demand two incompatible behaviours, leaving the listener confused and open to criticism following a response in one way or the other. Frequent exposure to confusing messages, the double-bind theorists maintained, may eventually prove so perplexing and distressing that they precipitate a psychotic breakdown. This account may have a certain 'face validity', but again the relevant evidence has failed to provide confirmation. Studies have consistently shown that double-bind communications are no more frequent in families of schizophrenic patients than in other families (Helmerson, 1983).

Recent studies of family communication and atmosphere   A number of recent studies have provided some support for the idea that families with a schizophrenic member are marked by a relatively high level of communication deviance. For example, it appears that parents of schizophrenic patients tend to be less clear and less accurate than other parents in their communication with their offspring (Goldstein and Strachan, 1987). Further support for the idea that aspects of family interaction may not be totally irrelevant to the development of schizophrenia comes from a Finnish study of the adopted children of schizophrenic parents (Tienari et al., 1987). The data showed a clear association between the psychological health of the adopted children and a number of interactional characteristics of their adoptive family. Thus it is possible that family factors may play some role in the development of schizophrenia, although there is no evidence to suggest that such factors may be sufficient in themselves to produce the disorder.

Stressful events   There is some evidence to suggest that a stressful life event may trigger a schizophrenic episode in someone who is particularly vulnerable (usually, someone who has experienced one or more acute episodes before) (Brown and Birley, 1968; Rabkin, 1980; Tennant, 1985). One study found that certain types of event, especially critical family events and pet deaths, were especially prevalent in the six months before a first episode of schizophrenia (Jacobs and Myers, 1976). However, in most cases it is not possible to identify a major life event as having triggered an episode (as it is, for example, in many cases of depression and anxiety disorder). Studies of psychological responses to major catastrophes have not identified schizophrenic breakdown as a frequent consequence, and there have been very few reports of a schizophrenic episode being triggered by combat stress.

Primary causes: summary

Twin studies, adoption studies and high-risk studies have produced overwhelming evidence indicating that genetic factors act as a primary cause of schizophrenia. But these same studies also show that genetic factors are not the sole primary cause of the disorder. Having a genetic make-up that can lead to schizophrenia does not make it inevitable that the person will actually develop the disorder. A particular genetic make-up may be necessary (although, in principle, we must allow that some schizophrenic patients may not have a 'schizophrenic' gene complement) but it is not sufficient (since many MZ co-twins of schizophrenic patients do not develop the disorder).

Other possible primary causal factors include several that that are associated with the perinatal stage of development (physical trauma during birth, for example, and infections contracted either during the foetal stage or in early infancy). However, the evidence for many of these suggestions remains somewhat equivocal. The evidence for the involvement of psychological factors as primary causes of schizophrenia is decidedly weak. Several coherent psychological theories have been put forward, but none of them have attracted convincing empirical support. Family communication patterns, parenting practices and responses to stressful events all appear to have, at most, a very marginal effect.

Mediating mechanisms: biochemical factors

For a long time it has been suggested that 'madness' in general and schizophrenia in particular may be produced by some abnormality in brain biochemistry. Kraepelin maintained that 'dementia praecox' resulted from a malfunctioning of the sex glands, producing a chemical imbalance in the brain, and Bleuler suggested that schizophrenia might be mediated by an abnormality in the protein content of the cerebrospinal fluid. Even the psychoanalyst Carl Jung hypothesized that some unknown substance, which he labelled 'toxin X', might be responsible for the symptoms of schizophrenia. In recent years attention has focused upon possible irregularities in the functioning of various neurotransmitter chemicals. Particular significance has been attached to one of these substances – dopamine.

The dopamine hypothesis of schizophrenia   The dopamine hypothesis suggests that schizophrenia results from overactivity in the brain dopamine systems. Many years ago, a number of British scientists (Owen et al., 1978; Iversen, 1982) reported evidence of increased levels of dopamine and a relative excess of dopamine receptors in the brain tissue of schizophrenic patients, and post-mortem studies later confirmed high dopamine concentrations in various subcortical brain regions and high densities of dopamine receptors in these areas (Davis et al., 1991). Brain scans used to examine the density of dopamine receptors in the brains of living patients have also found an excess of such cells in schizophrenic patients, including some who have never been treated with anti-psychotic drugs (Waddington, 1989).

Large doses of certain stimulant drugs which are known to increase dopamine production tend to produce psychotic-like symptoms in normal people. Thus high doses of amphetamine ('speed') may produce an 'amphetamine psychosis', a state that somewhat resembles paranoid schizophrenia. High doses of levodopa, a drug that is quickly broken down by the body to form dopamine, also produce delusions and paranoia in normal people. And dopamine administered directly to the brains of animals produces a severe disruption of the attentional processes. Finally, drugs such as amphetamine and levodopa, which increase dopamine levels, increase the severity of the symptoms of some schizophrenic patients (Haracz, 1982).

Thus increasing the level of dopamine tends to produce psychological effects that bear some resemblance to the symptoms of schizophrenia. And reducing the dopamine levels has the opposite effect. All of the effective antipsychotic ('neuroleptic') drugs block dopamine receptors, thus reducing the activity of the dopamine pathways. Moreover, the clinical effectiveness of such drugs is directly related to their power to block the dopamine receptors. The neuroleptic drugs also relieve the symptoms produced in normal people by those drugs which increase the rate of dopamine production.

Overall, then, the dopamine hypothesis is supported by a good deal of evidence (it has received more support, for example, than competing biochemical explanations). However, the dopamine hypothesis has certainly not been proven, and the available evidence leaves many issues unresolved. For example, although neuroleptic drugs are effective in reducing dopamine action, they only alleviate *some* of the symptoms of psychosis (mainly the 'positive' symptoms such as hallucinations and delusions) and they certainly do not 'cure' schizophrenia. Another unanswered question is why, although drugs which block the dopamine receptors work within hours, the symptomatic relief produced by the neuroleptics follows only after several weeks of regular drug administration. Such difficulties have led to numerous revisions and caveats being added to the dopamine hypothesis. One suggestion is that the symptoms of schizophrenia result not from a simple excess of dopamine but from a more complex dysregulation of dopamine functioning. For example, schizophrenic patients may have excess dopamine in some areas of their brain and particularly low levels in others. A specific proposal along these lines is that an abnormally low level of dopamine activity in the prefrontal regions may lead to excessive dopamine activity in the mesolimbic region (Davis et al., 1991). However, some authorities in the field highlight the fact that dopamine is not a solo player but an ensemble player in the metabolic orchestra, and suggest that schizophrenia may result from a major disturbance to the delicate balance that normally holds between different neurotransmitter regulating systems.

It may eventually be established that aberrant dopamine metabolism is one of several important mediating factors in the development of schizophrenia, and that such abnormalities are involved in just some cases of the disorder. Thus, it has been suggested that dopamine is implicated primarily in those cases characterized by positive symptoms and by a good response to anti-psychotic drugs.

Other biochemical factors Many other biochemical agents have been included in attempts to provide accounts of the chemistry of schizophrenia. These include serotonin, acetylcholine, GABA, neuropeptides and prostaglandins. It is likely that at least some of the many hypotheses implicating these substances have some degree of validity. This supports the view that several different patterns of neurochemical aberration may give rise to schizophrenic symptoms, and the key factor may be the balance of activity between several neurotransmitter systems.

Mediating mechanisms: neuroanatomical studies

A number of studies have reported finding gross anatomical abnormalities in the brains of some schizophrenic patients. The original studies were based on post-mortem examinations, but recent innovations in technology have made it possible to obtain 'brain scans' from living patients. The research has focused on two neuroanatomical features in particular, ventricular size and cerebral asymmetry.

Ventricular size Inside the brain there are four cavities or 'ventricles' filled with cerebrospinal fluid. Enlargement of these ventricles occurs when there is atrophy of the tissue surrounding the ventricle. Several studies have reported abnormally large ventricles in a proportion of schizophrenic patients (especially older, chronic, patients), although other studies have failed to find such an effect (Pearlson et al., 1989). It is of course possible that enlarged ventricles may be the result of the disorder, or its treatment, rather than being a mediating cause. For example, prolonged use of anti-psychotic medication may cause brain damage leading to ventricular enlargement. On the other hand, it has been suggested that relatively large brain ventricles may be the long-term result of brain damage sustained during birth.

Cerebral asymmetry   The two hemispheres of the brain (the left brain and right brain) have somewhat different functions. This functional lateralization means, for example, that the left ('dominant') hemisphere has the responsibility for controlling language functions (at least, in the majority of right-handed people). A number of studies, including several that have employed brain scan technology to monitor the distribution of blood flow across different regions of the brain, suggest that the balance of activity between the hemispheres may be disturbed in some schizophrenic patients (Birchwood et al., 1988). More specifically, it appears that some patients have a low level of activity in their dominant hemisphere. Some studies have indicated that there is often a dysfunction in the frontal lobe of the brain, and it has also been suggested that there may be abnormalities of functioning in the medial temporal lobe (Roberts, 1991). Aberrant genetic mechanisms might be the primary cause of these temporal lobe abnormalities, and asymmetries that appear during the normal course of development might be responsible for the more extreme effect on the dominant hemisphere. Such structural abnormalities, Roberts suggests, could lead to many of the familiar schizophrenic symptoms, since the medial temporal lobe appears to play a crucial role in integrating information.

The two hemispheres communicate via a dense mass of neural fibres (the corpus callosum), and several studies have now reported an enlargement of this structure in schizophrenic patients, particularly in the frontal area. On the other hand, other investigations have indicated that some schizophrenic patients have an abnormally thin corpus callosum. One hypothesis for which there is some empirical support is that a thickened corpus callosum is associated with early onset schizophrenia and negative symptoms, whereas a thin corpus callosum is associated with late onset and positive symptom schizophrenia (Coger and Serafetinides, 1990).

Thus there is a considerable body of evidence indicating the presence of gross neuroanatomical abnormalities in people suffering from schizophrenia. However, there appears to be relatively little consensus between studies as to which neurological features, if any, can be said to be characteristic of 'the schizophrenic brain'. The evidence is diffuse, and in some cases there appear to be contradictions between the findings from different studies. There is certainly no characteristic which is universal, and the best estimate is that only around a quarter of schizophrenic patients have any form of gross brain abnormality (Seidman, 1983). Furthermore, at least some of the observed structural defects may be the result of physical treatment (including prolonged use of anti-psychotic drugs, and electroconvulsive therapy) or other extraneous factors (Reveley, 1985).

Mediating mechanisms: psychophysiological studies

Electroencephalography (EEG) is widely used, both clinically and in research, to monitor the electrical activity of the brain. Electronic sensors are placed against the scalp and tiny changes in voltage are monitored as 'brainwaves'. Brain electrical activity may be monitored while the subject is at rest or is engaged on a mental task. Some research has indicated an abnormality of communication or integration between the two hemispheres, while other evidence has pointed to a particular disturbance in the functioning of the dominant hemisphere. Since the dominant hemisphere has major control over language functions, the prediction from EEG studies, and other studies of brain function, would be that schizophrenic patients are more likely to be impaired on verbal than on non-verbal tasks. A number of studies have offered some support for this suggestion (Flor-Henry, 1976). Another fairly consistent finding is that the amplitude of a particular brainwave, referred to as 'P300' (a positive wave which peaks some 300 milliseconds following a stimulus), is reduced in schizophrenic patients. It has been suggested that this might be related, at the cognitive level, to difficulties in organizing stimuli into meaningful elements.

Mediating mechanisms: models of cognitive dysfunction in schizophrenia

Selective attention People would be immediately overwhelmed if they were to pay attention simultaneously to all of the stimulation available to them. They therefore focus their attention on stimuli which are particularly intense or salient and disregard the rest. Following Broadbent's (1958) proposal that attention is focused by means of a 'filter' which screens out irrelevant information, McGhie and Chapman (1961) suggested that schizophrenia may involve a disturbance in the functioning of the hypothetical filter. Thus a problem in focusing attention might lead a schizophrenic patient to attend to inconsequential stimuli rather than to important aspects of the environment, or to be bombarded by excessive stimulation. Several studies have suggested that schizophrenic patients fail to make use of the redundancy and patterning of sensory input which would allow them to reduce information processing demands, and that as a result they continually experience 'information overload' (Hemsley, 1988).

Automatic versus controlled processing Many human actions are automatic, rather than being controlled by conscious processes. Automatic processes involve direct access to long-term memory and occur outside conscious awareness, and when such processes have been established they tend to be inflexible and difficult to suppress. Controlled processes, on the other hand, require continual attention. They are under the individual's conscious control and are relatively flexible. Some theorists have suggested that while schizophrenic patients may have considerable difficulties with controlled processing tasks, they remain relatively unimpaired on tasks that have become automatic. It has even been suggested that schizophrenic patients are especially aware of automatic processes, and that this awareness interferes with their ability to handle tasks that demand controlled processing (Frith, 1979).

Slow rate of information processing   Schizophrenic patients respond very slowly across a broad spectrum of tasks. Part of the reason for their apparent sluggishness may be a lack of interest and motivation, but various studies suggest that schizophrenic patients also process information at a slow rate. The patient may be struggling to understand a situation and may then take an inordinate time to consider alternative responses. Attempting to deal with a situation which appears to be changing very rapidly may be very confusing, and this could help to account for patients' reports of being overwhelmed by stimulation, for example in conversation with other people (Sternberg, 1975).

Poor perceptual organization   Schizophrenic patients also tend to perform particularly poorly on tasks which make special demands on perceptual processing. From a review of the research evidence relating to schizophrenic patients' problems in the early stages of the processing of visual information, Knight (1984) suggests that poor performance often results from a specific problem in differentiating between meaningless and meaningful information. Such an impairment might lead patients to concentrate on superficial details rather than attending, for example, to the gist of a verbal message.

Aetiology: summary

Schizophrenic symptomatology can be seen as the outcome of a causal chain involving 'primary causes' and 'mediating mechanisms'. The primary causes appear to include both genetic and environmental factors. The precise mode of genetic involvement is not yet established, but it seems likely that risk for schizophrenia may reflect the additive effects of several different genetic abnormalities. Various environmental factors have been suggested as having a primary causal effect, but the evidence has not been particularly strong for any of these. The most likely candidates appear to be perinatal complications and infections. Stressful life events may play a minor role in the onset of a schizophrenic disorder, and the hypothesis that family interaction styles are implicated cannot be completely discounted.

There is fairly strong evidence to suggest that the primary causes lead to disruptions in the metabolism of various neurochemicals which then serve as principal mediating mechanisms leading to the production of many of the familiar schizophrenic symptoms. A considerable body of evidence implicates dopamine, although several neurotransmitter systems are probably implicated. Gross structural brain abnormalities are found in a minority of schizophrenic patients, and as well their impact on brain biochemistry, such abnormalities may impose on cognitive functions. The nature of the basic cognitive deficits observed in schizophrenic patients suggests that they are the product of physical (or physiological) rather than psychological antecedents. Primary symptoms will have a major impact on the patient and on other people's responses, and these are likely to generate a range of secondary symptoms. Thus a patient may engage in bizarre actions in an attempt to reduce stimulation, or may become aggressive when other people respond unsympathetically to disturbed behaviour patterns.

◀Treatment and Management▶▶▶

There is no cure for schizophrenia, but there is much that can be done to treat the symptoms of the condition and to help those in remission to avoid a further acute episode. Fifty years ago the outlook was much bleaker. In those days straitjackets were in common use and many psychiatric wards had one or more padded cells. Before the 1950s, over half of those who were admitted to a mental hospital and given the diagnosis of schizophrenia remained in the hospital for the rest of their days. Despite the occasional use of many different forms of intervention, including such radical techniques as psychosurgery, 'insulin shock' and electroconvulsive therapy (ECT), there was rarely any major improvement. For most patients, 'treatment' consisted of little more than long-term care and custody (a practice now described, in retrospect, as 'patient warehousing'). However, the introduction of powerful neuroleptic drugs in the 1950s brought enormous changes.

The impact of drug treatments

The effectiveness of neuroleptic drugs, both in the treatment of acute schizophrenia and in the prevention of relapse, has been well established in a number of highly sophisticated double-blind trials (e.g. Caffey et al., 1964). The management of schizophrenic patients was revolutionized by these drugs, because they rapidly reduced many of the most disturbing symptoms, and sharply decreased the length of time for which a patient might be expected to remain in hospital care. Schizophrenia became a 'short stay' rather than a 'long stay' condition, although it was found that many patients needed to return to hospital from time to time when experiencing further acute episodes.

Of the 300 000 people in Britain who have suffered at least one acute psychotic episode, fewer than 3 per cent are now cared for permanently in mental hospitals. Many schizophrenic patients are now treated mostly on an outpatient basis, and of those who are admitted to hospital, the vast proportion are discharged within a few weeks or months of admission.

The phenothiazines   The first neuroleptic drugs to be introduced were the phenothiazines. These are now known to block dopamine receptors. The phenothiazines are highly effective in relieving the positive symptoms of schizophrenia, including thought disorder, hallucinations and delusions, but they have relatively little effect on negative symptoms such as withdrawal and apathy (Leff, 1992). The beneficial effects are likely to continue for as long as the drug is taken, but many of those who stop taking the drug suffer a major relapse within weeks. Thus patients need to be maintained on medication over the longer term. Although the phenothiazines are extremely useful in treating acute episodes, and are highly effective in preventing relapse, they certainly do not constitute a 'cure' for schizophrenia.

Phenothiazine medication can have a number of unfortunate side-effects, including increased sensitivity to sunlight, insomnia, muscle trembling (Parkinsonism), drowsiness and visual disturbances. Fortunately, most of these side-effects can be controlled by the use of appropriate medication. However, there is one serious side-effect that cannot be effectively controlled, and which develops in around one-fifth of those who use relatively high doses of the phenothiazines over a prolonged period. This is the condition known as 'tardive dyskinesia', a neurological disorder which causes the patient to make slow involuntary rhythmical movements of the limbs and continuous oral movements (lip-smacking, sucking and tongue movements). The gestural disturbances associated with tardive dyskinesia can be very embarrassing for the patient, and the condition may also impair the person's ability to speak and eat. In extreme cases respiration is also affected.

Clozapine   The drug clozapine often brings substantial symptom relief to patients who fail to respond to other neuroleptic drugs (Kane et al., 1988), and it also has the advantage of reducing both positive and negative symptoms. However, it is a very expensive drug to use and the full benefits may not become apparent for many months. Whereas most anti-psychotic drugs produce their effects by inhibiting the action of certain groups of dopamine receptors, most of the effects brought about by clozapine appear to result from the impact of the drug on the functioning of serotonin receptors.

Psychological treatments

Psychoanalytic therapy   Freud did not feel that psychoanalytic therapy was useful in treating schizophrenia, but many psychoanalysts did attempt to work with schizophrenic patients, even during acute psychotic episodes. However, controlled studies have failed to find any evidence that significant improvement results from such interventions, even after two years of intensive treatment (Grinspoon et al., 1968).

Milieu therapy   Schizophrenic patients who sit for hours in drab surroundings may adopt the role of a chronically sick person, and are said to be 'institutionalized'. One of the first to make radical changes was Maxwell Jones (1952), who set up a 'social rehabilitation unit' at the Belmont Hospital near London. Most hospitals and hostels now provide a stimulating (but not too stimulating) physical environment. They encourage social contact and implement a structured but flexible timetable. A number of studies have demonstrated that enhancing the physical and social milieu can bring about a significant improvement in the condition of some schizophrenic patients (Hogarty et al., 1986; Liberman et al., 1986). However, some patients respond unfavourably to such changes.

The self-control of symptoms Some schizophrenic patients develop an awareness of the factors likely to exacerbate their condition and evolve effective coping strategies. Strategies include avoiding people who are perceived as threatening and staying close to those who are judged to be supportive and trustworthy. Some patients retain enough insight to be able to imagine how their conduct must appear to other people, and make strenuous attempts to keep their behaviour in check. For example, the person may prompt himself or herself not to reply overtly to disembodied voices when other people are around. Meyers et al. (1976) reported the case of a patient who was taught to monitor his social behaviour and to control his speech so that it became more coherent and less disturbed. He learned a set of phrases which he was able to use (covertly) when trying keep himself on a topic and to remain coherent. Among the self-instructions he used were: 'I mustn't talk sick', 'I must talk slowly', 'I must stay on the topic', 'I mustn't ramble on'. The patient improved considerably after learning to use such stock phrases, and he expressed his appreciation of the fact that that the covert self-instructional technique had 'stopped me talking like a crazy man'. Within the past decade, there have been several important developments in the application of cognitive intervention techniques to acute psychotic conditions.

Predicting relapse

In most cases, a person's schizophrenic 'career' will be marked by several relapses and remissions. Acute symptoms will be absent during remission, although a number of disabling personality features may still be apparent. Thus the person may find it difficult to relate comfortably to other people and may become totally absorbed in bizarre pastimes. The key factors determining whether an individual will relapse are whether medication is maintained, the emotional climate in the patient's home (or other residential setting) and the amount of time the patient spends with certain relatives (Leff, 1976).

Medication Sustained use of neuroleptic medication is extremely important for the prevention of relapse. Every one of the 30 studies reviewed by Davis et al. (1980) showed that such medication clearly prevented relapse. However, some schizophrenic patients do not relapse when they stop using neuroleptic medication, and most patients may eventually reach a stage when they no longer need these drugs. Unfortunately, there is as yet no way of telling when it is safe for an individual to discontinue medication.

Social environmental factors The course of a schizophrenic disorder is strongly influenced by the person's social context. Acute symptoms may be attenuated or exacerbated by the atmosphere in the home. During a remission phase, the likelihood of relapse increases if the person's circumstances are unfavourable. Relapse may follow a stressful life event, or may be brought on by living in an environment marred by constant harassment, discord or disturbance. Particular aspects of the family environment are highly predictive of relapse, and for the past twenty-five years one complex variable – 'expressed emotion' – has been the subject of intensive study. This research has been extraordinarily fruitful and has resulted in the development of a number of important relapse prevention programmes.

Expressed emotion   In a seminal study, Brown et al. (1972) found that the level of emotion expressed by a key relative at the time of hospital admission provided the single best predictor of symptomatic relapse during the nine-month period following the patient's discharge from hospital. Fifty-eight per cent of patients living with a high 'expressed emotion' (EE) relative relapsed within nine months of discharge, compared with only 16 per cent of those living with low-EE relatives. Vaughn and Leff (1976) later found the EE effect to be particularly pronounced when the patient was in close contact with the high-EE relative for prolonged periods (more than 35 hours per week). They also demonstrated the additive effects of continued phenothiazine medication and an optimal (low-EE) environment. Among patients who did not take regular medication, and who had prolonged contact with a high-EE relative, the nine-month relapse rate was 92 per cent. Among those living in a low-EE environment, and who continued to take neuroleptic drugs, the nine-month relapse rate was only 12 per cent.

The relationship between EE and schizophrenic relapse has now been confirmed by studies conducted in many countries, including the USA, Australia, Italy, Denmark and India (Parker and Hadzi-Pavlovic, 1990). Furthermore, the EE variable has now been shown to be an important factor influencing the course of several other conditions, including depression and anorexia nervosa.

Relapse prevention

Recognition of the factors that contribute significantly to a high risk of early relapse has been vital in the development of relapse prevention programmes. It is clearly essential that the person be maintained on suitable neuroleptic medication, and various programmes have focused on ensuring that patients and their families are fully aware of the significance of medication. Another approach to relapse prevention involves attempts to encourage the patient's family to provide an environment in which the patient will not be subjected to unnecessary demands, or undue criticism, or the attention of relatives who are emotionally intense and over-involved.

Family intervention   When the atmosphere in a patient's family, or the behaviour of key relatives, threatens an early relapse, there is an urgent need to instigate change. It may be decided that permanent residence in the family is too hazardous, and it may be necessary to arrange some alternative accommodation for the patient. Alternatively, a day-care facility may be seen as useful way of reducing the degree of contact between the patient and the family to manageable proportions.

Another possible solution is to facilitate changes within the family that will reduce the scale of threat. Several family-based programmes have focused on attempts to lower the level of expressed emotion within certain families. Thus Leff et al. (1982) devised a family intervention programme aimed at modifying the behaviour of families rated as particularly critical and over-controlling of the schizophrenic member. The programme included: (a) educational sessions dealing with the nature of schizophrenia, the common symptoms and the best ways of dealing with difficult behaviour; (b) group meetings with non-critical families who coped well with their schizophrenic family member; and (c) family sessions in which social workers and other professionals met the whole family in the home to discuss the family's specific problems.

When the effects of the programme were evaluated, significant reductions were found in the number of critical comments made about the patient, and in the degree of emotional over-involvement (two of the major elements of the composite EE factor). Furthermore, the programme appeared to have had a marked effect on relapse. During the two years following the end of the programme, 78 per cent of patients in a control group had been readmitted to hospital on at least one occasion, compared to only 14 per cent of those whose families had taken part in the intervention programme (all patients continued to take phenothiazine medication throughout the study period).

A number of other successful intervention programmes have been reported. Many involve whole families, are home-based and span a considerable period of time (usually at least a year). However, there are indications that much more modest interventions may also be useful. Smith and Birchwood (1987) described a brief educational programme to increase relatives' knowledge of schizophrenia and to modify their attitudes towards the patient. They, too, were able to show that the family's involvement had been of benefit to the patients. The educational component common to all the family-intervention programmes may be particularly important. Families that are well informed about the nature of schizophrenia are likely to show more understanding, to criticize the patient less, to make fewer demands for the patient to act 'normally' and to help the schizophrenic patient achieve and maintain an agreeable lifestyle.

Adaptive responses to prodromal symptoms   A relapse may have a sudden and unexpected onset, but in some cases the patient and other people will recognize certain 'prodromal' effects that signal an oncoming episode. Interviews with schizophrenic patients and their relatives (Herz and Melville, 1980; Birchwood et al., 1989) have helped to identify the signs that may warn of an imminent relapse. Overall, about two-thirds of patients and their relatives notice such signs, which include loss of interest, fears of going crazy, problems with concentration, disturbing dreams and withdrawal. A prodromal phase is likely to be followed by a full relapse after a week or so, although in some cases the symptoms do not develop into an acute episode and simply disappear.

If patients and their families appreciate the significance of prodromal symptoms, they may be able to prevent the occurrence of an acute psychotic episode. If they seek urgent professional help, a number of interventions are possible. One obvious strategy is to increase the level of medication. But a family facing the threat of an imminent acute episode may also benefit from psychological support and counselling. In addition, the patient can be encouraged to employ strategies that often reduce the severity of the prodromal symptoms and may even be effective in evading relapse. Such strategies include various stress management manoeuvres such as relaxation and the use of reassuring self-statements. It is important for the patient not be become highly stressed by the prodromal symptoms, because a powerful emotional reaction to the symptoms may actually trigger the onset of a full-blown relapse (Birchwood, 1992). Stress is often generated as a result of the patient's thoughts about the significance and likely outcome of the prodrome, and it is useful if clients are helped to avoid catastrophic think-ing and to appreciate the degree to which prodromal symptoms can be controlled (Smith et al., 1992).

Long-term care

Many of those who have experienced an acute schizophrenic episode remain in a somewhat delicate psychological state for a long time, whether or not they continue to show any clear sign of the disorder. About half will experi-ence another acute episode within two years. Many who are suffering from 'schizophrenia, in remission' are not well enough to live a completely au-tonomous life. Some will be able to live in the family home, but others will need some form of sheltered accommodation.

In a specialized community setting such as a 'half-way house', a group home or a semi-permanent hostel, the schizophrenic person's particular needs are likely to be recognized. The relatively 'uncharged' emotional envi-ronment that can be provided in such homes means that the person may be somewhat shielded from the normal demands and pressures of independent living. In such a context, the person may receive regular counselling, partici-pate in therapeutic groups and be gently encouraged to take further steps towards independence. Help may also be provided in finding employment, perhaps initially in a sheltered workshop. When several people with a simi-lar history share accommodation, they may gain confidence and may de-velop mutually supportive friendships. There is good evidence that a suitable living environment can significantly reduce the rate of relapse (Fairweather et al., 1969; Watts and Bennett, 1983).

Care in the community For several decades professionals have been aware of the dangers of 'institutionalization' and have sought to remove schizo-phrenic patients from hospitals and to place them in the community. Recent policy changes favouring 'care in the community' reflect a movement that has long been developing (Murphy, 1991). However, if community care is to be a better option for patients than hospitalization, community resources need to include a variety of hostels, day centres and sheltered workshops, and good cover needs to be provided by community psychiatric services and family practitioners. There should also be provision for 24-hour crisis help. Professionals need to monitor each patient's progress carefully, and to ensure that medication is continued. The relatively high risk of suicide also needs to borne in mind. At the same time, professionals need to avoid becoming overprotective or too intrusive. Services have to be well planned and coordinated, with close collaboration between professionals from different disciplines and agencies (including voluntary agencies).

Despite widespread enthusiasm about deinstitutionalization (or even 'decarceration', as it is sometimes labelled), many individuals, and many voluntary and professional groups, have expressed scepticism about whether community care policies will in fact promote better patient care (Bean and Mounser, 1993). If the policy is pursued too aggressively, a critical safety net will be removed. The traditional mental hospitals did at least offer asylum, and 'asylum', despite its modern connotation, means 'sanctuary' – a place where vulnerable people can be protected from exploitation, abuse and privation (as in 'political asylum').

Ultimately, the move away from long-term hospitalization is to be welcomed, although this should not be regarded as a 'cheap option'. Adequate (let alone 'ideal') community care is bound to require huge resources in terms of capital expenditure and recurrent costs. A necessary feature of a well integrated and universally applicable programme is a spectrum of different kinds of community care, and a variety of residential options. There will probably always be a need for short-term inpatient facilities. In the treatment of at least some cases of acute schizophrenia there are certainly advantages of a brief period of hospitalization followed by a term of day care before the person returns to the family home, or to sheltered or independent living.

◀Conclusions▶ ▶ ▶

Schizophrenia is a severely disabling condition and the most common form of psychotic disorder. Several different subtypes can be distinguished, each with its characteristic symptom pattern. Symptoms associated with schizophrenia include various disturbances of the process and content of thinking, emotional flattening and various dysfunctions of perception, motivation and movement. Many schizophrenic patients experience hallucinations, and many are subject to extreme delusions. The condition usually has an onset in early adulthood, and then runs a variable course. In many cases, a number of acute episodes are separated by extended periods of remission. The presence of 'florid' symptoms, including hallucinations and paranoia, predicts a relatively good outcome, while an insidious loss of normal functioning, including a blunting of emotional affect and social withdrawal, suggests a less favourable prognosis.

It is not yet possible to produce a comprehensive aetiological account of schizophrenia, although there is abundant evidence suggesting the involvement of an assortment of heterogeneous factors. Some of these may be identified as primary causes and others as mediating causes. There is strong evidence for the involvement of genetic factors in determining vulnerability to schizophrenia, and somewhat weaker evidence for the involvement of certain environmental factors, including perinatal complications and both pre- and post-natal infections. The primary causes do not lead directly to symptoms, but appear to be mediated by a number of physiological and psychological mechanisms. A good deal of evidence points to the involvement of the neurotransmitter systems in general, and dopamine metabolism in particular.

A relatively high proportion of schizophrenic patients have gross brain abnormalities, although there is a lack of consensus regarding their nature and significance. Psychological mediating mechanisms include both cognitive and non-cognitive abnormalities of functioning. Thus, the interplay of primary causes gives rise to mediating mechanisms, which in turn result in the primary symptoms of schizophrenia. These primary symptoms are then likely to produce additional secondary symptoms (arising, for example, from the person's attempts to cope with the primary symptoms).

The most effective way of reducing the symptoms of an acute schizophrenic episode is by administering neuroleptic drugs, most of which work by blocking dopamine receptors in the brain. However, such treatment does not provide a 'cure' for schizophrenia and medication needs to be maintained over a long period in order to reduce the risk of relapse. High expressed emotion by a key relative is another highly significant predictor of relapse, and the risk of relapse can also be reduced by means of family interventions.

Further Reading ▶ ▶ ▶

Gottesman, I.I. (1991) *Schizophrenia Genesis: the Origins of Madness*. New York: Freeman.

Thorough and well argued review of the evidence relating to the involvement of genetic factors in schizophrenia, by one of the leading contributors to the field.

David, A. and Cutting, J. (Eds.) (1995) *The Neuropsychology of Schizophrenia*. Hove: Psychology Press.

Contributors consider how abnormalities in the brain may produce the signs and symptoms of schizophrenia. Perspectives range from the neurophysiological to the phenomenological.

Fowler, D., Garety, P. and Kuipers, L. (1995) *Cognitive Behaviour Therapy for Psychosis: Theory and Practice*. Chichester: Wiley.

Reviews the current major growth in the development of cognitive interventions for psychotic conditions.

Boyle, M. (1993) *Schizophrenia – a Scientific Delusion*. London: Routledge.

An alternative view, challenging all aspects of orthodox accounts of schizophrenia. The main thesis is that there is no illness or disease that can be objectively diagnosed as 'schizophrenia'.

◄Discussion Points►►►

1 What distinctions have been made between different forms of schizophrenic disorder?
2 Describe the cognitive symptoms associated with schizophrenia.
3 Review the evidence for the claim that a predisposition to develop schizophrenia is transmitted genetically.
4 Does the available evidence now lead to the conclusion that schizophrenia is a biological disorder and that psychological factors play little or no part in the causation of the disorder?
5 What can be done to reduce the risk of relapse in a person suffering from 'schizophrenia, in remission'?
6 Discuss the social policy of 'care in the community' as it applies to people suffering from schizophrenia.

6   **Drug Abuse**

Human beings have always, it seems, eaten, drunk, chewed or smoked substances that produce intoxication, stimulation or euphoria. There are many natural sources of such drugs. Over 4000 plants contain psychoactive chemicals, and hallucinogenic mushrooms, cannabis and other intoxicants have been used for thousands of years in tribal ceremonies and religious rituals, including rites associated with initiation, marriage and death. Many psychoactive drugs are also self-administered by those who wish to alter their psychological state. Drugs such as alcohol, amphetamine and the opium narcotics are used to reduce anxiety, to lower social inhibitions, to increase arousal or to attain a state of euphoria. In many cases, the abuse of such substances produces highly disturbing experiences and long-term use may precipitate serious psychological and physical damage.

There appears to be little relationship between the danger associated with particular drugs and the degree of cultural prohibition they attract. Thus alcohol has a very high potential for causing harm, and the smoking of tobacco leads to millions of deaths per annum worldwide. Yet the use of these substances is more or less accepted within most societies. Compared to these drugs, cannabis might appear to be a relatively harmless substance, yet its use is almost universally condemned. Even coffee, which attracts very little prohibition, is not without its dangers. Many people who drink five or more cups a day may be dependent on caffeine and may be running a health risk.

The Psychological Effects of Psychoactive Drugs▶▶▶

Expectations

People's subjective drug experience is often markedly affected by their expectations of drug effects, even if the substance they have ingested is chemically neutral. Such inert substances, or dummy tablets, are known as 'placebos', and strong placebo effects are often found when people believe that they have ingested a particular psychoactive drug. Placebo responses include intoxication, changes in mood, drowsiness and relief from pain. The strong placebo effect associated with alcohol and several other psychoactive drugs has been demonstrated in many controlled experiments (for example, by Marlatt and Rosenow, 1980).

Previous experience

The psychological effects produced when a psychoactive drug is taken for the first time are often very different from those experienced by regular and long-term users. For example, few people who use cannabis for the first time experience the 'high' described by seasoned users. Similarly, an individual's first experience with alcohol and nicotine is often unpleasant or neutral, but many people soon develop a taste for these drugs and learn to appreciate and enjoy their effects.

Mood

Although many psychoactive drugs affect mood (for example, by producing euphoria), it is also true that the mood a person is in when he or she takes a drug will affect the psychological effects that are experienced. Although drugs are often taken in order to obtain a specific mood effect, some drugs appear rather to augment the mood that the person was in before taking the drug. Alcohol provides a familiar example. Drinking when happy may produce something akin to euphoria, but drinking when sad may lead to misery and tearfulness. Thus a person's frame of mind when taking a drug can make a substantial difference to the psychological effects that the drug produces. An individual's current mood and preoccupations, together with any expectations he or she has regarding the likely drug effects, are together labelled the 'psychological set'. This 'sets' the conditions for the psychological effects of the drug.

The context ('setting')

Experienced drug users are also aware that the physical and social setting in which a drug is taken can have a marked impact on the effects the drug produces. Many LSD users, for example, take great care in choosing whom they spend time with while they are experiencing the effects of the drug. Realizing that the drug can invoke paranoia, they may strenuously avoid those whom they feel unable to trust. A number of animal studies have demonstrated that drug effects are changed substantially by the physical environment and by the social situation (for example, by the presence of either subordinate or dominant animals; Palfai and Jankiewicz, 1991).

Tolerance, dependency and addiction

Repeated use of certain drugs leads the body to develop a tolerance, so that increased doses are necessary to achieve the effects previously achieved with smaller doses. Thus a person who uses amphetamine for the first time will typically feel the effect at a dosage of around 10 milligrams, whereas some-one who has a long history of amphetamine addiction may ingest over 150 times this amount without ill effects (Palfai and Jankiewicz, 1991).

The term 'drug dependent' can mean a number of different things. The distinction is commonly made between physical dependence and psychological dependence. In either case the individual feels a powerful craving or drive to take the drug, but in the case of physical dependence this feeling arises from changes in the person's metabolism, leading to physical discomfort ('withdrawal symptoms') when the drug is unavailable. The term 'psychological dependence' best refers to cases in which lack of access to the drug produces a substantial disruption in the person's life. Rather than being able to 'take it or leave it', the person feels a strong 'need' for the drug.

The term 'addiction' implies that the person feels a compulsion to take the drug, or that very high quantities of the drug are being used habitually and that the person could suffer substantial withdrawal effects if the drug were not constantly available.

'Withdrawal' refers to the adverse physiological and psychological effects that occur when a person stops using a drug. The term is generally restricted to cases in which physical dependence has become established. Although withdrawal effects result primarily from biological changes, there is good evidence to suggest that social and psychological factors also play an important role in shaping the experience (Hodgson, 1988). Thus, being in a situation in which the drug is still being used by other people may increase craving and other withdrawal effects.

Use, misuse and abuse

The terms 'misuse' or 'abuse' clearly reflect value judgements, and opinions differ sharply on the issue of where lines should be drawn. Many would subscribe to the view that any use of a prohibited substance is 'abuse', but legal proscriptions are relative. Although the law in many countries classifies different psychoactive substances according to their judged dangerousness, these classification systems are far from perfect.

◀Types of Psychoactive Drug▶▶▶

Cannabis

Cannabis comes from the Indian hemp plant (*Cannabis sativa* L). The active ingredient is tetrahydrocannabinol (THC), a drug which can act as a sedative, an analgesic, a stimulant or a mild hallucinogen. There are three main forms: marijuana ('grass'), which resembles chopped dried grass and is smoked, sometimes with tobacco; resin ('hash'), which is compressed into brown-black blocks and either smoked with tobacco or eaten; and hash oil, the most potent form, which is usually spread on the tip of a cigarette and then smoked.

Cannabis has been used in Asia for at least 4000 years. The plant was cultivated in North America in the early seventeenth century (the fibre was used to provide rigging for ships), and the drug enjoyed some popularity among European intellectuals in the nnineteenth century. In more recent times the drug has been used extensively, particularly by young people. In both the USA and the UK it is estimated that at least one-third of those between 18 and 30 have tried the drug and that around 10 per cent of those in this age range are regular users.

When it is smoked, the effects of cannabis begin within a minute or two and can last for an hour or more. The drug usually produces relaxation and enhanced sensory awareness. Time perception may be distorted, so that there is an illusion of time passing very slowly.

Physical dangers? There is no known fatal dose of cannabis, and it is generally accepted that physical dependence does not develop. However, there is evidence to suggest that men who regularly use high doses of cannabis have low testosterone levels and relatively low sperm counts. There is also some evidence that persistent use of the drug may disrupt a woman's menstrual cycle. Cannabis is often smoked mixed with tobacco, which is a danger in itself, but cannabis burns at a higher temperature than tobacco, the smoke has a very high tar content and users tend to hold the smoke in their lungs for a long time. As with all other drugs, the use of cannabis during pregnancy is inadvisable.

In Victorian England, cannabis was used for a number of medicinal purposes, including the treatment of asthma (it was smoked as 'Indian cigarettes'). In more recent times it has been used to reduce the fluid pressure in the eyes of patients suffering from glaucoma, and to decrease the vomiting and nausea that results from the treatment of cancer by chemotherapy (Gossop, 1987).

Psychological dangers? Although millions of people have used cannabis recreationally without encountering adverse psychological effects, the drug sometimes produces confusion, paranoia and panic attacks. Such adverse reactions are most likely to be experienced by novice users and by those who are in a poor state of psychological health when they take the

Table 6.1   Commonly abused psychoactive drugs

Alcohol	Has a depressant effect on the central nervous system. Low doses produce relaxation, disinhibition and mild euphoria. High doses lead to 'drunkenness', a state which includes disorientation and gross impairments of perceptual-motor functions.
Cannabis	Produces a pleasurable 'high' and may give rise to vivid perceptual experiences.
Amphetamines and similar substances	Increase central nervous system arousal, making the user feel more alert and energetic.
Cocaine	Acts as a stimulant and produces euphoria.
Hallucinogens (LSD etc.)	Produce perceptual changes, ecstatic detachment and euphoria.
Opiates	Natural or synthetic drugs that act like morphine, reducing pain and producing strong euphoric feelings.
Volatile inhalants (gasoline, glue and cleaning fluids)	Produce intoxication and may lead to hallucinations.
Ecstasy	Increases sense of well-being and feelings of social intimacy.
Barbiturates	Lower the arousal level of the central nervous system, producing a very relaxed and pleasurable feeling.

drug. Regular use of cannabis may also produce temporary deficits in memory.

Progression to other drugs   One of the most frequent arguments advanced against the use of cannabis is that those who use this drug are likely to progress to experimentation with other, more dangerous, drugs. People who take this view therefore regard cannabis as a 'gateway drug'. It is certainly true that the vast majority of those who use cocaine and opiate drugs have previously used cannabis, but most of those who have used cannabis do not go on to use other drugs, and there is no pharmacological reason why such a progression should occur. For example, although cannabis is used among a relatively high proportion of the West Indian population in Britain, heroin addiction is not a special problem in this group.

Amphetamines

Amphetamine ('speed') is the general name for a group of synthetic drugs, the first of which (Benzedrine) was produced in 1927. The amphetamines are usually swallowed in pill or powder form, but are sometimes sniffed or injected. Ingestion often induces a marked euphoria, with increased self-confidence and sociability. The user feels very alert and energetic and may go for very many hours without sleep. Another effect is a pronounced loss of appetite for food (the amphetamines were once used as hunger suppressants or 'slimming pills').

Amphetamine produces a number of adverse effects. It can make the person feel very tense, anxious and panicky, and paranoia or depression may also develop. Frequent use of the amphetamines can lead to psychological dependence. Withdrawal from the drug often leads to a number of symptoms, including depression and extreme fatigue. If a person overdoses on amphetamine the effects can be very serious. Muscle spasms and an extremely fast heartrate may be followed by convulsions and coma. Another serious condition which may be precipitated by the drug is the so-called 'amphetamine psychosis'. This disorder is associated with hallucinations, delusions, paranoia, panic attacks and extreme aggression.

Long-term excessive use may cause brain damage and can also lead to serious heart problems. There are additional dangers if the drug is injected, especially if needles are shared between users (HIV and other serious infections may be transmitted in this way). Most illicitly obtained speed is also heavily 'cut' (adulterated) with substances such as chalk and glucose, which can be extremely dangerous, especially if injected into the bloodstream.

Cocaine

Cocaine is a powerful stimulant obtained from the leaves of the coca plant. For many centuries Andean Indians have chewed the leaves to obtain the effects of the drug, and early European invaders learned to make a powerful potion by brewing the leaves. Pure cocaine was first extracted from coca leaves in the mid-nineteenth century and was then widely used as an anaesthetic.

Today, two forms of cocaine are used illicitly. One is cocaine hydrochloride and the other, obtained by combining cocaine with baking soda, is known as 'freebase cocaine' or 'crack'. Cocaine is a white powder which is usually sniffed, or 'snorted', through a rolled banknote or straw (or sometimes with a special coke spoon), but it may also be injected. The effect begins a few minutes after ingestion and then builds to a peak at around 15 minutes. Freebase cocaine ('crack') is a crystalline substance. It may be smoked in a pipe, or a piece of crystal may be heated on a piece of tin foil and the vapours inhaled. Crack produces intense pleasurable psychological effects very quickly and these usually continue for 10 minutes or so. This form of the drug is cheaper, more powerful and more likely to lead to dependency than pure cocaine.

Cocaine tends to make people feel strong, confident and very alert, and reduces or eliminates hunger. After the peak, however, the effect of the drug quickly diminishes, leaving the user feeling tired and often somewhat depressed. There is little or no tolerance effect with cocaine. The question of whether physical dependence develops remains highly controversial. However, the intense feelings of well-being produced by the drug certainly lead some users to become psychologically dependent.

The use of cocaine does involve a number of physical and psychological dangers. Adverse physical effects include increased blood pressure and irregular heartbeat. There is also a possibility of damage to the nasal passage if the drug is snorted, and the risk of cross-infection if the drug is injected with a needle previously used by someone else. Extremely high doses depress the breathing reflexes, leading to delirium, convulsions and unconsciousness, which can lead to death.

Frequent use of cocaine may also produce harmful psychological effects, including insomnia, irritability, paranoia, depression, psychotic states and a symptom known as 'formication' – the delusion that insects are crawling on or under the skin. Victims of this delusion have been known to mutilate themselves in order to produce bleeding wounds so that 'the trapped insects' can escape.

Alcohol

Alcohol is the excretion of yeast, a one-celled fungus, and is produced by the process of fermentation. This occurs in nature, but for several millenia people have known how to stimulate and control the process of alcohol production. The first recorded breweries were established in Egypt around 3000 BC.

Alcohol is a central nervous system depressant, despite its common description as a 'stimulant'. It does, however, reduce the activity of certain neurons which may inhibit particular behaviours, thoughts and feelings, so the apparent stimulant effect would more appropriately be labelled 'disinhibition'. The ingestion of small amounts of alcohol tends to lower inhibitions, produces a mild euphoria and reduces anxiety. Higher doses adversely affect the person's performance of motor skills. Gait may become unsteady and vision may be impaired. Such effects increase the risk of accidents in the home, at work and on the road. Enormous social costs are incurred each year as a result of drink-related motor vehicle accidents. In recent years, around 20000 people have been injured, and 800 killed, annually in England and Wales as a result of alcohol-related road accidents. But there are also many other detrimental effects of excessive alcohol use. Adverse effects on social judgement and emotional control may lead a person who has been drinking heavily to become aggressive, depressed or manic. Severe intoxication can instigate violent uncontrolled outbursts and short-term amnesia, and a blood alcohol level of 0.40 per cent is likely to produce stupor and coma and may lead to death.

Tolerance to alcohol often develops rapidly. A person who would become intoxicated on two pints of beer at the beginning of a drinking career may soon find that two pints has relatively little subjective effect. As tolerance develops, drinking increases, and eventually the person may become dependent on alcohol. A conservative estimate suggests that in the United Kingdom there are at least 300000 people who are 'alcohol dependent'. Chronic abuse of alcohol exacts a very high toll on drinkers and their relatives, and on society. In 1990 about 6000 people in the UK died from alcohol-related diseases. Physical problems associated with prolonged excessive use of alcohol include cirrhosis of the liver, hepatitis and acute gastritis (bleeding in the stomach), enlarged heart, heart arrhythmias and hypertension. Chronic drinkers are also likely to suffer from malnutrition, including

Box 6.1
Alcohol and Violence

There is a clear association between alcohol and violence. Evidence from studies of criminal violence invariably show that a high proportion of people who commit violent acts are intoxicated at the time of the offence. Studies of domestic violence show, similarly, that many men who beat their partners have been drinking for some time before the attack (Hotaling and Sugarman, 1986). However, violence is not a direct effect of alcohol, and drinking, even in large amounts, does not inevitably lead to aggression. In many cases, indeed, alcohol seems to decrease aggressiveness and leads the drinker to become especially affable, sympathetic and hospitable. The connection between alcohol and aggression cannot be accounted for by reference to a single mechanism but needs to be explained in terms of the social context in which drinking is likely to take place, and various fundamental psychological effects of the drug.

Alcohol is often consumed in bars, and many bars are overcrowded and noisy. At busy times, it may take some time to get served (which may be very frustrating), and fellow drinkers may be loud, uncoordinated in their movements and provocative in their verbal and physical behaviour. The atmosphere may be noisy, smoky and hot. Such situations give rise to more than their fair share of frustration and provocation. Thus part of the association between alcohol and aggression may reflect the conditions of the drinking environment. A person who becomes angry in a bar-room situation might become aggressive then and there or might displace his or her anger on to a hapless victim in another setting (particularly the home).

The effects of alcohol include changes in social judgement. Thus the drug may lead to anger because it affects the way in which the drinker perceives, or 'appraises', other people's actions. A person who is intoxicated is more likely to misinterpret other people's behaviour, and may fail to make due allowance for the context. Another kind of distortion which can affect the drinker's judgements of events is 'shortsightedness'. People who are drunk may fail to take account of anything beyond the immediate context and may see things 'out of perspective' and become angry as a consequence (Steele and Josephs, 1990).

As well as promoting anger, the effects of alcohol may also facilitate the progression from anger to overt aggression. A good deal of the anger that people experience usually remains hidden, or may be expressed in subtle and safe ways. However, alcohol tends to reduce inhibitions, and when a person has been drinking, normal apprehension regarding possible physical retaliation, social embarrassment and other costs of open aggression may be so reduced that anger is expressed in an explosive fashion.

The social construction of the relationship between alcohol and aggression is also relevant. Public awareness of a link between drinking and increased aggressiveness means that alcohol may be used to explain, and sometimes to 'excuse', a drinker's violence. Thus, following an act of drunken aggression, a person may cite the drinking as a mitigating factor ('it wasn't me, it was the drink'). Some authorities on family violence have even suggested than some men may drink deliberately in order to engage in acts of violence which can later be blamed on the drinking (Gelles, 1987).

Thus the relationship between alcohol and aggression is rather complex. Increased aggression is not a direct pharmacological effect of the drug, although pharmacological effects do play a critical role (Bushman and Cooper, 1990). A comprehensive explanation needs to take into account social and physical aspects of the drinking environment, the effects of alcohol on social perception and the disinhibiting effects of the drug. There is also good evidence to show that the emotional and behavioural effects of alcohol, especially with regard to aggression and other forms of social behaviour, reflect the drinker's presumptions about the likely effects, and that these presumptions are largely culturally determined (MacAndrew and Edgerton, 1969) vitamin deficiency. Prolonged deficiency in thiamine and other vitamins can lead eventually to a serious brain disorder known as 'Wernicke's encephalopathy'. Another brain disorder, 'Korsakoff's psychosis', which can result from brain damage following chronic alcohol abuse, is characterized by severe disorientation, profound confusion, hallucinations and amnesia.

The opiates

Heroin   Heroin is derived from the opium poppy. Opium contains morphine and codeine, and morphine can be used to produce heroin (which has twice the potency of morphine). Pure heroin is a white 'fluffy' crystalline powder, but when obtained from illegal sources it is generally mixed ('cut') with other substances such as glucose. Other additives may also be present and some, such as talcum powder, are very dangerous when injected.

Heroin can be taken in a number of different ways, but is usually dissolved before being injected. Because of the health dangers involved in injecting, particularly when needles are shared between users, smoking heroin ('chasing the dragon') has recently become more popular. The heroin is heated on a piece of metal foil held over a candle or match and the smoke then inhaled. The common belief that this form of using heroin avoids dependency is erroneous.

If the drug is injected into a vein there is an almost immediate 'rush' – a short-lived burst of extremely pleasant feelings. The drug then produces a number of pleasurable effects which generally last for a few hours. The user generally feels somewhat drowsy, contented and relieved of all stress and discomfort.

Heroin users rapidly develop a tolerance to the drug, so that higher and higher doses are needed to produce the same effect. However, there eventually comes a point at which no amount of the drug will produce the original euphoria. Users then continue to use the drug in order to avoid withdrawal symptoms, which may include cramps, sweating, shaking, vomiting and muscle pains. Some of those who have experienced withdrawal from heroin describe the effects as similar to those of a particularly bad bout of influenza.

People who inject heroin and other opiates face a number of dangers. Their veins may become inflamed or obstructed, and adulterants used to 'cut' the heroin can clog blood vessels in the lungs. The use of dirty needles can cause infections, and HIV, hepatitis and other infections may be passed from one user to another when needles are shared.

Methadone   Methadone hydrochloride is a synthetic drug, first developed at Rockefeller University in 1966. It is widely prescribed as a heroin substitute. Compared with heroin, methadone appears to be a relatively safe drug, although there is a strong physical dependency effect. Sudden cessation of methadone use leads to withdrawal symptoms which can be particularly unpleasant. However, it is sometimes possible to achieve a gradual withdrawal without severe effects.

The hallucinogens

LSD   Lysergic acid diethylamine 25 (LSD) is derived from ergot, a fungus which grows on rye, and was first synthesized in 1938. However, its halluci-nogenic effects were not discovered until 1943, when Dr Albert Hofmann accidentally ingested a minute quantity of the drug and experienced the first LSD 'trip'.

LSD is a white crystalline material. Typically, a liquid containing the drug is mixed with other substances and eaten in the form of a capsule or a tablet, or on blotting paper or a sugar cube. After ingestion, certain effects are noticeable within half an hour. The effects peak after about three hours, and may then continue for up to 12 hours. Physical effects of the drug include muscular weakness, trembling, numbness and an impairment of coordina-tion. Feelings of nausea are quite common, and there are increases in blood pressure and heart rate.

The main psychological effects are a profound heightening of sensation, with vivid visual effects and extreme perceptual distortions of time and space. When the eyes are closed the visual field may appear very bright and highly coloured, with stunning geometric and kaleidoscopic patterns. Music may be experienced as a visual pattern, such intermingling of the senses being known as 'synaesthesia'. A loosening of associative thought processes may increase creativity, and thought content may follow magical, surrealis-tic or religious themes.

LSD can also produce severe adverse psychological reactions, including paranoia, extreme fearfulness, violence and suicidal behaviour. A 'bad trip' is often so alarming that the person resolves never to use the drug again. Another disturbing feature reported by some users is the experience of brief episodes of 'flashbacks' to the intoxicated state which may occur for up to a year after the trip.

Although some degree of tolerance may build up when the drug is used a number of times in quick succession, physical dependence does not occur, and psychological dependence is very rare. Most LSD users ingest the drug only occasionally and stop using it after a few months or years.

Psilocybin ('magic mushrooms')   Psilocybin is obtained from the 'liberty cap', a mushroom that was used in religious ceremonies by the Aztecs. The plant is usually dried or crushed before being either eaten or made into a tea. The effects include light-headedness and enhanced sensations, sometimes of an hallucinatory nature. Unpleasant physical effects, including nausea and stomach pains, may also be experienced. There are no withdrawal symp-toms, and the greatest danger associated with experimenting with magic mushrooms may be the risk of using poisonous fungi in mistake for the liberty cap.

Phencyclidine (PCP, 'angel dust')   This 'designer drug' was used as an anaesthetic in veterinary medicine before it began to be used illicitly in the USA in the early 1960s. It is smoked or eaten. PCP produces euphoria, gross perceptual distortions, disorientation and a decreased response to pain. Delusions and antisocial behaviour are common, and the drug sends some users into a state of uncontrolled agitation and rage. There is no evidence of physical or psychological dependence.

Ecstasy (MDMA)

MDMA (methylenedioxymethamphetamine), known as Ecstasy or 'E', is sometimes referred to as a 'hallucinogenic amphetamine', although in terms of its psychological effects it is particularly difficult to categorize. At street level, it is commonly recognized as a 'dance drug'. The compound was first synthesized in 1914, but its illicit use did not become widespread until the late 1980s. Ecstasy is sold in the form of capsules and tablets, the ostensible dose of the drug being between 100 and 120 mg. However, the purity and strength of pills sold as Ecstasy vary widely, and they often contain amphetamine, LSD or other psychoactive drugs. The drug begins to have an effect between half an hour and an hour after ingestion, and the peak effect is then maintained for two to four hours. The effects resemble those of both stimulant and hallucinogenic drugs to some degree, although hallucinations are rarely experienced. The sought-after effects are euphoria and increased energy, together with a heightened sense of intimacy with other people, and acute tactile sensations.

Negative side-effects are relatively common and may include nausea, anxiety, fatigue, confusion, loss of coordination and depression. Ecstasy produces an accelerated heartrate and a sharp increase in blood pressure. The drug also leads to a rise in body temperature which can lead to heatstroke, especially if the drug is used in hot environments, if the person dances continuously and if cool liquids are not taken regularly. There is some evidence that the positive effects of the drug decrease with increased use, while the negative effects increase (Solowij et al., 1992).

There are rare fatal cases (the annual ecstasy fatality figure in the UK is around ten cases), and most of these appear to be related to increased blood pressure and hyperthermia. There are also occasional reports of the acute onset of psychosis, extreme anxiety states and other psychiatric conditions following the ingestion of ecstasy (McGuire, 1994). There is some concern regarding possible long-term effects of using the drug. MDMA appears to produce the experienced effects by disturbing neurotransmitter metabolism, and it seems to have a toxic effect on serotonin neurons (McCann and Ricaurte, 1991). Some people have therefore suggested that ecstasy may permanantly disturb the natural neurotransmitter balance, which might then render the individual vulnerable to various forms of psychological disturbance.

Ecstasy has become very widely used within the United Kingdom and many other countries over the past decade. It was originally closely associated with house music and parties, and later with 'raves', and is now mostly used at weekends in dance clubs. Current estimates suggest that around 500 000 people use the drug each week in Britain (ISDD, 1996).

Barbiturates

Barbiturates are usually ingested orally and produce relaxation, euphoria and a decrease in inhibitions. Negative effects include impaired judgement, slurred speech and a disturbance in the user's ability to concentrate. High doses of the drug will eventually produce sleep, and overdosing can lead to breathing difficulties and the loss of consciousness. Extremely high doses may prove fatal.

People develop a tolerance to barbiturates and easily become both physically and psychologically dependent on them. Withdrawal effects may be severe and may include fever, tremors, insomnia and extreme anxiety.

Benzodiazepines

Two quite separate groups of people have problems with the use of benzodiazepine drugs. One group consists of illicit users, many of whom use particular benzodiazepine drugs as a substitute for opiate drugs. The other group consists of people, many of whom are suffering from an anxiety disorder, who are prescribed a benzodiazepine drug by their physician and then find it difficult to stop taking the drug.

The benzodiazepines are 'anxiolytic' (anxiety-reducing) drugs and are widely prescribed for acute anxiety conditions. They are also given to surgical patients as a form of premedication. Most of the familiar minor tranquillizers – including Valium, Librium and Ativan – are benzodiazepines. Because they are low in toxicity, they are relatively safe to prescribe for patients who may be tempted to take an overdose. This safety factor gave the benzodiazepines a major advantage over the barbiturates. The benzodiazepines are usually swallowed as pills, although some are also available in injectable form. The effects of 'medium-acting' benzodiazepines last for up to six hours, while the effects of 'long-lasting' benzodiazepines continue for at least 24 hours.

Benzodiazepine prescribing practices have changed considerably over the past 15 years. During the 1960s, 1970s and early 1980s, these drugs were used extensively as maintenance medication for people diagnosed as suffering from a persistent anxiety disorder. Following the recognition of certain dangers associated with long-term use, however, benzodiazepine prescription was recommended only as a short-term measure for patients facing acutely stressful situations.

Symptoms now recognized to be associated with long-term benzodiazepine use include depression, anxiety, aggressiveness and disinhibition. Some users become unconcerned about the possible consequences of their actions and engage in shoplifting, for example, or drive dangerously. Driving under the influence of a benzodiazepine drug can be particularly hazardous, not only because of the disinhibition effect, but also because the drug may produce drowsiness, dizziness and poor coordination. Furthermore, the benzodiazepines interact with alcohol. In addition to the

Box 6.2
Withdrawal from Prescribed Benzodiazepines

A national UK survey conducted in the early 1980s found that 7 per cent of men and twice as many women had been prescribed benzodiazepine medication at some time in the previous 12 months. In a third of these cases the drug had been used for less than a month, but around a quarter had been using the drug regularly for over a year (Balter et al., 1984). Although the situation has changed considerably following the recognition of side-effects resulting from long-term use, recent estimates suggest that many adults still continue to be long-term users.

Early assurances that the benzodiazepine drugs were relatively free of side-effects and could be stopped at any time without any adverse consequences can now be seen as grossly inaccurate. However, only a relatively small proportion of patients experience severe side-effects, and many people are able to stop taking a benzodiazepine drug, even after a considerable period of use, without experiencing extreme withdrawal symptoms.

On the other hand, many people do experience intensely distressing effects when they suddenly stop using a benzodiazepine. Common withdrawal symptoms include a sharp increase in anxiety, insomnia, loss of energy and difficulty in concentrating. Depression may also be experienced, as well as a number of somatic symptoms, including headache, muscle pains and an increased sensitivity to tactile, visual or aural stimula-tion. Thus sudden withdrawal of the drug is certainly not advisable. However, even gradual withdrawal can cause problems. There may be a 'rebound' effect, so that the person feels extremely anxious for up to several days, and sleep may be poor and disturbed. Nausea, sweating and cramps may occur, together with perceptual disturbances. Withdrawal effects may persist for several days or weeks, and some people continue to experience disturbing effects for several months. Curiously, administering benzodiazepines during the withdrawal phase does not appear to alleviate these symptoms.

One strategy suggested for those who experience severe withdrawal effects is simply to maintain them on benzodiazepine medication indefinitely, but very prolonged use of these drugs may lead to memory and attention deficits (Hayward et al., 1989). A preferable alternative is to implement a careful and gradual management programme (using various forms of medication to alleviate persistent withdrawal symptoms, if necessary), while at the same time providing the patient with training in the use of psychological techniques for anxiety reduction. A number of such programmes have been described and evaluated positively by a number of clinical research teams since the 1980s (e.g. Tyrer et al., 1984; Higgitt et al., 1987).

various side-effects, around a quarter of long-term users (those who have used benzodiazepines for six months or more) show marked symptoms when attempts are made to withdraw the drug (see Box 6.2).

The benzodiazepine drug temazepam is often used illicitly. Opiate users sometimes resort to it when they are unable to obtain their preferred drug, sometimes injecting the soluble form as a substitute for heroin or, in some cases, mixing the temazepam with heroin (Forsyth et al., 1993). Temazepam is also used orally by those who have no history of opiate use. One study in

Scotland found that 6 per cent of 13–16 year olds had used temazepam orally (without prescription) (RBL, 1989).

Volatile inhalants

'Glue sniffing' is the term applied to the inhalation of a wide range of solvents, including those used in glue, lighter fuel, paint thinners, metallic paints, antifreeze and cleaning fluids. The active ingredients vary, but many contain compounds of chlorine and fluorine, and some contain dangerous metal particles. Recent estimates suggest that approximately one in fifteen 11–16 year olds in the UK have sniffed solvents on at least one occasion (ISDD, 1992).

One effect of such substances is to reduce the amount of oxygen reaching the brain, producing a form of intoxication. Following inhalation, the user is likely to experience dizziness, disorientation and visual distortions. Nausea is also likely, and speech may become slurred. The effects generally last for up to half an hour.

A number of immediate dangers are associated with the use of these substances. Butane gas or aerosols sprayed directly into the mouth can cause the tissues to swell, and may lead to suffocation. Most products used are highly inflammable, and so there is also a danger of fire. In the longer term, several of the volatile inhalants can produce serious physical damage to the lungs, kidneys and circulatory system.

Patterns of Use ▶ ▶ ▶

A British national survey found that 29 per cent of a sample of 15–24 year olds had used an illegal drug or solvent on at least one occasion (ISDD, 1992), and a major US study found that over 60 per cent of those aged between 18 and 34 had used an illicit drug at least once (Schuster and Kilbey, 1992). Cannabis is the drug most widely used, and the majority of those who have used any other illegal drug have also used cannabis.

It is estimated that in Britain in any one year between one million and one and a half million people use cannabis and that over a quarter of those in their mid-twenties have used cannabis on at least one occasion (ISDD, 1992). The corresponding figures for LSD and Ecstasy are in the region of 5 per cent, and for heroin the figure is less than 1 per cent (ISDD, 1992).

Estimates of the extent of use of various psychoactive drugs by 19–20 year olds in England and Wales are provided in Table 6.2.

A number of characteristics are associated with a relatively high frequency of drug use (whether occasional or regular). Most of those who use illicit drugs are young (in their teens, twenties or thirties), although some people continue to use illicit substances beyond this age. Certain drugs (particularly solvents) are used by young teenagers more than by adults. More males than females use illegal drugs, the male : female ratio reported by most surveys being in the region of 2:1. People from every social class use

Table 6.2 The prevalence of psychoactive drug use: percentage of 19–20 year olds who have ever used psychoactive drugs (England and Wales)

Drug	Prevalence (%)
Cannabis	29
Hallucinogenic mushrooms	12
Amphetamine	10
LSD	7
Ecstasy	7*
Cocaine	3
Heroin	1

Source: RBL (1989).
*The RBL survey was conducted before the recent sharp rise in the use of Ecstasy. The figure quoted is from a more recent survey conducted by Gallup for Wrangler (Gallup and Wrangler, 1992), although this, too, may now be an underestimate.

drugs, but particularly high levels of illicit drug use are often associated with conditions of poverty and social deprivation (Peck and Plant, 1986). There is something of a social stratification effect, with different drugs being used by those from different social groups. Thus cocaine, which is an expensive drug, is used more by those from middle and upper social class groups, whereas crack cocaine, which is considerably cheaper, is used more by those from lower socioeconomic groups. People who use illegal substances also tend to be frequent users of alcohol and tobacco. Compared to use who use drugs only occasionally, those who indulge in regular use appear to be less socially conforming, less religious and more rebellious and impulsive (Stein et al., 1987).

Some social subgroups have distinct attitudes to drugs, and membership of a particular group is often associated with an especially high or low rate of drug use. Thus those who have a strong affiliation to an orthodox religious group are unlikely to use illegal drugs, whereas those who identify with a 'counter-culture' in which pro-drug values are openly expressed (at least with respect to cannabis, LSD or Ecstasy) are very likely to use one or more illicit drugs. Many of those who use one illegal substance also use others (they are sometimes described as 'polydrug users'), and in some groups considerable prestige is attached to the extent and breadth of one's experience with drugs. The connection between drug use and identification with particular cultural subgroups reflects a two-way association. Those who use cannabis are likely to be attracted to a subculture which endorses the use of this drug. And those who are attracted to such a subculture for other reasons (because they like a particular kind of music, for example) are likely to experiment with the drugs that are favoured by the social group and are therefore likely to be readily available.

It is certainly inappropriate to classify experimental users as 'drug dependent' or as 'addicts' or 'junkies'. Of those who have ever taken an illegal drug, only a very small proportion develop a dependence on the drug. Very few drug users ever inject, and in most cases drug experiences do not interfere with the person's normal lifestyle. For most people, drug-taking is merely one, rather minor, aspect of their leisure activity.

◄A Psychological Model of Drug Use►►►

It is often imagined that the use of illicit drugs must result from some personality defect or incapacity, but very few users have a history of psychiatric illness or have any recognizable 'personality defect'. Viewing drug use, abuse or dependency as a 'symptom' of some underlying personality problem is inaccurate and unhelpful. Nevertheless, a proportion of drug abusers do have a history of difficulties (stress, for example, or loneliness) which may have played some part in leading them to experiment with, or to over-indulge in, the use of psychoactive drugs.

Drug taking is not as 'irrational' as it may at first appear. Most of those who use drugs do so because of the benefits they gain, or expect to gain, from using them. These benefits may include pleasant or exciting physical sensations, euphoria, relief from anxiety, social disinhibition and increased prestige with peers. Most drug users acknowledge that their use of drugs entails some risks, but they are likely to underestimate the real dangers and real costs involved. Even if they were to judge the overall costs and benefits of drug use to be roughly equal, continued use might well remain attractive because the positive effects tend to be immediate (and therefore highly compelling), whereas the negative effects tend to be longer term. Many smokers, for example, accept the prospect of eventual damage to their health, but the immediate pleasure (or relief from craving) they obtain from smoking a cigarette usually outstrips such fears. If the immediate negative effects of smoking were experienced as greater than the immediate positive effects, very few people would smoke.

People use a drug the first time because they anticipate that the consequences will be positive. The expected benefits may include direct psychological effects such as euphoria and anxiety reduction, and social effects such as higher prestige among peers or acceptance by a particular subcultural group. Those who experiment with a drug may find that the first experiences confirm the expectation of pleasant or exciting effects, and they may then continue to use the drug even if other people voice their disapproval of the drug-taking.

For many drugs, frequent use produces a bodily adaptation that results in increased tolerance, and in such cases progressively higher doses are needed to re-create the original effects. If physical dependence occurs, continual use of the substance may be necessary to avoid withdrawal symptoms, and withdrawal effects may be so unpleasant that the person constantly 'needs' the drug to make life tolerable.

The account given here suggests that at no stage in the process is the drug user 'thoughtless' or 'stupid'. The drug-taking, although ill-advised, is a 'rational' behaviour, at least from the user's own perspective. The model

Table 6.3   Commonly abused psychoactive drugs: some 'sought-after' psychological effects

	Euphoria	Reduced inhibitions	Anxiety reduction	Perceptual changes
Alcohol	**	***	**	*
Cannabis	**	**	*	**
Amphetamines	**	**		*
Cocaine	***	**		*
Hallucinogens	*	*		***
Opiates	***	*	*	*
Volatile inhalants	**	**		**
Ecstasy	**	*	*	**
Barbiturates	**	***	**	*

*Some effect; **moderate effect; ***intense effect.

This table provides only a rough guide to some of the psychological effects of these drugs. Responses to the drugs depend on the dosage, the level of tolerance, the user's psychological 'set' and the social setting in which the drug is taken.

avoids the conclusions, so beloved of tabloid newspapers, that drug-taking is a wilful process of self-destruction (although such a description might be appropriate in isolated cases) and that drug-takers are weak, careless, or are suffering from a personality disorder.

Most users of illicit drugs appear to confine themselves to casual experimentation and occasional recreational use. If the pleasurable effects of the drug diminish over time, or if it becomes evident that the drug is causing problems, most users will 'rationally' decide to stop using it. In many cases they are able to do this without difficulty. Again, this picture of self-monitored and self-regulated drug use differs sharply from that presented by many press reports. 'Drug horror' stories often depict the typical drug user as a crazed zombie-like individual whose life is totally out of control.

A considered and informed view which stands in sharp contrast to the 'moral panic' evident in media representations is presented by a leading British researcher in the drug abuse field, Martin Plant:

Drug taking is generally restricted so that it does not interfere with primary obligations. An office worker appearing drunk on the job, or a student 'stoned' in lectures would rapidly be confronted with censure or mockery in consequence. Most drug taking is a facet of leisure. It is part of 'time out' and usually an aid to relaxation. The rules of leisure are different from those of work. At a party one might quite acceptably get 'high' ... flirt and engage in a wide variety of behaviour unthinkable during working time. Drug taking is largely engaged in as a pleasure-producing activity. Individuals who, under the influence of drugs, become obnoxious or interfere with the enjoyment of others will usually be treated with disapproval or disdain by their associates ...

Box 6.3
Adolescent Drug Use

Buckhalt et al. (1992) surveyed over 130000 12–16 year olds in the United States and enquired about their use of drugs and other aspects of their lives. The drugs most frequently used by these adolescents were tobacco, alcohol and cannabis. A relatively low frequency of drug use was reported by those who indicated a high level of involvement in school, family and church activities, but participation in sports activities was not associated with lower levels of drug use. There was a fairly strong relationship between the extent of drug use and how long the adolescents were allowed to stay out for at night. Those granted a good deal of autonomy were more likely to have used drugs than those whose freedom was more limited.

A review of research concerning the relationship between adolescent drug use and peer, family and community variables (Dielman et al., 1991) suggested that the best single predictor of drug use is whether the adolescent's peers use drugs. Parental behaviour and values, and the degree to which parents monitor their children's behaviour, are also significant predictors, but the effects of these variables are not generally found to be as strong as those of peer variables.

Shedler and Block (1990) investigated the relationship between psychological health and adolescent drug use. The same subjects were studied over 15 years, into late adolescence. It was found, as expected, that heavy drug use was associated with a number of indices of maladjustment, including interpersonal alienation, poor impulse control and manifest emotional distress. However, adolescents who had never experimented with any drug also tended to have problems. Many were anxious and lacked social skills. The group of adolescents who had engaged in a moderate degree of experimentation with drugs appeared to be the best adjusted (cannabis accounted for most of their illicit drug use). Retrospective analysis of childhood data collected earlier in this study suggested that personal and social maladjustment was often evident before the development of a drug problem, so that extreme drug use in adolescence appeared to be an effect, rather than a cause, of psychological difficulties. The quality of parenting received during the early years of childhood accounted for a number of the differences between those who used drugs frequently, those who had experimented occasionally, and those who had never used drugs.

Most drug taking is sporadic, moderate and discreet. (Plant, 1987, p. 119)

This may be a reasonable overview of the general business of drug-taking in our society, but we should not forget that many people do get into very serious psychological, social and physical difficulties through their use of drugs. For this reason experimentation with psychoactive drugs is something to be discouraged. In the next part of this chapter we consider the process of change and the treatment methods available for working with people who find themselves in difficulties as a result of their drug use.

◀The Process of Change▶▶▶

Many of those who use illegal drugs do so only once or twice. Their curiosity may be satisfied after trying a particular drug, they may find that the drug effects fail to live up to their expectations or they may be alarmed when they experience adverse effects. Other people continue to use a particular drug in moderation over a longer time. They may take it when it is offered to them, but may make little effort to obtain supplies of their own, or they may confine their use to special occasions.

Having used one drug, such as cannabis, an individual may be more inclined or less inclined to try another illicit drug. People often have their own simple classification system that categorizes drugs in terms of different levels of power or danger. Very often cannabis is regarded as low power (or 'soft'). Those who experience powerful effects as a result of using cannabis, or who find that the drug produces adverse effects, are likely to avoid substances that they regard as more dangerous. On the other hand, those who find that cannabis produces mild pleasant effects might well be tempted to try other drugs which they believe might produce a stronger pleasurable experience.

Most of those who become regular drug users eventually reach a point at which they wish to stop. Some merely place an intention to quit on their personal agenda for future action, but many make a firm resolution and attempt to change their behaviour. Some manage to quit without much effort and without external help. Others find that they can succeed in changing their behaviour only with the aid of professionals or voluntary groups. Many struggle through a number of attempts and successive relapses before they eventually achieve a permanent change in their drug-related behaviour.

A model of change in drug use

Prochaska and DiClemente (1984) provided a useful model of the process of change in drug use. They suggest that it is helpful to recognize a number of stages leading from initial denial or lack of recognition of the problem to eventual abstinence from the drug. They distinguish six stages in the process of change.

1 *Precontemplation.* Initially, the person may not recognize that the drug use presents anything of a problem and may therefore have little or no motivation to change the behaviour.
2 *Contemplation.* At a later stage the person may recognize that the use of the drug incurs a number of costs (including adverse effects on health) and may begin to assess these against the judged benefits of continued drug use.
3 *Decision.* If the cost–benefit analysis leads the person to conclude that the overall value of using the drug is positive, he or she may return to the first

stage. If the overall value is judged as negative, however, he or she is likely to move towards changing the drug-related behaviour.

4   *Active change*. Those who are motivated to stop using a drug are likely to seek out strategies for bringing about a positive change. They may try to do this alone, or they may ask for help from friends and/or professionals. Change may involve reducing the amount of the drug, shifting to a less powerful drug or changing to a safer means of administration. For many people, successful change comes about through participation in a structured intervention programme.

5   *Maintenance*. If a treatment or self-managed change is to be judged wholly successful, the initial change in behaviour has to be maintained for some time. During this time, the person may need to develop special coping strategies to reduce craving and to avoid succumbing to temptation; for example, when in a celebratory mood or when experiencing stress.

6   *Relapse*. A failure to maintain change is likely to result in the person returning to the former pattern of drug use. However, a single infringement of planned abstinence ('a lapse') should not be interpreted as signifying a total relapse. Many people relapse several times before they finally achieve a consolidated and permanent change in their behaviour.

The decision to change

People decide to give up taking a drug or to seek help in giving up for a variety of reasons. In many cases the trigger is pressure from other people, such as parents or a partner. Sometimes the change stems from a realization of the long-term costs of the drug, in terms of health and relationships, and sometimes it follows a prosecution for possession. Another common stimulus for change is a sudden awareness of the potential danger of the drug as a result of a traumatic incident (a near-fatal overdose, for example, or a 'bad trip'). Sometimes a serious drug-related accident involving a friend will bring home the dangers.

A change of attitude towards drug-taking may reflect a major adjustment in the person's disposition or circumstances. In some cases it is merely one aspect of a much wider 'personal revolution' in which the person makes a decision to transform his or her whole lifestyle. In other cases the change results from a radical shift in the person's environment. A remarkable example of this phenomenon involves US military personnel who served in the Vietnam War. A high proportion of these soldiers used drugs, including opiates, while on active service. However, fears that these individuals would continue to use drugs when they returned to the United States, thus producing a massive rise in the national drug problem, proved to be groundless. Many authorities were astonished by the fact that 95 per cent of the soldiers who had been regularly using opiates while in South East Asia stopped using these drugs immediately upon their return, with very few reporting any special discomfort or difficulty (Robins, 1978).

Let us consider some of the factors that might help to account for this phenomenon. It is likely that one of the key factors was simply availability. Drugs were easily available in Vietnam, whereas few of the soldiers had experience of using opiates before active service and were not in contact with drug sources when they returned home. Thus drugs were no longer 'there for the taking'. Another important factor may be the highly aversive context of the former drug-taking. For many of the soldiers, the use of opiates would have been closely and specifically associated with the Vietnam experience. With a dramatic change in their life situation (and a likely desire to turn away from everything associated with the fearful experience of the war), many of the soldiers who returned home may have rejected drugs because they identified drug-taking with the horrors of participating in the war. Furthermore, the cost–benefit situation would have changed considerably upon the soldiers' return. A general social tolerance or approval of drug-taking among fellow military personnel would have been replaced, for many soldiers, with a strong level of disapproval from family, friends and civilian colleagues.

During the Vietnam War, many soldiers were often in a state of profound fear and lived for the present, not knowing how long they would survive. In such circumstances the opiates would have provided immediate relief from stress, intense physical pleasure and a powerful distraction from the menacing environment. With a high risk of imminent death, the potential longer-term dangers associated with drug use must have seemed relatively unimportant. Upon their return, however, there would have been no need for the desperate measure of seeking temporary oblivion by means of opiates, and many veterans must have decided that it was now worth renewing their concern for their longer-term health and well-being. Thus the benefits of drug use had sharply declined for these people, while at the same time the potential costs had sharply increased. While drug-taking had been judged a 'positive value' activity in Vietnam (that is, the judged benefits had outweighed the judged costs), it had now become a 'negative value' activity for almost all of the veterans who behaved 'rationally' and immediately discontinued their drug use.

◀Treatment▶ ▶ ▶

Those who end their drug-taking without external intervention are often said to undergo a 'spontaneous recovery', but this term is inappropriate for two reasons. First of all, the term 'recovery' may imply that the person had been suffering from a disease, and it is now generally agreed that a disease model of drug use is inappropriate. Second, the term 'spontaneous' suggests that there was no particular reason for the change, whereas in most cases there is a perfectly rational explanation of why the person chose to stop using the drug and of why the attempt was successful. Thus a term such as 'self-managed change' is preferable to 'spontaneous recovery'. In a study that explored how 100 heroin addicts managed to stop using the drug without treatment, Biernacki (1986) found evidence of many perceptive and elaborate strategies.

Most drug-taking 'careers' do reach an end-point, and in the majority of cases this occurs through self-managed change. In other cases the drug user quits with the help of a professional or voluntary agency that offers advice, support and, in some cases, a structured treatment programme. There is likely to be a particular need for such a programme if the person has become physically dependent on a drug.

Many diverse approaches have been developed for the treatment of drug problems. This is partly because different drugs, and different patterns of drug use, require different forms of intervention. A person who contacts an agency seeking help in reducing the use of a drug such as cannabis or LSD, for which physical dependence does not develop, will probably be counselled and given practical advice on how to regulate drug use and how to limit harmful effects. On the other hand, a person seeking help for a longstanding heroin habit may be invited to discuss the possibility of detoxification, although initially the focus may be on the safer use of the drug. The treatment provided may be constrained, to a large degree, by local policies and practices. Thus, for opiate addiction, variations in prescription rules and practices between different areas mean that some centres are able to prescribe heroin, or a substitute drug such as methadone, whereas others are not.

Some treatment programmes focus directly on the drug problem, while others take a much broader approach and principally address psychological or lifestyle issues that may have helped initially to make the drug attractive or which may be playing a part in maintaining the drug use. Most programmes begin with a detailed assessment of drug-related attitudes and behaviours and an examination of the person's current lifestyle.

Few programmes now reflect an earlier view that drug users are addicts who have no choice over their drug-taking. Most now emphasize the importance of self-control and argue that change must come from the drug user himself or herself rather than being imposed from outside (Van Bilson, 1986). It is recognized that success in treatment depends largely on the degree of motivation for change, and that this will reflect the drug user's attitudes and beliefs about the drug and the treatment regime. One variable that has been identified as central to the attitude/belief/motivation domain is 'self-efficacy' (Bandura, 1977). In general, 'self-efficacy' refers to a person's judgement that he or she will be able to deal with problems successfully; it is the strength of belief in one's personal effectiveness. In the context of drug treatment, self-efficacy refers to the user's confidence that he or she can overcome the drug problem. A number of studies have shown that those who are confident (i.e. have high self-efficacy) are more successful in coming off drugs than those who lack such conviction.

The objectives of treatment programmes have changed somewhat over recent decades. Formerly, the principal aim was to achieve and maintain abstinence from all drug use. Today, much more significance is attached to harm limitation. Thus greater emphasis is placed on the safer use of dangerous substances and on broader aspects of rehabilitation (the achievement of a more favourable lifestyle). Although abstinence may still be regarded as the ultimate goal, total abstention from all illegal drugs is no longer regarded as the sole measure of outcome success. Thus many of those working in the field would accept that a reduction in the amount of drug used, a switch to a safer drug or a change to a safer method of administration (from injection to oral ingestion, for example) all represent worthwhile achievements.

The various strategies used to bring about change include drug prescription (of the original drug or a substitute drug), controlled detoxification, various counselling approaches and many different forms of social intervention. Many programmes combine a number of these strategies.

Controlled drug prescription

The drug prescription strategy remains highly controversial and is not universally available (i.e. constraints are often imposed by the law or by medical practice guidelines). The strategy applies mainly to opioid use. Those who use heroin, for example, face a number of problems in addition to their underlying dependency on the drug. Illegal supplies of the drug may be difficult to obtain, and the user has scant means of determining the strength and purity of the substance obtained. Street heroin is often 'cut' with additives that can be very dangerous indeed, especially when the mixture is injected. The variation in the strength of different supplies means that it is impossible for the user properly to monitor or control the amount of drug being taken, and this can lead to an accidental overdose, the consequences of which may prove fatal. Another problem relates to the high price of street heroin. Those who need a constant supply often have to turn to crime or prostitution to pay for their habit. Financial constraints and problems with the availability of needles also mean that needles ('works') are frequently reused and may be shared between users.

If, instead of relying on street dealers, the user is able to obtain a medical prescription for heroin, many of these problems disappear. The substance obtained is pure and of known strength, an adequate supply of needles can be provided and the financial burden is reduced. Even when the drug itself cannot be supplied, the availability of a free needle exchange scheme can do much to reduce the hazards associated with opioid use. Another widely used strategy involves prescribing another opioid drug, methadone, as a substitute for heroin and supplying it in a form that is taken orally rather than by injection.

The methadone maintenance strategy offers the user continued access to an opioid (and freedom from withdrawal symptoms) through the use of a substance which is pure and of known strength, which does not impose a heavy financial burden and which is administered by a safe route. Many ex-users of heroin are maintained on methadone over several years, but the agency prescribing the drug remains in control of the dosage and can endeavour to reduce this when it seems appropriate to do so. The methadone strategy is certainly not a 'cure' for heroin dependence (it simply transfers dependence from one drug to another), but methadone has fewer side-effects than heroin, it is safer and it may be somewhat easier to give up gradually. It eliminates, or at least greatly reduces, the craving for heroin, although it does not produce the same pleasurable effects as that drug.

Pharmacological substitutes are also available for a number of other psychoactive drugs, and other useful strategies involve progressively reducing the dosage and changing the route of administration. Familiar examples include low-alcohol drinks (which 'lower the dose'), and nicotine chewing gum and patches (which deliver nicotine in ways that are considerably safer than smoking).

Detoxification

Detoxification involves stopping all supplies of the drug on which the person is physically dependent and then caring for the person through the period of withdrawal. Although withdrawal can be exceptionally unpleasant, the media image of the addict battling through a living hell for several days is a highly exaggerated representation of the real situation. Even the effects of heroin detoxification, which is widely held to be one of the most traumatic examples of drug withdrawal, have been described by many ex-users as similar to those of severe influenza, and the majority of Vietnam veterans who had used opiates regularly reported very few ill-effects of withdrawal when they returned to the United States. Similar, relatively 'painless', withdrawal experiences are reported by many dependent drug users who undergo withdrawal at home or in a clinic.

However, if severe withdrawal symptoms are experienced, the drug-dependent person is likely to crave for the drug and may return to drug use in a bid to attenuate the symptoms. Faced with the prospect of an immediate relapse, those supporting the client may have to work very hard to encourage the person to persevere. In addition to offering support and encouragement, various drugs and psychological strategies may be employed to alleviate withdrawal symptoms. Vitamin C, tranquillizers, relaxation and acupuncture have all been used to some effect. The withdrawal stage can be a period of relatively high health risk, and close monitoring of the person's physical and psychological state is certainly advisable. Detoxification should be seen as an initial stage of treatment rather than as a complete treatment. There is no guarantee that a successful detoxification will result in long-term abstention from using the drug. Indeed, for many drugs (including heroin and alcohol), the majority of clients do in fact relapse following detoxification.

Residential treatment

Many treatment programmes are carried out on an outpatient basis, but some programmes require the client to be resident for a while in a hospital or hostel. In such residential settings the treatment can be more elaborate and more intensive, and the person is protected from unwanted contact with people who might encourage an early return to drug-taking. A specialist hostel can often provide a high level of psychological support and regular group therapy meetings. Most residential programmes aim to empower clients and to encourage them to take control of their own life, while at the same time offering respite and support. Other people (fellow residents and staff – some of whom may be ex-drug-dependent) may act as important models for the individual who is struggling to establish a viable drug-free lifestyle.

Must abstinence be the goal?

Must the aim of treatment for a drug problem be a complete abstinence from drug use? In recent years there has been a major shift in emphasis in many treatment programmes. Rather than striving exclusively to 'cure' the person of a 'need' for a particular drug, many current programmes focus principally and explicitly on harm limitation. Goals may include reducing the frequency of drug use, substituting a relatively safe drug for one that is highly danger-ous or ensuring that the person is fully aware of the dangers of using dirty needles and of sharing needles.

Thus a programme may be successful in its aims even if the person does not renounce the use of all dangerous substances. Some programmes have a hierarchy of goals, with harm limitation as a first step and complete absti-nence as a possible long-term objective. Certain users, however, refuse to accept a total rejection of the drug as their target, and decide that their personal goal is to continue to use the drug in a controlled and safe way. Such an aim is not entirely fanciful, for it appears that even some opiate addicts may return to limited and non-dependent drug use. Thus Stimson et al. (1978) provided evidence to show that people who had once been dependent on heroin were able to use opiates on isolated occasions for 'recreational' purposes without returning to their former dependence.

◄ Relapse ► ► ►

Only a minority of those who manage to stop using a drug remain abstinent forever, and in many cases it is only a matter of days or weeks before the drug is used again. In a study of an intensive treatment programme for opiate addicts, Gossop et al. (1990) found that 42 per cent of the sample had used an opiate drug again within one week of ending the treatment. How-ever, a single violation of a rule of abstinence does not necessarily signal a return to chronic drug use, and it is important to distinguish between a momentary 'lapse' and a return to regular drug-taking – a 'relapse' – which may or may not follow from this.

A lapse is usually triggered by exposure to a high-risk situation. This may be a situation in which the person becomes highly emotional, in which there is considerable peer pressure to start taking the drug again or in which environmental cues (such as needles and other drug paraphernalia) stimulate powerful craving. Once a lapse has occurred, the issue of whether or not this then leads to a complete relapse will rest largely on how the person judges the lapse and whether he or she perceives it as indicating a total loss of control over the use of the drug.

Factors which make relapse likely

A number of factors are known to increase the probability of relapse following treatment or self-managed change. Several of the most significant are:

1 Adverse effects of abstinence.
2 Exposure to high-risk situations.
3 Low self-efficacy.
4 High craving.
5 Abstinence violation effect orientation.
6 Absence of 'protective factors'.

In examining each of these factors, we will address the issue of how the risk of relapse might be reduced.

Adverse effects of abstinence The first days or weeks of abstinence constitute something of a trial period, and unpleasant withdrawal effects frequently provoke a relapse. If life without the drug turns out to be agreeable then the person is less likely to relapse than if life has become dreary or unpleasant. In the area of personal relationships, for example, abstinence may be greeted with warm enthusiasm by family members, but the person may miss the company of friends who are still using the drug. In terms of the direct effects of the drug, escape from any adverse physical symptoms will be recognized as a benefit, while the loss of the drug 'high' (or the loss of any 'therapeutic' effects of the drug) may be judged as a substantial cost. Thus, during the first days or weeks after coming off the drug the person will assess the value (the benefits minus the costs) of continued abstinence and compare this with an evaluation of the effects of a returning to the use of the drug (Sutton, 1987). The risk of relapse will be higher for those who regard a return to drug use in positive terms than for those who recognize that any further use of the drug would be damaging.

The initial effects of using a drug after some days or weeks of abstinence may be exceptionally positive, for the full power of the drug may be restored as a result of a decrease in the person's tolerance level. The drug may produce intense euphoria or may be extremely effective in reducing stress. Moreover, the use of the drug will alleviate craving, at least in the short term. Drug-related dangers are likely to be played down, and the fact that abstinence was maintained for some time before the relapse may convince the person that the next attempt to quit will be successful. Thus the manifest benefits of renewed drug use may be high, and the apparent costs low, resulting in a high positive value being assigned to continued use.

These considerations suggest a number of important ways of reducing the probability of relapse. It is helpful if any adverse withdrawal effects are minimized and if a high level of support is offered, particularly by friends and family, during withdrawal and for some time afterwards. Successful withdrawal should be seen as a major achievement, and a cause for congratulation (including self-congratulation). The potential rewards of a drug-free life should be emphasized, and the person helped to find alternative ways of attaining at least some of the benefits previously obtained by using the drug (for example, other ways of achieving stimulation or stress relief).

Exposure to high-risk situations   Studies of relapse following treatment for the abuse of alcohol, the opiates, nicotine and a number of other drugs indicate that the majority of lapses are triggered by exposure to high-risk situations (Cummings et al., 1980; Bradley et al., 1990). Particular elements associated with high risk include 'emergency', 'social pressure' and 'craving'. 'Emergency situations' are marked by extreme excitement or stress, often in response to some change in the external environment. An accident, a serious argument, the loss of a job or some other stressor (or a positive event such as a celebration) may lead a person to focus on short-term rather than long-term goals. Such a change in time perspective, together with an extreme mood state – anger, anxiety, boredom or elation – may prove a major challenge to the individual's resolve.

Some people who are striving to remain abstinent are subjected to strong social pressures to begin using the drug again. They may feel awkward and out of place in a social situation in which most other people are using the drug. Inveterate users may regard it as a challenge to talk someone who has recently rejected a drug back into using the substance, and they may be very forceful in their efforts at persuasion. Finally, some situations are associated with high risk because they increase the individual's craving. A visit to a setting previously associated with drug use, the sight of other people using the drug or the presence of needles and other drug equipment and trappings may increase the person's level of craving to an unbearable degree.

People can protect themselves from high-risk situations by means of three broad strategies: situation avoidance, situation escape and situation coping. A return to drug use is often the final step in a chain of behaviour that begins, for example, with a visit to a familiar place where drugs are readily available. This chain may be broken at several points; for example, by avoiding the venue altogether, by avoiding interaction with particular users who may exert pressure or by refusing any offer of a drug.

It is usually an easy matter for the person to identify potentially hazardous situations, and avoidance of dangerous venues and dangerous people may be something a counsellor might usefully explore. Positive alternatives also need to be explored, because a person is more likely to relapse if abstinence brings a lifestyle which is lonely and boring. As well as attempting to reduce the client's exposure to risk, a therapist may help the person to rehearse ways of escaping from hazardous situations. For example, clients may be encouraged to be assertive in the cause of their own safety and may be helped to practise such actions as withdrawing from a difficult social situation and refusing to discuss drug-related issues with anyone who might be concerned to challenge the necessity for continued abstinence.

Many different programmes have been devised to teach ex-users how to anticipate and cope effectively with high-risk situations. Marlatt's (1982) relapse-prevention programme teaches clients how to recognize dangerous social contexts and how to monitor their own reactions. The programme includes the use of cognitive restructuring techniques and training in behavioural skills. Effective responses to situations that might precipitate a relapse are described and practised, and various coping strategies rehearsed in imagination and role-play, before being tested in situations likely to present a real threat. Other programmes focus on helping the individual to develop coping strategies that will increase emotional control, reduce craving and maximize the individual's potential to resist temptation.

Low self-efficacy   'Self-efficacy' (in this context, a person's degree of confidence that he or she can overcome the drug problem) is an important factor in determining whether a person will follow a treatment programme conscientiously and whether treatment will be followed by relapse. People who have a high level of self-efficacy are less likely to relapse than those with a low level of self-efficacy (Rist and Wazl, 1983). Marlatt and Gordon (1985) suggest that exposure to high-risk situations may threaten the individual's self-efficacy, but that self-efficacy often increases significantly when the person develops effective coping skills.

Beck and Emery (1977) suggested that clients' judgements about relapse reflect certain automatic thoughts and images associated with drug use and drug abstinence. They developed a cognitive therapy programme to change clients' 'silent assumptions' – distorted cognitions and unrealistic attitudes that undermine confidence in the ability to control one's own behaviour. The aim is to empower clients and to help them to discover that they are not enslaved by the drug. Clients come to recognize that their behaviour need not be determined by external factors such as drug availability or social pressure.

Behavioural interventions have also been used to increase people's confidence in their ability to resist an available drug (Hodgson, 1982). For example, exposing clients to high-risk situations while helping them to cope can break the previously established link between 'drug situations' and drug-taking. This intervention demonstrates to clients that they can control their own responses and can cope effectively with situations in which drugs are present. A user who believes that he or she is powerless to resist any opportunity to use a particular drug will regard it as a foregone conclusion that any attempt at treatment will fail. Thus interventions which modify this view, and increase confidence in the ability to handle drug situations successfully, overcome an important barrier to effective treatment.

High craving   Relapse is likely if the person continues to experience a high level of craving for the drug over a long period. Generally, high craving derives from recollections of pleasurable drug effects and from negative withdrawal effects. Strategies devised to help individuals to cope with the effects of craving involve such elements as self-distraction, planned escape to a situation where drug-taking will be impossible and self-management of stress.

Certain situational cues, such as the sight of the drug or drug paraphernalia, or the presence of other people taking the drug, may greatly increase the level of craving. One way to attempt to reduce such 'reactive craving' is to expose the person to 'craving cues' (hypodermic syringes, for example, or videotapes of people injecting) in a clinic situation. Exposure to drug-related cues without the possibility of the usual drug-taking response will weaken the customary association and may reduce the strength of cue-triggered craving in real-life situations (Powell et al., 1993).

The ingestion of a small dose of the drug often stimulates intense craving. A single puff of a cigarette, for example, may sharply increase the desire to smoke. This is known as the 'priming' effect. Whether this has a physiological basis or whether it is entirely psychological remains a matter of controversy, but in many cases the priming effect is responsible for an initial lapse developing into a serious binge (which may then bring about a total relapse). Some therapists have attempted to weaken the priming effect by providing the client with a very small dose of the drug on a number of separate occasions, in a clinic situation in which further consumption of the drug is not an option. The idea is that this regime will weaken the priming effect and thus inoculate the person against the potentially serious consequences of a lapse occurring.

Abstinence violations effect (AVE) orientation   Some ex-users respond to any lapse by concluding that they are now 'back on' the drug, that their 'cure' has failed and that their attempt to quit, or their treatment programme, has failed. They may infer that they will never be able to remain abstinent, and that the drug will always have a powerful hold over them. Such thinking may lead the person to conclude that further resistance would be futile, and in deciding to 'give up giving up', the person effectively gives himself or herself permission to continue using the drug indefinitely (Eiser, 1978).

The tendency to infer that total relapse is inevitable from the fact that there has been a single lapse has been labelled the 'abstinence violation effect' (AVE) (Marlatt, 1978). The AVE has been shown to be relevant to smoking, dieting and the misuse of many drugs (including alcohol). An ex-smoker who smokes a single cigarette after many months of abstinence may conclude 'I'm back on cigarettes again' and therefore carry on smoking.

Ex-users who are committed to complete abstinence are especially likely to regard a momentary lapse as signalling a total return to problematic drug use. Thus treatment programmes that insist on total abstinence tend to reinforce the AVE by emphasizing the dire consequences of a single lapse. They deliver the message: 'as soon as you use the drug again, all your efforts to quit will have been completely wasted'. Portraying even the most minor lapse as totally critical (or 'very costly') may help some people to avoid a lapse forever, but it delivers quite a different message to anyone who does lapse on even one occasion. In effect, it informs such people that they are now 'back on' the drug. And those who believe this are likely to indulge further so that the minor lapse becomes a major relapse.

The alternative view, that a single slip does not signal an inevitable return to dependency, is much more helpful in such circumstances. Thus an ex-smoker who smokes one or two cigarettes at a party might conclude 'I broke my no-smoking rule on one exceptional occasion' and resolve never to let this happen again. The assumptions a person makes about a lapse are extremely critical, and some cognitive therapists have gone as far as guiding patients through 'planned relapses', so that they learn to avoid the defeatist thinking that may follow a minor infringement.

Absence of 'protective factors'   Relapse is less likely if the person who has recently stopped using a drug enjoys high levels of social and environmental support. Certain people (often family and friends) may have a powerful influence in encouraging continued abstinence and helping the person to cope with stressful events. Being in regular employment, having frequent social contact and having interests or hobbies can all help the person to lead a fulfilling life without drugs and to avoid the temptation to begin using the drug again (see Box 6.4). Thus, many effective intervention programmes follow clients through a rehabilitation period, helping them to re-establish and maintain relationships which are likely to prove supportive, helping to increase employment prospects and in some cases providing sheltered accommodation.

A realistic view of relapse

Although relapse rates are very high for some drugs (the opiates, in particular), relapse following a single treatment programme does not mean that all future attempts are doomed to failure. Many users have to pass through several treatment opportunities before they reach a stage of permanent abstinence or controlled drug usage. As the relapse process has become better understood, it has been possible to build into treatment programmes a number of features that make relapse less likely. Counselling, group therapy, cognitive and behavioural strategies help an individual to avoid or escape from situations in which there is a high risk of relapse, to cope with craving and to come through an occasional lapse without becoming dependent on the drug again. Such programmes seek to increase the individual's level of self-efficacy, to neutralize any feelings of being overwhelmed by the power of the drug and to strengthen 'protective factors'.

Gossop et al. (1990) suggest that treatments which help dependent drug users to gain self-confidence and to benefit from protective factors are likely to be associated with relatively low relapse rates. Following the model introduced by Prochaska and DiClemente (1984), they suggest that several attempts at treatment may be necessary before permanent change is achieved. The cumulative impact of several 'unsuccessful' treatment programmes, however, might be largely responsible for the eventual success.

Box 6.4
Factors Affecting the Outcome of Treatment for Opiate Dependency

Gossop et al. (1990) studied the factors which predicted the outcome of treatment given to dependent opiate users. When 77 clients who had successfully withdrawn from drugs were followed up six months after treatment, a high proportion were found to be using opiates again. In fact, 42 per cent of the sample had used such a drug within one week of completing their treatment.

The study attempted to discover what distinguished those who had relapsed from those who had managed to stay free of opiate use, and a particular focus of the study was an examination of the relationship between outcome and a number of possible 'protective factors'. Clients had been interviewed when first admitted for treatment, and were interviewed again immediately following treatment, and at a follow-up stage six months later. On admission, clients had been asked to rate a number of protective factors – people, activities or aspects of their social environment which they thought might prove helpful in their efforts to stay off drugs following treatment. Assessments were also made of the clients' coping strategies and skills, and the degree to which they were confident of their ability to avoid the use of opiates in the future.

From the many variables examined, two were found to be consistently predictive of the non-use of opiates following treatment – the overall number of protective factors reported by the client, and the client's level of confidence about remaining abstinent.

Prevention

Because many psychoactive drugs pose a serious health threat, considerable efforts have been made to deter people from using them. One important strategy for preventing the use of drugs is to limit their availability. Most societies have passed laws which ban the sale and possession of certain drugs, and continual efforts are made to curtail the growing of source plants, and the manufacture and distribution of illicit drugs.

The other major prevention strategy involves making drugs less attractive to potential users. This may be attempted by attaching heavy penalties to drug possession and drug use. The idea is that if legal sanctions increase the potential costs associated with drug use, some people will evaluate drug use as too costly ('not worth it') and will not indulge. However, the effectiveness of this tactic may depend on a (perceived) high rate of detection, and for some potential drug users the fact that a behaviour is illegal, and the slight threat of discovery and punishment, will actually add to the mystique and excitement of drug use. Another tactic used to make drug use less attractive involves informing people about the health dangers associated with the use of particular drugs. Most health promotion programmes have employed this strategy. The rationale is quite simple. If people know about the dangers associated with using psychoactive substances, it is argued, they will respond rationally and avoid using them.

However, health promotion programmes aimed at persuading people not to experiment with drugs have generally met with little success. One possible reason for this relates to the 'image' of agencies which typically devise and deliver anti-drug messages. In persuasive communication, the effectiveness of a message depends largely on the credibility and attractiveness of the source of the communication. People are likely to be persuaded by messages when they regard the source as well informed, unbiased and reasonable. They tend to dismiss information from a source that they regard as prejudiced and ill-informed. The relatively high effectiveness of AIDS-related health education targeted at homosexuals may relate to the fact that many of the agencies which provide the cautionary information were created by gay activists who are accepted as sympathetic rather than authoritarian. The agencies' use of street language in their documentation is also perceived as natural rather than phoney, and their literature is able to suggest attractive alternatives (i.e. various forms of 'safe sex') to the dangerous practices they are warning about.

By contrast, many of the health promotion agencies which attempt to persuade people not to use drugs are regarded by their target audience as moralistic, patronizing and shroud-waving. Cautions regarding drug use by sources perceived as 'straight' and 'establishment' may actually encourage drug-taking as an act of defiance by those who wish to rebel and to kick against social orthodoxy. Warnings issued about the risks involved are often viewed as highly exaggerated and may be dismissed as biased and unfounded. Furthermore, some people are likely to be attracted by the dangers described, and they may regard experiments with drugs as acts of daring.

Approaches to drug prevention that are highly medicalized, too legalistic or too 'respectable' are likely to be disregarded or ridiculed by the target audience. Recognition of the need to avoid such alienation has produced a number of innovations in drug prevention work in recent years. Increasingly, anti-drug messages are delivered by influential sports and music personalities, and peer models, rather than anonymously or by authority figures. People who have a history of drug use may be in a particularly powerful position to dissuade others from experimenting with drugs. Other changes relate to the content of anti-drug messages. Exaggeration of the dangers associated with drug use has been recognized as counterproductive, and current health promotion material is unsensational and acknowledges the distinction between the occasional recreational use of less harmful substances and the regular use of dangerous drugs. Furthermore, such material often includes advice on such 'harm limitation' practices as changing to a safer route of administration, limiting the amount of drug ingested and using only clean syringes. Some critics, however, protest that such advice may convey the false impression that dangerous drugs can be used safely and may encourage non-users to experiment with drugs.

Many health promotion efforts to prevent drug abuse have been directed at children and adolescents through school-based educational programmes and campaigns in the mass media. Early campaigns which focused on providing children with information about the dangers of drug use generally met with little success (Des Jarlais et al., 1987). More recent programmes have often employed young people to inform their peers about the negative effects of drug use, and they have focused more on immediate than on longer-term costs. Children have also been provided with suggestions about how to resist peer pressure towards drug use. By modelling resistance tactics (i.e. showing how the offer of a drug may be rejected), such programmes hope to inoculate children against dangerous influences.

Although campaigns following these lines tend to be more effective than traditional programmes (Botvin and Wills, 1985), even highly sophisticated programmes generally meet with only limited success. Thus one study involved five thousand 12 year olds, half of whom were given a series of 12 lessons aimed at the prevention of the early use of tobacco, alcohol and cannabis. Follow-up studies suggested that although the programme was successful in dissuading the children from using cigarettes and alcohol, it had very little effect on the use of cannabis. Furthermore, the programme had significantly less influence on boys than on girls (Graham et al., 1990).

◀Conclusions▶▶▶

Drug-taking is a social and psychological phenomenon. It is not a disease, although the persistent and heavy use of most drugs may eventually lead to serious physical or psychological disorders. Drug-taking is almost always a voluntary and considered action designed to maximize personal payoff. However, the judged benefits tend to fade over time, while the judged costs tend to rise, so that most people eventually reach a point at which they wish to stop using the drug. Many find that they are able to abstain with relatively little effort, but others find the task difficult or impossible. Some embark upon a prolonged struggle to overcome their drug use, either alone or with the help of professionals or voluntary workers. Many eventually succeed as a result of their own efforts, or as a result of counselling or another form of psychological intervention.

Many intervention programmes focus initially on harm limitation, and help users to avoid particularly dangerous practices such as injecting substances of dubious composition, or sharing needles. Detoxification is recognized as an early step in the treatment of cases involving physical dependence, and programmes now include many strategies focused on rehabilitation and relapse prevention.

It is accepted that a high proportion of those who participate in drug treatment programmes will relapse, but it is also recognized that a succession of treatment attempts may have an additive effect. Prevention programmes have traditionally emphasized (and sometimes exaggerated) the longer-term dangers of drug use, but contemporary programmes communicate more authentic and more credible messages. This change, and the increased use of peers as sources of drug information, may have increased the effectiveness of drug prevention programmes to some degree, but most programmes still have a very limited impact.

◄Further Reading►►►

Palfai, T. and Jankiewicz, H. (1991) *Drugs and Human Behavior*. Dubuque, IA: Wm C. Brown.

A detailed presentation of the nature and effects of psychoactive drugs, focusing more on pharmacological and behavioural aspects than on social and applied aspects.

McMurran, M. (1994) *The Psychology of Addiction*. London: Taylor & Francis.

An overview of psychological approaches to understanding addictions (not only to drugs and alcohol but also to gambling, overeating and excessive sexuality). Describes initiation, maintenance, dependence and change, and emphasizes the social, psychological and emotional consequences of addiction.

Gossop, M. (1987) *Living with Drugs*. Aldershot: Wildwood Smith.

Places drug use in a broad social and psychological context. Includes material on the social history of drug use and provides a balanced and non-sensational view of contemporary drug-taking.

Biernacki, P. (1986) *Pathways from Heroin Addiction: Recovery without Treatment*. Philadelphia, PA: Temple University Press.

Report of an extensive social psychological study of how 100 heroin addicts managed to give up their use of the drug without formal treatment. Describes their strategies and subsequent feelings about heroin and addiction.

Marlatt, G.A. and Gordon, J.R. (1985) *Relapse Prevention: Maintenance Strategies in the Treatment of Addictive Behaviors*. New York: Guilford Press.

The key work describing the model of relapse and relapse prevention developed over many years by Marlatt and his colleagues.

◄Discussion Points►►►

1   Consider the various reasons why a person might decide to take an illegal psychoactive drug. Can such a decision ever be regarded as 'rational'?
2   Discuss the meaning of the terms 'tolerance', 'dependence' and 'addiction'. Illustrate your account with examples relating to commonly used and abused substances (including alcohol).
3   Why might a person who has been using a drug for some time decide to stop using it? Discuss the processes involved in making such a decision.
4   Why do many people who are initially successful in giving up drugs relapse? What can be done to help prevent relapse?
5   Informing drug users about how potentially dangerous drugs might be used in relatively safe ways is known as the 'harm reduction' strategy. Discuss the possible psychological effects of adopting this intervention strategy.
6   Most 'drug prevention programmes' appear to have had very limited success in dissuading people from taking illegal drugs. Focusing on relevant psychological aspects, suggest how the effectiveness of such a programme might be optimized.

7 Sexual Dysfunction and Sexual Disorders

Human sexual behaviour reflects biological, psychological and social influences. A distinction is made between problems of sexual 'performance' (commonly labelled 'sexual dysfunction') and problems of gender identity and sexual orientation (often labelled 'sexual disorders').

Sexual dysfunction is experienced by approximately half of all married and cohabiting couples at some time during their relationship, and may take the form of a low level of sexual desire, difficulties with sexual arousal or problems in controlling or achieving orgasm.

Before considering unusual forms of sexual orientation, we will examine the nature and origins of homosexuality, not because this is a dysfunction or a disorder, but because it provides an opportunity to discuss a number of general issues relating to sexual orientation. We then discuss gender identity disorder, or 'transsexualism', which raises fundamental issues relating to personal identity. Finally, we will address the 'paraphilias', a broad range of sexual disorders that includes paedophilia, transvestism, exhibitionism, fetishism, voyeurism and sadomasochism.

◄Human Sexuality►►

Sexual behaviour is the means to reproduction in most animal species, which will survive only if mating is successfully accomplished. Thus the major biological function of sexual behaviour is procreation. In mammalian species, at least, effective sexual performance is dependent on sexual interest and sexual arousal.

There is no single 'sex centre' in the brain. Instead, many different areas play different roles. The level of sexual desire is largely controlled by activity in certain areas of the lower brain, particularly within the hypothalamus, but in higher mammals sexual arousal is also strongly influenced by the activity of 'higher' cortical structures. This is especially true of humans. The sex hormones, which are essential for the normal development and functioning of the reproductive system, are produced by the gonads (the testes and the ovaries) under the control of the anterior lobe of the pituitary gland. The male sex hormones are known as androgens, the principal androgen being testosterone. The oestrogens are female sex hormones produced primarily by the ovaries.

Although the sex hormones are extremely important in regulating physical changes at puberty and many of the physiological aspects of sexuality and reproduction, they seem to play a limited role in human sexual motivation and behaviour. An injection of testosterone may increase the sexual interest and sexual activity of a man with a marked androgen deficiency, but surgical castration, which markedly reduces the rate of testosterone production, has a limited effect on sexual appetite and sexual behaviour. Some castrated men experience a decreased interest in sex and have problems in achieving and maintaining an erection, but many castrated men remain potent and sexually active for many years.

Similarly, the oestrogens are responsible for the bodily changes during puberty, for the regulation of the menstrual cycle and for a host of effects throughout pregnancy and during the stage of breastfeeding, but they appear to have little effect on women's sexual interest or behaviour. On the other hand, if an androgen is administered to a woman it tends to increase her sexual sensitivity and level of sexual desire (Bancroft, 1984; Riley, 1988). By contrast, the oestrogens appear to lower male sexual desire and performance.

A consideration of only the biological aspects would provide a very distorted picture of human sexuality. Psychological and social factors must feature prominently in any satisfactory account of the nature of the human sexual response and the nature of sexual dysfunction. The cultural context, and the individual's beliefs, attitudes and personal history, are all critical determinants of sexual behaviour. For this reason, studies of the sexual behaviour of other species cannot provide a satisfactory basis for understanding human sexual activity. One of the pioneers of research into the psychobiology of sex, C. S. Beach, concluded from his extensive studies of the sexual behaviour of many species that 'human sexuality is about as closely related to the mating behaviours of other species as human language is related to animal communication, a relationship that is distant indeed' (Beach, 1977, p. 334).

Human sexuality is not simply instinctual but is massively influenced by social learning. Human sexual attraction and sexual expression are shaped to a considerable degree by personal experiences, attitudes and values, which are in turn affected by powerful cultural forces. The similarities and differences between cultures with regard to sexual prohibitions, for example, are interesting and instructive. Thus sexual relationships between parents and children, and between siblings, are universally proscribed, but cultures differ widely regarding which other sexual liaisons are forbidden. And as well as laying down rules concerning sexuality, all cultures have a set of beliefs about sex which together constitute the sexual knowledge of that culture. Ignorance concerning sexual matters, and stringent rules concerning sexuality, have a powerful influence on sexual behaviour and may play a significant part in triggering or maintaining dysfunction.

Studies of human sexuality

Alfred Kinsey and his colleagues published the book *Sexual Behavior in the Human Male* in 1948. This was followed five years later by a companion volume, *Sexual Behavior in the Human Female*. These reports were the product of detailed interviews with 17 000 subjects about their personal sexual history. At a time when many people still believed that masturbation would inevitably lead to all manner of serious physical and psychological ills, Kinsey and his colleagues showed that ultimately 95 per cent males and 60 per cent females masturbate to orgasm.

Kinsey also found that homosexual activity was much more common than had previously been believed, with a third of males and one in eight females reporting that they had experienced an orgasm during a homosexual encounter. Furthermore, 4 per cent of males and 2 per cent of females were categorized by Kinsey as 'exclusively homosexual'. Many estimates since that time have quoted similar proportions, although some studies have produced sharply contrasting results. Thus a large-scale British survey (Wellings et al., 1994) found that only 5.2 per cent of the males and 2.6 per cent of the females in the sample (of over 18 000 adults) reported having experienced any homosexual contact and that only 1 per cent of men and 0.3 per cent of women reported their sexual experiences as 'mostly homosexual' or 'only homosexual'.

◄The Sexual Response Cycle►►►

Sexual arousal follows a general course whereby it increases, reaches a peak and then decreases. The first detailed analysis of the human sexual response cycle was produced by Masters and Johnson (1966), following their close monitoring of the sexual responses of thousands of subjects in extensive laboratory studies. Further analysis was then provided by Kaplan (1974). Four phases are now commonly distinguished. The initial phase (sometimes labelled the 'appetitive phase') is one in which the person becomes sexual interested and experiences sexual desire. The next stage ('the excitement phase') involves a gradual increase of excitement, which may build up until it reaches a plateau. This level of arousal may be maintained for some time until the acute 'orgasm phase' occurs, following which there is a rapid decrease in sexual excitement ('the resolution phase'). This widely accepted model of the human sexual response is outlined in Box 7.1.

Box 7.1
The Human Sexual Response Cycle

The appetitive stage

The person becomes interested in sex, perhaps engages in sexual fantasies and is motivated to engage in sexual activity. Sexual arousal is often stimulated by environmental aspects, and the person may seek out stimuli that will induce sexual excitement.

The excitement stage

A subjective feeling of sexual arousal and pleasure accompanied by physiological changes. These include erection of the penis and retraction of the testes in men, and clitoral and nipple erection and increased vaginal lubrication in women. Peripheral changes include raised blood pressure and heart rate changes.

Orgasm

The peak of sexual excitement. Subjectively experienced as intensely pleasurable and exhilarating, and sometimes involving feelings of loss of control (or even partial loss of consciousness), orgasm is accompanied by elevated muscle tension and many other physiological changes. Male orgasm is almost always accompanied by ejaculation, with most men becoming aware that ejaculation is imminent (the point of 'ejaculatory inevitability') some 2 seconds or so before it actually occurs. A volume of semen (usually between 1 and 6 millilitres) is ejected in rhythmic contractions at a rate of just under one per second.

There has long been considerable controversy about the nature of the female orgasm. Some authorities maintain that there are two distinct types of orgasm – vaginal and clitoral. Freud made this distinction and claimed that women who could achieve orgasm only by means of clitoral stimulation were psychologically immature. Kinsey, and later Masters and Johnson, asserted that all female orgasms were similar whatever the means of stimulation used. Many women do report that they can distinguish subjectively between two types of orgasm (Fisher, 1973), but it has not been possible to make such a differentiation in physiological terms. The female orgasm involves a number of intense rhythmic contractions (usually five to eight in number) of the muscles in the outer part of the vagina.

Starting just before orgasm, heart rate and blood pressure increase, and hyperventilation occurs. The majority of women and around a quarter of men develop a short-lived rash on the chest and neck ('the sex flush'). Male orgasm (with the ejaculation of semen) clearly has an important reproductive function, but the female orgasm does not appear to have such a function.

The resolution stage

The decrease of arousal following orgasm. Subjectively, there is an experience of calmness. Physiologically, the symptoms of arousal return towards normal levels.

Following the male orgasm there is a period within which the man cannot be further stimulated to erection or sexual excitement. The duration of this 'refractory period' increases with age. Women, however, may be further stimulated immediately after orgasm, and this means that some women are capable of multiple orgasms.

◀Sexual Dysfunction▶▶▶

Sexual problems can be broadly classified in terms of the stage of the response cycle at which the dysfunction becomes apparent. Thus lack of sexual interest is a problem of the appetitive stage. Problems associated with the excitement stage include, for men, failure to achieve or maintain an erection and, for women, failure to produce adequate lubrication. Finally, both men and women may have problems at the orgasm stage. No special problems are associated with the resolution stage.

Male sexual dysfunction

Low sexual desire   Men who rarely or never experience a desire for sexual activity engage in few sexual fantasies and have little motivation to initiate sexual contact, although they may become aroused if they are sexually stimulated. A partner may be particularly disturbed by the man's lack of sexual desire if she feels that it reflects his general dissatisfaction with the relationship or that it signifies that he no longer finds her sexually attractive.

Premature ejaculation   Estimates of the prevalence of premature ejaculation vary substantially, reflecting major differences in the criteria used to define the dysfunction. Thus, according to one definition, premature ejaculation is a habitual inability to delay ejaculation for 30 seconds after the penis has been inserted into the vagina, whereas another definition states that it is the inability, on at least 50 per cent of occasions of sexual intercourse, to delay ejaculation until the partner has achieved orgasm. Clearly, these two extremely different attempts at an 'objective' definition will lead to very different prevalence estimates. In clinical practice the principal criterion for recognizing a problem of premature ejaculation is likely to be the man's dissatisfaction with his capacity to delay ejaculation.

Primary erectile disorder   The term 'impotence' was previously used to refer to an inability to achieve an erection. The term 'erectile disorder' is now preferred, and men who are said to be suffering from primary erectile disorder have never been successful in maintaining an erection long enough to complete the act of intercourse.

Secondary erectile disorder   Men who suffer from secondary erectile disorder have previously been able to maintain an erection long enough to reach a satisfactory climax but are no longer able to achieve this. It should be noted, however, that occasional difficulties in achieving or maintaining an erection are almost universal and do not constitute 'a dysfunction'. If a man is no longer able to achieve an erection under any circumstances, the dysfunction may be the result of a physical problem, perhaps involving either the vascular system or the nervous system. However, if a man is able to maintain an erection when masturbating, but cannot maintain an erection throughout intercourse, then psychological factors are probably responsible, at least in part.

Ejaculatory failure   Ejaculatory failure is a relatively uncommon problem in which the man is unable to ejaculate into the vagina even though he has no difficulty in maintaining an erection. Most men who have this problem are able to masturbate to a climax, suggesting that the problem is psychological rather than physiological.

Painful intercourse (dyspareunia)   Few men experience pain during intercourse, and when pain does occur it is usually the result of an infection or of a slight anatomical defect that prevents the foreskin from fully retracting.

Female sexual dysfunction

Sexual desire disorders   Some estimates suggest that as many as one-third of women lose interest in sex for one or more prolonged periods. For many women this does not cause difficulty or distress, but some women do become anxious or depressed, often because they feel their lack of interest in sex to be 'unnatural'. The partner may interpret the woman's low sexual responsiveness as a sign of rejection.

'Sexual aversion' is a more extreme condition which also affects the appetitive phase of the sexual response cycle. Some people develop a profound distaste for all sexual activity, or for all genital contact, or for all heterosexual contact. The problem appears to be uncommon in men and affects only a small proportion of women.

Primary orgasmic dysfunction   Women who have never been able to achieve an orgasm by any means (including masturbation) are said to be suffering from primary orgasmic dysfunction (but see Box 7.2 for an alternative view).

Secondary orgasmic dysfunction   Women who have previously experienced orgasm regularly during intercourse but then fail to achieve a climax over a prolonged period may be said to be suffering from 'secondary orgasmic failure'. However, it should be emphasized that intercourse is rarely the most effective means by which a woman can achieve orgasm. Many women never experience orgasm during intercourse and it is not acceptable that such women should be identified as suffering from an abnormal psychological condition.

Vaginismus   Vaginismus is a severe tightening or spasm of the outer third of the vagina which usually makes it impossible for the woman to have intercourse.

Painful intercourse (dyspareunia)   Some women experience a burning or aching sensation in the vagina whenever intercourse is attempted. Such pain is commonly associated with infection, vaginismus or inadequate vaginal lubrication.

◀Aetiology of Sexual Dysfunction▶▶▶

There are many disparate causes of sexual dysfunction. Physiological factors are often implicated as primary causes, but many psychological elements also play a causal role. They may act as predisposing factors, precipitating factors or maintaining factors.

General lack of physical health   Any serious illness is likely to distract a person from sexual concerns. Those who are in pain or discomfort, who lack energy or who are anxious about their general state of health are likely to have little interest in sex. Thus a wide range of medical conditions which have no specific effect on sexual functioning may nevertheless have dramatic consequences for the couple's sexual activity together.

Specific physical (sexual) problems   Some physical disorders have a direct effect on sexual performance. Thus men with diabetes, vascular problems or certain neurological conditions may develop erectile problems, and sexual difficulties may result from spinal injuries and other disabling conditions, such as multiple sclerosis. A number of men lack sexual interest because they have an abnormally low level of sex hormone. Some women find sexual intercourse painful due to pelvic inflammatory disease or vaginal infection.

Drug effects   Sexual dysfunction may arise as a side-effect of drugs taken to alleviate physical conditions such as hypertension or epilepsy, although the newer drugs used to treat such conditions are generally free of such side-effects. Oral contraceptives may inhibit vaginal lubrication and in some cases appear to reduce sexual interest. A number of psychotropic drugs, including some anti-depressants and major tranquillizers, may also contribute to the development of various forms of sexual dysfunction.

The short-term effects of alcohol on sexual performance are well known. In small doses, alcohol may reduce inhibitions and increase the level of sexual desire, but excessive consumption often leads to temporary erectile failure in men. The chronic abuse of alcohol usually results in a lowering of sexual interest and performance, and can bring about persistent erectile failure (Hawton, 1985).

General lack of psychological well-being   People who are feeling depressed or anxious, for whatever reason, often lose interest in sex or find that they are unable to become sexually aroused. Stress generated in the work environment, for example, may lead to tension and anxiety during sexual intercourse. Low self-esteem and feelings of helplessness may also contribute to the development of various forms of sexual dysfunction.

Feelings of unattractiveness   People who have negative feelings about their body are likely to be reticent and anxious about relating sexually to their partner. Many men and women are highly sensitive and self-critical about their general body shape or about some specific aspect of their appearance. The onset of menopause is a time of a rapid decline in sexual confidence for some women (Studd and Thom, 1981), and certain disfiguring conditions often result in sexual avoidance and low sexual motivation. Disfiguring surgical interventions such as a colostomy or a mastectomy often lead to a substantal and immediate reduction in sexual interest (Maguire et al., 1978).

Sexual ignorance and negative sexual attitudes   Masters and Johnson suggested that ignorance of sexual physiology was responsible for much of the sexual dysfunction that they encountered. The widespread dissemination of research findings and the extensive discussion of sexual matters in the media may have helped to correct certain misperceptions. However, many people remain ignorant of key facts about sexuality, many couples remain too embarrassed to talk openly together about their sexual relationships and many still hold on to the irrational and dysfunctional attitudes identified by Masters and Johnson (including, for example, a 'double standard' applied to male and female sexual conduct).

Sexual fears and performance anxiety   Anxiety can be a powerful inhibitor of sexual responsiveness. A fear of pregnancy or of contracting a sexually transmitted disease may lead to tension when the person engages in sexual activity. However, it would be erroneous to assume that anxiety is always antagonistic to sexual arousal. In many circumstances mild anxiety can in fact act as a sexual stimulant (Norton and Jehu, 1984). Thus some people deliberately engage in various forms of reckless or 'naughty' behaviour in order to achieve heightened sexual arousal.

General relationship problems   Sexual dysfunction is sometimes, but not always, a sign of fundamental problems in the relationship between the partners. Couples may find it difficult to engage in sexual activity together when their relationship is insecure or highly conflictual.

Sexual relationship problems   Even if a relationship is gratifying and harmonious in other respects, the partners may find that they are in some way 'sexually incompatible'. There may be substantial discrepancies between the partners, for example, in their views on how often they should have intercourse or what activities their love-making should include. Such differences are particularly likely to lead to long-term resentment if the couple find it difficult to discuss sexual matters openly. Reticence about communicating sexual preferences can produce long-term frustrations, and if there is a lack of dialogue a minor problem may become a major source of distress. If other aspects of their life together are gratifying, such a couple may seek to preserve their relationship by simply avoiding all sexual contact. This can be a successful strategy, but for many couples prolonged sexual abstinence becomes a source of growing dissatisfaction and may eventually jeopardize the relationship.

Previous sexual trauma In some cases, sexual dysfunction is a legacy of a chilhood sexual attack. Some survivors of child sexual abuse develop an aversion to sex, and others experience low sexual interest, difficulties with arousal or orgasm, or pain during intercourse (Jehu, 1988). Although many adults who were sexually molested as children do experience sexual problems, it is important to recognize that such long-term effects are by no means inevitable or universal, and that when they do occur they can often be successfully treated (Baker and Duncan, 1985; Jehu, 1988).

Rape and other forms of sexual assault in adulthood are associated with many kinds of post-traumatic effect, including sexual dysfunction (Kilpatrick and Amick, 1985). Many rape victims report long-term feelings of being 'soiled', and some find it difficult or impossible to resume sexual contact with their partner. It must be emphasized, however, that rape, like child sexual abuse, has a very variable psychological outcome (Ellis, 1985).

Complex multicausal patterns Most sexual problems arise from a combination of causes, and it is important to recognize the distinction between the initial causes (or the 'precipitating factors') and the factors which serve to maintain the problem. It should also be recognized that there are many vicious circles which may have helped to shape the situation by the time the problem is brought to the attention of a therapist.

◀Treatment of Sexual Dysfunction▶ ▶ ▶

Sexual dysfunction can arise from any of a large number of different causes, and the combined effect of several factors may be involved in the development and maintenance of such a dysfunction. The complex causal nature of sexual dysfunction suggests that effective intervention might be achieved through a variety of different approaches, and that different modes of treatment might be appropriate for different cases. We can use the list of aetiological factors considered above as a framework for considering the therapeutic elements often included in treatment programmes. The specific strategies used for treating particular forms of sexual dysfunction will then be discussed.

General lack of physical health If a person is freed from pain or discomfort, or becomes more agile, sexual activities are likely to be less of a problem. However, in some cases medical treatment will prove ineffective, or the person may be suffering from á chronic disabling condition. In such circumstances, couples may be helped to explore alternative positions for intercourse, and other forms of sexual contact, so that mutual satisfaction can be gained by means of activities which produce less discomfort, or are less demanding of physical effort (Davies, 1988).

Specific physical (sexual) problems   When a physical disorder has a direct effect on sexual performance, the sexual problem may be addressed by treating the primary disorder. If this is not possible, then intervention may focus more specifically on the sexual symptoms. Thus vaginal dryness, which may occur during the menopause as an effect of hormonal imbalances, may be remedied simply but effectively by the use of lubricant creams or jellies. When erectile failure results from a vascular or neurological condition, it may be possible to produce an erection by means of a physical intervention. Thus a drug might be injected directly into the penis or a prosthesis might be implanted surgically.

Drug effects   When sexual dysfunction is a side-effect of a prescribed drug, it may be possible to adjust the individual's medication so that the unwanted effects disappear. When the sexual problem relates to the use of non-prescribed drugs or alcohol, treatment may be directed towards the provision of help for the drug use.

General lack of psychological well-being   Depression, anxiety, stress and low self-esteem are often implicated in sexual dysfunction, and may be treated using various forms of psychological therapy or psychotropic medication. Such treatments therefore focus on the underlying psychological problem rather than on the sexual problem which has arisen as a consequence. If the sexual dysfunction appears to be the result of stress generated within the relationship, marital psychotherapy may be useful. This may focus on the sexual or the non-sexual aspects of the relationship, or on both.

Feeling of unattractiveness   Oversensitivity about body shape, or about breast or penis size, can often be eliminated through supportive counselling, and marital therapy will often reveal to one partner that the other is less critical than had been imagined. However, in some cases, the negative feelings which people have about their bodies may be reasonable. In some cases such feelings relate to aspects that are anemable to change, and it might prove useful to give advice about dress sense, dieting or even cosmetic surgery. In all such cases the aim will be to increase the person's self-confidence so that he or she will be less self-critical and more relaxed and responsive in sexual situations. Those who have been through surgery (a colostomy or a mastectomy, for example) may benefit from psychological help aimed at maintaining their sexual self-esteem and from practical advice about sexual contact after recovery from surgery.

Sexual ignorance and negative sexual attitudes   Many sexual problems reflect an ignorance about sexual physiology and sexual psychology, and accurate information about such issues can provide reassurance, reduce uncertainty and enable the person to arouse a partner more successfully.

Therapists who apply specific cognitive change strategies endeavour to identify and modify problematic assumptions about sex, such as 'intercourse is the only satisfying form of sexual contact' (Baker, 1993). They may also attempt to change cognitions which may interfere with sexual performance, including thoughts about the possible consequences of 'sexual failure' (Baker and de Silva, 1988). Thus, cognitive interventions are used not only to change individuals' (or couples') general belief systems regarding sex but also to change the nature of cognitive responses to sexual difficulties and setbacks.

Sexual fears and performance anxiety   The educational component of sex therapy may do much to allay fears and guilt about particular aspects of sexuality, and the promotion of communication between the partners often helps to dispel anxieties about the partner's judgements. A therapist is likely to highlight the dangers of 'spectatorism' (obsessive self-monitoring of sexual performance) and to encourage the couple to be more relaxed during their sexual encounters.

General relationship problems   If it is recognized that sexual dysfunction is a sign of basic relationship problems, then therapy may focus on solving these difficulties. Marital psychotherapy may focus on long-term conflicts, on insecurities in the relationship or on hidden resentment.

Sexual relationship problems   Partners who maintain respect for one another, but who regard themselves as sexually incompatible, can be helped to articulate the nature of their apparent incompatibility. In some cases the partners need space and 'permission' to discuss their sexual preferences, and the couple may benefit from a relaxed discussion of possible routes back to a satisfactory sexual relationship.

Previous sexual trauma   When sexual dysfunction is associated with a partner's previous sexual trauma (as a victim of child sexual abuse, or of rape, for example), individual psychotherapy or couple therapy can often help the survivor to come to terms with the earlier victimization. Jehu (1988) has described a variety of interventions used to treat female survivors of child sexual abuse for sexual dysfunction and other problems, and a detailed treatment programme for women who become sexually dysfunctional following rape was developed by Becker and Skinner (1983).

Treatment programmes

Sex therapy is now widely available, and between a half and two-thirds of sexually dysfunctional couples experience considerable improvement following treatment (Barlow et al., 1973). Some therapists pay special attention to possible physical reasons for the couple's problem, while others are especially concerned with the dynamics of the partners' relationship.

Many of the techniques now used extensively to treat sexual dysfunction were introduced by William Masters, a gynaecologist, and Virginia Johnson, a social scientist, who collaborated on a long-term and wide-ranging human sexuality research programme at the Reproductive Biology Research Foundation in St Louis, Missouri. Following 15 years of research involving over 500 sexually dysfunctional couples, they published a detailed report of their work in the book *Human Sexual Inadequacy* (1970), and this revolutionized thinking and practice in the field of sex therapy. Indeed, in a review of developments in the field up to the mid-1980s, Cole and Dryden (1988) concluded that there had been little dramatic change since the publication of the Masters and Johnson book.

The Masters and Johnson approach The 'classical' Masters and Johnson treatment programme involved intensive therapy with a couple over a two-week period. Couples booked into a hotel near the clinic and took part in a full-time therapeutic programme with two therapists, one male and one female. During the first stage of the treatment programme, the nature of the therapeutic approach was explained and couples were asked to refrain from any form of sexual activity until directed by the therapists. Detailed medical and sexual histories were then taken, and physical examinations conducted.

Couples were first introduced to the practice of the 'sensate focus', which is still widely used and focuses on touching. Although touch is a key element in intimate communication, few couples exploit the full potential of non-genital touching as a way of arousing loving and sexual feelings. The sensate focus strategy encourages partners to explore the power of touch, to massage each other and to fondle and caress each other in non-sexual ways. It teaches partners how to give and how to receive pleasurable touch.

When both partners are comfortable and unselfconscious in applying the sensate focus, the next phase involves each partner directing the other's hands to perform the movements that provide the most (non-genital) pleasure. Gradually, the body areas included in the sensate focus manipulations are extended to include the genital regions, although therapists caution couples that this should not prompt them to attempt intercourse.

Following the exploratory, educational and sensate focus stages of treatment, couples who participated in the Masters and Johnson programme were helped to overcome the particular dysfunction that had brought them to the clinic. They were guided in a step-by-step fashion through various techniques for achieving sexual satisfaction and overcoming any problems encountered at various stages of the response cycle. Many of the techniques introduced by the team involve the use of special positions for intercourse and a gradual controlled build up of sexual excitement.

Specific forms of male dysfunction

Low sexual desire and aversion to sex For men, low sexual interest is often a symptom of depression, and treatment for depression will often lead to a return of sexual drive. In some other cases, the problem is secondary to another form of sexual dysfunction. For example, a man who is constantly embarrassed by a failure to maintain an erection, or who invariably ejaculates within a few seconds of entering the partner's vagina, may simply 'give up on sex'. If the primary sexual problem is satisfactorily addressed, however, the man's sexual interest is likely to return. In rare cases, a lack of sexual interest results from a major deficiency in androgen levels, and in such cases hormone therapy can be an effective treatment.

Premature ejaculation   As a treatment for premature ejaculation, Masters and Johnson introduced the highly effective 'squeeze technique'. When erection is achieved, the woman holds the penis between the thumb and two fingers, just below the glans of the penis, and squeezes hard for a few seconds. Further stimulation may then be needed to restore the full erection, and the squeeze is then applied again. The cycle may need to be repeated several times until the man is able to maintain the erection while the penis is squeezed.

When the squeeze technique has been successfully applied a number of times, the penis is inserted into the vagina, and remains motionless. The 'woman superior position' is adopted (the man reclines and his partner squats on him), because this is a much easier position in which to maintain ejaculatory control than the customary 'male superior position'. After practising the squeeze and the so-called 'quiet vagina' technique for some days, the man is instructed to make slight movements inside the vagina for about 15 minutes, following which he proceeds to ejaculation. After six months or so, ejaculatory control may be possible in any position. This approach is widely used and is highly effective. In their initial report, Masters and Johnson cited a 96 per cent success rate.

Erectile disorders   Masters and Johnson suggested that erectile difficulties usually stem from psychological precursors. They linked primary erectile disorder to such causes as homosexual feelings which are 'denied' by the man, rigid adherence to religious views that identify sexuality with 'sin' and traumatic sexual experiences (for example, of initial failure at intercourse). The development of secondary erectile disorder, following perhaps years of successful sexual acitivity, was found to be related to a wide variety of causes, including various psychological disorders, excessive use of alcohol and a growing awareness of a homosexual orientation. Masters and Johnson suggested that the problem frequently followed a major loss of confidence or acute stress, and they reported that it sometimes developed after a history of premature ejaculation.

Recent research has led many people to revise their views of the causes of both primary and secondary erectile failure, and to assign more importance than Masters and Johnson to physical causes. It has been suggested that organic conditions, including diabetes, neurological disorders, hormonal disorders and vascular conditions, may be the primary cause in up to a half of all cases (Mohr and Beutler, 1990).

Approaches to the treatment of this condition reflect the various factors that have been identified as possible causes. Counselling or psychotherapy has been used, for example, to address issues relating to religious views of sexuality, or a homosexual orientation, so that the client comes to recognize the link and can decide whether any change would be desirable. Other cases have been treated using sensate focus followed by a gradual progression to full sexual contact, usually employing the female-dominant position.

Masters and Johnson reported success with 60 per cent of cases of primary erectile failure and 74 per cent of cases of secondary erectile failure. Although these figures appear high, the authors reported that of all the conditions they treated, erectile failure was the most resistant to treatment.

In the 1980s several physical methods of treatment came to be used more widely (Kaplan, 1990). Drugs such as papaverine and prostaglandin, when self-injected directly into the erectile tissue of the penis, produce an erection which usually lasts for over an hour. Surgical procedures have also been developed which allow various types of prosthesis to be implanted into the penis.

Ejaculatory incompetence   Some men have no difficulty in maintaining an erection but are unable to ejaculate into the vagina. The antecedents of ejaculatory incompetence include a strong fear of impregnating the partner, and a lack of interest in (or active dislike of) the partner. In some cases the ejaculatory response appears to have become blocked following the experience of a traumatic event. Thus Masters and Johnson reported several cases of men who had been severely criticized or punished during adolescence when their parents discovered them masturbating.

A therapist will attempt to identify any traumatic experiences, fears or attitudes that might explain why the problem has arisen. In addition, a detailed assessment of changes in the severity of the problem over time, and any variation over different situations (and, perhaps, with different partners), will often lead to the identification of a useful focus for treatment.

It will be emphasized that ejaculation is something which happens naturally, and that failure to ejaculate does not reflect a lack of skill or motivation. In many cases sensate focus is used, and gradually progress to the woman masturbating her partner to a climax. Following this there is a gradual transfer from masturbation to intercourse. Thus, while maintaining the female-dominant position the woman teases the penis to erection before inserting it into the vagina. As the therapy proceeds, the penis is inserted into the vagina at earlier stages until eventually the man is able to ejaculate during intercourse without the need for an intervening phase of masturbation.

Specific forms of female dysfunction

Female sexual dysfunction has become an issue of considerable controversy. While the majority of sexologists, sex therapists and health professionals concur with the 'established' view of female sexuality and female dysfunction, derived principally from the work of Masters and Johnson, many critics claim that the field misrepresents female sexuality and is grossly inaccurate in its characterization of the sexual problems women experience. The 'orthodox' picture of the nature and treatment of female dysfunction is presented below. The alternative perspective on female sexual dysfunction is presented in Box 7.2.

Box 7.2
Female Dysfunction: an Alternative Perspective

A number of writers and therapists, many of them feminists, have sharply criticized sexology and sex therapy as value-laden and biased towards the male sexual experience and male sexual values. Such critics complain that sex therapy is 'performance-oriented' and that 'sex' is often equated with heterosexual penetrative intercourse. Men may equate 'the sexual act' with penetrative intercourse culminating in orgasm, it is argued, but female sexuality is essentially different. It is asserted that women's natural sexual interests focus on intimacy within the context of a relationship. Women who have discovered their own sexual nature, it is suggested, do not equate sex with penetrative intercourse and are unconcerned about attaining orgasm during intercourse.

It is recognized, however, that many women are influenced by the dominant cultural view of sexuality (sometimes referred to as the 'phallocentric view'), and it is claimed that gender-biased research and clinical work, and misrepresentations of sexuality in the media, lead many women to judge their own sexuality (including their own sexual adequacy or inadequacy) according to inappropriate 'male' criteria. One commentator wrote: 'In the case of sex, it appears that men, via science, have gained control of what is considered "normal" and "healthy"' (Nicholson, 1993, p. 38). Some authors attribute the male bias to lack of vision and perspective, but others claim that it is the result of a conscious manipulative process: 'Theories of sexuality and definitions of sexual dysfunction within psychology have been seen as being based on misogynistic theorising, functioning to pathologize women who do not seek or achieve pleasure within the phallocentrically biased heterosexual relationship' (Ussher, 1993, p. 30).

One effect of the widespread acceptance of the phallocentric view, it is argued, is that women whose sexual performance or sexual interests do not match up to male-defined norms are identified as 'pathological' or 'dysfunctional'. Such an inappropriate identification is made not only by men (including male partners), but also by sex therapists (including female sex therapists) and by women themselves. Furthermore, women who reject the male view of sexuality and refuse to judge their own 'sexual adequacy' in male-defined terms are often regarded as having a distorted view of sexuality.

Each of the common types of female dysfunction can be reinterpreted in accordance with the alternative perspective on female sexuality, and these reappraisals frequently 'depathologize' the condition. Preferences and behavioural patterns that many people (including therapists) might regard as 'symptoms' of female sexual dysfunction may be seen, instead, as a woman's exercise of free choice, as an expression of 'true' female sexuality or as an adaptive way of coping with disagreeable aspects of a current sexual relationship (such as a partner's failure to engage in foreplay).

Such reinterpretations are outlined below. It should be noted, however, that even those who are most outspoken in rejecting the prevailing cultural view of female sexuality generally agree that some women are sexually dysfunctional. Thus, many critics of the traditional approach would accept orthodox accounts of female dysfunction as applying to at least some of the women who refer themselves for advice and therapy.

Sexual desire disorders

The characterization of a low level of sexual desire as a pathological condition reflects a particular value judgement. Some women have moderate or high levels of sexual interest, whereas others have relatively little interest in sex. However high or low a woman's level of interest, it is neither appropriate nor justifiable to identify a woman, on that basis, as 'suffering' from a 'pathological condition'. Similarly, if a woman chooses to remain celibate, her celibacy should not be regarded as a disorder or a dysfunction. People have a right to engage in as little or as much sexual activity as they choose, and choices which fail to match a particular prescriptive stereotype should not be identified as 'pathological'.

All sexually active people have preferences for certain kinds of sexual activity, and almost all find certain acts unappealing. Graphic (and often highly exaggerated) media representations of the extremes of sexual activity ('gourmet sex'), and the presentation of such behaviours as universally acceptable and palatable, can distort judgements of what is 'normal' and lead people to feel that their own sexual activity is dull and deficient. Whether a woman draws the line at intercourse, oral–genital contact or anal intercourse, it remains her right to choose which sexual activities she will engage in (and of course she remains free not to engage in any sexual activity at all). It is no more pathological for a woman to wish to refrain from intercourse than for her to wish to refrain from anal intercourse or acts of extreme sadism. The view that a woman 'should' engage in intercourse with her partner reflects questionable value judgements which are endemic within the culture.

'Aversion to sex' is often an understandable response to intolerable past experiences. Some women develop an aversion to sexual contact from an early age because they have experienced various forms of sexual exploitation in childhood or adolescence. Many older women lose interest in sex, become disenchanted with sex or develop a sexual aversion because their experiences with their partner are unfulfilling, painful or oppressive. Men generally have little understanding of female sexuality and often assume that a woman's sexual interests are (or ought to be) very similar to their own. They imagine that women's sexual priorities concern intercourse and orgasm, they have little interest in discovering their partner's true preferences and they disre-gard many important aspects of psychological intimacy. Thus many men make unsatisfactory sex partners for women, and many women understandably lose interest in sex. Some men, indeed, are sexually aggressive or oppressive, and their sexual behaviour frequently constitutes abuse. The natural inclination of the partners of such men to avoid or reject further sexual intimacy should not be categorized as a pathological response.

Orgasmic dysfunction

According to the predominant male view of sex, 'the sexual act' is penetrative intercourse and 'sexual satisfaction' means orgasm. Thus, for most men satisfactory sex involves (simply) intercourse leading to orgasm. This may be true for a majority of men, but it is categorically untrue for the great majority of women. Yet the same 'recipe' for satisfactory sex is incorrectly applied to women, and this means that a woman who fails to have an orgasm during intercourse may be regarded as abnormal and 'dysfunctional'.

Although the phallocentric view of female sexuality predominates, even in the work of many sex therapists, it is demonstrably inappropriate. There is clear evidence that the majority of women do not regularly experience orgasm during intercourse, although few women have difficulty in achieving orgasm by manual stimulation. Thus the judgement that vaginal penetration is the 'normal' or 'natural' route to female orgasm is inaccurate (and 'fraudulent'). The fallacy is pernicious because it establishes a criterion by which a clear majority of women might be labelled 'anorgasmic' (or, to use the older term, 'frigid').

It needs to be stressed that most women who come forward for treatment for 'failure to achieve orgasm during intercourse' do not complain that they fail to gain pleasure from their sexual relationship, or that they lack sexual satisfaction. The principal anxiety of most of these women is that they are 'abnormal' and are 'unable to function as other women do'. Such judgements can often be traced to criticism by partners or to inappropriate expectations derived from inaccurate media representations of normal female sexual responses.

Vaginismus

A woman who has had painful or exploitative sexual experiences may develop a fear of penetration or may find the act of intercourse abhorrent. In many cases the woman will be aware of such feelings, but in some cases her apprehension will remain unconscious. Natural physiological responses to such fear or revulsion may include a constriction of the vagina (known as 'vaginismus'). Women obviously have every right to reject penetration, but many such women regard themselves (and are regarded by others) as sexually inadequate or dysfunctional. Nicholson is particularly critical of physical treatments for vaginismus. She writes of women who allow themselves to be subjected to 'most severe punish-

ment ... such as inserting penis-shaped instruments of ever-increasing size into the vagina in the name of gynaecological therapy (i.e., graduated glass vaginal dilators)' (Nicholson, 1993, pp. 70–1).

Painful intercourse (dyspareunia)

Women may feel under considerable pressure to proceed with intercourse even if they have little sexual interest, are not aroused by their partner and would prefer not to continue. In such circumstances, attempts at penetration are likely to prove painful because of vaginal constriction or a failure to lubricate. The more painful intercourse has been in the past, the more aversive will be the anticipation of penetration, and a vicious circle is thus likely to develop. The avoidance of painful situations is a perfectly natural response and should not be construed as pathological.

Low sexual desire and aversion to sex Low sexual desire is the most frequently reported form of female sexual dysfunction (Hawton, 1985). Some women who seek therapy maintain that they have never had a high level of sexual desire, whereas others report a substantial reduction in interest. Such a loss often follows a traumatic experience (such as rape), or a major change in lifestyle. Some women fail to regain their previous level of enthusiasm for sex after the birth of a baby, while others lose all interest in sex following disfiguring surgery.

Some women are disturbed by their lack of sexual drive, but others are not. Some who would be happy to live a celibate life seek therapy for the sake of their partner and the continuation of their relationship. If both partners are content to exclude sex from the relationship then the absence of desire will not be problematic, and many relationships do indeed continue very happily on this basis.

If a woman's loss of interest in sex (or aversion to sexual contact) is linked to a traumatic experience, a fear of pregnancy or fundamental relationship problems, it would be appropriate to address the cause directly. If no instigating cause can be identified, the discussion is likely to focus on details of the couple's sexual activity together, and particular attention will be paid to the nature of the partner's sexual overtures. The therapist may emphasize the appropriate use of foreplay and the importance of non-genital touching in the initial stages of sexual contact, and use of the sensate focus strategy may be recommended.

Although treatment is sometimes successful, outcome is highly variable (LoPiccolo and Friedman, 1988). Whether or not intervention is effective depends partly on the nature of the problem (whether it is a response to a traumatic experience or reflects a 'natural' low level of interest, for example), and partly on the level of motivation for change by both partners (Leiblum and Rosen, 1988).

Orgasmic dysfunction   Women who have never experienced an orgasm by any means are said to suffer from 'primary orgasmic dysfunction', and those who regularly fail to experience orgasm during intercourse are said to suffer from 'secondary orgasmic dysfunction'. However, both of these concepts have been sharply challenged, partly as a result of new evidence concerning female sexuality and partly as a result of the efforts of critics who have 'deconstructed' issues around the female orgasm, 'anorgasmia' and 'frigidity' (Ussher and Baker, 1993; see also Box 7.2).

With regard to 'primary orgasmic dysfunction', it now appears that women who have never experienced an orgasm have simply never been stimulated sufficiently in such a way that they reach orgasm. Some women have never masturbated and have never been manually stimulated to climax by a partner. The concept of 'secondary orgasmic failure' is based on an assumption that women 'normally' experience orgasm during intercourse, whereas a number of studies have shown that unless additional stimulation is provided, orgasm during intercourse is the exception rather than the rule. Thus Sanders's (1985) study of over 4000 women found that 60 per cent of married and 80 per cent of unmarried women had never achieved an unassisted orgasm during intercourse.

Masters and Johnson (1970) maintained that, in many cases, difficulty in achieving orgasm can be attributed to a 'double standard' that applies to male and female sexuality. Many of the women they treated had received strong negative cues about sex and many had been taught from an early age that sex was 'dirty'. A woman who holds generally negative and prohibitive attitudes towards sexuality is unlikely to be able to relax sexually.

Some couples share the erroneous assumption that 'successful' sexual intercourse involves each partner having an orgasm. When the woman then fails to reach orgasm during intercourse, the couple may feel that they have failed, and any subsequent dialogue might involve accusations in which each partner blames the other for the failure. Alternatively, both partners might engage in a high level of self-blame and feel sexually inadequate.

In an initial phase of treatment, the couple are likely to be informed of the current thinking about the nature of the female orgasm. The information that few women regularly achieve orgasm during intercourse may come as a huge relief and may help to dispel guilt, blame and feelings of inadequacy. Many couples, however, will still feel that their sexual interaction could be more fulfilling and satisfying and will request further help.

Couples may first be instructed in the practice of sensate focus, and the male partner may be given instructions on the most effective ways of masturbating the woman to a climax. If the couple wish to go beyond this stage, so that female orgasm is achieved during intercourse, then they are first taught how to use manual stimulation to achieve this. Eventually, the woman may achieve orgasm on some occasions without such stimulation, but this is not held out as the key criterion of success. Most evaluation studies have reported improved orgasmic ability in the majority of women who receive treatment (Cole and Dryden, 1988).

Vaginismus Vaginismus is an involuntary physiological response (a tightening of the outer part of the vagina), which is usually attributed to an unconscious fear or loathing of penetration. Such feelings may relate to past experiences, to anxieties about penetration itself or to fears concerning the possible consequences of intercourse.

Treatment is likely to begin with an attempt to identify any likely source of apprehension or fear which may be responsible for the condition. Sensate focus may also be used, with a gradual progression to genital touching. A more direct treatment for vaginismus involves gradual physical vaginal dilation. The woman inserts first her fingers and then plastic 'dilators' of different sizes into her vagina. When she is able to accommodate a fairly large dilator without discomfort the woman is encouraged to keep it in place for several hours every night.

Of all the sexual dysfunctions, vaginismus is the condition which most readily yields to treatment (Bancroft, 1993). All the women treated for this dysfunction in the original Masters and Johnson clinical sample became sexually functional, and the follow-up data indicated that none of these women had suffered a relapse.

Painful intercourse A woman may find intercourse painful for a number of reasons. Pain may be caused by a failure to lubricate owing to a lack of sexual arousal. Underarousal may stem from a low level of sexual interest, fear of pregnancy, a traumatic sexual episode, generalized negative attitudes towards sex or the sexual inadequacy of the partner. Pain may also be due to various medical conditions, including infections that lead to an inflammation of the vagina. Treatment will be tailored to the identified cause, and may include instructing the partner about effective foreplay, individual psychotherapy, relationship therapy, the use of dilators, treatment for infection or hormone replacement therapy. Symptomatic relief from pain during intercourse can often be achieved by the use of a vaginal lubricating cream or jelly, but this should not be used as a substitute for the treatment of any underlying cause.

◄The Homosexual Orientation►►►

Homosexual behaviour has now become widely accepted as a 'legitimate' form of sexuality and in many countries homosexual acts between adults are no longer illegal. The change in public attitudes to homosexuality over the past fifty years has been matched by profound changes in legislation and in the views of mental health professionals. DSM-II listed homosexuality as one of the sexual deviations, but in 1973 the American Psychiatric Association decided that homosexuality was not a psychiatric disorder and the 'condition' was then removed from the Diagnostic and Statistical Manual of Mental Disorders. DSM-III included only 'ego-dystonic homosexuality' (that is, a homosexual preference that is distressing to the individual). When the revised edition, DSM-IIIR, was published in 1987, neither 'homosexuality' nor 'ego-dystonic homosexuality' was included, although the category 'Sexual Disorder not otherwise specified' did allow for the inclusion of conditions in which there is 'persistent and marked distress about one's sexual orientation'. The position remains unchanged in DSM-IV.

Although homosexuality is no longer regarded as a 'psychiatric condition', a brief examination of some of the explanations put forward to explain why some people are gay will be useful in helping us to understand some of the other aspects of human sexuality discussed in this chapter.

Psychoanalytic accounts   According to one prominent psychoanalytic theory, male homosexuals are likely to have had an especially close relationship with their mother during boyhood and to have been somewhat alienated from their father. As a result, it is suggested, these boys identify more with their mothers than with their fathers, and take on a female identity. This account clearly implies that adult homosexual feelings stem from gender confusion which has its origins in childhood and then persists into adulthood. However, if there is any gender confusion it is certainly deeply hidden, because most homosexuals do not report such confusion with respect to either their childhood or their adult life. Most gay men and lesbian women fully accept themselves as male and female, respectively, and simply prefer to develop intimate relationships with other people of their own sex.

The social learning account

According to accounts based on social learning theory, individuals who find their initial homosexual experiences rewarding and their initial heterosexual experiences threatening, embarrassing or unfulfilling will tend to seek out further homosexual encounters and to avoid further heterosexual liaisons. As long as the homosexual encounters prove gratifying, it is suggested, the person will continue to engage in homosexual behaviour, while at the same time accepting and developing a self-image which includes homosexuality as a major element.

This explanation is unconvincing for most homosexuals, however, for many insist that they were aware of their sexual orientation a long time before they had engaged in any overt sexual activity. And although some do recall their early heterosexual activities as traumatic or threatening, many male homosexuals, at least, remember these experiences as pleasurable, sexually arousing and satisfying.

The social learning account may be somewhat more convincing as an account of the origins of female homosexuality. For example, there is evidence that a relatively high proportion of lesbian women experienced early heterosexual encounters which they found frightening or disgusting. Many of them report a history of childhood sexual abuse by older males and remember being forced into early heterosexual activities. By contrast, any early sexual experiences with women tend to be remembered as particularly exciting and loving.

A major study

A good deal of light was shed on the various psychological theories of the origins of homosexuality by a major study conducted by Bell et al. (1981). This research team conducted in-depth interviews with approximately 1000 homosexual and 500 heterosexual people living in the San Francisco Bay area and tested several major theories of the development of homosexuality. The data failed to provide support for the view that male homosexuals had 'special' relationships with their mothers or that the parents of homosexual men had treated their boys in gender-inappropriate ways. Furthermore, there was no evidence to show that homosexuals were more likely to have had traumatic early sexual experiences or to have been seduced by an older same-sex person, although homosexual males did report less enjoyment of their early heterosexual experiences than heterosexual men.

The most striking findings from this study were those which revealed the early age at which many homosexual men had first become aware of their sexual preference. The authors concluded that in the majority of cases the homosexual preference is determined before adolescence and that this sexual preference therefore appeared to be a 'a deep-seated predisposition'. Speculating about the basis of such a predisposition, they suggested that their findings were 'not inconsistent with what one might expect to find if . . . there were a biological basis for sexual preference' (Bell et al., 1981, p. 216).

A biological basis for homosexuality?

In recent years, there have been a number of reports of differences between homosexual and heterosexual men in the size of certain brain structures (LeVay, 1993), and studies of gay males, their brothers and other male relatives have given some support to the view that genetic factors may play a role in whether a man becomes homosexual or heterosexual. The case was considerably strengthened in 1993 when a research team announced that they had discovered direct evidence indicating that some cases of male homosexual orientation do reflect an individual's genetic constitution (Hamer et al., 1993; see Box 7.3).

Box 7.3
Genetics and Homosexuality

In 1993, when investigating why certain cancers often develop in gay men infected with HIV, a team from the National Cancer Institute in the United States produced evidence which appears to show that genetic factors may play a role in the development of a male homosexual orientation (Hamer et al., 1993). As part of their work, the team examined the family backgrounds of 114 gay men and found relatively high rates of homosexuality among certain groups of male relatives. For example, 13 per cent of the gay men's brothers were homosexual, compared with only around 2 per cent in the general population. Relatively high rates of homosexuality were also found among maternal uncles and maternal male cousins. For some of the families, gay relatives could be traced back three generations.

The chromosomal composition of 40 pairs of gay brothers was then investigated, and in 33 of these pairs the team found an unusual structural pattern in one part of the X chromosome (known as Xq28). The X chromosome is a sex-linked chromosome which men inherit from their mother, and the region specified carries hundreds of genes. The team had not, therefore, identified any specific gene or genes involved in a predisposition towards homosexuality, although they had found that some homosexual men differ from the majority of heterosexual men in their genetic composition. Thus the scientists suggested that genetic attributes may influence male sexual orientation just as they influence such characteristics as height, trait anxiety and certain other personality features.

The researchers emphasized that the involvement of genetic factors had not been demonstrated in every case of homosexuality they examined. They also acknowledged that genetic factors interact with environmental factors, so that if an individual is genetically predisposed to a particular sexual orientation, the expression of the predisposition in terms of subjective experience or overt behaviour will depend on the individual's personal history. Family, cultural and social environmental influences, together with personality characteristics, will have powerful effects on shaping the individual's sexual interests and behaviour. It is therefore likely that when the genetic characteristics which predispose an individual to homosexuality can be specified in detail it will be found that many men who have such a biological predisposition have never recognized any homosexual feelings and have never engaged in homosexual activity.

Because homosexuals are less likely than heterosexuals to reproduce, it might be expected that any genetic characteristic which predisposes an individual to become homosexual would soon become rare and might disappear over time. However, many men who are genetically predisposed to be homosexual may never feel attracted to others of their sex, and many of those who do recognize their homosexual preference may nevertheless choose to engage exclusively in heterosexual relationships. Many people are guided in their sexual preference and their sexual behaviour by prevalent social values and the attitudes and prejudices expressed by relatives and peers. In a social context in which homosexuality is strongly condemned, many of those who feel an attraction towards others of their sex might suppress their homosexual feelings. Thus it is possible that, until fairly recently, a majority of those who recognized their own homosexual inclination would have settled into heterosexual relationships and had children. If this analysis is accurate, then the recent liberalization of attitudes and laws, providing fewer sanctions against homosexual relationships, might lead to less reproduction by those who are genetically predisposed towards becoming homosexual. And this might lead to the relevant genetic pattern becoming less widespread over time.

Media announcements regarding 'a gay gene' brought a wide range of responses from gay men and lesbian women. Some welcomed the announcement as confirmation of their conviction that their sexuality was an inherent part of their 'nature'. Others, however, were suspicious of a possible implication that homosexuals were genetically abnormal or defective. They expressed a fear that the research might be used as a basis for 'diagnosing' homosexuality and, eventually perhaps, for 'correcting' the 'genetic defect'.

While some made the point that those who are gay have a right to equality regardless of whether they are 'born gay' or choose to become gay, others expressed the hope that if homosexuality were confirmed as partly determined by a normal genetic variation, akin to skin colour, this might strengthen the case for more powerful anti-discrimination laws. Many argue that it should be an offence to discriminate between people on the basis of a genetically determined characteristic, and the hope was expressed that this principle, which now applies to sex and race, would extend to homosexual orientation if the evidence of genetic involvement were confirmed.

The media coverage also led to a widespread discussion of the possibility of eugenic intervention. It was acknowledged that some prospective parents might wish to abort a foetus shown to have genetic characteristics predictive of homosexuality. Even if such abortions were forbidden, or if parents decided not to abort, a 'positive' indication of future sexual orientation might well influence the parents' attitude to the child and would also raise the issue of whether (or when) the child should be told of the pre-natal test result. The formidable advances in genetic knowledge in recent years, and the unprecedented availability of tests for the pre-natal identification of a wide range of individual characteristics, raises many such practical, ethical and political dilemmas, all of which need to be urgently addressed.

At present, there is little evidence to support the view that a homosexual orientation in females is related to genetic factors, although the results of studies that are now under way may help to establish whether or not genetic influences are involved in the development of lesbianism as they appear to be for male homosexuality.

Although work in genetics may help us to understand the nature of sexual orientation, we should be wary of interpreting findings in terms of 'genetic determinism'. And as in so many other areas of individual differences, we should not assume that any single explanation of why people are homosexual will be equally applicable to all cases.

◄Transsexualism► ► ►

A transsexual has a gender identity which conflicts with his or her biological sex. Transsexualism (or 'gender identity disorder') can be a highly distressing condition, and many transsexuals become severely depressed. Some engage in self-mutilation (in a number of reported cases male transsexuals have endeavoured to cut off their genitals) and a relatively high number attempt suicide.

Developmental aspects

It is possible to distinguish between different types of transsexual in terms of their developmental history. Some transsexuals appear to have identified with 'the other sex' from early childhood (see box 7.4). As children they may have shown a distinct preference for playing with children of 'the opposite sex' and they may have engaged in frequent 'cross-gender play', which may have included 'cross-dressing'.

The developmental history of other transsexuals is very different. They appear to have had orthodox childhood experiences, and to have identified with others of their biological sex without any reservation. During adolescence or early adulthood, however, their masturbatory explorations may have led them to handle, and later to dress in, women's clothing. At this point the person would be identified as a 'transvestite'. Some transvestites, however, pass beyond the stage of cross-dressing for sexual excitement, and enjoy being 'in role' and acting 'as if' they were women. And in a small minority of cases the role-play becomes much more intense and the person gradually develops the conviction that he or she really 'belongs' to the opposite sex. If this belief is strongly held over a considerable time period then the person would no longer be labelled a 'transvestite' but would be recognized as a transsexual.

Many transsexuals make strenuous efforts to suppress their thoughts and feelings about their true gender over a number of years, during which time they try to conform to the social roles expected of them. Many of those who try to repress their transsexual feelings, however, later conclude that they are 'living a lie' and that the future will be bleak unless they acknowledge and reveal their true nature. Many therefore decide to change their social identity, and some complete their gender reassignment with the help of hormonal treatment and surgery.

Transsexualism: sexual disorder or gender disorder?

Transsexualism is not a sexual disorder. Many transsexuals report that their motive for sex reassignment is not sexual and, indeed, it appears that many transsexuals have a rather low sex drive. Although a number have engaged in 'homosexual' activities during adolescence and early adulthood, many say that their thoughts and fantasies during these encounters were heterosexual in nature (thus the transsexual man will imagine himself to be a woman engaging in sex with a man).

Prevalence

Transsexualism is certainly a rare condition. It is impossible to gauge the prevalence with any accuracy, but the figures usually quoted suggest that the condition affects around 1 in 30000 males and 1 in 100000 females.

Box 7.4
Two Male-to-female Transsexuals

A number of transsexuals have written autobiographical accounts of their experiences before and after sex-reassignment surgery, and these provide a fascinating insight into many of the personal dilemmas that result from transsexualism. The various memoirs reveal the difficulties experienced by children who feel that they belong to 'the other sex', and describe the enormous relief that came when the authors realized that their predicament was shared by others, that it had a name and that there might be a solution through gender reassignment. The intensity of the desire for sex reassignment surgery is often remarkable, and the determined efforts to convince professionals to agree to surgery often make harrowing reading. The British male-to-female transsexuals Jan Morris and Caroline Cossey are two among several who have contributed book-length accounts of their experiences.

Jan Morris James Morris was a leading journalist and travel writer for many years before undergoing sex-reassignment surgery in a Casablanca clinic in 1972. By this time James had been a soldier, had married and had fathered four children. Following surgery, Jan Morris has continued her work as a writer, and her autobiographical account of her transsexualism, *Conundrum*, was published in 1974.

Caroline Cossey Barry Cossey was born in 1954. Convinced from an early age that he was female, he learned about transsexualism in his late teens and then began to dress and live as a woman. He then worked as a 'female' professional dancer before having sex-reassignment surgery in 1974. Caroline Cossey then began a highly successful modelling career (taking the professional name 'Tula') and was featured in Vogue and many other leading magazines. In recent years she has been a prominent campaigner on issues relating to transsexualism. In 1989 she was unsuccessful in her appeal to the European Commission of Human Rights for the right for a male-to-female transsexual to marry as a female. Caroline Cossey published her autobiography, *My Story*, in 1992.

Both these writers insist that they were aware of their gender identity dilemma from a very early age. Caroline Cossey wrote: 'Even in the infant classes I failed to integrate. In the nativity play at Christmas I was utterly humiliated to be playing the part of a shepherd . . . I longed to be cast as Mary, or at least one of the pretty angels all in white with wings and tiny haloes. I identified entirely with a female world.' Jan Morris writes: 'I was three or perhaps four years old when I realized that I had been born into the wrong body, and should really be a girl. I remember the moment well, and it is the earliest memory of my life.' She adds: 'Not that I dreamt of revealing it. I cherished it as a secret, shared for twenty years with not a single soul.'

Both writers describe their great relief when they realized for the first time, during early adulthood, that many other people shared their predicament, and that they might be helped through surgery to change their body structure radically. Both had to contend with immense obstacles in order to obtain surgery, and both felt an extreme sense of release following the surgical transformation.

It is clear throughout both accounts that the major issue facing these two people was one of identity rather than one of sexuality. Before her operation Caroline Cossey had several sexual relationships with men, but she insists that her feelings during these encounters were not the those of a gay man but those of a woman. It is clear from Morris's account that sexual feelings played relatively little part in her desire for change. Indeed, she makes it clear that for her surgery represented a kind of cleansing, a removal of parts of the body which she had come to loathe. Yet the physical restructuring was just one step towards a more fundamental personal reshaping: 'that my conundrum might simply be a matter of penis or vagina, testicle or womb, seems to me still a contradiction in terms, for it concerned not my apparatus but my *self*' (italics in original).

Causes

There is no evidence that transsexualism is related to any genetic characteristic, although the evidence might be difficult to obtain – a condition as rare
as transsexualism hardly lends itself to twin studies or adoption studies.
Neither is there evidence to suggest that transsexuals are atypical in terms of
hormone levels, although it has been suggested that some cases might be
marked by irregularities in the interactions between hormonal sub-systems.

The earliest psychological theory of transsexualism was put forward by
the psychoanalyst Stoller (1968). According to this theory, extreme stress in
adult life profoundly disturbs all aspects of the person's identity, and in
some cases it may disturb gender identity. Stoller's theory remained highly
influential for a number of years but has since been widely criticized (Eber,
1980), and empirical studies have generally failed to confirm predictions
from the theory. Another analyst, Lothstein (1987), suggested that a child
becomes a transsexual as a result of complex family communication
processes in which the parents continually express their aversion towards
the child's genitals and their contempt for his or her developing gender
identity. Again, however, there is no convincing empirical support for this
suggestion.

It might be relatively easy to account for cases in which transsexualism
develops later in life following an extended period of transvestism. A transvestite wears clothing normally worn by the opposite sex, initially as a form
of auto-erotic play. Most transvestites are happy to engage in cross-gender
role-playing on an occasional basis, but in a minority of cases the cross-
gender role-play takes on a completely different character and the man may
eventually become convinced that he is really a woman.

Treatment

Transsexuals do not wish to be 'cured of a gender delusion'. They want to
live, and to be accepted, in the gender with which they identify. Rather than
seeking psychological help for their predicament, therefore, they are much
more likely to seek social acceptance for their changed role (and, in many
cases, they are likely to seek bodily change through surgery).

Given the almost universal lack of motivation for a 'change of mind', it is
not surprising that very few transsexuals come forward for psychotherapy
for their 'gender dysphoria', although they may seek help for the emotional
problems which often arise from their difficult situation. It is also widely
(although not universally) accepted that psychotherapy is invariably ineffective in changing the gender self-image of the transsexual.

Sex reassignment Sex reassignment for transsexuals involves social
changes – living openly as a member of the preferred sex – and, in many
cases, hormonal and surgical procedures. Some transsexuals are content
with social reassignment and are satisfied as long as they are accepted by

others in their preferred sex role. Some join groups in which they are taught gender-specific social skills and deportment, and some are given elocution lessons so that their voice quality accords with their reassigned gender.

In the United States a person may legally change sex by arranging for his or her birth certificate to be changed, but in many European countries the legal reassignment of sex is often a much more complex procedure, and in some countries, including the United Kingdom, legal reassignment is not possible.

Biological interventions to aid reassignment include hormonal treatment and, in some cases, sex-reassignment surgery. Hormones are administered to promote the development and maintenance of certain physical characteristics. For male-to-female transsexuals, oestrogen is used to enlarge the breasts and to change the distribution of body hair. However, this hormone does not stop the growth of facial hair (the beard is removed by electrolysis) or raise the voice pitch. Oestrogen inhibits the action of the naturally produced androgens, which may reduce a biological male's level of sexual desire and diminish the strength of the orgasm. When male sex hormones, the androgens, are given to female-to-male transsexuals these suppress menstruation, promote the growth of facial and body hair and deepen the voice. They may also increase erotic sensitivity.

Sex-reassignment surgery   A high proportion of transsexuals are highly motivated to undergo sex reassignment surgery, so that 'inappropriate' parts of their body will be removed and replaced with more appropriate genitalia. Following successful surgical intervention most transsexuals are able to perform sexually, although of course it is impossible to change a woman into a fertile man, or to change a man into a woman who can conceive a child. While social, legal and hormonal forms of sex reassignment may be reversible, surgical intervention is not, and most clinics which offer such surgery therefore operate a rigorous selection procedure. They often programme the sex reassignment over a number of years, so that only those who maintain a high level of motivation over the longer term, and are emotionally stable, will finally be permitted to undergo surgery.

The first sex-change operation was performed in 1930 and from the 1950s onwards there has been a steady growth in the demand for this type of surgery. Approximately 1000 transsexuals now undergo sex reassignment surgery each year in the USA. In the UK the figure is around 100. In the USA and most West European countries the ratio of men to women who undergo sex reassignment surgery is about 4:1. However, the ratio varies considerably between countries. In Poland, which is exceptional in this respect, around five times as many women as men undergo the operation for sex reassignment (Godlewski, 1988).

In the male-to-female operation the testicles and penis are removed, the skin of the penis being used to construct a 'vulva' and 'vagina'. Further operations may be used to insert breast implants and to elevate the voice pitch. Female-to-male surgery involves successive operations to remove the breasts, the uterus and the ovaries. The clitoris is left intact to preserve erotic sensitivity. Plastic surgery may then be used to construct a 'penis', although the results of this operation, in terms of 'penile' effectiveness during intercourse, are variable. Some surgical procedures allow the constructed penis to become erect by means of an additional prosthetic device (these days, this often takes the form of an inflation device implanted inside the patient's body).

Although sex reassignment surgery is often impressively successful, serious physical complications do arise in a relatively high proportion of cases (up to a half, according to Lindemalm et al., 1986).

Psychological outcome following surgery Most follow-up studies of people who have undergone sex reassignment surgery have found major improvements in their psychological well-being following the operation (Kuiper and Cohen-Kettenis, 1988; Blanchard et al., 1989). However, satisfaction is not universal, and some patients do eventually regret having had the operation. Ross and Need (1989) found that the best predictors of psychological outcome were the quality of the surgical effects, the person's current level of social support and the reactions of family members.

Lothstein (1987), a psychoanalyst, is one of the fiercest critics of sex reassignment surgery. He argues that transsexualism is a psychological problem and that psychotherapy must therefore be the appropriate treatment. Surgery, he argues, is no way to solve an identity problem, and he paints a pessimistic picture of the psychological outcome of surgical intervention.

The Paraphilias ▶ ▶ ▶

Some forms of sexual proclivity and sexual behaviour are generally agreed to be 'abnormal' and 'disturbed'. Many of these are now labelled 'paraphilias' (from 'para', meaning 'to the side of', and 'philia', meaning 'preferred'). The term covers an apparently diverse group of behaviours and orientations, which includes transvestism, paedophilia, fetishism (see Box 7.5), voyeurism, exhibitionism, sado-masochism (Box 7.6) and a number of others. A common feature is a compulsive quality which is generally absent from 'normal' sexual behaviour.

The many different specific forms of paraphilia may be seen as variations on a limited number of common themes. For example, many paraphiliacs, whatever their specific sexual interest, lack control over their sexual fantasies (Abel and Rouleau, 1990), and many are motivated to explore 'forbidden' sexual territory. However, it would be foolish to assume that different cases, even of any one form of paraphilia, must reflect a similar causal pathway or the same pattern of antecedent conditions.

Biological accounts

The possibility that paraphilias reflect some biological disturbance has received relatively little attention, although Money (1990) contends that all the paraphilias are essentially 'brain diseases'. Anomalies in EEG patterns have

Box 7.5
Fetishism: Some Classic Cases

The following classical case reports of fetishism are adapted from Richard von Krafft-Ebing's book *Psychopathia Sexualis* (1886).

Shoe Fetishism (Krafft-Ebing Case No. 77)

A minister of religion, aged 50 years, was a regular visitor to his local brothel. On entering a bedroom with a woman he would look lustfully at her shoes, take one off and bite it ecstatically. He would then press the shoe on to his genitals, ejaculate and rub the semen over his chest. When he woke from his sexual ecstasy he would beg the woman to allow him to keep the shoe for a few days. He always returned the shoe as promised, with thanks.

Glove Fetishism (Krafft-Ebing Case No. 122)

A 33-year-old manufacturer, married with children, had developed a glove fetish from an early age. It started when, as a boy, he had used a chamois leather as a masturbatory aid. At puberty his sexual interest centred on ladies' kid gloves. Merely touching his penis with such a glove would produce an erection and even lead to ejaculation. Men's gloves did not excite him, although he loved to wear them. The only thing that attracted him to a woman was her kid gloves, and for him the ultimate erotic stimulus was a pair of long gloves, with many buttons, dirty and saturated with perspiration. Even shaking hands with a woman wearing such gloves could bring him to orgasm. He used such gloves when he masturbated, and when he visited a prostitute he would take one of the many hundreds of pairs in his collection. When having intercourse with his wife he would place a pair of gloves by her head so that he could kiss them during the sexual act.

been reported for several paraphiliac groups, including exhibitionists and paedophiles (Flor-Henry et al., 1991), and the results of a number of studies have suggested that some of those who engage in unusual sexual behaviour have a localized abnormality in the left temporal lobe (Lang, 1993). The idea that paraphiliac sexual interests might reflect a biological predisposition may appear more plausible following the research linking a homosexual orientation to genetic characteristics. Most explanations of the paraphilias, however, are psychological in nature.

Psychoanalytic accounts

Most psychoanalytic accounts suggest that the paraphilias stem from arrested psychosexual development. According to Freudian theory, a child normally passes through a series of psychosexual stages before reaching the final ('genital') stage, but may become fixated at an early point. Such a

Box 7.6
Auto-erotic Asphyxiation

In February 1994, Stephen Milligan, a 45-year-old Member of the British Parliament and parliamentary private secretary to a defence minister, was found dead in the kitchen of his home. He was naked apart from a pair of women's stockings and a suspender belt, and had a flex around his neck and a plastic bag over his head. Mr Milligan appeared to have strangled himself accidentally as a result of a practice known as 'auto-erotic asphyxiation'. The fact that the flex had been specially prepared and padded, and that other similar apparatus was found in the house, led to the conclusion that the fatal incident was not the first time that Stephen Milligan had engaged in such a practice.

It was decided at the inquest that Mr Milligan had died when the main artery in his neck had been constricted by a flex which appeared to have been placed like a noose, with one end tied to his leg. This arrangement should have allowed him to control pressure on the neck by means of leg movements, but it seemed that a reduction in blood flow to the brain may have caused Mr Milligan to faint in such a way that the noose tightened until he was dead.

The Stephen Milligan case gave rise to newspaper headlines over several weeks, but this was one of many such fatalities which occur in the UK every year. Why do men (and invariably it is only men) engage in the practices which lead to such accidents? Controlled asphyxiation is usually employed as part of a masturbatory routine because a lack of oxygen to the brain ('anoxia') may increase the vividness of sexual fantasies and lead to an especially powerful orgasm. Devices used to achieve the optimum level of anoxia include plastic bags placed over the head or a controllable noose placed around the neck.

Two Canadian studies of auto-erotic asphyxial death show that in many ways the circumstances of Stephen Milligan's death were typical of such fatalities. In a study of 19 such deaths, Tough et al. (1994) found that the sexual activity was usually performed in isolation, that there was usually evidence of similar activities having been repeated a number of times, and that death was generally caused when the person was unable to relieve compression on the neck. Blanchard and Hucker (1991) studied 117 fatalities resulting from auto-erotic asphyxiation and found that pornographic material, sexual aids and toys and special clothing (bondage gear or items of women's clothing) were often present at the scene of death. In some cases it also appeared that the person had been observing his activities by using a carefully positioned mirror. There was greater evidence of sadomasochistic and transvestite involvement among the older men in the group, suggesting that the masturbatory ritual might become progressively more elaborate over time.

fixation, some psychoanalysts claim, may lead to the formation of strong emotional attachments ('object cathexes') to objects which would normally evoke little affective response. An alternative psychoanalytic explanation links the development of the paraphilias to the Oedipal complex and suggests that fear of castration, associated with a sexual attraction towards the mother, induces some males to search for non-threatening ways of fulfilling their sexual needs.

Behavioural (conditioning) explanations

According to behavioural accounts, the paraphilias are learned responses. Within the framework of the classical conditioning paradigm, paraphiliac behaviours are regarded as conditioned responses to stimuli that have acquired the power to arouse sexual feelings as a result of close association with inherently sexual stimuli (that is, unconditioned stimuli). Explanations based on the operant learning paradigm emphasize the degree to which paraphiliac behaviours are progressively shaped and then maintained through positive reinforcement.

In a study conducted to explore the possibility that a fetish might be acquired through a classical conditioning process, Rachman and Hodgson (1968) exposed normal male subjects to slides of naked women (an 'unconditioned stimulus'), which elicited a sexual response ('an unconditioned response'). Slides of women's boots were then repeatedly paired with the erotic slides, and eventually the slides of footwear (now the 'conditioned stimulus') were sufficient to produce a weak sexual response (the 'conditioned response'). Although classical conditioning usually involves the repeated pairing of two stimuli, a single sexual experience may instigate a conditioning process if the experience (of the 'pairing') is repeated many times in imagination. Thus an object which regularly features in the individual's masturbatory fantasies is likely to acquire fetishistic properties (McGuire, Carlisle and Young, 1965).

One reason why the vast majority of fetishists are attracted to one of a very limited assortment of objects might be that certain stimuli tend to resonate with biologically determined sexual interests. Thus human beings might be biologically prepared to develop sexual responses towards particular types of stimuli (Laws and Marshall, 1991).

The operant conditioning paradigm can be used to explain how paraphiliac behaviour is strengthened and shaped. If a behaviour is followed by positive reinforcement it will tend to be repeated, whereas if it is not reinforced, or if it is followed by punishment, it is likely to be dropped from the person's behavioural repertoire. Hence, as the person explores variations on a paraphiliac theme (perhaps in masturbatory fantasies), he will experience different levels of sexual arousal and will gradually be led towards the variation which produces the most powerful positive reinforcement (that is, the maximum sexual excitement).

Finally, once a paraphiliac interest has been established, it is likely to be maintained by the arousal generated in response to memories of past exploits and the cognitive rehearsal of future paraphiliac activities. Masturbatory fantasies play a powerful role in maintaining many forms of paraphilia (McGuire, Carlisle and Young, 1965; Blair and Lanyon, 1981). Fantasies can activate sexual arousal, heighten excitement and eventually induce orgasm. Pornography may well play an important role at this stage, stimulating and shaping fantasies and leading the individual to anticipate the sensual pleasures that might be derived from new sexual adventures.

Personality and motivation

While it is generally assumed that the principal motive for engaging in paraphiliac activities is that of gaining sexual gratification, other possible motives relate to social intimacy or personal power. Thus it has been suggested that some exhibitionists expose themselves in order to exert power over their victims rather than to gain sexual satisfaction. And some transvestites claim that although their cross-dressing was initially motivated by sexual concerns, they continue to dress in women's clothes principally to feel feminine and relaxed.

There is some evidence to support the contention that in certain cases the primary motive for the paraphiliac act might be a quest for intimacy. Many paraphiliacs lack partners and friends, and some have a very high level of social anxiety (Marshall, 1989). Gosselin and Wilson (1980) found that many paraphiliacs were shy and introverted, and a number of other studies have also shown that many (but certainly not all) lack social confidence and are deficient in social skills. Thus some will seek out 'social' encounters which they regard as 'safe' and 'intimate'; for example, by engaging in voyeurism or exhibitionism, or by pursuing the company of children.

This model suggests that some people are 'pushed' towards paraphilia through a fear of normal social and sexual relationships, rather than being 'pulled' by a sexual attraction to inappropriate people, objects or situations.

Management

Some of the paraphilias, but not all, lead to behaviours which are proscribed by law, and a sex offender will usually first come into contact with clinical services after he has been arrested (or following sentencing by a court). In many cases a person who is caught exposing himself, or peeping, or interfering with a child, will protest his innocence, or otherwise deny the reality or the seriousness of his offence. Such a person will not be motivated to undergo a process of therapy in order to change his sexual orientation. Hence, considerable effort may be expended during the initial stages of therapy in addressing and challenging denial and attempting to motivate the client to change his sexual orientation and his sexual behaviour.

Treatment programme components

Most current programmes for sex offenders follow a cognitive behavioural approach, although they may also include a wide range of techniques borrowed from other approaches. A comprehensive package may include behaviour therapy techniques, social skills training, role-plays and group discussion. The psychological intervention programme may be complemented by the use of drugs which lower levels of circulating male sex hormones, and ancillary interventions may focus on such issues as stress reduction, anger management and other life management skills. Almost all cognitive programmes now include specific strategies designed to prevent relapse. The increased used of cognitive programmes, and the greater emphasis now placed on structured relapse prevention strategies, has meant that other approaches, including psychodynamic psychotherapy, now account for only a minor part of therapeutic activity in this area.

Most sex offender treatment programmes, whether based in a hospital, in a prison or in a community setting, involve groups of offenders working together. Participation in a group may bring a number of benefits. For example, it may help the person to become less detached and less evasive, and he may benefit from witnessing other people's testimony and observing their responses to therapeutic interventions. However, the group setting may not be suitable for all clients. An individual who denies his offence, for example, or who minimizes the effects of his offending on victims, may inhibit progress by other participants in the group (Barker and Beech, 1993).

Physical treatments

Several kinds of physical treatment have been used in a bid to curtail paraphiliac behaviours. In the past these included psychosurgery (involving the ablation of parts the hypothalamus) and surgical castration. Despite their severity, however, these techniques were of limited effectiveness, and ethical concerns over the irreversibility and the detrimental effects of these methods gradually led to their abandonment. These days the only form of physical intervention used to aid the treatment of paraphilia is pharmacological. Considerable use is made of anti-androgen drugs such as medroxyprogesterone acetate (MPA, trade name Depo Provera) and cyproterone acetate (CPA) to help the client to maintain control over his sexual behaviour (Money, 1987). These drugs may reduce the strength of the client's sex drive, but usually have little impact on the focus of the client's sexual interest. Used alone, they do little to inhibit sexual offending, and they are therefore invariably used as part of a comprehensive programme in which psychological interventions form the major part.

The effect of these drugs on the level of sexual response has been demonstrated in a number of studies. For example, in a double-blind cross-over study, Bradford and Pawlak (1993) compared the effects of cyproterone acetate and a placebo. They found that the use of CPA was associated with a significant reduction in several aspects of sexual behaviour, and had particularly marked effects on sexual fantasies. The drug reduced the levels of circulating sex hormones and also produced a reduction in subjective estimates of sexual arousal.

Drugs may also be useful in preventing relapse in the longer term. Federoff et al. (1992) followed 46 paraphiliac patients for five or more years, during which time they all continued to receive group psychotherapy. There was a striking difference in the frequency of relapse between those who were maintained on MPA and those who were not. Whereas two-thirds of the patients not receiving this drug relapsed at some time during the period studied, the rate of relapse among those taking MPA was only 15 per cent.

Buspirone, a relatively new anxiolytic drug, may have more specific effects than the established drugs because it appears to facilitate non-paraphiliac arousal while inhibiting paraphiliac sexual arousal. Its effectiveness may stem from its action in reducing certain effects normally associated with obsessive–compulsive disorders (Fedoroff and Fedoroff, 1992).

The anti-androgen drugs tend to produce unpleasant side-effects, which helps to explain why a high proportion of clients fail to continue using them. Although continued use may facilitate the curbing of anti-social responses, these drugs certainly do not represent a 'cure' for the paraphilias. This is to be expected, because the association between levels of circulating sex hormones and human sexual behaviour is weak, and paraphiliac behaviour rarely stems from an excessive sexual appetite. Paraphiliac clients differ from other people not because their level of sex drive is particularly high, but because their sexual interests differ in kind from those of most other people.

Cognitive–behavioural programmes

Cognitive restructuring, which is the major focus of most cognitive–behavioural programmes, is used to challenge false beliefs and to correct the cognitive distortions that help to maintain inappropriate behaviours. One technique used to achieve such restructuring is psychoeducation. The client's beliefs are likely to change as he is provided with accurate information on such matters as sexual physiology, the human sexual response cycle, the nature of sexual fantasies, gender differences in sexuality, childhood sexuality and the effects of sexual attention on children. Those implicit beliefs and attitudes which relate to the client's disturbed behaviour patterns need to be identified and made explicit to the client before being challenged. In addition, any self-verbalizations likely to prompt offending behaviour must be recognized, and efforts made to replace them with self-statements that are likely to inhibit undesirable actions.

Most cognitive treatment programmes also include an 'empathy training' element. Few paraphiliacs have a realistic idea of the impact of their actions on other people. This is clearly the case for paedophiles, but may also be true of those who expose themselves or make obscene telephone calls. Empathy training involves efforts to make offenders aware of the likely impact of their behaviour on victims and to encourage feelings of compassion towards former victims. Various techniques have been developed to encourage such empathy, including role-playing (in which the offender may be asked to take on a victim role), and discussions following exposure to 'victim testimony'. Such testimony may be presented in the form of videotapes or written accounts by victims who have been seriously disturbed by unwanted sexual attention.

Modification of fantasy and fantasy-induced arousal It is clear that paraphiliac interests are shaped and maintained to a considerable extent by sexual fantasies. Some of these may relate to pornographic material (including visual images and narrative passages), but many will reflect the person's own paraphiliac experiences or anticipated future actions. Furthermore, it seems that many of the fantasies that most men would find highly arousing have relatively little impact on those whose interests are paraphiliac in nature. This suggests that an intervention which would 'normalize' a sex offender's repertoire of sexual fantasies might prove useful in shifting his sexual orientation. The effect of highly arousing paraphiliac fantasies might be reduced either by encouraging the person to avoid engaging in such fantasies or by 'de-eroticizing' or neutralizing these fantasies so that they lose their power to provoke sexual excitement. At the same time it might be possible to increase the individual's sexual response to appropriate non-paraphiliac fantasies. A number of therapeutic strategies have been designed to meet one or both of these objectives.

An example of a technique used to neutralize paraphiliac fantasies is 'covert sensitization'. The person is taught to visualize images which he finds particularly aversive (for example, images of being arrested by the police, or of being beaten by fellow prisoners) and is then taught to bring such images to mind whenever he has a fantasy involving his paraphiliac interest or whenever he feels tempted to engage in a paraphiliac activity. The rationale behind covert sensitization is that the disturbing image will produce a psychological shock (comparable to an electric shock) which, when repeatedly associated with a paraphiliac image, will reduce the power of that image to arouse the person sexually (Barlow et al., 1969).

In 'habituation therapy', the person is first helped to achieve a relaxed state and is then guided through thoughts and fantasies relating to his sexual preference. He may be asked to verbalize his fantasies and to describe his feelings. This activity is sustained over a prolonged period without the client having any opportunity to engage in overt sexual activity. The idea is that if the fantasies are maintained for a very long time without sexual relief they will eventually lose their power to arouse the individual. As the person becomes 'satiated' with particular erotic fantasies, the physiological responses and subjective feelings which would normally accompany these fantasies will diminish. Although this technique has not yet been thoroughly evaluated, preliminary evidence suggests that it might be useful in helping paraphiliac clients (Hunter and Goodwin, 1992).

Other techniques are designed to increase the individual's sexual response to appropriate (non-paraphiliac) fantasies. The term 'orgasmic reconditioning' is applied to some of these techniques. In its simplest form, such treatment involves instructing the client to restrict his masturbatory fantasies to those which follow appropriate themes and invoke appropriate images. He may be helped to identify new erotic images, perhaps with the aid of 'suitable' pornographic material, so that he establishes a repertoire of arousing fantasies that do not depict abnormal or unlawful situations. As a result of such reconditioning, the focus of sexual interest, in real life as well as in fantasy, may change from paraphiliac concerns towards more acceptable themes.

Another form of orgasmic conditioning, 'stimulus satiation', attempts to increase the erotic response to appropriate fantasies while at the same time diminishing the sexual response to inappropriate fantasies. The client is first helped to devise a set of acceptable sexual fantasies (not involving paraphiliac elements). As a 'homework assignment', he is then instructed to masturbate to climax using only the approved set of fantasies, but then immediately following ejaculation to switch to inappropriate (paraphiliac) fantasies and to work hard on playing and replaying these fantasies while he continues to masturbate for another hour (Marshall, 1979). The technique relies on the fact that following ejaculation most men remain unaroused for at least an hour or so. Fantasizing paraphiliac images when arousability is at its lowest point will diminish the power of these images to arouse the man sexually on later occasions. Thus the technique is an attempt to switch the erotic response from paraphiliac images (which become associated with the discomfort of masturbation following orgasm) to appropriate images (which become associated with the pleasures of masturbation prior to and during orgasm).

Relapse prevention   There is increasing emphasis on 'relapse prevention' as an essential component of any cognitively based programme, and a number of clinicians now describe their entire programme as following the relapse prevention model (Neidigh, 1991; Abel et al., 1992). Relapse prevention involves a range of techniques (including psychoeducation and behavioural skills training) designed to help paraphiliacs to anticipate and cope with situations in which they might yield to a temptation to reoffend. Clients learn to identify situations, cognitions and feelings that might trigger paraphiliac activity and are helped to understand why in the past they have made decisions that lead to offending (for example, the decision to enter a park or to travel near a student residence at night).

By means of role-play and cognitive rehearsal techniques, offenders also learn specific verbal and behavioural strategies for dealing with high-risk situations. It is particularly important for clients to recognize that if a single lapse should occur this must not be understood as a 'relapse' (a total failure of treatment, for example). A lapse is regarded as a temporary suspension of abstinence and an opportunity for further learning; it should increase the person's motivation to succeed and lead to a redoubling of efforts, rather than causing the person to 'give up giving up' (a common response known as the 'abstinence violation effect').

Social skills training

Another component of many sex offender treatment programmes is social skills training. It is well established that many paraphiliacs (but certainly not all) are deficient in social skills and that many lack social confidence and experience high levels of anxiety in social situations. Difficulties may be experienced in almost any social encounter, only in intimate situations or (in the case of some paedophiles) only in interactions with adults. Because a high level of social anxiety will obviously reduce opportunities for meeting an appropriate sexual partner, it is suggested, those who are afflicted with such anxiety may resort to engaging in sexual behaviours which, although abnormal and unlawful, are experienced as less threatening. Increased social skills and enhanced self-confidence would be expected to increase a person's opportunities for forming an orthodox sexual relationship, which might then lead to a discontinuation of paraphiliac activities.

There is good evidence of the general effectivenesss of social skills training (SST) as a means of increasing interactional skills and self-confidence. Hopkins (1993) showed that sex offenders who were provided with a social skills training programme improved in their social functioning. Compared with a control group, these offenders showed an increase in self-esteem, a reduction in anxiety and less fear of negative evaluation by others. Similarly, Graves et al. (1992) found that social skills training, used as part of a comprehensive treatment programme with adolescent sex offenders, improved social performance and enhanced self-concept.

Unfortunately, however, there is little evidence to suggest that an enhancement of social skills alone is sufficient to curb paraphiliac behaviour. Such training may be a valuable component of a comprehensive treatment package, but the elimination of a paraphiliac interest appears to require the use of techniques that will change unreasonable beliefs about sexuality, reduce the arousing effects of paraphiliac fantasies, enhance victim empathy and offer strategies for preventing relapse.

Treatment effectiveness

There is a popular belief that once a person has committed a sexual offence he is likely to go on committing such offences for the rest of his life, and that any attempt at intervention is almost bound to fail. It must be said that some clinicians share this view, and some recent reviews have painted a rather gloomy picture (for example, Quinsey et al., 1993). However, many authorities in the field have vigorously challenged this position. Marshall (1993), for example, reviewed recent outcome studies and suggested that many treatment programmes do lead to a marked reduction in re-offending for at least some types of sex offender, especially if a comprehensive treatment programme is used, if it is based on the cognitive–behavioural approach and if it includes a relapse prevention component (Marshall and Pithers, 1994). Marshall also emphasized the possible value of anti-androgen drugs in supplementing the effects of psychological treatment programmes.

Although the claim that 'nothing works' with these clients therefore appears unjustified, it must be recognized that many paraphiliacs are not motivated to undergo treatment, and that many of those who do engage in a therapy programme do not appear to change as a result. Because motivation for treatment is a strong predictor of outcome, considerable effort may be needed in the initial stages of a programme to ensure that the sex offender client is genuinely concerned to change his pattern of sexual behaviour. When the client does have a strong level of motivation, change is possible, but short-term gains need to be reinforced by arming the individual with effective relapse prevention strategies.

◀Conclusions▶▶▶

Human sexual behaviour reflects biological, psychological and social influences. Forms of sexual dysfunction include a low level of sexual desire, difficulties with sexual arousal and problems in controlling or achieving orgasm. The causes of sexual dysfunction include physical or mental health problems, the experience of sexual trauma in childhood or adulthood, a lack of self-confidence (perhaps related to feeling unattractive) and relationship factors. Much of the knowledge about the nature and causes of such dysfunction and many of the relevant treatment techniques are based upon research by Masters and Johnson. Highly effective treatments are available for most forms of sexual dysfunction.

Homosexuality is no longer regarded as a 'psychiatric condition' or a disorder. The idea that homosexuality results from gender confusion has not been borne out by evidence, and there is similarly little support for the view that sexual orientation is determined by the impact of the earliest sexual experiences (although many lesbian women do report early heterosexual trauma). Many homosexual people discover their sexual orientation early in life, and recent evidence suggests that genetic factors may be implicated, at least in the homosexual orientation of some males.

A transsexual has a gender identity which conflicts with his or her biological sex. Transsexualism, which is very rare, may be evident from early childhood, or it may develop during adolescence or early adulthood. Although the causes of early transsexualism are not known, it is likely that late-onset transsexualism arises as a result of sexual experimentation involving gender-inappropriate clothing. Very few transsexuals seek to change their gender conviction. Instead, most are motivated towards sex reassignment, which may include surgical intervention.

The term paraphilia covers an apparently diverse group of behaviours, including transvestism, paedophilia, fetishism, voyeurism, exhibitionism and sado-masochism. The behavioural expression of some of these forms of sexual interest is illegal, and the criminal records of many sex offenders testify to the compulsive quality of many of these behaviours (although it must be remembered that not all sex offenders are paraphiliacs). Biological factors may play some role in a predisposition to some paraphilias, but development and expression may depend largely upon inappropriate associative learning during early sexual experimentation, in conjunction with a progressive 'shaping' of the paraphiliac behaviour through instrumental (reinforcement) processes.

Paraphiliac behaviours are often resistant to treatment, but drug treatment may reduce sex drive, cognitive–behavioural techniques may modify inappropriate learning and social skills training may improve the person's ability to form appropriate sexual relationships. Programmes which combine several different elements are most likely to be effective, particularly if they include techniques for motivating the client to change his behaviour and techniques for preventing relapse.

◀Further Reading▶▶▶

Bancroft, J. (1989) *Human Sexuality and Its Problems*, 2nd edn. Edinburgh: Churchill Livingstone.

A comprehensive presentation of sexuality and sex therapy, with a particular emphasis on physiological and medical aspects.

Ussher, J.M. and Baker, C.D. (eds) (1993) *Psychological Perspectives on Sexual Problems: New Directions in Theory and Practice*. London: Routledge.

Various contributors challenge orthodox views of female sexuality and sexual dysfunction. Also includes chapters on cognitive approaches to therapy and on sexual problems in physically and learning disabled people, women with eating disorders and gay men.

Howitt, D. (1995) *Paedophiles and Sexual Offences against Children*. Chichester: Wiley.

Detailed examination of alternative explanations for the origins of paedophilia, and the social context of paedophilia. Includes extensive interview material and offers controversial views of the role of pornography and the role of professionals.

Hollin, C.R. and Howells, K. (eds) (1991) *Clinical Approaches to Sex Offenders and Their Victims*. Chichester: Wiley.

Contributors to this volume examine why people engage in offensive sexual behaviour against adults and children, the effects on victims, and interventions with both perpetrators and their victims. The major focus is on the sexual abuse of children.

Marshall, W.L., Laws, D.R. and Barbaree, H.E. (eds) (1990) *Handbook of Sexual Assault: Issues, Theories, and Treatment of the Offender*. New York: Plenum Press.

A handbook, providing excellent summaries of research on biological and social factors in sexual assault, including the influence of pornography on sexual crimes. Also includes detailed accounts of (mainly behavioural or cognitive–behavioural) assessment and treatment strategies and techniques.

◀Discussion Points▶▶▶

I   To what extent is the human sexual response biological, and to what extent is it psychological and social? Consider whether different answers need to be given to this question with respect to male and female sexuality.

2 How important are psychological factors in the causation and maintenance of sexual dysfunction?

3 Some feminist critics maintain that the orthodox understanding of female sexuality and female sexual dysfunction is based on distorted 'phallocentric' views. To what extent do you agree with this claim?

4 Can an understanding of the nature and origins of homosexuality help us to understand the nature and origins of transsexualism and the paraphilias?

5 What is understood about the nature of transsexualism? Does sex reassignment offer the optimal solution to the plight of the transsexual?

6 Consider paedophilia and one other major type of paraphilia and attempt to explain how these conditions develop.

8 Organic Disorders

Damage to brain tissue often produces deficits in cognitive functioning, and in some cases the damage will also have direct effects on behaviour and mood. Neurological problems arise from many different causal antecedents, including strokes, brain tumours and head injuries. In addition to any primary psychological effects, directly due to the structural brain damage, there are likely to be secondary symptoms, reflecting the individual's psychological response to the primary symptoms. Thus a person who has had a stroke is likely to become depressed about the resulting disabilities and life changes.

◀The Description of Neurological Disorder▶▶▶

Neurological disorders can be categorized in various ways. The 'anatomical approach' distinguishes between cases on the basis of the anatomical site and type of physical pathology involved. The 'functional approach' focuses on the different types of disturbances of psychological functioning associated with brain damage. Finally, the 'aetiological approach' distinguishes between different conditions or syndromes identified on the basis of a clustering of symptoms. The assumption is made that each condition probably reflects a particular causal pattern.

◀The Anatomical Approach▶▶▶

The brain is not an undifferentiated mass of tissue. Areas are specialized in terms of their functioning (see Table 8.1). This 'localization of function'

Table 8.1 Localization of functions within the brain

Frontal lobes	Adaptability
	Action planning
	Motor control
	Problem-solving
	Verbal fluency
	Impulse control
	Social behaviour
	Expressive speech
Temporal lobes	Hearing
	Attention
	Integration of information from different modalities
	Sexual behaviour
Right temporal lobe	Visual recognition
	Spatial long-term memory
	Musical skills
Left temporal lobe	Hearing
	Reading
	Verbal long-term memory
Parietal lobes	Short-term auditory memory
	Speech reception
	Tactile and bodily perceptions
	Left–right discrimination
	Movement sequencing
	Visual recognition
	Spatial orientation
	Reading
	Drawing
	Calculation
Occipital lobes	Visual perception (including colour, movement, depth, orientation, stereopsis, and some object recognition)
	Reading
Brainstem and diencephalon	Arousal
	Alertness
	Drive
	Mood
	Hunger and thirst
	Libido

means that damage to different areas of the brain will have different effects. Damage may be highly localized – for example, following a knife wound – but in many cases it is more diffuse (following a major stroke, for example) or may be pervasive, as when, in some degenerative disorders, the brain tissue as a whole begins to 'break down'.

If the anatomical approach is used to delineate organic conditions,

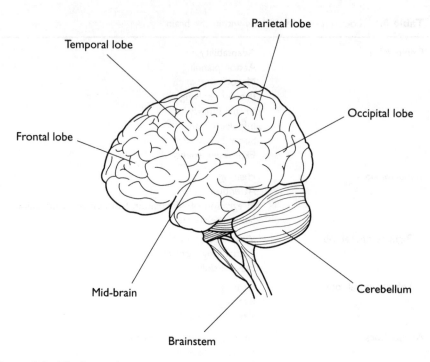

Figure 8.1 The human brain

distinctions might first be made in terms of the anatomical specificity or diffuseness of any damage. In the case of diffuse conditions, differentiation might be made at the cellular level. Thus multiple sclerosis is caused by a dysfunction of the glial cells that produce and maintain the myelin sheath around the axons of neurons. A breakdown in this protective sheath produces weakness, reduced sensation and other symptoms. Another degenerative condition, Alzheimer's disease, involves the atrophy of neurons that produce acetylcholine, a vital neurotransmitter substance.

When damage is less diffuse it is useful to specify which area or areas of the brain are affected. The fact that psychological functions are localized means that such anatomical mapping can be used as a means of anticipating the likely effects of the damage on psychological functioning. The association also works in the other direction. An appreciation of the pattern of deficits in an individual's psychological functioning can generate hypotheses about the likely site of any brain damage. Thus lesions in the frontal lobe are associated with disinhibited behaviour, extreme distractability and problems in thinking about abstract issues (see Box 8.1 for a brief account of the classic case of Phineas Gage). Lesions in the right temporal lobe, however, are associated with certain difficulties in visual and auditory perception. Table 8.2 provides a list of some of the main effects on psychological functioning of damage to particular areas of the brain.

Box 8.1
A Classic Case of Frontal Lobe Damage: Phineas Gage

In 1858, a 25-year-old American, Phineas Gage, was working on the Vermont railroad when an explosion caused an iron bar to pass through the front of his skull, destroying a large quantity of the frontal part of his brain. Following this his whole personality seemed to change. A contemporary report by Harlow (1868) states: 'He is fitful, irreverent, indulging at times in the grossest profanity (which was not previously his custom) ... at times perniciously obstinate, yet capricious and vacillating, devising many plans for future operations, which are no sooner arranged than they are abandoned in turn for others ... his mind is radically changed, so decidedly that his friends and acquaintances said he was "no longer Gage"' (Harlow, 1868, p. 340).

Table 8.2 Some effects of localized brain dysfunction

Frontal lobes	Apraxia
	Perseveration
	Poor quality of thinking (special difficulties with abstraction and synthesis)
	Impulsiveness
	Regressive behaviour
	Disinhibited behaviour
Temporal lobes	Amnesia
	Dementia
Right temporal lobe	Loss of musical ability
	Perceptual deficits with regard to complex visual stimuli
	Difficulties with auditory perception
Left temporal lobe	Aphasia
	Poor verbal memory
	Intellectual loss
Parietal lobes	Body agnosia
	Spatial disorientation
	Apraxia
	Spatial neglect
	Dyslexia (specific reading problem)
	Dyscalculia (specific arithmetic problem)
Occipital lobes	Disturbances of visual recognition
	Hallucinations
	Visual agnosias
Brainstem and diencephalon	Amnestic syndrome
	Emotional instability
	Extreme aggressiveness
	Extreme under-responsiveness
	Excessive or reduced libido
	Anorexia (or excessive eating)
	Coma

◄Psychological Effects of Brain Damage►►►

Influential Factors

Site and extent of brain damage   The nature and degree of deficits depend on whether the damage is diffuse or localized, and, if localized, which particular parts of the brain are affected.

Handedness   Because the brain is asymmetrical in its functioning, damage to tissue on the right side will result in a different pattern of deficits from comparable damage on the left side. There is an association between which side of the brain is 'dominant' for language and the person's handedness. For 99 per cent of right-handed people and for about 60 per cent of left-handed people, language is mainly under the control of the left hemisphere. Left hemisphere damage is therefore likely to result in language deficits. If damage is restricted to the left frontal lobe, language comprehension is likely to be preserved, but an involvement of the left temporal lobe usually leads to some degree of impairment in comprehension.

Rate at which damage occurs   In some cases damage occurs instantly, following a gunshot wound, for example. In other cases, however, the anatomical change may take place gradually over many months. As a general rule, there is a less dramatic disturbance of functioning when the damage evolves slowly.

Type of pathology   The effects of damage arising from a stroke are somewhat different from those arising from a tumour, for example, even if the same area of the brain is involved.

Elapsed time since occurrence of damage   There is often some degree of recovery of function following traumatic brain damage, and thus the greatest deficits are usually observed immediately after the damage has been inflicted.

Age   Lesions in young children tend to have less serious long-term effects than similar lesions in older people, due to the greater plasticity and adaptability of the young brain.

◄The Functional Approach►►►

Another way of describing different neurological conditions is to specify the associated psychological dysfunctions or deficits. Neurological damage can lead to generalized impairments (delirium and dementia) and to a range of more specific, or 'focal', deficits.

Generalized impairments

Delirium The basic features of delirium are a clouded state of consciousness, difficulty in sustaining attention, disorientation in time and place and a disordered stream of thought. Sensations are often misinterpreted, and the person may experience hallucinations (visual, auditory and tactile). Delusions (including the paranoid variety) are also common. The patient may be drowsy, or even stuporous or comatose, although in some cases the condition is marked by extreme agitation.

Delirium can result from a severe infection such as pneumonia and is one of the key symptoms of specific brain infections such as encephalitis and meningitis (an inflammation of the 'meninges', the thin membranes which cover the brain and spinal cord). Children and older adults are most at risk of delirium from such conditions. Delirium also arises as a result of head injury and brain tumours, and other causes include metabolic failures, low blood sugar ('hypoglycaemia') and nutritional deficiencies. The state is sometimes an effect of drug intoxication or drug withdrawal. It is also associated with epilepsy, and may follow surgical intervention. The severity of delirium may vary considerably over time, and tends to be worse at night. Rapid recovery sometimes occurs, perhaps because an underlying cause has been removed. Following recovery, most people are unable to remember what occurred during the period of delirium.

Dementia Dementia is a general impairment of intellect and memory, usually without a disturbance of consciousness. In most cases it is insidious and irreversible. Difficulties with memory are usually among the first signs, with the person having particular problems in recalling recent events. Thinking is often slow and inflexible, and speech may contain grammatical errors. The person may also experience difficulty in finding words.

These various cognitive impairments lead to changes in behaviour and personality. For example, the person may begin to avoid social gatherings and may engage in stereotyped routines in order to make life manageable. Embarrassing gaps in memory may be 'filled' by fictional accounts of recent events (in a process known as 'confabulation'), and any exposure of such a fiction may bring about a depressed response or trigger an aggressive outburst.

As the dementia progresses, the symptoms gradually become more severe. Eventually, there may be little emotional response and the patient may become totally mute. There is a loss of control over voluntary movement, confusion may become total and the person may begin to suffer convulsions. In the final stages the patient is likely to become paralysed and doubly incontinent.

Dementia is not a specific disorder but a pattern of signs and symptoms associated with a number of different disorders and causal antecedents. It is often the result of a widespread degenerative process, although in some cases it is brought about by a tumour or a metabolic dysfunction. Other possible causes include anoxia (lack of oxygen to the brain), head injury, an infection or a cerebrovascular accident (a 'stroke'). In some cases the dementia can be reversed – for example, when it is owing to a metabolic dysfunction or alcohol poisoning – but in the majority of cases the condition is essentially irreversible.

Dementia is particularly associated with old age. As many as a quarter of those aged 85 or older may be suffering from severe or mild dementia, and up to two-thirds of the elderly who suffer from dementia have Alzheimer's disease (see below). Two-thirds of the remainder suffer from 'multi-infarct dementia', which reflects the cumulative brain damage resulting from repeated major or minor strokes. Other, rarer, causes of dementia in older people include tumours, infections and various metabolic disorders.

Focal symptoms

Aphasia The term 'aphasia' refers to a loss in language skills. Particular forms of the symptom affect speech fluency, language comprehension and the ability to repeat phrases and sentences. Aphasia is a deficit in language skills rather than a difficulty in the physical articulation of speech. In non-fluent aphasia the person has a problem in finding words and therefore speaks in a hesitant and faltering way. In fluent aphasia the person speaks without hesitation but uses words inappropriately. Problems with verbal expression may or may not be accompanied by difficulties in reading, writing or understanding other people's speech.

Because language functions are usually localized in the left hemisphere, an acquired language impairment often signals left hemisphere damage. In 'expressive aphasia' language comprehension remains intact but the person has difficulty in finding words, and constructs ungrammatical sentences. This pattern is associated with damage to a region in the left frontal lobe known as Broca's area. By contrast, in 'receptive aphasia' language production is fluent and grammatical (although it may include many invented words, or 'neologisms'), but the person also finds it very difficult to understand speech. Receptive aphasia is associated with damage to a part of the left temporal lobe known as Wernicke's area.

Amnesia 'Amnesia' refers to any pathological loss of memory. Information received via the sense organs enters a series of temporary sensory stores, after which there is a transfer of some information to a 'short-term store'. Two short-term stores may operate, one for visual information and the other for verbal information. Short-term memory, or 'working memory', has a limited capacity and operates for about 15 seconds. Short-term memory operates, for example, when someone looks up a telephone number and then immediately dials that number.

Some of the material in short-term memory is selected for transfer to the long-term memory store, which has a virtually limitless capacity. It is useful to distinguish between long-term memory for personal experiences, called 'episodic memory', and long-term memory for general knowledge, termed 'representational memory'. It is also appropriate to subdivide

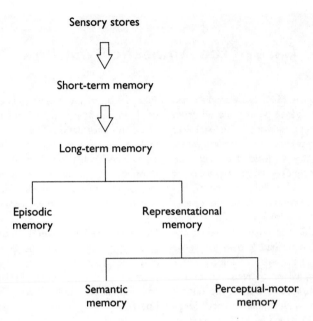

Sensory stores

Short-term memory

Long-term memory

Episodic memory

Representational memory

Semantic memory

Perceptual–motor memory

Figure 8.2 The organization of human memory

representational memory into 'semantic memory' and 'perceptual–motor memory'. The semantic memory is the store of words and their meaning. Perceptual–motor memory facilitates the understanding of perceptual information and the performance of routine action patterns such as dressing or riding a bicycle. Effective memory functioning requires that information be perceived, appropriately selected for transfer to the long-term store, retained and later retrieved.

Amnesia following head injury Most of those who sustain a severe head injury lose consciousness at least momentarily, and then suffer some degree of amnesia when they regain consciousness. There is often an inability to recall events which occurred immediately prior to the accident and when regaining consciousness. Difficulties in recalling new information may then persist for some time after consciousness has been fully restored. The duration of post-traumatic amnesia provides an indication of the seriousness of the injuries which have been sustained (Fortuny et al., 1980) and of the likely outcome of the person's condition.

The amnestic syndrome The amnestic syndrome is a specific pattern of memory deficits in the absence of any general deterioration in intellectual functioning. Short-term memory is unaffected, there is usually good word recall and long-established memories can be recalled without much difficulty. However, there are severe deficits in episodic memory, with a

Box 8.2
A Classic Case of the Amnestic Syndrome: H.M.

A patient known as 'H.M.' is a Canadian man of normal intelligence who suffered from very severe epileptic seizures. The focal sites of these seizures were the temporal lobes, and eventually it was decided to treat the condition by surgically removing parts of both of these lobes. Following surgery, the epilepsy was well controlled, but the operation left the patient with a profound memory impairment. H.M. was unable to recognize hospital staff that he had known for some years, and he was also unable to find his way around the hospital or to recall important events from a few years before the operation. He was, however, able to recall long-distant events. In later life, H.M. can retain information in short-term memory (as long as he has 'kept it in mind') but is unable to store this information. Thus he can read and reread the same magazine article, and it appears new to him on each occasion. He is constantly surprised at seeing himself in a mirror, because he remembers himself as he was before the operation, some forty years ago. He describes his experience as that of 'constantly waking from a dream', and is aware that he has serious disturbance of memory functioning. Despite the severe memory problems, H.M.'s intelligence level has remained stable since before the operation.

profound loss in the ability to remember recent events. The inability to recall ongoing events for more than a few minutes after they have happened means that there is no memory of the recent past. Those who suffer from the most severe form of amnestic syndrome therefore live, in effect, only in the present and in the long-term past (see Box 8.2 for a brief account of the classic case of 'H.M.').

Although the amnestic syndrome is associated with difficulties in both recalling and recognizing new information, there is generally less impairment on recognition tasks, and this suggests that special difficulties may arise at the retrieval stage (Warrington and Weiskrantz, 1972). One theory suggests that the memory deficits shown by those suffering from the amnestic syndrome arise because information is stored in long-term memory in an unorthodox way which does not facilitate the process of retrieval (Hirst, 1982).

The amnestic syndrome may result from a cerebral infection, a haemorrhage, epilepsy, a stroke, a tumour, surgical trauma or carbon monoxide poisoning. However, it is most often associated with Korsakoff's syndrome, a condition which may develop following severe and long-term alcohol abuse. Persistent drinking may lead to a severe deficiency in vitamin B_1 (thiamine), which then precipitates an acute neurological condition known as Wernicke's encephalopathy, the main features of which are acute delirium, disorientation and ataxia (loss of motor coordination). Many of those who suffer from this condition then go on to develop Korsakoff's disease. Anatomically, this is associated with damage to certain subcortical structures, atrophy in the frontal region and haemorrhaging in certain areas. The main psychological symptom of Korsakoff's disease is a severe form of the amnestic syndrome.

Apraxia   Apraxia is an impairment in the ability to perform a skilled motor task appropriately, even though there is no loss of basic physical functioning. Thus the person may lose the ability to imitate gestures, to copy drawings or to carry out routine action sequences successfully. It appears that most apraxic patients are able to perform skilled tasks in the natural setting (thus they may be able to brush their teeth in their own bathroom), but cannot accomplish the same tasks when out of their normal context. Apraxia is generally associated with left hemisphere dysfunction following stroke-induced damage to the parietal lobe.

Agnosia   Agnosia is a loss of ability to understand and interpret sensory stimuli even though the sense organs and the nerves leading to the brain are functioning normally. Such a deficit may be apparent in just one modality (auditory or visual, for example) or in several. Some agnosias are very specific. Thus 'astereognosia' is a loss of ability to recognize objects in their three-dimensional form. Those who suffer from this symptom are therefore unable to recognize familiar objects by touch alone. 'Prosopagnosia' is a form of visual agnosia in which there is a specific loss of ability to recognize faces. Like the apraxias, the agnosias are associated with damage to the parietal lobes.

An extreme case of visual agnosia was reported by the neurologist Oliver Sacks, in his book *The Man who Mistook His Wife for a Hat* (Sacks, 1985). The patient, a professor of music identified as 'Dr P.', did not have a sensory visual impairment but could make little sense of what he saw. He was able to recognize and name complex geometric forms, and could describe the shapes in detail, but he was totally unable to identify everyday objects. Asked to describe a glove presented to him, he offered the following description: 'A continuous surface infolded on itself . . . it appears to have five outpushings, if that is a word.' His difficulties were quite specific and his perception of music, for example, appeared totally unaffected. Neurological investigations eventually revealed that Dr P. had a large tumour in the visual-processing region of his brain.

Perseveration   Perseveration is a disturbance in which a person finds it difficult to change from one kind of activity to another. The patient may find it difficult to release objects that are being held, and may constantly repeat the same action. Those who suffer from severe perseveration show extreme inflexibility both in their motor actions and in their cognitive functioning. This symptom is sometimes referred to as the 'stuck-needle syndrome', and often indicates damage to the frontal lobes.

Distractibility   'Distractibility' is another symptom associated with damage to the frontal area of the brain. Those who suffer from this deficit find it difficult to focus on a task and to discriminate between relevant and irrelevant cues. Experimental studies show, for example, that patients with frontal damage perform particularly poorly on the Stroop colour word test. This test consists of a list of names of colours, each printed in a colour which does not match the name. Most people experience some difficulty when asked to specify the printed colours, due to interference from the incompatible word meanings. People with frontal lobe damage, however, find the task especially onerous because they are powerfully distracted by the irrelevant semantic content of the printed words.

◀ The Diagnosis of Brain Disorders ▶ ▶

The diagnosis of a brain disorder may be made on the basis of a wide range of information relating to pathology, functional deficits and aetiology. The pattern of functional deficits often establishes the likely nature of the disorder, and the history of the condition (whether it developed rapidly or slowly, for example) will usually aid the preliminary diagnosis. Investigations designed to assess functional aspects include examinations of physical responses and mental status, and formal neuropsychological testing routines. Investigations designed to assess pathology include biological assays, brain imaging techniques and, indirectly, investigations to assess psychological functioning.

It is often possible to suggest the probable site and extent of any brain damage from the pattern of functional deficits. Damage may be highly diffuse – as in the senile degenerative disorders – but in the case of strokes and brain tumours there is likely to be a focal area of damage.

The investigation of brain damage

Physical evaluation   Physicians (especially neurologists) can gain a good deal of information about the functioning of the patient's central nervous system by means of a physical examination that includes an assessment of reflexes, motor coordination and perceptual thresholds. Examination of the retina may provide evidence of damage to blood vessels.

Mental-status examination   The mental-status examination assesses the patient's degree of consciousness and the extent of any disorientation. It establishes levels of awareness in various domains, attention span and memory functioning. Orientation is assessed by asking the patient where he or she is and what year, month, day and time it is. Short-term memory may be assessed by asking the patient to repeat a series of numbers, and long-term memory functions are examined by means of questions concerning recent personal and world events, early personal history (the name of the first school attended, for example) and various aspects of general knowledge. Other functions that are assessed include language ability (speech, comprehension, repetition, reading, writing), stream of thought (whether the patient is able to produce a coherent narrative account of some event), mood and social judgement. There are standard procedures for assessing each of these aspects of cognition and affect. In recent years a streamlined version of the mental state examination, the Mini-Mental State Examination (MMSE), has been shown to be practical and reliable (Ferris, 1992).

Neuropsychological testing Neuropsychology is a highly developed specialism within clinical psychology. Some neuropsychological testing provides a more structured and sophisticated way of examining the various functions assessed by the mental-status examination (visual memory, verbal memory, perceptual-motor skills etc.). Groups of tests are often administered to the patient in the form of a 'test battery', the results of which provide a complex profile of the individual's abilities and deficits.

Some test batteries have been devised to establish whether a patient is likely to be suffering from an organic, rather than a psychogenic, disorder. Where there is good preliminary evidence of an organic disorder, further test batteries may be used to investigate the pattern of performance deficits (on memory tasks or language tasks, for example). This can then allow the clinician to offer suggestions about the probable nature of underlying brain dysfunction. The subtest pattern of a sophisticated intelligence test such as the WAIS (the Wechsler Adult Intelligence Scale) can provide some such indication, but a number of more specialized test batteries have been developed. Two of the most widely used are the Halstead–Reitan Battery and the Luria–Nebraska Battery.

The Luria–Nebraska Battery consists of over 250 items relating to intellectual processes, motor skills, memory, verbal and spatial skills, expressive and receptive speech abilities, reading, writing, arithmetic, tactile skills and simple musical skills. The battery takes over two hours to administer, but is very sensitive. The diagnostic power of the battery is unaffected by the patient's level of education. As well as the adult version of the battery there is an adaptation suitable for use with children between eight and 12 years old.

Major developments in brain scanning techniques over the past thirty years have meant that psychological tests now play a much more limited role in the identification of focal brain damage. However, such tests are still useful for a number of purposes. A detailed assessment of the patient's cognitive functioning can provide a baseline against which further deterioration, or recovery of function, can be judged, and it can lead to recommendations concerning the patient's care and possible rehabilitation.

Biological assays A sample of cerebrospinal fluid taken from the base of the spine can be examined for evidence of bleeding, infection, toxins etc. which might be causing, or may result from, brain dysfunction.

EEG The EEG (electroencephalogram) provides a record of the electrical activity of the brain. Patterns in the firing of neurons create fluctuations in voltage that can be picked up through electrodes pasted to the scalp. Amplified up to two million times, these variations can be recorded as a pattern of oscillations or waves. Rhythms of particular frequencies are associated with certain states in the normal waking person, and with various stages of sleep.

Deviations from normal patterns, and abnormal patterns across various positions on the scalp, can indicate different types of brain abnormality.

Brain imaging techniques

Scar tissue, diseased tissue and tumours differ from normal neurons in their density and other properties. Various means of scanning the brain can produce images in which such abnormalities can be identified:

X-rays and CAT scans It is sometimes possible to detect the presence of a tumour by means of an X-ray examination, but CAT (computerized axial tomography) scans are much more sensitive than conventional X-rays. The brain is scanned repeatedly at different angles with an X-ray that records different 'slices' of the patient's brain over the 360 degrees, to produce a 'map' of brain structure, including signs of haemorrhaging, changes in the size of ventricles and variations in the density of brain tissue.

PET scans PET (positron emission tomography) scans are reconstructions of X-ray pictures that show patterns in the use of glucose in the brain (an index of brain activity). A glucose-like substance containing a short-lived radioactive isotope is injected into the patient's bloodstream and the PET scan shows the varying strength of biochemical processes occurring in different parts of the brain.

NMR scans NMR (nuclear magnetic response imaging) scans are produced by placing the patient's head inside a large circular magnet and recording the movement of hydrogen atoms as the magnetism is switched on and off. The resulting electromagnetic signal is subjected to computer analysis so that a representation of variations in the brain tissue can be obtained.

Exploratory neurosurgery In some cases there is no real alternative but to undertake exploratory brain surgery in order to investigate the nature and extent of disease.

◄Brain Disorder: an Aetiological Classification►►►

There are many different causes of brain dysfunction, and in the next section we will follow the aetiological approach to the classification of brain disorder. Table 8.3 provides a simple outline of the many different causes of brain dysfunction.

Brain damage often follows a severe blow to the head. Head injury may lead to haemorrhaging and structural damage to the brain tissue. A punch, a kick or forceful shaking may lead to concussion and bruising. Gunshots

Table 8.3   Brain dysfunction: outline of some causes

Brain trauma	Concussion Contusion Laceration
Cerebrovascular accidents ('strokes')·	Cerebral occlusion (blockage in blood vessel(s)) Cerebral haemorrhage
Hypoxia	(Shortage of oxygen – may be due to heart attack, drowning, respiratory disorders etc.)
Brain tumours	(Also other forms of 'space-occupying lesion' including cerebral abscesses)
Cerebral infection	Encephalitis Meningitis Neurosyphilis HIV
Toxins	Mushroom toxins Lead Other heavy-metals (mercury, manganese etc.) Psychoactive drugs (alcohol, barbiturates, opiates etc.) Carbon monoxide
Metabolic dysfunction	Electrolyte disturbance (potassium, sodium, calcium) Uraemia (retention of waste materials in the blood) Hypoglycaemia (low blood sugar)
Nutritional deficiencies	Korsakoff's disease Pellagra (deficiency of vitamin B_3 – niacin) Beriberi (deficiency of vitamin B_1 – thiamine)

Endocrine dysfunction	Thyroid syndromes
	Adrenal syndromes
	  Addison's syndrome (hypoadrenalism)
	  Cushing's syndrome (hyperadrenalism)

Degenerative disorders	Dementia due to ageing Alzheimer's disease Pick's disease Multi-infarct dementia Huntington's disease Parkinson's disease
The epilepsies	

and motor vehicle accidents will produce multiple lacerations and can result in a substantial loss of brain tissue. A 'cerebrovascular accident' or 'stroke' is said to occur when the blood vessels in the brain become blocked, or tear, interrupting the cerebral flood flow. Growths in the brain ('tumours' and abscesses) may damage structures, disrupt blood flow and increase pressure. Some brain tumours are benign, whereas other are malignant. Brain dysfunction may occur as the result of infections, including those of encephalitis, meningitis and syphilis (in its tertiary stage), and several forms of neurological damage are associated with AIDS.

Many different substances have a toxic action on brain tissue, including lead and other heavy metals, carbon monoxide and a wide range of psychoactive drugs. Various nutritional deficiencies also cause serious brain damage. A severe deficiency in vitamin B_1 (thiamine) may lead to the acute neurological condition known as Wernicke's encephalopathy, which is often followed by Korsakoff's syndrome. Symptoms of pellagra, which is caused by a deficiency in niacin (vitamin B_3), include confusion, delirium, hallucination and ultimately dementia. Brain dysfunction can also develop as the result of a number of endocrine disorders, including thyroid and adrenal syndromes.

The most frequent cause of severe brain dysfunction is the degeneration of brain tissue. Such deterioration may result from normal ageing processes or from specific degenerative disorders such as Alzheimer's disease or Huntington's disease. Finally, certain abnormalities in neuronal functioning produce the spasms and seizures associated with the group of brain disorders known as 'the epilepsies'.

The epilepsies

An epileptic seizure (or 'fit') is an episode of altered consciousness resulting from bursts of abnormal discharges in large neuronal groups. A seizure is marked by perceptual disturbances and loss of muscle control. Around 7 per cent of the population have had at least one epileptic seizure at some time (mostly during childhood), and about half of these will have had a number of seizures. However, only about 0.5 per cent of the adult population suffer from an active and ongoing epileptic disorder. There is some evidence of a weak hereditary effect, but the precise nature of the genetic involvement is not understood.

Seizures may occur as a result of a tumour, intoxication, drug withdrawal, an infection or head injury, and people who show such symptoms are sometimes said to be suffering from 'symptomatic epilepsy'. But in around three-quarters of cases none of these factors appears to be responsible, and the individual is then said to be suffering from 'idiopathic epilepsy'.

In fact, a number of rather different conditions are included within this category. All the conditions involve seizures, but the seizures take a number of different forms. The most severe type is the *grand mal* seizure, which can be characterized as involving four stages. The first stage is the 'aura', a partial seizure that often involves an odd sensory or affective experience. For example, some people report that they smell a strong odour during the aura, others develop a sense of profound apprehension and others experience cramps or dizziness.

When the aura has persisted for some little while (often no more than a few seconds), the major seizure begins. The person loses consciousness and collapses while entering the second, 'tonic', phase. The voluntary muscles begin a series of contractions lasting up to 20 seconds. Typically, the person's legs are outstretched and the fists clenched. Breathing may be interrupted, and control over the bladder and bowel may be lost. In the third phase, the 'clonic' phase, jerking movements occur as the muscles relax and contract in rapid alternation. At this stage some people bite their tongue, and this sometimes leads to a serious injury.

The clonic phase lasts for between one and three minutes, and the person then generally passes into a sleep or 'coma', eventually waking in a highly confused state and typically having no memory of the fit or of the events leading up to it. In rare cases people do not revive, but continue to have seizures. This condition, known as *status epilepticus*, is extremely dangerous and may be fatal unless emergency treatment is administered.

A quite different form of seizure is the *petit mal*. This involves a loss of consciousness for a few seconds. The person remains immobile, stops speaking and may turn pale, but does not collapse and does not perform jerking movements. Those who suffer a *petit mal* seizure are often unaware of the temporary loss of consciousness and simply resume their activity when the seizure is over. Some individuals have *petit mal* seizures as often as three or four times an hour.

Both *grand mal* and *petit mal* seizures involve neuronal disturbances across a large part of the brain. By contrast, the physical disturbances which give rise to 'focal seizures' are restricted to a particular part of the brain.

The location of the epileptic focus determines, to a large degree, the nature of the symptoms experienced during a seizure. Of special interest and concern is temporal lobe epilepsy. This usually produces memory deficits and may cause the person to experience hallucinations and specific distortions of awareness labelled *déjà vu* (the sense of having had precisely the same experience before) or *jamais vu* (the sense of not recognizing things which are in fact familiar). Temporal lobe seizures do not render the person unconscious, but they do usually produce some degree of confusion and dreaminess. The person may continue to perform automatic and skilled behaviours throughout the seizure.

There are two other important types of epileptic disorder, known as 'Jacksonian epilepsy' and 'psychomotor epilepsy'. Jacksonian epilepsy (named after Hughlings Jackson, one of the pioneers in the field) involves partial seizures which primarily affect motor responses. The seizure begins with a twitching or tingling in the hands and feet, and these sensations may then spread to other parts of the body. In psychomotor epilepsy, an initial aura is followed by a loss of contact with reality, usually for a few minutes. Following the seizure, the person has little awareness of anything which occurred during the fit. Some psychomotor seizures are marked by bizarre or psychotic-like behaviour. For example, the person may undress or urinate in public, become aggressive or appear to be responding to hallucinated voices.

Although it is often impossible to identify any environmental stimulus as having provoked a particular epileptic seizure, some fits do appear to be triggered by certain situational features, such as specific sounds or stroboscopic lights operating and a specific frequency. Seizures are sometimes induced by a blow to the head, or an abnormal metabolic state resulting from fatigue, hyperventilation or low blood sugar. And some women appear to be at higher risk of having a fit during a particular stage of their menstrual cycle.

In the majority of cases, both generalized and focal epilepsy can be effectively controlled by the use of anti-convulsant medication. In very extreme cases in which medication is not effective, and in which the person continues to suffer from severe focal epilepsy, surgery may be used to remove the part of the brain that is acting as the site for the seizures.

The psychosocial consequences of epilepsy   Epilepsy remains a socially stigmatizing condition, and those who have recurrent seizures often find that they are treated unfairly in the employment market. Discrimination may be related in part to fears about safety – for example, with respect to driving, or controlling industrial machinery – but it also reflects the embarrassment which many people feel when they witness someone having a fit, and it reflects a general attitude towards those who are suffering from a 'psychiatric condition'.

Such stigmatization is highly regrettable, and is keenly felt by many people whose epilepsy is well controlled by anti-convulsant medication. Most of those who have had one or more epileptic seizures have no psychiatric symptoms, although about one-third of those who suffer from epilepsy will develop some kind of psychological disorder at some time (Fenwick, 1987). This is partly because seizures can lead to structural brain damage, particularly if they are focal. But whereas it was once believed that epilepsy inevitably led to a deterioration in personal behaviour and a decline in intelligence, it is now established that such consequences are rare. And any personality change which occurs is likely to reflect the social effects of being a person suffering from epilepsy, rather than a direct consequence of the epilepsy itself.

Neurosyphilis

Syphilis is a relatively common sexually transmitted disease which can now be treated very effectively with antibiotics. If treatment is not obtained when the condition first develops, the acute symptoms will eventually disappear, but the apparent recovery may mask a secondary incubation phase that can last for up to 25 years. In some cases of secondary-stage syphilis the central nervous system is invaded by an organism that produces an inflammation and degeneration of the central nervous system. Eventually, the neurological effects at a tertiary stage become apparent as 'neurosyphilis'. There are various forms of neurosyphilis, but in around a half of the cases which reach this stage a disorder develops which is known as 'general paresis' (formerly GPI, or 'general paralysis of the insane').

The first symptoms of this condition are emotional changes. The person becomes irritable, depressed and apathetic. Soon afterwards an intellectual deterioration may become apparent. Certain psychotic symptoms can also develop, including delusions and hallucinations. Delusions of grandeur, or paranoid delusions, may be present. If the condition goes untreated, the dementia will become more severe, tremors are likely to develop and the person may be subject to seizures. Profound memory deficits develop, and the person may become manic or severely depressed. The condition eventually leads to paralysis, and unless treatment is provided death will usually occur within five years of the onset of the tertiary symptoms. Post-mortem examination reveals profound atrophy throughout the cerebral hemispheres and a thickening of the meninges.

Timely treatment with antibiotics can eliminate the early symptoms and return the person to relatively healthy functioning. Treatment at a later stage with high doses of penicillin is usually effective in preventing further deterioration in functioning. Because most people suffering from syphilis have been effectively treated since antibiotics became widely available, general paresis, which was once quite common, is now rarely encountered.

AIDS-related neurological disorders

The acquired immune deficiency syndrome (AIDS) was first recognized in 1981, and two years later it was discovered that a virus (the human immunodeficiency virus, HIV) was responsible for the condition. The clinical manifestations of full-blown AIDS are infections, including pneumonia, and various forms of tumour, the most common of which is Kaposi's sarcoma, a malignant growth which develops in the skin and the gastrointestinal tract. AIDS patients may also develop a malignant proliferation of lymph tissue (lymphoma), which can affect the central nervous system, bone marrow, gastrointestinal tract the skin.

Nearly 80 per cent of those who die from AIDS are found at autopsy to have neuropathological abnormalities. In addition to tumours and infections, HIV (the virus) causes widespread atrophy in many areas of the brain (particularly the central white matter). The virus does not appear to invade neurons, but it does invade non-neuronal brain cells, causing them to produce substances which have a toxic effect on neurons. The end result is a form of dementia known as the 'AIDS dementia complex', which affects a third of AIDS patients (Kennedy, 1988). This condition is marked by severe memory loss, confusion, impaired concentration and other cognitive effects (which sometimes include hallucinations). Most of those who suffer from this condition become withdrawn and depressed, although some become hyperactive and agitated. Many patients develop a tremor, become unsteady in their gait, become very weak and lose motor coordination. The condition progresses to total dementia, usually within weeks or a few months, following which the person enters the terminal stage.

Cerebrovascular accidents ('strokes')

A 'stroke' is an acute disturbance of brain functioning following an interruption in the cerebral blood supply. In the majority of cases the interference with arterial blood flow leads to the death of some brain tissue. The disturbance in blood supply is usually the result of a blockage ('cerebral occlusion') due to atheroma (the build-up of fatty substances on the arterial walls), but in some cases it follows a rupture in one or more of the small arteries inside the brain. This then produces bleeding – cerebral haemorrhaging. Untreated high blood pressure is a major risk factor for strokes.

About a third of those who have a stroke die within a month, and strokes are one of the most frequent causes of death in Europe and the USA. About half of those who survive are disabled in some way, the most frequent form of disability being a weakness or paralysis on one side of the body ('hemiplegia'). The majority of strokes are unilateral (they involve only one of the cerebral hemispheres) and, because motor control is organized 'contralaterally' (i.e. the left hemisphere controls the movement of the right side of the body, and the right hemisphere controls the movement of the left side), a stroke in one hemisphere will produce weakness, loss of sensation and limb paralysis on the opposite side of the body. Strokes that occur in the brain stem tend to have more generalized effects, and strokes in other areas may increase the pressure throughout the brain and lead to various brain stem effects, including unconsciousness and respiratory paralysis.

The person's clinical condition immediately following a stroke provides some indication of the prognosis. In general terms, the outcome is likely to be poor if the immediate deficits are severe. Certain symptoms, including prolonged unconsciousness, incontinence and a tendency for the eyes to deviate to one side, also signal an unfavourable outcome.

Strokes may lead to any of a wide range of cognitive dysfunctions. A very severe stroke can produce dementia, although this is more likely to follow a series of smaller strokes ('multi-infarct dementia'). Localized damage will lead to more specific difficulties. For example, if the visual pathways of one hemisphere are damaged the person may experience what amounts to a 'blindness' in the contralateral visual field. Thus a person who has suffered a severe right hemisphere stroke may be unable to see objects on the left side of the field of vision. This perceptual deficit is referred to as 'hemianopia'.

Strokes that occur within the left hemisphere tend to produce disturbances of language functioning, including anomia (a loss in the ability to name familiar objects) and the receptive and expressive forms of aphasia. Conversely, patients who have suffered right hemisphere damage frequently show abnormalities of spatial orientation, including apraxia and agnosia (Wade et al., 1986). They may also show evidence of 'anosognosia', or 'left-sided neglect' – a loss of awareness of the left side of the body and of the left side of the external environment.

Many people change in their behaviour and personality following a stroke. Some show gross behavioural disturbances and some become very irritable. There may be an extreme lability of mood, but many people become very apathetic and some become profoundly depressed. Such emotional states may reflect the long-term disruption of brain functions precipitated by the stroke, but they are also understandable psychological responses to the sudden infliction of a major disabling condition.

The process of rehabilitation can usually begin a week or two after the stroke and is likely to involve physical training to improve limb movements.

Specific interventions may also be needed to deal with cognitive difficulties. In the longer term, those who remain disabled as the result of a stroke often have considerable difficulty adjusting to new constraints on their lifestyle. The frustration resulting from their limitations and their dependency on other people may lead to persistent irritability and frequent expressions of anger, although some patients become very passive, withdrawn and depressed. Various appliances and modifications to the home environment may aid mobility and reduce dependency, and counselling may help to alleviate the emotional effects of the disability. Marital and family work can help not only the patient but also other family members, many of whom are considerably stressed as a result of the relative's stroke and its aftermath.

Huntington's disease

Huntington's disease is a hereditary syndrome which was first recognized in 1872. It is estimated that about 100000 people worldwide suffer from the condition. The average prevalence figure quoted for Huntington's disease is around five per 100000 of the population, but pockets of unusually high prevalence occur in some areas of the world. This is related to the hereditary nature of the disease and reflects the presence of a number of affected families within particular localities. One small region in Venezuela has the highest prevalence, the rate being over 500 times that of the UK or the USA.

The symptoms of Huntington's disease are both neurological and psychological and usually begin to appear between the ages of 30 and 50. The signs of neurological dysfunction include a number of motor disturbances and the psychological symptoms include both cognitive and affective abnormalities. Following such early signs as occasional grimaces, involuntary shrugs, difficulties in pronouncing words and an unsteadiness of gait, more striking movement abnormalities become apparent. The person may show pronounced facial twitching and nodding, together with gross writhing ('choreiform') movements. Eventually, the motor abnormalities affect all aspects of the person's behaviour, including speech, eating and swallowing, walking and respiration.

Signs of psychological dysfunction may become apparent either before or after the first neurological signs. Some people who suffer from Huntington's disease have an earlier history of schizophrenia and other psychiatric conditions. The first cognitive symptom of Huntington's disease itself is often a pronounced distractibility. There is usually a slow decline in intellectual functioning, although memory often remains relatively unimpaired until a late phase of the illness. Many patients therefore retain an insight into their condition until they reach an advanced stage. The dominant affective symptom is usually depression, although outbursts of anger are not uncommon. Eventually the person is likely to withdraw into a state of profound apathy. Huntington's disease is progressive and eventually leads to death, the life expectancy following the onset of symptoms being around 15 years.

The pathology of Huntington's disease includes a general atrophy of the cortex, particularly in the frontal areas. The ventricles become enlarged and there are major losses of neurons in the corpus striatum and at the head of the caudate nucleus. Autopsy studies show a deficiency in the neurotransmitter substance GABA in several parts of the brain. GABA has an inhibitory effect on dopamine activity, and it is suggested that at least some of the symptoms of the disorder arise from abnormalities in the action of dopamine.

Although there is no cure for Huntington's disease, some of the symptoms (including the choreiform movements) may be relieved temporarily by means of neuroleptic drugs. These may be effective because they act on the dopamine systems. In addition, anti-depressant drugs and minor tranquillizers may be used to treat the depression and anxiety which often accompany the neurological and cognitive dysfunctions.

Hereditary factors are implicated in many types of psychological disorder, but in most cases such factors play a modest role in adjusting the individual's level of vulnerability to the disorder. However, in the case of Huntington's disease the person's genetic make-up is the sole and determinate cause, and all those who are born with the relevant genetic anomaly do eventually develop the disorder. The means of genetic transmission is now well understood. It has long been established that transmission is by means of a single dominant gene, and in 1983 it was shown that this was located on chromosome 4. In 1993 the relevant gene was itself identified (IT15) (Huntington's Disease Collaborative Research Group, 1993).

The single dominant gene transmission means that 50 per cent of the offspring of an affected person will develop Huntington's disease in adulthood. The other half of the offspring will not develop the disease themselves and will not pass it on to any of their children. Thus the disorder would be eradicated (almost – some spontaneous genetic mutations do occur) if those who had the relevant gene abnormality did not have children.

Although it would clearly be unethical to coerce people into remaining childless, the need for young adults at risk of developing the disorder to receive genetic counselling has long been recognized. In the past, those who received such counselling came to realize that there was a 50:50 chance that they might have the relevant gene abnormality and that they might not know for certain whether they were at risk of passing on the abnormality until the age of 50 or so. It was impossible to determine in advance of the first symptoms which of the offspring of a Huntington's patient would develop the disorder (i.e. there was no presymptomatic test).

The situation changed dramatically in 1983 with the production of a test which could predict with limited accuracy which people would develop the disorder. Further refinements since that time mean that it is now possible to predict accurately which vulnerable people (i.e. the close relatives of a Huntington's patient) possess the aberrant gene (Tyler et al., 1992). These developments have raised many fundamental questions, including the degree to which people should be encouraged to take the test and how far those who test positive should be exhorted to remain childless. There is clearly a need to provide intensive emotional support for those who learn that they will one day develop Huntington's disease. Such information is likely to make the person feel severely depressed and may lead to attempts at suicide.

Indeed, ever since the disorder was first recognized it has been appreciated that there is a relatively high rate of suicide among relatives of Huntington's patients A test which will in many cases confirm the individual's worst fears needs to be administered in a context which is adequately resourced to provide a high level of continuing psychological support.

Alzheimer's disease

Alzheimer's disease is an insidious, crippling and eventually fatal disorder. It is the most common cause of dementia and affects between 5 and 10 per cent of people over 65 and 20 per cent of those over 80 (Henderson, 1986). Over the whole population, the rate is increasing as life expectancy increases, and in no fewer than a third of families at least one parent will die of the disease. Alzheimer's is more common in women than in men. Risk factors include a family history of dementia or Down's syndrome, advanced maternal age at the time of the person's birth and previous head injury (Amaducci et al., 1992).

Various subtypes of Alzheimer's disease have been differentiated, but the most significant distinction is that made between the 'early onset' form (which begins before the age of 65) and the 'late onset' form. Although Alzheimer's disease mostly affects older people, it can occur in people as young as 40. Early onset is associated with a more rapid course, with greater loss of neurons and with more substantial disturbances of perceptual and motor functions. Hereditary factors are also said to be more important in determining an individual's vulnerability to the early onset form of the disease.

Alzheimer's disease involves the progressive degeneration of brain tissue, leading to a gradual deterioration in intellectual ability, skilled performance and emotional integration. The primary symptoms are cognitive, and one of the earliest symptoms is a difficulty in remembering recent events. Other early signs include problems in recalling words or people's names, and irritability. The person may also show some degree of disorientation.

Diagnosis It is not an easy matter to distinguish Alzheimer's disease from other forms of dementia. Indeed, absolute certainty of diagnosis may be established only when brain tissue is examined after death. When the German physician Alois Alzheimer first described the syndrome in 1906, he raised a number of diagnostic issues which are still not totally resolved. For example, it is not yet possible to make a clear distinction between senile dementia and the normal processes of brain ageing, and it remains unclear whether Alzheimer's disease should be considered a variant of senile dementia or a distinct disorder.

In the early stages of the disorder, a tentative diagnosis may be given on the basis of psychological competence. A procedure such as the Mini-Mental State Examination (MMSE) may be used to assess aspects of cognitive functioning (Ferris, 1992), but will often need to be supplemented with a detailed neuropsychological assessment. This may reveal mild impairments in language expression and comprehension, verbal and non-verbal memory, the organization of skilled tasks, attention and abstract thinking. In addition to the various psychometric and neuropsychological test batteries available to test such functions, assessments are often made of the person's daily living skills.

Establishing that there is a loss of intellectual functioning, or dementia, does not of itself establish that the person is suffering from Alzheimer's disease. Possible alternative diagnoses, including those of a brain tumour, multi-infarct dementia, Parkinson's disease, depression and acute confusional state, may be eliminated by the use of appropriate psychological tests, EEGs and brain scans.

Clinical picture Following initial difficulties with orientation and memory for recent events, deficits eventually become apparent even in simple, well established and overlearned tasks. Thus the person may become unable to recall the names of close relatives, and may have difficulty in dressing and washing. Forgetfulness and other symptoms may cause accidents in the home. Aphasia, agnosia, apraxia and alexia are all common in Alzheimer's patients. Language impairments include difficulties with naming, word fluency, comprehension and word association. Semantic (word meaning) aspects appear to be affected more than phonological and syntactic aspects. Language performance is also likely to be adversely affected by the person's general state of confusion and disorientation, or by deficits in perception, memory and intellectual functioning (Miller, 1989).

Suspiciousness, paranoia and delusions are common in Alzheimer's, and around a quarter of patients experience hallucinations (Cummings and Victoroff, 1990). There are also many behavioural symptoms, including restlessness, agitation, pacing and wandering. The level of the person's appetite may change and many patients display idiosyncratic patterns of sleeping and waking. When they wake at night their confusion and disorientation may be profound. Urinary incontinence may also develop. Changes in personality and mood may include increased anger and irritability and a loss of inhibitions, sometimes to an embarrassing or dangerous degree. Many patients become apathetic and depressed, although major depressive episodes rarely occur.

The progressive deterioration in the person's intellectual abilities and memory, together with changes in affect and motivation, will eventually mean that the person is unable to function independently in the home. The extent of the disability needs to be closely monitored so that the person can be provided with adequate care and helped to avoid danger. Several standardized instruments for assessing such aspects are available. The Instrumental Activities of Daily Living (IADL) scale provides information concerning the person's competence on such tasks as food preparation, washing and cleaning, and handling money (Lawton and Bordy, 1969). The Clifton Assessment Procedures for the Elderly (CAPE) provides an assessment of behavioural and cognitive functioning and can also be used to gauge the level of the person's dependency on others (Pattie and Gilleard, 1979).

Pathology and aetiology   Alzheimer's disease involves a loss of neuronal material. Abnormal proteins produced by the brain appear to have a toxic effect on neurons and lead to substantial atrophy across several areas. The brain tissue of the Alzheimer's patient also includes twisted nerve fibres (known as 'tangles') and small lesions in the neurons ('plaques'), and metabolic dysfunction leads to a deficiency in the neurotransmitter substance acetylcholine. There is a close association between the extent of biological deterioration and the degree of cognitive and behavioural dysfunction. Thus the clinical state in the terminal stage is correlated with the extent of neuron loss, the number of plaques and tangles, and the degree of acetylcholine deficiency, all of which may be assessed at autopsy. Although the biological basis of many of the symptoms of Alzheimer's disease is fairly well understood, the primary causes of the disorder are still subject to much speculation. Why do some brains develop plaques and tangles, produce abnormal proteins and suffer a reduction in acetylcholine levels, while other brains do not?

The results of a number of family studies (including twin studies) indicate that genetic factors influence an individual's level of vulnerability to Alzheimer's. This is also supported by the fact that the majority of people with Down's syndrome (a form of mental deficiency caused by a chromosomal abnormality) eventually develop Alzheimer's disease. However, many MZ (identical) twins are discordant for the disorder, indicating that environmental influences also play a part (Rapoport et al., 1991). The mode of genetic transmission is not known, although a number of possible modes have been suggested (Kay, 1989). A number of hypotheses have also suggested that the disorder may be linked to viral effects, to the toxic effects of aluminium, and to specific dysfunctions of the immune system (Deary and Whalley, 1988).

Treatment   There is no cure for Alzheimer's disease, although some studies have demonstrated that a number of drugs (including nicotine) may act as 'cognitive enhancers' for Alzheimer's patients (Warburton, 1992). It is possible that drugs now under development may help to stimulate the production of acetylcholine or to inhibit the production of abnormal proteins in the brain (Bartus, 1990).

Drugs are currently used to relieve the emotional and psychotic-like symptoms which often develop in people suffering from Alzheimer's disorder. Anxiolytics may relieve anxiety, although they do sometimes make the symptoms worse. Anti-depressants may be prescribed, and neuroleptic drugs are occasionally used to deal with such symptoms as delusions or hallucinations. Hypnotic drugs may be used to promote regular sleeping.

Psychological intervention in dementia

No amount of psychological treatment can reverse the intellectual deterioration or memory deficits evident in Alzheimer's patients, but a number of psychological interventions can help to reduce the impact of such deficits, and to make life less burdensome for patients and their carers, particularly in the early stages of the disorder.

For example, the physical environment may be arranged to reduce the effects of disorientation and impaired memory. Notice boards can be placed in prominent places within the home with useful information, and a standard shopping list might be provided. Important phone numbers can be pinned above the telephone, and a 'visitor's book' placed near the door, so that callers 'sign in' and leave reminder messages. A calendar with the day, month and year clearly marked may help to reduce disorientation. Safety in the home may be enhanced by installing hand-rails, replacing gas fires with storage heaters, placing a non-slip mat in the bath and fitting special locks and alarms. Low-power nightlights provide a useful aid for those who leave their bed during the night. Slip-on shoes may be far easier for the person to manage than shoes which require laces to be tied.

Goal planning   One specific and structured approach to helping people suffering from dementia is labelled 'goal planning' (Barrowclough and Fleming, 1986). This involves first identifying individuals' needs and resources. Needs are stated in positive terms ('Mr Smith needs to consult the newspaper to check when his favourite television programmes are on'), and resources include personal assets, personal skills and social resources (carers, friends and available services). Realistic goals are set, and small steps planned to enable each objective to be achieved. The process is highly structured, and the planning involves direct communication with the patient as far as possible, although carers may be involved in guiding the person through the successive steps and monitoring progress.

Reality orientation   'Reality orientation' (RO) is the name given to strategies that help people to orient themselves in time and place and to maintain a sense of identity. RO often takes the form of structured sessions in which a small group of people are encouraged to note the day and the time, to appreciate where they are and to use each other's names. The group members are then encouraged to talk about aspects of their current and past life. Newspapers and magazines may be used to stimulate conversation, and materials relating to events thirty or forty years ago are often used with elderly people to stimulate 'reminiscence' (Coleman, 1986). Recalling happy memories, and sharing them with others, may enhance the person's mood and stimulate a satisfying social interaction.

In informal RO, or '24-hour RO', care staff and relatives enhance the person's orientation by making frequent references to the time, for example, or announcing which meal will be served next. Carers may look through a newspaper with the patient, commenting on various pictures and stories and making links to the person's own life. Evaluation studies have shown that RO is effective in reducing disorientation and increases the satisfaction and interest of those suffering from dementia (Holden and Woods, 1988).

The course of the disease   Although the course of Alzheimer's disease is highly variable, the general pattern is one of progressive deterioration.

Some authorities distinguish between three phases or stages of the disorder. In the 'forgetfulness stage' the person experiences difficulty in recalling recent events. Objects are frequently 'lost', there may be difficulty in recalling names and there is some degree of disorientation. The person often finds it difficult to maintain concentration and may become anxious or irritable.

In the 'confusional stage', memory abilities weaken further, there is a clear intellectual deterioration and the person is likely to wander. Fictional accounts of recent events may be offered in a bid to conceal the extent of memory problems (confabulation), and there may be frequent errors of speech. There is likely to be a lack of emotional responsiveness, the person may show little interest in ongoing events, and he or she may act as a silent witness to social interactions rather than becoming actively involved.

In the final stage of dementia, people are unable to perform even the simplest of tasks, and the severity of the intellectual impairment is apparent in the person's inability to construct a coherent sentence. At this stage the person will be profoundly disoriented and will need assistance in all aspects of care, including toileting and feeding.

There is considerable variation in how rapidly people progress through these stages. There may be apparently random fluctuations within the general course of deterioration, but an adverse environmental change or a physical illness (especially an illness involving delirium) may lead to a sudden decline in the person's level of functioning. Most people survive for between five and ten years after the first signs of the disorder became apparent (although a diagnosis may not have been established until some time after this). Eventually, the need for continual nursing care may require the person to be accommodated within a residential home or a hospital. Relatives sometimes insist that they will continue to provide for the patient's needs. However, many such carers are themselves of advanced age, and they may not be in the best of health.

Effects on care-givers Many of the relatives who care for Alzheimer's patients experience extremely high levels of strain, become very fatigued and feel physically run down (Gilhooly, 1984). Many become socially isolated during their period of caring for the person suffering from dementia, and many suffer from serious emotional problems including anxiety and depression (Morris et al., 1988). Although many Alzheimer's patients are very passive, some are extremely demanding and frequently irritable. In some cases the relationship between the sufferer and the carer deteriorates to such a degree that there are conflictual flare-ups which result in physical aggression. The situation is often one of desperation, particularly if the carer has little contact with and support from other people. In recent years the plight of relatives caring for Alzheimer's patients has been more widely recognized, and in some cases this has been met with the provision of help, including domiciliary support and respite care. A number of self-help and support groups have also been formed.

Severe head injury

Severe head injuries may be the result of violent attacks (gunshots, stabbings, kicking etc.) or accidents (particularly falls and motor vehicle accidents). A number of those who suffer such injuries are young children or older adults, but teenagers and young adults are also at a relatively high level of risk. The primary effects of head injury include a wide variety of sensory, motor, cognitive and affective symptoms, the pattern of psychological deficits reflecting the site and extent of the neurological damage. In extreme cases, head injury will lead to death or to lifelong coma ('a persistent vegetative state').

As well as the primary psychological effects of brain damage, there are also many secondary effects. Prigatano (1987) described a number of personality changes frequently found in patients following severe head injury. Many become extremely anxious and a high proportion become severely depressed. The depression often stems from a 'learned helplessness', and may be associated with paranoia, social withdrawal and a loss of motivation. The individual's mood may fluctuate erratically between despair and euphoria.

Behavioural disruption may take the form of frequent aggressive acts or 'catastrophic reactions' (anger and tearfulness, together with restlessness and stereotyped movements). Many people appear to lose self-control very readily. Some become very disinhibited, and many make highly inappropriate judgements of social situations (Brooks and McKinlay, 1983). Such difficulties often persist for a considerable time after the injury was inflicted, and the frequency of threatening and aggressive behaviour may actually increase over the months and years (Brooks et al., 1986).

Many cases of traumatic head injury are complicated by the person having sustained other injuries at the same time, or by an involvement in protracted legal proceedings. Thus involvement in a serious industrial accident or motor vehicle accident may have left the person with physical disabilities or sensory impairments in addition to severe brain damage. Unresolved issues about the causes of and responsibility for an attack or accident may add to the person's confusion and to feelings of anger, anxiety or guilt. And adjustment is not facilitated by criminal proceedings or personal injury litigation which may remain unsettled for several years.

The primary and secondary effects of severe head injury often exact a considerable toll on the person's family (Brooks, 1991). Living with a relative who has undergone a major personality change and who has become irritable, aggressive and depressed often proves extremely stressful, and adverse effects on care-givers are particularly intense when there is a high 'burden of care' (i.e. when the person is highly dependent and the responsibility for care falls on just one or two people). A number of studies have shown that many close family members of severely head injured people are frustrated, socially isolated and depressed.

Various 'stage models' have been suggested as useful frameworks for describing how the families of head-injured people adjust over time. Lezak (1982) proposed a model involving six stages: (a) preoccupation with helping; (b) bewilderment and anxiety; (c) guilt and despair; (d) acceptance of change; (e) active mourning; and (f) adaptation. Groveman and Brown (1985) use a five-stage model: (a) denial and isolation; (b) anger; (c) bargaining; (d) depression; and (e) acceptance. Such models can be helpful, but it is unlikely that any one could be applied usefully to all cases.

◄Recovery following Brain Damage►►►

Many infections, nutritional deficiencies and hormonal imbalances can be treated, and it may be possible to reduce levels of toxic agents within the brain. Neurosurgery can be used to excise tumours, to stop haemorrhaging and to remove the focus of a severe epilepsy. However, once brain tissue is dead it is not replaced. Although damaged neurons may recover, no new neurons are produced beyond infancy. And although it is sometimes possible to slow the rate of deterioration in the case of degenerative disorders, or even to halt the atrophy, by treating the underlying cause, any tissue which has died is permanently lost.

In the long term, it may be possible to understand the inhibitory mechanisms which preclude the regeneration of central neural tissue, and some way might then be found of stimulating regeneration. This is an area which is currently attracting a good deal of research activity. An alternative approach, which has already met with some success in a limited number of brain-damaged patients, involves the grafting of healthy neural tissue into the damaged brain. However, this form of treatment is still at a very early stage of development.

Although brain tissue cannot be recovered, many patients who suffer traumatic head injury or a stroke do achieve a substantial degree of recovery of *function*. For example, about three-quarters of disabled stroke survivors who are unable to walk immediately after the stroke do eventually learn to walk again, although many fail to regain their former gait or speed of walking. Around 15 per cent of stroke patients who suffer a paralysed arm regain normal function in the arm. A follow-up study of severely head-injured patients found that, some years after their injury, almost all the patients retained some degree of disability, although 40 per cent had made a 'good recovery' and had been able to resume their previous social, educational and occupational activities. Just 20 per cent remained severely disabled and dependent on other people to perform routine daily tasks (Jennett et al., 1981).

Initially, recovery of function may be rather rapid, but the rate of recovery then tends to slow down. Factors which affect the pace and extent of recovery include: the person's age (younger people tend to recover more fully); the extent of the lesion (more extensive lesions are associated with a less complete recovery); and the degree to which a skill has been 'overlearned'.

Long-established and often-practised skills tend to recover quickly and more completely. Similarly, information acquired a long time before the onset of the brain damage tends to be less disrupted, and is usually more completely recovered, than recently acquired information (Miller, 1984). Psychological characteristics which have been shown to affect the rate and extent of recovery include intelligence, motivation and degree of emotional adjustment (Golden, 1978). Many environmental and social aspects are also relevant.

Various explanations have been offered for the recovery effect. Miller (1984) classifies these as 'artifact theories', 'anatomical reorganization accounts' and 'functional reorganization accounts'. Artifact theories suggest that head injuries lead to both 'primary deficits' resulting from the destruction of brain tissue and 'secondary deficits' resulting from temporary functional disturbances of the brain. Thus the physical shock of an impact on the head may temporarily suppress the functioning of certain brain areas. Artifact theories suggest that recovery of function results from the reactivation of those parts of the brain which have been temporarily disturbed, and is not due to the restoration of activity in damaged areas.

The anatomical reorganization account suggests that other parts of the brain take over the functions previously carried out by the damaged area, and the functional adaptation account suggests that people learn new ways of performing tasks that were previously accomplished by the damaged part of the brain. Thus the functional adaptation model implies that people develop new ways of executing 'lost' skills.

The three explanations are not mutually exclusive, and several of the processes described may be involved in the recovery of function. However, while there is no question about the reality of functional adaptation, and clear evidence for the effects referred to by artifact theories, the issue of anatomical reorganization within the adult brain remains a matter of considerable controversy. The controversy does not extend to the case of young children, however, for it is well established that the young brain possesses a 'plasticity of functioning' which can sustain a radical reorganization of functions.

Rehabilitation and retraining

'Rehabilitation' is a broad concept which includes treatment, resettlement and adjustment to disability (Tyerman and Humphrey, 1988). Those who sustain an injury to the brain can rarely be said to make a complete recovery, and most brain-damaged people continue to experience formidable psychological difficulties. Rehabilitation programmes aim to promote optimum recovery across a wide range of areas by attending to the patient's physical, emotional, social and vocational needs.

Many of the intervention strategies used to help people recover following a stroke or severe head injury are directed towards restitution – the regaining of lost functions. For example, a person who has suffered a stroke may be provided with speech therapy. The patient may be encouraged to use simple sentences, to speak slowly and to make full use of gestures and non-verbal cues. Role-plays of everyday situations, such as those involving shopping, using the telephone or travelling by public transport, may be enacted to help the person to practise new ways of using language. The 'melodic intonation' strategy capitalizes on the fact that people who find it difficult to enunciate speech following head injury often retain the ability to sing. Patients are initially encouraged to 'chant' the words they wish to say before gradually learning to produce utterances that are more like normal speech.

People suffering from apraxia are often able to perform automatically any action sequences which have been overlearned, but falter badly when they focus consciously on the task at hand. Dressing apraxia, for example, is often made worse if the person deliberately concentrates on the process of getting dressed. Such people may be trained in the use of self-distraction strategies, so that they pay less attention to those actions which they are able to perform mechanically. In other cases help with complex tasks can be provided by means of step-by-step instructions (perhaps in pictorial form) and objects which are colour coded for ease of identification. People who suffer from one-sided neglect (anosognosia) are likely to find it useful if relatives and other initially place themselves on the 'attended' side of the patient rather than the 'blind' side. Gradually, it may be possible to extend the field of attention by introducing strategic manipulations which encourage and help the patient to attend strategically to the 'blind' field.

Rehabilitation programmes may also focus on emotional problems, and may include elements of vocational counselling and training (Tyerman and Humphrey, 1988). A comprehensive rehabilitation project may include social skills training, behavioural therapy, counselling and, in some cases, some form of family-based intervention. Family members are sometimes invited to act as 'co-therapists' and may help with both the planning and the implementation of rehabilitation strategies (McKinlay and Hickox, 1988; Durgin, 1989).

Amelioration

Because there are often serious limits to the effectiveness of treatments aimed at helping brain-damaged people to overcome their primary deficits, many clinicians now place an additional emphasis on helping people to manage with their handicaps. The term used to describe such efforts is 'amelioration', and the procedures employed reflect two basic strategies for assisting brain-damaged people. The first strategy involves teaching the patient alternative ways of reaching desirable goals. For example, those who have lost the power of speech may be taught sign language as a means of communication. The other strategy involves adapting the environment to the patient's needs. This might be achieved by arranging various *aides mémoires* in strategic locations in the home of a person suffering from a memory impairment, or attaching labels to domestic objects to help a person suffering from agnosia to communicate more effectively with other family members.

◀Conclusions▶▶▶

Psychological disturbances, and deficits of psychological functioning, are often associated with identifiable brain pathology. Damage to brain tissue may occur as the result of severe head injury, cerebrovascular accidents ('strokes'), tumours, infections and tissue degeneration. Because different areas of the brain have different functions, the effects of brain damage largely depend on the site and nature of the damage.

It is possible to represent the field of organic psychological disorders by reference to anatomical aspects (the location and nature of damage) or psychological functions (for example, disturbances of perception, memory, language and mood). There are also a number of specific syndromes, including Alzheimer's disease, Huntington's disease, the epilepsies and AIDS-related disorders.

The investigation of organic conditions has traditionally relied on neurological examination and neuropsychological assessment, although biological assays, X-rays and exploratory surgery have also played a role. In recent decades, powerful new brain imaging techniques have been developed, and these can now provide highly detailed diagnostic information.

As well as the primary symptoms directly caused by damage to the brain, the organic disorders often lead to severe secondary symptoms, many of which are disturbances of mood and social behaviour. These secondary symptoms are highly variable and change with the course of the organic disorder. The course may include some recovery of function (in many cases of stroke, for example) or a gradual deterioration (as in Alzheimer's disease). Caring for a brain-damaged patient often places a very great strain on relatives, and various forms of psychological intervention may be useful in helping patients and their families. Such interventions include procedures designed to facilitate the recovery of cognitive functions, a range of rehabilitation, retraining and amelioration strategies, counselling and family-based psychotherapy.

◀Further Reading▶▶▶

Beaumont, J.G. (1988) *Understanding Neuropsychology*. Oxford: Blackwell.

A general introduction to neuropsychology, beginning with a description of the structure and functioning of the nervous system and providing a concise account of the structure and functions of cortical and subcortical areas of the brain. Includes a number of neuropsychological case studies.

Hart, S. and Semple, J.M. (1990) *Neuropsychology and the Dementias*. London: Taylor & Francis.

Discusses clinical features and neuropathological aspects of the dementias (particularly Alzheimer's disease). Also examines rehabilitation and management.

Miller, E. and Morris, R. (1993) *The Psychology of Dementia*. Chichester: Wiley.

Detailed examination of the psychological impairments associated with dementia, with additional discussion of assessment, management and psychosocial aspects.

McCarthy, R. and Warrington, E.K. (1990) *Cognitive Neuropsychology: a Clinical Approach*. New York: Academic Press.

Balanced psychological and neurological account of cognitive deficits in patients with brain lesions. Organized around specific cognitive functions, including perceptual recognition, speech, reading, memory and problem-solving.

◀Discussion Points▶ ▶ ▶

1 What factors are known to affect the psychological consequences of brain damage (include the site of the damage as well as other factors)?
2 Write an essay: 'Brain damage and memory deficits'.
3 Describe the possible primary and secondary symptoms associated with cerebrovascular accidents ('strokes').
4 Consider the course of Alzheimer's disease, including the progression of symptoms and the possible impact on the patient's relatives.
5 Write an essay: 'Recovery from head injury'.
6 Discuss the various strategies that have been developed to aid the rehabilitation of brain-damaged patients.

9　Learning Disability

Some people have broad intellectual deficits which limit their capacity to function in educational, vocational and social situations. In most cases the condition is present from birth, although it may not be diagnosed until some time later, and it continues throughout the person's lifetime. Many different terms are used to label the condition, and it is not easy to find a term which everyone finds acceptable. A frequent criticism of many terms, including 'mental retardation', 'mental subnormality', 'mental deficiency', 'mental handicap' and 'intellectual impairment', is that they are stigmatizing and demeaning. Some of the terms are also imprecise. Thus the term 'mental handicap' could be applied to people suffering from a psychotic condition such as schizophrenia as well as to those who have an intellectual deficit.

Even the term 'learning difficulties', which is widely used by clinicians and educationalists, attracts critical comment. Taken literally, this term would include specific learning problems (such as dyslexia) as well as global intellectual impairment. Furthermore, some parents of children with a profound intellectual deficit argue that 'learning difficulties' is a euphemism which does nothing to convey the breadth and severity of their children's disability. Both of the major psychiatric diagnostic systems (DSM and ICD) retain the term 'mental retardation', which, although not particularly agreeable, does have the virtue of being specific.

An unfortunate effect of applying any single term is that it tends to imply a certain degree of uniformity, whereas, in fact, people with learning difficulties vary hugely in their intellectual abilities, their clinical condition and their ability to function independently. The 'true prevalence' of mental handicap is usually estimated at between 2 and 3 per cent of the population, although fewer than half of this number of people are ever formally recognized or diagnosed.

Table 9.1   Differences between subcategories of mentally handicapped people

	Mild	Moderate	Severe and profound
Prevalence as % of the handicapped population	80	12	7 severe <1 profound
Causes	Mostly familial	Mix of familial and pathological	Almost all pathological
Background	Majority from lower social class background Family members often mentally handicapped	Tendency for lower social class background Family members sometimes mentally handicapped	No particular social class pattern Family members rarely mentally handicapped
Physical	Physical abnormalities rare Brain damage rare Epilepsy rare	Physical abnormalities often found Sometimes brain damage Epilepsy common	Almost always physical abnormalities Brain damage common Epilepsy very common
Speech and communication	Good understanding of speech. Expressive language skills may also be well developed	Often speech problems, but expressive and receptive skills generally adequate	Very limited vocabulary and language skills. Speech may be absent
Social skills	Adequate social skills. Able to form and maintain close relationships	May make friends but often encounter difficulties in social situations	Little or no social skill. Limited interaction and very few relationships formed
Self-help	Usually few difficulties, except with official forms, etc. Many can read and write, use the telephone, etc. May be vulnerable to exploitation	Can achieve adequate self-help skills with training Can feed, bathe, and dress self Highly vulnerable to exploitation	Some limited self-help might be achievable with intensive training Will always need care Highly vulnerable to exploitation
Vocational	Can usually work at unskilled tasks in normal settings	Usually need supervision in sheltered workshop	No employment Some may join in structured daily activities
Adult living	Usually form stable relationships, marry and have children May live independently, but likely to need help when problems arise	Usually remain dependent, and form few stable partnerships	Never achieve independence Need constant care and supervision in a highly structured environment

There will be many exceptions to the generalizations in this summary table. Each person has peaks and troughs of ability relative to a general level of functioning, and many aspects of performance and behaviour will reflect education, training, and social environmental factors.

Definition ▶ ▶ ▶

Traditional definitions of mental retardation emphasized intellectual performance as the key defining element, and diagnosis traditionally depended on an assessment of the person's intelligence quotient (IQ). Current definitions of learning disability may still refer to low intelligence as a necessary element, but the major emphasis now tends to be placed on difficulties which the person has in coping with everyday tasks.

The UK Mental Health Act of 1959 defined severe subnormality as 'A state of arrested or incomplete development of mind which includes subnormality of intelligence and is of such a nature and degree that the patient is incapable of leading an independent life or of guarding himself against serious exploitation, or will be incapable when of an age to do so.' A more recent definition of mental retardation offered by the American Association on Mental Retardation (AAMR) is even more explicit in rejecting a diagnosis based exclusively on IQ: 'Mental retardation is present when specific intellectual limitations affect the person's ability to cope with the ordinary challenges of everyday living in the community. If the intellectual limitations have no real effect on functioning, then the person does not have mental retardation' (AAMR, 1992, p. 13).

The American Psychiatric Association (in DSM-IV) specifies three necessary criteria for the diagnosis of mental retardation. There must be a significant intellectual deficit (this is usually said to be equivalent to an IQ score of 70 or below), and the person must have deficiencies in 'adaptive functioning' (that is, in behaviour relating to social responsibility and the capacity for independent living). The third – developmental – criterion (the condition must have been apparent from childhood) is included in order to distinguish between mental retardation and dementia.

Classification ▶ ▶ ▶

Four levels of severity of learning disability (or 'mental retardation') are commonly distinguished: mild, moderate, severe and profound. Each level may be identified with a particular range of IQ scores, but categorization also reflects a number of other factors, including the person's communication abilities and self-help skills, social behaviour and the degree to which the person is able to function independently. Many educationalists employ a somewhat different classification and distinguish between those considered to be educable and those who are not.

Another basis for classification is the cause of the disability. In the majority of cases there is actually no identifiable cause; the person simply happens to be at the lower end of the normal distribution of intelligence. Because this form of disability often reflects the individual's family background (genetically and also, perhaps, environmentally), it is sometimes labelled 'familial' (alternative terms used are 'non-specific' and 'subcultural'). If, however, the condition reflects some form of organic pathology, it will be identified as a case of 'pathological' disability. A number of specific syndromes are distinguished within the pathological category, the most familiar being Down's syndrome.

Using the classification system based on the level of intellectual performance, it is possible to characterize the 'typical' abilities and disabilities of people who might be considered to be mildly, moderately, severely or profoundly mentally handicapped (see Table 9.1).

Mild mental handicap (IQ 50–70) Some people who are mildly handicapped differ very little from people with IQ scores towards the lower end of the 'normal' range. Most appear normal, can communicate reasonably well and can live an independent life. However, many will have been identified as 'slow learners' during their school years, and as adults they may experience difficulties in coping with some of the more demanding aspects of everyday life. In most cases the condition is 'familial' rather than 'pathological', and other members of the person's family are also likely to have rather low IQ scores. Most mildly handicapped people form stable relationships and eventually have children of their own.

Moderate mental handicap (IQ 35–49) Moderately handicapped people are likely to have conspicuous learning difficulties and communication problems. Most are able to acquire effective self-care skills but some require continual help and supervision. Although they may be capable of simple routine work, close supervision will often be necessary. Many people with moderate learning disabilities have some form of brain damage, but some do not.

Severe mental handicap (IQ 20–34) People who are severely mentally handicapped have multiple physical abnormalities and profound communication difficulties. They may require supervision most of the time and generally show little or no initiative. Brain damage is often severe and may render the person inactive.

Profound mental handicap (IQ below 20) The profoundly mentally handicapped person is unable to care for himself or herself except in the most rudimentary ways. Speech is often completely absent, social responses may be minimal and the person will require nursing care throughout life. Severe physical problems are invariably present.

Diagnosis

Whereas familial handicap can only be diagnosed when it becomes apparent that the child is failing to develop intellectually in the usual way, pathological conditions linked to mental handicap can sometimes be diagnosed even before birth. Since the first antenatal diagnosis of Down's disorder in 1966, major advances have been made in antenatal testing and an increasing range of disorders can now be identified before birth. The tests available are described in Box 9.1.

Foetal distress in the days or hours before the birth, or complications during the birth itself, may lead health professionals to suspect that brain damage has occurred. Certain physical features apparent at birth, or abnormalities of reflex responses, also suggest neurological damage, and particular syndromes associated with mental handicap (including Down's syndrome, spina bifida and microcephaly – an abnormally small brain and skull) can also be diagnosed at birth or shortly afterwards. Other problems become apparent only after diagnostic tests have been carried out.

In some cases emergency surgical or medical treatment can minimize damage. For example, in cases of hydrocephalus, in which an excess of cerebrospinal fluid exerts pressure on the brain, it may be possible to relieve the pressure inside the head by draining off the superfluous fluid.

In many cases, however, a pathological condition leading to mental handicap will not become apparent until a much later stage. A lack of responsiveness or a failure to achieve various developmental milestones at a normal rate may lead to an investigation of possible pathological causes. Details of the family background and of the pregnancy and birth will be considered, measurements will be made of various physical characteristics, including head circumference and shape, and the nature and extent of any sensory or motor impairments will be assessed.

However, the majority of people with a learning disability have no discernible biological abnormality that might be held responsible for their low level of intellectual functioning. At least three-quarters of those who have a learning disability are handicapped simply because they happen to fall at the lower extreme of the normal distribution of intelligence. Their condition is familial rather than pathological.

Standardized batteries of tests can be used to measure a child's intelligence from the age of about three years, although assessments at this age tend to be unreliable and may be substantially revised at a later point. For older children, and adults, a number of reliable intelligence tests are available.

Assessments of a child's social maturity and level of adaptive behaviour will rely primarily on information collected from the parents, teachers, nurses and others. Adaptive functioning is primarily assessed in terms of personal independence, with emphasis on age-appropriate dressing, eating and communication skills. Commonly used scales include the Adaptive Behavior Scales (ABS) (Nihara et al., 1974) and the Vineland Adaptive Behavior Scale (VABS) (Sparrow et al., 1985). The VABS assesses communication, daily living skills, socialization, motor skills and maladaptive behaviour, and the manual provides normative data on many different groups, including those with a mental handicap and those with sensory handicaps who function intellectually within the normal range.

A full clinical appraisal will also include an evaluation of any behavioural problems. Parents and others will be asked about difficulties with eating, sleep patterns, toiletting, aggressiveness etc. Those who are severely

Box 9.1
Antenatal Testing

Over the past thirty years or so, there have been major developments in antenatal testing. It is now possible to diagnose a wide range of abnormalities, including many that are associated with mental handicap, from ultrasound scans, maternal blood tests and chromosomal tests made on foetal material.

Ultrasound scans

These may be used to monitor foetal growth throughout the pregnancy. At 10–12 weeks, ultrasound scans can be used to detect major structural abnormalities, including neural tube abnormalities (such as spina bifida) and certain signs that may indicate Down's syndrome. Foetal head measurements can also be made to detect hydrocephalus.

Amniocentesis

In this procedure, a sample of amniotic fluid (the fluid in which the foetus is immersed) is taken from the uterus. This fluid contains cells from the foetus which are cultured in order to examine the chromosomal composition. Particular attention is paid to the number of chromosomes present, and to their shape and size. This type of assessment of chromosomal material is known as karyotyping. An amniocentesis is usually carried out between 16 and 18 weeks into the pregnancy and it can reveal a number of abnormalities, of which the most common is Down's syndrome. DNA analysis of the material can also detect phenylketonuria (PKU).

Chorionic villi sampling (CVS)

This is an alternative to amniocentesis and can often be carried out as early as the ninth week of pregnancy. A small amount of tissue from the chorionic villi (which later become the placenta) is taken from the uterus and analysed to provide genetic information. A thorough analysis may take as long as two weeks, although preliminary information is available much earlier.

Foetal blood sampling (cordocentesis)

In this technique blood is taken from the umbilical vein and some of the blood cells are used for karyotyping. Thus the test produces information similar to that which would be obtained from amniocentesis and CVS, but the results can be obtained more rapidly. This method can also be used to test for Fragile X syndrome (the second most common genetic cause of mental handicap, after Down's syndrome), and a range of metabolic disorders (including Lesch–Nynan syndrome) and infections (including rubella and cytomegalovirus).

Tests performed on maternal blood samples

Various analyses may be performed on blood samples taken from the pregnant woman. In terms of the assessment of foetal malformation, these are only screening methods (any sign of abnormality will need to be confirmed by means of other tests), but they are perfectly safe for the foetus (the invasive techniques of amniocentesis, CVS and foetal blood sampling are associated with a risk of miscarriage of about 1 per cent).

If an analysis of maternal blood indicates a relatively high probability of a specific foetal abnormality then further tests are carried out on foetal tissue. Unfortunately, the blood screening techniques return many false positive results which may cause a good deal of unnecessary anxiety. On the other hand, a woman who is given a negative result can rest assured that this is reliable.

MSAFP (maternal serum alphafetoprotein)
This test is performed on a sample of the mother's blood between 16 and 18 weeks into the pregnancy and is used to screen for neural tube defects, including spina bifida and anencephaly.

The triple test
This is really an extension of the MSAFP, and involves an additional assessment of two hormones in the maternal blood sample. The biochemical information, together with the woman's age, is used to estimate the risk that the woman is carrying a foetus with the Down's chromosomal pattern.

handicapped may engage in stereotyped behaviours such as rocking and head banging, and parents, nursery workers and teachers may be asked to keep a careful record of such problematic behaviours.

Some young children who appear to have substantial learning difficulties are later found to have problems with hearing or, more rarely, vision. Mild hearing loss may be difficult to detect because it tends to be intermittent in nature. 'Clumsy' children, and those with more severe motor difficulties (such as spasticity), may also be misjudged as being mentally handicapped, but careful testing may reveal that such a child has an average or a high IQ.

An initial diagnosis should not be regarded as conclusive or unalterable. As the child develops, and perhaps following medical intervention, educational help and special training, the initial assessment may be seen as having provided a low baseline against which progress has evidently been made.

◀The Causes of Mental Handicap▶ ▶ ▶

The range of specific causes or conditions covered by the term 'mental retardation' is said to exceed 300 (Baumeister and Baumeister, 1989). However, it is useful to distinguish between the two broad types, 'familial' and 'pathological' (or 'organic').

Familial mental handicap

Many authorities suggest that between one-half and three-quarters of the variation in IQ scores is determined by genetic factors, leaving other factors responsible for between one-quarter and one-half of the variation (Zigler and Hodapp, 1986). Genetic factors may determine an upper limit to an individual's potential intellectual ability, with environmental factors determining how far the person's potential is actually achieved.

Close relatives of mildly mentally handicapped people tend to have low IQ scores themselves, supporting the idea that the condition may have a genetic basis. However, because close relatives usually share a common environment, the familial pattern might reflect shared disadvantages in the form of poverty, stress, poor education or poor medical care. Factors such as inadequate medical care, poor nutrition, inferior housing, lack of antenatal care, smoking and drug use during pregnancy and second-rate education may all be involved. Thus adverse environmental factors, as well as genetic elements, may conspire to limit a child's intellectual development.

Pathological mental handicap

Severe learning disability is often linked to identifiable pathology. The causes of pathological mental handicap include chromosomal and genetic abnormalities present before conception, problems that arise during pregnancy, birth complications and serious childhood medical problems (for example, meningitis). Weatherall (1983) provided a useful breakdown of the causes of severe handicap (see Table 9.2). In about a third of cases of pathological handicap the precise cause is not identified, although it may apparent that the person has a congenital brain abnormality or has suffered brain damage.

Chromosomal abnormalities   Learning disability sometimes results from an abnormality in the number or structure of the chromosomes. Down's syndrome was first described by the British physician Langdon Down in 1866, although the genetic basis of the condition was not established until 1959. The normal human chromosome complement is 46, comprising 22 pairs and either two X chromosomes (in the case of females) or an X and a Y chromosome (in the case of males). Down's syndrome results from the presence of an extra chromosome. In the majority of cases (around 95 per cent) there is an extra chromosome number 21 (a condition referred to as 'trisomy 21'). The abnormality arises from a malformation of the ovum, and the fact that the risk of such a malformation increases with the mother's age means that older mothers are more likely to conceive a Down's child. Before accurate and routine antenatal testing became available for older mothers, approximately 1 in 50 women who gave birth at the age of 45 or over gave birth to a Down's child (compared with 1 in 1000 teenage mothers).

Until recently, the overall incidence of Down's syndrome was 1.5 in every 1000 live births, and about 1 in 12 of those who were handicapped had the condition. However, the incidence of Down's has decreased significantly in recent years, partly because women now tend to have their last child at a relatively young age (because effective means of contraception are readily available) but partly because when Down's is detected at the antenatal stage many couples decide to terminate the pregnancy.

Down's people vary widely in their intelligence. Many are in the moderate range, but some are only mildly handicapped and others are severely handicapped. The majority develop a wide range of self-care skills and about half eventually develop some reading and writing skills. Many Down's people are socially adept, and there appears to be some validity in a long-

Table 9.2   Causes of severe mental handicap

Cause	Prevalence (%)
Pre-fertilization (single gene or chromosomal)	55 (of which 60% Down's)
Intrauterine problems	2
Perinatal (asphyxia etc.)	7
Post-natal (encephalitis, meningitis etc.)	2
Unknown aetiology	34

Source: Based on Weatherall (1983).

held stereotype which depicts Down's people as being particularly affection-
ate and as having an easy temperament.

Down's syndrome is associated with many physical abnormalities. The
term 'mongolism' was formerly applied to the condition because Down's
people have a distinctive and somewhat 'mongoloid' appearance – the inner
corner of the upper eyelid folds over the eyes, which appear narrow and
slanted. Down's people have a large tongue, a small mouth, a flattened skull
(especially at the back), a stocky build and short fingers. Around a third have
congenital heart abnormalities. Around one in ten babies with Down's syndrome die during the first year, but those who survive this initial period
usually live to middle age, and an increasing number now live to old age.

A number of other chromosomal abnormalities can also lead to intellectual deficits, including 'Fragile X syndrome', which results from an inherited
defect of the X chromosome. This is the second most common cause of
moderate and severe mental handicap after Down's syndrome, affecting 1 in
every 1000 male births (it is a sex-linked disorder and occurs much more
frequently in males than in females). People with this disorder show poor
muscle tone and are likely to have special difficulties with speech and
language.

Cranial malformation and neural tube defects   Mental handicap sometimes
results from a congenital malformation of the central nervous system. Such
malformations include abnormalities of head size (microcephaly, an unusually small head; or macrocephaly, an unusually large head) and neural tube
defects, including spina bifida. In another neural tube defect, anencephaly,
a large part of the brain is absent at birth. The incidence is around 1.5 per
cent of all conceptions, although there is a high rate of both spontaneous
and therapeutic abortion. When the pregnancy continues to term, the
anencephalic baby is likely to be stillborn. For those who are born alive,
death invariably follows within hours or days.

Cranial malformations may result from maternal infection or irradiation
during pregnancy. In the condition known as hydrocephalus, an increased
volume of cerebrospinal fluid produces an enlargement of the cerebral ventricles and a significant increase in head circumference. The young brain is

put under considerable pressure and may be severely damaged as a result. It is sometimes possible to relieve the pressure inside the head by providing a valve (or 'shunt') which drains excess cerebrospinal fluid off into the circulatory system. Hydrocephalus may be the result of an infection, a neural tube defect or a chromosomal abnormality.

Spina bifida is another neural tube defect in which a number of vertebrae fail to develop completely, so that part of the spinal cord is left exposed. The body is usually paralysed below the site of the abnormality. Spina bifida sometimes leads to hydrocephalus, which may then produce brain damage that leads to intellectual disability. There are wide national and even regional differences in the incidence of spina bifida. Thus, within the UK spina bifida is more than twice as common in South Wales and Northern Ireland as it is in London and the South East.

Problems of metabolism and nutrition Some cases of mental handicap result from inherited metabolic errors, certain types of hormonal imbalance or particular forms of nutritional deficiency. The best known example of such a condition is phenylketonuria (PKU) a very rare inherited disorder present in about 1 in 15000 live births. In this disorder, a deficiency of the enzyme phenylalanine hydroxylase leads to a build-up of phenylalanine, a chemical which has a toxic effect on the developing brain. Unless preventive action is taken in the early years, neurological problems will lead to disruptions of reflexes and disturbances of speech and walking. Older children are likely to experience seizures and may become extremely hyperactive. Without treatment, children with PKU become severely or profoundly mentally handicapped. However, a test for the condition can be carried out immediately after birth, and if PKU is diagnosed the infant is placed on a low phenylalanine diet which must be strictly followed for at least the first six years. By this time the brain will have achieved a level of maturity which allows the special diet to be discontinued. Most PKU children who adhere to the special diet have an IQ within the normal range.

Lesch–Nynan syndrome is another abnormality of enzyme metabolism. It occurs almost exclusively in males and produces uncontrolled writhing movements of the arms, mental handicap and severe self-injurious behaviour. Those who suffer from this condition have severe difficulties in articulating speech, and most are unable to walk.

Infections Certain maternal infections during pregnancy are associated with a high risk of mental handicap. These include rubella ('German measles'), cytomegalovirus (a herpes virus) and syphilis. Many of these infections produce widespread damage which affects many different bodily systems. Thus rubella may lead to profound sensory impairments and heart defects, as well as learning disability.

Infection by cytomegalovirus (CMV) is very common in the general population, with around 50 per cent of people having been infected by the time they reach their twenties. If a woman becomes infected during pregnancy she may give birth to a child who is later shown to have an intellectual disability (deafness is another effect which is relatively common). Although only 5 per cent of babies born with a CMV infection will become noticeably handicapped, the relatively high prevalence of this infection makes CMV a relatively common cause of learning disability.

Profound effects on intellectual development may also result from certain infections which may occur during infancy and early childhood. Two of the most dangerous of these are encephalitis and bacterial meningitis. The meninges are the protective membranes immediately surrounding the brain, and an acute inflammation of these membranes (meningitis) can cause permanent brain damage. Encephalitis is an acute inflammation of the brain itself, and is usually the result of a viral infection. The disease can be fatal, although therapy with antiviral agents is often effective. Depending on how much damage has been caused by the infection (and possibly by subsequent hydrocephalus), longer-term effects may include various degrees of mental handicap, epilepsy and deafness. However, permanent neurological damage is not inevitable and learning disabilities result in only a proportion of cases.

Toxins   The developing foetus, especially during the earliest months of development, is exceptionally vulnerable to the toxic effects of chemicals circulating through the mother's body. Some of these are produced as the result of the mother's faulty metabolism (as in toxaemia), or arise as a result of an incompatibility between the Rh (rhesus) factor in the maternal and the foetal blood. Other toxic effects in pregnancy result from the ingestion of harmful substances. Special care needs to be taken with medication at this time, and pregnant women are advised to drink alcohol only in moderate amounts, and not to smoke. Epidemiological studies have shown consistently that women who smoke have lower birthweight babies (Werler et al., 1985), and some studies have reported links between maternal smoking during pregnancy and the child's height and intelligence even at the age of eleven.

Excessive use of alcohol during pregnancy can have particularly serious effects on the foetus, an extreme manifestation of this being the 'foetal alcohol syndrome' (FAS). Signs of FAS include low birth weight and a specific pattern of congenital malformations (small head, flattened face and widely spaced eyes). Mild to moderate mental handicap becomes apparent as the children develop and they also tend to exhibit extreme behavioural problems. The incidence of foetal alcohol syndrome in the general population is generally estimated at 1 or 2 per 1000 live births. Among women who continue to drink very heavily throughout their pregnancy, however, the risk of giving birth to a child suffering from FAS may be as high as 20 per cent. Some studies suggest that binge drinking at certain stages of the pregnancy (particularly in the fourth and fifth months) may in fact be as dangerous as drinking heavily throughout the pregnancy. Maternal addiction to drugs such as heroin and the cocaine derivative 'crack' can also result in a baby being born damaged and addicted.

Exposure to various toxins during early childhood can also lead to learning disability. One substance which causes particular concern is lead, and the issue of possible adverse effects of lead from motor vehicle exhaust fumes has proved particularly controversial (Smith, 1986).

Trauma The developing brain may be damaged before birth by physical insult (for example, if the mother is involved in a motor vehicle accident), through exposure to radiation or through a lack of oxygen. A traumatic birth delivery or delayed spontaneous respiration may result in cerebral palsy. This is principally a motor disorder in which the person has difficulty in controlling the movements of one or more limbs, the lack of control being apparent in characteristic 'spastic' movements. Although cerebral palsy is associated with mental handicap, up to a half of those affected have an IQ within the normal range and many, indeed, have an IQ score which is well above the average.

The significance of prematurity and low birthweight Babies born weighing less than 2500 grams (around five and a half pounds) are described as 'low birthweight babies'. Those who are born before the thirty-seventh week of pregnancy are labelled 'premature', and those who are small relative to the length of their gestation are termed 'small for dates' or 'small for gestational age' (SGA). Each of these conditions is associated with a somewhat heightened risk of intellectual impairment. However, each of these risk factors is associated with other risk factors, including foetal and maternal medical problems, poverty, poor nutrition and maternal smoking.

◀The Nature of the Psychological Deficits▶▶▶

People with learning difficulties tend to perform poorly on tasks involving visual-spatial ability, motor ability, learning, short-term memory and social skills. There may be peaks of ability in certain areas (Vicari et al., 1992), but deficits are usually evident across a spectrum of cognitive abilities. A large body of research has attempted to identify the nature of a general cognitive deficit which might be responsible for such widespread problems. One possibility is that people with learning difficulties are generally slow in processing information, and that this slowness is responsible for many of the observed performance deficits.

After reviewing a number of relevant studies, Kail (1992) concluded that slowness of information processing is indeed a pivotal problem, and Ellis and Dulaney (1991) made reference to a 'widespread cognitive inertia'. In order to respond appropriately to an environmental situation, information must be acquired, retrieved and manipulated. Many experimental studies have compared the performance of learning disabled and other people on tasks relating to each of these stages.

Information acquisition

Learning disabled people are slow to encode information and take longer to scan information that they hold in a temporary memory store. Thus if two lines are briefly flashed on a screen, and the person is asked to judge whether or not the two lines are of the same length, those with learning difficulties need the image to be presented for a relatively long time before they are able to make such a judgement accurately (Nettlebeck and Lally, 1979). Zeaman and his colleagues have shown that those who are intellectually impaired have a number of difficulties in detecting and identifying stimuli and that abnormalities in attentional processes lead to difficulties in selecting relevant aspects of a stimulus for further processing (Zeaman and House, 1979).

Storage and retrieval

The difficulties that learning disabled people experience in remembering things may reflect a limited capacity for storing information or a failure to employ effective strategies for memorizing material. For example, when asked to learn a list of items, they tend not to employ the useful strategy of grouping similar items (such as animal names or colour names). They may be taught to use such strategies, but have generally failed to develop them as a natural cognitive skill.

Cognitive functioning: delay or difference?

The differences in cognitive functioning between learning disabled people and others might be quantitative or qualitative in nature. A quantitative difference would mean that cognitive skills develop in the same way, but that development takes place at a slower pace for those with learning difficulties, and fails to develop beyond a certain point. This 'delay' model is implied by the term 'retarded'. An alternative model, the 'difference model', suggests that those with learning difficulties differ qualitatively from other people in terms of their cognitive development.

The issue of which of these two models presents a more accurate picture remains unsettled. Both models have their adherents, while some claim that learning disabled people are both cognitively delayed and cognitively different from other people. One model might be more applicable to some disabled people and the other model more applicable to others. For example, it has been suggested that familial handicap may be marked by a delay in cognitive development but that pathological handicap may reflect idiosyncrasies of cognitive style.

The delay model suggests that normal educational techniques and materials are likely to be appropriate to the education of the learning disabled, but that teaching should progress at a slower pace. On the other hand, if there are substantial cognitive differences between most people and those who have learning difficulties, a totally different educational approach might be necessary.

◄The Clinical Picture► ► ►

Psychological disorders

A little under a half of those recognized as having learning difficulties will suffer from a psychiatric disorder at some time during their life. This relatively high rate may partly reflect the fact that many learning disabled people have some form of brain dysfunction which may leave them particularly vulnerable to the development of an organically based psychiatric disorder. Disturbances in brain chemistry may precipitate disturbances of behaviour, thinking and mood. But psychosocial factors are also relevant. Many learning disabled people live in difficult circumstances in which they exert relatively little control over their lives. They may be frustrated and lonely, and they may have difficulties in forming and maintaining satisfactory relationships. Such aspects are likely to undermine self-esteem and may generate considerable psychological distress, which becomes evident in the form of behavioural disturbance, anxiety or depression.

Psychological disorders in childhood   In a survey of learning disabled children aged between 9 and 11 years old, Rutter et al. (1970) found that over a quarter were rated by their parents as 'disturbed' and that behavioural problems were three times more common in this group than in a sample of non-disabled children of the same age. Gath and Gumley (1986) also found that parents reported a relatively high rate of behaviour problems, including hyperactivity and extreme distractibility. Of those children who have a severe mental handicap, around half exhibit some form of serious behavioural disturbance.

Psychological disorders in adulthood   There is a relatively high prevalence among learning disabled adults of a wide range of abnormal psychological conditions, reflecting the influence of social environmental factors and organic factors. Many severely handicapped adults (and children) engage in various actions, including self-mutilation, aggression, hyperactivity and stereotyped behaviours, which are sometimes referred to collectively as 'challenging behaviours' (see Box 9.2).

Compared to others with a pathology-based learning disability, adults with Down's syndrome appear to be at low risk of psychiatric problems (Collacott et al., 1992). It appears that only around 25 per cent of people with Down's syndrome are ever diagnosed as suffering from a psychiatric condition, compared with around 40 per cent of those with other forms of mental handicap. Down's people are also less likely to engage in challenging behaviours than others with a similar level of intellectual impairment. On the other hand, the rate of depression in Down's people is relatively high (around 10 per cent). There is also a high prevalence of presenile dementia, and eventually a very high proportion of Down's people exhibit the symptoms of Alzheimer's disease, including memory deficits, withdrawal, apathy and a decrease in language and self-care skills (Oliver and Holland, 1986). Physical signs of Alzheimer's disease can in fact be detected in the brain tissue of all older Down's people (and some who are considerably younger), although the clinical signs and symptoms of this condition do not always become apparent, even in those who reach a relatively old age.

Box 9.2
Challenging Behaviours

Many mentally handicapped people engage in 'challenging behaviours'. These include acts of aggression, screaming, spitting, food throwing, undressing and making inappropriate sexualized gestures. Other challenging behaviours – labelled 'stereotyped behaviours' – include rocking, head banging and self-biting. Some of these actions clearly represent a serious risk to the person's physical safety, as well as having a number of other potentially deleterious effects (Mansell, 1994). Many stereotyped behaviours, for example, are problematic not only because they may lead to self-injury, but also because they interfere with the acquisition of new skills and bring negative social consequences (Jones, 1991).

There are many different reasons why mentally handicapped people engage in challenging behaviours, and the contributory causes include many different biological, environmental, emotional and cognitive factors. Some that appear to have a special relevance to particular cases include organic brain disorders, sensory impairments, low self-esteem, inconsistent discipline, poor communication skills and poor social skills. Many learning disabled people have poor self-control and a low boredom threshold, and these elements often occur in combination with a craving for attention, excitement and stimulation. There is likely to be a strong motive for immediate gratification, and there may be little awareness of the possible longer-term consequences of actions.

Lowe and Felce (1995) studied carers' responses to the challenging behaviours of mentally handicapped people living in a variety of hospital and community settings. They found that carers were particularly stressed by clients' aggression, temper tantrums, disturbing noises, straying beyond the home and sexual delinquency. Bromley and Emerson (1995) found that challenging behaviour provoked a number of emotional responses in staff, including despair, anger, annoyance, fear and disgust. Difficulties in understanding and predicting clients' actions were found to contribute significantly to staff stress (Bromley and Emerson, 1995). From their review of studies concerning staff responses to challenging behaviour, Hastings and Remington (1994) concluded that such responses were often counter-productive and sometimes maintained or even increased the frequency of challenging behaviours. These authors highlighted the need for care staff to be specially trained in the management of problem behaviour.

Attempts to eliminate or reduce the frequency of challenging behaviours take a number of different forms. One approach is psychopharmacological, and many adults who frequently engage in socially disruptive behaviours are maintained on anti-convulsant or anti-psychotic medication (Kiernan et al., 1995). Another approach involves changing relevant aspects of the environment or the living conditions (house rules, for example) which may have been identified as provoking hostile or disruptive responses. A number of studies have now reported significant reductions in challenging behaviours following a move from hospital into community care (Meera et al., 1994; Allen and Lowe, 1995), although it must be added that some case studies have shown increases in problem behaviours following such a move. Factors which may contribute to beneficial changes include the provision of a 'normal' or 'enriched' environment, and increased autonomy (more privacy, for example, and greater freedom to exercise personal choice).

Behavioural approaches have also been used to reduce the frequency of challenging behaviours, and they have often proved successful. Some behavioural interventions make use of aversive stimuli, particularly when there is a high risk of serious self-injury, and there is of course considerable controversy regarding the use of such strategies. An effective behavioural strategy which does not involve aversive stimulation, or punishment, and which has been used to reduce high rates of self-injurious and stereotyped behaviour, is based on a reinforcement schedule described as 'the differential reinforcement of incompatible behaviour' (Jones and Baker, 1990). A positive reward is given at the end of a preset interval during which no instances of the target behaviour occurred. If the proscribed behaviour does occur, the interval is immediately reset, thus delaying the opportunity for reinforcement. What is actually being reinforced by using this schedule is the omission of the unwanted behaviour. From a review of interventions used to treat self-injurious biting, Hile and Vatterott (1991) concluded that differential reinforcement procedures are the most effective, especially if the time-out strategy is also employed (that is, if the opportunity to obtain reinforcement is removed for a brief period).

Zarkowska and Clements (1988) developed a comprehensive behavioural approach to understanding challenging behaviours and devising appropriate intervention programmes. The approach focuses on the 'STAR' model, the four components of which are 'settings' (stable features of the environment in which the challenging behaviour normally takes place), 'triggers' (situations which commonly 'set off' specific actions; triggers include being told off, and being bored), 'actions' (the problem behaviours) and 'results' (the events which follow problem behaviours). Results can be divided into reinforcers (which increase the likelihood that the behaviour will be repeated) and punishers (which decrease the likelihood that the action will be repeated). Challenging behaviours can be viewed as 'skills' acquired through learning and maintained by results. Thus a client may learn that engaging in a challenging behaviour brings attention or provides a way of avoiding chores.

One way to eliminate problem behaviours is to replace them with alternative behaviours which are more rewarding. Other strategies focus on modifying settings and triggers, using appropriate reinforcers to change the results that follow challenging behaviours and encouraging self-management. Zarkowska and Clements (1988) suggest that a management plan should be established for each client, following a detailed assessment of the client's behaviour problems, skills and motivators. An action plan is devised, with goals clearly specified, and an attempt is made to reduce problem behaviours by altering settings, triggers (for example, by relieving boredom) and results. Results can be changed using extinction procedures (never providing the hoped for result) and following inappropriate actions with a cost (such as instant deprivation of television viewing). Specific cost techniques recommended by these authors include 'time-out', the imposition of a 'fine' or short-term physical restraint.

Physical disorders

Most people with mild learning difficulties are physically healthy, but many of those who are more severely disabled have malformations, metabolic disturbances and other abnormalities that seriously affect their physical health. Thus people with spina bifida are likely to suffer some degree of paralysis and are often incontinent. Around a third of Down's people have a convergent squint, and a third have a congenital heart problem. Many moderately, severely and profoundly learning disabled people also have serious visual impairments and/or hearing difficulties. Those whose mother was infected with rubella during pregnancy may be blind or deaf and may also suffer from cardiovascular disorders. Motor disabilities associated with intellectual deficits include spasticity, ataxia (the inability to coordinate voluntary movements) and athetosis (involuntary movements, especially of the fingers and toes). Various speech defects may also contribute significantly to the social problems faced by mentally handicapped people.

Mortality There has been little change in the overall prevalence of severe mental handicap over the past fifty years, although the incidence of new cases has fallen substantially. This pattern is explained by the fact that fewer severely and profoundly handicapped children are now being born (because of improved antenatal care and the availability of both antenatal diagnosis and abortion), while at the same time improved medical care has substantially increased the life expectancy of those who are severely and profoundly disabled. Thus, whereas, fifty years ago, relatively few people with Down's syndrome survived to adulthood, around a half of today's young Down's people are expected to live to the age of 60 (Carr, 1994).

◄Treatment, Training and Education►►►

Interventions to reverse or arrest an underlying pathology

In some cases, physical interventions are able to prevent organic damage likely to reduce or limit intellectual capacity. Thus surgery can greatly attenuate the damage that may be caused by hydrocephalus, and antibiotics can be administered in the early stages of bacterial meningitis. Providing a strictly controlled diet to a baby who has been diagnosed as suffering from phenylketonuria (and maintaining this for at least the first six years of life) will usually be successful in preventing intellectual impairment.

Interventions to improve basic intellectual abilities

In recent years the relationship between vitamin intake and intelligence has attracted a good deal of publicity, and a number of studies have appeared to show that supplying children of normal intelligence with vitamin supplements can significantly increase their IQ score (Benton and Cook, 1990; Schoenthaler et al., 1991). This work has led some people to suggest that the administration of extremely high doses of vitamins might improve the intellectual abilities of people with learning difficulties. However, research has failed to provide support for this supposition, and most authorities dismiss the hypothesis as absurd (Kozlowski, 1992).

There is, however, a good deal of evidence demonstrating the effectiveness of psychological interventions designed to improve performance on fundamental learning and memory tasks. Forness and Kavale (1993) conducted a meta-analysis of over 250 studies of cognitive training in learning disordered people and concluded that performance can be enhanced significantly by teaching specific strategies designed to improve learning and memory.

Interventions to treat psychiatric disorders and behaviour problems

Many handicapped people are prescribed neuroleptics (anti-psychotic drugs), anxiolytics (anti-anxiety drugs) and anti-depressants. Anti-convulsants may also play a useful role in controlling seizures and these and other drugs are sometimes used to repress disruptive behaviour.

Counselling and other forms of psychotherapy generally depend on clients being verbally fluent and having a reasonable degree of insight into their condition, and for a long time it was considered that such methods were not applicable to clients with learning disabilities. In recent years, however, there have been major developments in the adaptation of psychotherapeutic methods for use with learning disabled clients (Conboy-Hill and Waitman, 1992).

Several forms of behavioural intervention have been used to great effect with learning disabled people for several decades. Some of these interventions are based on the classical conditioning paradigm and others are based on the principles of operant conditioning. They can be highly effective in reducing specific dangerous or problem behaviours, and in widening the handicapped person's repertoire of useful skills (Watson and Uzell, 1981; Zarkowska and Clements, 1988; Demchak, 1990; see Box 9.2).

Interventions to assist the development of academic, social and self-care skills

Special education is the most widespread form of intervention provided for those with learning disabilities. There is a clear association between the degree of intellectual impairment and the extra effort needed to provide training and education. After a good deal of instruction and practice, most people with moderate learning difficulties do acquire a fairly wide range of skills. The majority of Down's people learn to feed and toilet themselves, and around a half are eventually able to dress and bathe unaided. Those who are considered to be educable also acquire certain academic skills, and around a half of Down's people develop some ability to read and to do simple arithmetic (Carr, 1994).

People whose intellectual impairment is more severe are regarded as 'trainable'. They are not usually expected to achieve academic goals and the special education they receive will focus largely on the acquisition of basic self-help skills, social skills and speech. If toilet training has not been successful by late childhood, this is likely to be a special target for intervention. Most learning disabled people learn to use a telephone and to recognize public signs indicating, for example, male and female toilets and no-smoking areas.

The acquisition of relevant skills increases the person's ability to function independently as well as helping to build confidence and self-esteem.

Many different techniques are used to train those who are learning disabled. Verbal instruction, patiently given, simply expressed and often repeated, can be very effective, but new behaviours may be learned more rapidly if the teacher first demonstrates, or 'models', the appropriate action and then encourages the student to imitate. Considerable prompting may be needed in the early stages, but it is usually possible to 'fade' the prompts gradually so that the person is eventually able to perform the action independently (Demchak, 1990).

Another technique which may be used to augment the person's repertoire of skills is 'shaping'. When a child is being taught to speak, for example, basic sounds are first demonstrated by the teacher (possibly the child's parent), who will then reward any noise that approximates to the target sound. As the child progresses, rewards are given for closer and closer approximations. Complex skills like washing and dressing may be broken down into simple component parts and the person can be gradually trained to perform each element before the actions are combined together in an appropriate sequence.

In all such training, an experienced teacher sets realistic goals and breaks elaborate tasks into small, manageable, steps. Such teachers also recognize the need to encourage and praise the student continually. There is good evidence for the short-term effectiveness of training in self-care skills, although the degree to which such learning will generalize to everyday situations does depend to a large extent on the cognitive and linguistic abilities of the person being trained (Ferretti et al., 1993).

Parents are often tireless in their efforts to train their special child, and a number of structured programmes have been developed to help them to maximize their effectiveness as teachers. One of the most widely adopted home-teaching services for young mentally handicapped children is the Portage programme, originally developed in Portage, Wisconsin (Shearer and Shearer, 1972). Parents are guided by a visiting professional who instructs them in a wide-ranging programme designed to build on the child's existing skills. An initial checklist of questions is used to assess the child's competency in each of five key areas: socialization, language, self-help, cognitive skills and motor skills. The parents learn how to structure tasks, how to encourage and help the child and how to monitor achievements. The parents maintain the prime responsibility for carrying out the programme, and they are supported in their efforts by a professional instructor who visits the home regularly to give encouragement and assistance and to monitor the child's progress. Research has shown that the use of this programme typically results in a substantial extension of the child's skills (Pugh, 1981).

Since the original Portage scheme was introduced, many other skills development and 'enrichment' programmes have been devised (Hedderly and Jennings, 1987). Hanson (1981) described a method for providing Down's children with enhanced stimulation from the age of a few months, a major objective of this programme being the prevention of the developmental decline often evident for Down's children in the early years.

◀Lifetime Management and Care▶▶▶

There has been a growing recognition, over the past forty years or so, that people with learning disabilities have rights, that they have preferences and are able to make choices, and that they need to be allowed and encouraged to exercise control over their own life as far as possible. Contemporary trends in care provision reflect this more humane outlook. 'Normalization' is now a fundamental goal, although it is recognized that mentally handicapped people are likely to need some degree of special support throughout their adult years.

Adolescence

People who have a learning disability often face special difficulties during adolescence (Dossetor and Nicol, 1989). Issues relating to independence from parents, sexuality and planning for the future may all raise problems. They may become resentful when they recognize that their own lifestyle is substantially different from that of others of the same age. Such an awareness may lead to feelings of resentment and humiliation and may undermine the person's self-confidence. There is a particular danger that relatives and other people will continue to treat them as children long after they have attained adulthood.

Employment

Many mildly handicapped people are able to manage an unskilled job in a normal work setting, but others may secure a position especially designated for a handicapped person, either in an ordinary workplace or in a sheltered work environment. Many remain without any form of employment. Those who have a moderate learning disability may be given a full-time or a part-time job in a sheltered workshop, while those who are more severely handicapped often continue to receive training in a special unit.

Such training is aimed at developing a range of basic skills, but it also provides an occupational atmosphere with a structured day and regular activities. Work may offer some degree of financial support as well as extending opportunities for making and maintaining social contacts, and it often has the added benefit of relieving family members of 24-hour care provision for at least some days of the week.

The home

Constant nursing is necessary for those with the most severe forms of learning disability, and for such people there may be no viable alternative to continual hospital care. Most disabled people, however, live either in their own homes (with their parents or in their marital home) or in special community-based residential accommodation.

Over the past twenty years or so there has been a major change towards providing care in the community. This gives people much more independence and may make for a lifestyle which is congenial, stimulating and challenging. Attempts are made to promote autonomy while still offering support and some degree of protection from exploitation. Such provision is demanding of resources, however, and there is often a continual struggle by the agencies responsible for such accommodation to secure the funding necessary for continuation of the scheme.

Various residential arrangements are available as alternatives to traditional institutional care, including various types of hostel and 'group homes'. The latter are houses located within a community residential area in which a small number of people with learning disabilities live together. Residents are guided and supported by a team of professionals and voluntary helpers who work to develop the residents' practical living skills and self-confidence, and help them to live in harmony with others. The group home can offer permanent accommodation for those who would not be able to function on their own, although some residents are eventually able to take the next step towards independence and move to their own flat, or move in with a friend or partner.

In an early evaluation study, Malin (1983) compared the progress of residents of group homes with that of similar people living in hostel accommodation, and found that the group home residents showed significantly greater improvement in their cognitive abilities and self-help skills. A high level of staff support within a group home was associated with particularly high levels of skill acquisition.

Mentally handicapped people as victims of abuse

There is now substantial evidence showing that mentally handicapped people are at a high risk of being sexually and physically abused by family members and other carers (Morgan, 1987; McCormack, 1991). The increased risk of physical abuse may be partly explained as resulting from the high levels of stress often experienced by those caring for a handicapped person. Many people with learning disabilities are hyperactive, and some are frequently aggressive. Such behaviours may eventually provoke extreme anger in the carer, especially if they are judged to be deliberate acts of annoyance or provocation.

The increased risk of sexual abuse requires a different explanation. People with a moderate or severe learning disability are particularly vulnerable to sexual assault because they tend to be compliant and have little opportunity to voice their disapproval or to make a complaint against a person who is mistreating them sexually. Those who are emotionally insecure, and who have not been provided with teaching about sexuality and sexual exploitation, are relatively safe targets for the sexual attention of unscrupulous adults (Tharinger et al., 1990).

Although some physical and sexual abuse takes place within the family, abuse also occurs in other residential settings. Marchetti and McCartney (1990) examined the mistreatment of learning disabled people in public residential facilities and found that the staff most likely to be the perpetrators of abuse were those who had direct responsibility for the care of residents. Most of the victims of abuse in this study had either mild or moderate learning difficulties.

The task of helping mentally handicapped victims of physical and sexual abuse is likely to be even more difficult than that of helping non-handicapped victims, but in recent years a number of workers have developed methods of providing psychotherapeutic interventions for sexually abused handicapped children and adults (Sinason, 1989; Sullivan and Scanlan, 1990; Conboy-Hill and Waitman, 1992). Prevention strategies include close monitoring for any early indications of physical or sexual abuse, and the delivery of specially devised sex education programmes which refer specifically to the possibility of sexual exploitation.

Marriage

These days a major goal for the long-term care of mentally handicapped people is the provision of skills and resources that will enable them to live as independently as possible. The normalization goal implies that handicapped people should be free to form relationships, including sexual relationships, and should also be free to conceive, bear and rear children of their own. All these issues, however, pose substantial ethical problems.

When two moderately or severely mentally handicapped adults are physically attracted to one another, those responsible for their care must decide whether sexual behaviour is to be encouraged, merely 'permitted' or actively discouraged. The carers' decision may be influenced by rules and guidelines adopted in the particular residential setting, and it will reflect judgements regarding any possibility that the relationship might be exploitative or that the relationship might end in a pregnancy.

Many people insist that all mentally handicapped people have a right to sexual expression, whereas others feel that at some level of handicap the person simply cannot be fully aware of the significance of sexual relationships and the physical and emotional hazards often associated with physical liaisons. Although marriages in which one or both partners has a learning disability are often successful, the risk of marital distress is relatively high, especially when both partners have an intellectual handicap (Koller et al., 1988). Relatively high rates of marital violence have also been reported.

Mentally handicapped people as parents

There is a relatively high risk that a child of mentally handicapped parents will also have some degree of intellectual impairment. This is partly due to genetic factors, but it may also reflect the poverty of the social and physical environment. Dowdney and Skuse (1993) reviewed the evidence relating to the quality of parenting provided by adults with learning difficulties, and they also considered the effectiveness of schemes for training such parents in child-rearing skills. Adequacy of parenting has been assessed using a number of different criteria, including standards of physical care, the health of the child, whether or not agency support is necessary and whether there has ever been any indication that the child has suffered neglect or abuse.

Although the results of several studies testify to the fact that many adults with IQ scores of around 60 are competent and successful parents, those who function below this level invariably have problems in handling their children, and the results from a number of large-scale surveys give considerable cause for concern. Mentally handicapped parents tend to be highly controlling of and punitive towards their children, and a relatively high proportion are abusive (Whitman and Accardo, 1990). Many rarely involve themselves in their children's play and many appear insensitive to their children's needs. A high proportion of the children are described by the parents as difficult to handle, and the relationship between the parents and the child often becomes fraught. In around a third of cases the child is eventually taken away from the parents and placed in a foster home.

A number of programmes have been designed to train handicapped parents in basic caretaking and play skills. Although most of these programmes have been directed at families seen individually, some have brought groups of families together for demonstrations and discussions of issues relating to child safety, limit setting and methods of disciplining. Substantial improvements have often been reported, for both group-based and family-based interventions, although there appears to be a limit to what can be gained through group work alone.

Techniques used in family-based interventions include modelling, role-play and feedback, and an important element in all such programmes is the positive reinforcement of adequate parenting. Training programmes appear to be most successful when they are tailored specifically to the parents' abilities and to the characteristics of the particular child, and many skills need to be developed gradually in a number of incremental steps. However, even when it has been possible to build skills that are used successfully in the training situation, parents often fail to transfer these skills to everyday home situations with the child.

Other intervention programmes have been targeted specifically at learning disabled parents who are at risk of abusing their child. These programmes focus on issues relating to disciplining and anger control, and they may also include attempts to increase the parents' understanding and empathy for the child. Unfortunately, however, the results of these programmes have not been encouraging. Seagull and Scheurer (1986) described a highly intensive two-year programme with twenty 'at-risk' families. Despite a very high level of contact maintained throughout this period between the families and the professionals who were attempting to help them, the disappointing outcome was that eventually 78 per cent of the children needed to be taken into care.

◀The Impact of Mental Handicap on the Family▶▶▶

Responses to learning that a child has a mental handicap

In some cases, particularly if there is a pathological cause, the fact that a child is mentally handicapped is apparent immediately after birth. Professionals who have the task of informing parents about their child's condition are placed in an unenviable position, and the way in which they make the disclosure can have a marked effect on how well the parents cope. Parents of handicapped children are frequently critical of how they were informed of the child's condition. In most cases, the parents' initial reaction to learning of their child's handicap is one of profound shock, but they may also experience revulsion, embarrassment, guilt and anger. It is often said that such couples undergo a process of grief similar to that which follows a bereavement.

In their struggle to identify reasons for the child's condition, the parents may blame themselves, or may feel guilty about having brought the child into the world. In the most severe cases the parents have no option but to allow the child to be permanently cared for in an institution, but in border-line cases parents may face an agonizing decision about whether to place the child in a hospital or to devote themselves to caring for the child.

In the majority of cases, however, the question of institutional care does not arise. Indeed, there may be no sign that a child is handicapped until some months or even years after the birth. The first indication that all is not well may come with the realization that the child has taken considerably longer than most other children to achieve the various developmental markers that represent key advances in motor abilities, perceptual-motor skills and un-derstanding. The parents' progressive awareness of the child's limitations, together with their familiarity and affection for the child, often means that there is relatively little shock when a diagnosis of mental handicap is eventually confirmed.

Adaptation

After the initial shock of being told that their child will develop with an intellectual deficit, many parents struggle to accept the fact and begin to plan for a life with the handicapped child. They may be helped in their efforts by professionals who are able to offer specialist advice, and by other families who have faced a similar situation. However, the adjustment process may be hindered by other people's reactions, some of which will reveal the igno-rance and prejudice often associated with learning disabilities. Despite the difficulties involved, most of these families do eventually adapt to their exceptional situation. They are able to put things into perspective and gradu-ally begin to develop a new lifestyle which accommodates to the special needs of the child.

Longer-term effects on family life

Caring for a handicapped child is a long-term responsibility which places an onerous burden on parents and, to a lesser extent, on siblings. The emotional pressures and the relentless demands on energy can place an enormous strain on a family. The family may face additional financial hardship, because mothers of handicapped children are less likely to work outside the home, the child may have special medical or dietary needs, and it may be necessary for the family to make frequent trips to specialist clinics.

Some parents of learning disabled children become obsessed with caring for the child. They may take little account of their own or their partner's needs, and the needs of other children in the family may be disregarded. The presence of a handicapped child often has a marked impact on relationships between other family members, but whereas some studies have suggested that the effects are likely to destabilize the marriage, other studies suggest that in some cases the marital relationship is strengthened by the adversity (Frude, 1991).

The additional burden on the family is often shared unevenly. The major responsibility for the care of the handicapped child is usually taken up by the mother, although siblings (particularly older daughters) also tend to be assigned special duties. Fathers typically play a relatively minor role in rearing the handicapped child, and some endeavour to cope by withdrawing emotionally from the family (Lamb, 1983). The learning disabled person, whatever his or her age relative to the other children, may be assigned the role of 'the youngest family member'.

Many families with a learning disabled younger member are rather isolated and become somewhat housebound. They may engage in few activities beyond the home, and may be reluctant to call upon people to act as babysitters.

Parenting style

Parents need to judge when the child is realistically capable of achieving certain skills, and they need to avoid the danger of overprotection. Children who are learning to dress themselves or to use the toilet may fail many times before they eventually succeed, and if they are not provided with the chance to fail they will not have the opportunity to learn. Failures and embarrassments are also an intrinsic part of social development, and it is particularly unfortunate that many learning disabled youngsters develop few peer relationships. Byrne et al. (1988) found that Down's syndrome children who had several friends and were subject to few restrictions in their play activities developed a higher level of social maturity than those who lacked close peer relationships and whose play was highly controlled.

Many parents of children who have a mental handicap deliberately avoid being restrictive and overprotective. Many are extremely keen to encourage independent learning, self-sufficiency and exploration. Many become adept at ignoring failure and learn to understand the child's poorly expressed needs. Such parents adapt extremely well to their child's limitations and behavioural style. They take great pride in each minor accomplishment, and by praising hard-won successes they manage to boost the child's confidence and self-esteem.

The effects on parents

The physical and emotional strain involved in caring for a mentally handicapped child can lead to a deterioration in the parents' physical and psychological health. Quine and Pahl (1985) reported that over half of their sample of mothers of mentally handicapped children were depressed, and Byrne et al. (1988) discovered high levels of maternal stress in families with a Down's syndrome child, particularly when the child's behaviour was persistently disturbed. Many mothers caring for handicapped children consider any depression and anxiety they feel to be natural responses to their circumstances and relatively few seek professional help for their emotional problems (Gath, 1978).

Maternal stress is not universal, however, and many studies have reported that a high proportion of mothers derive a great deal of enjoyment from their interaction with the child. Emotional well-being has been found to be associated with having some free time, being able to make frequent excursions beyond the home and receiving help and support from other family members. The partner's support appears to be especially important in protecting the mothers of learning disabled children from distress (Gath, 1978; McKinney and Peterson, 1987)

Effects on siblings

The brothers and sisters of people with learning difficulties are likely to be affected by the handicap in a number of ways. They may become distressed by their parents' reaction to the diagnosis of a young sibling as handicapped, and they may become disturbed by signs that their parents are under stress or that the marital relationship is under some strain. Siblings sometimes feel that their parents devote all their attention to the special needs of the handicapped child, and feel themselves to be neglected. Older children may also become resentful about parental requests for help with the care of their brother or sister. Beyond the home, children are often teased about having a brother or sister with a learning disability (Byrne et al., 1988).

Bagenholm and Gillberg (1991) reported relatively high levels of behavioural problems and emotional symptoms among siblings, and revealed that many were lonely or had difficult relationships with their peers. Many viewed the handicapped child as a burden on the family. The results of other studies, however, suggest that there is rarely any evidence of serious adverse effects on siblings when the parents are coping well. Gath and Gumley (1987) found that siblings of learning disabled children were less likely to be 'deviant' when there was a high level of cohesion within the family.

Helping families with a mentally handicapped member

Only some of the families caring for a person with a learning disability need help for emotional problems, but all may benefit from practical help and information. Health professionals who are knowledgeable about appropriate medical, social and educational facilities should be able to help in arranging access to local resources. Parents may be encouraged to teach basic skills to their child using one of the available structured training programmes, and they may be encouraged to make contact with local nurseries or 'parent and toddler' groups.

When the child reaches school age, the family may need help in considering how best to meet the child's educational needs. In particular, the parents might need advice when evaluating the advantages and disadvantages of placing the child in a special school (the issue of 'mainstreaming' is considered in Box 9.3). In the UK, the 1981 Education Act introduced provision for a 'Statement of Special Educational Needs', a formal document drawn up following consultation with the parents and a detailed assessment of the child's capabilities and behavioural characteristics. Educational psychologists, who are responsible for drafting the statement, also take the feelings and perceptions of the parents and child into account when detailing the child's educational needs. The Statement of Special Educational Needs is a powerful tool because local education authorities are required by law to make the educational provisions specified within the document (Advisory Centre for Education, 1990).

Families often benefit from brief intervals of 'respite care'. For a few days or weeks the handicapped person moves to a special residential setting or stays with relatives. This provides an opportunity for the learning disabled person to broaden his or her experience, and it allows other family members to engage in activities that might be impossible when care needs to be constantly provided.

At a later stage, the handicapped person and the family may need help in choosing between available employment and training options, and may need to discuss the issue of longer-term living arrangements. Some handicapped people look forward to moving to a group residence or living independently, while others are content to remain in the family home for as long as possible. Parents, and siblings too, are frequently concerned about what will happen to the handicapped person when the parents become too old to continue with their caring role. Professionals are often able to help with what has become known as 'permanency planning'.

In addition to professional sources of advice and assistance, a number of voluntary and self-help groups exist to offer support to families of people with learning disabilities. By meeting other families, some of whom will have gained a good deal of knowledge about local resources, the parents may gain both emotional and practical support. However, some families

Box 9.3
Mainstreaming in Education: an Ongoing Controversy

Parents of children who have been assessed as having mild or moderate learning difficulties often prefer to have their child educated in an ordinary school. Their preference may stem partly from concern that attendance at a special school will stigmatize the child (and, perhaps, the rest of the family), and partly from the hope that a normal school setting will better enable the child to fulfil his or her academic potential. Parents may also believe that attendance at an ordinary school will facilitate their child's social adjustment and competence, and thus better prepare him or her for life beyond the school.

The provision of integrated education for children who have a mild or moderate learning disability is labelled 'mainstreaming'. Widely adopted as a key element in educational policy, this practice has now been implemented in many countries for the education of all but the most severely handicapped pupils. In the UK, the 1981 Education Act introduced legislation that promoted the integration of all children with special educational needs into ordinary schools, and directed that these children should engage with other children in the school in the broad range of activities. In the USA, a 1986 amendment to the Education of the Handicapped Act made it mandatory for children with disabilities to be educated in the 'least restrictive environment'.

Many people are highly enthusiastic about mainstreaming and believe that the accommodation of handicapped children in normal schools will reduce their isolation and stigmatization and enable them to integrate socially with non-handicapped peers both within and beyond the school. Advocates regard mainstreaming as an important part of a broader move towards the normalization of handicapped people, and they stress the fact that integration in schools may increase the understanding and acceptance by non-handicapped children of those with disabilites.

On the other hand, many educationalists and others have expressed serious doubts about the desirability of the move towards wholesale integration. They emphasize certain benefits that may be gained from special education, and identify a number of potential problems with the mainstreaming strategy. Some contend that mainstreaming exposes handicapped children to constant unfavourable comparison with their more able peers. Because they are likely to be constantly outperformed by their peers on a wide range of academic and non-academic tasks, it is argued, handicapped children may become more, rather than less, aware of (and self-conscious about) their limitations. The critics of mainstreaming point to the danger of a progressive lowering of the self-esteem of such children, particularly if their peers subject them to derision and sarcasm.

Critics also cite the fact that most ordinary schools have a much less favourable staff : pupil ratio than special schools, and that few of the teachers are trained to educate pupils with special needs. Thus, it is argued, handicapped children who are placed in integrated schools may fail to realize their academic potential precisely because their special education needs are not being met.

Few of the arguments around this issue reflect differences in values between the protagonists. Most of the disagreements concern predictions about the actual outcomes of mainstreaming. However, although it might appear an easy matter to subject the conflicting predictions to empirical test, the evaluation of the effects of mainstreaming has proved to be a highly complex task. It would clearly be unethical to assign children randomly to a segregated or integrated educational setting, without regard to their own preferences and those of their parents, yet without such allocation it is difficult to find two groups, one mainstreamed and one not, that are adequately matched on all relevant characteristics.

Furthermore, it is difficult to draw general conclusions from any one study because there is a huge variation in how mainstreaming is implemented. Apart from differences in terms of the ages of the children concerned, and the nature and severity of their handicaps, mainstreaming itself takes a number of different forms, and there is a wide variation in the degree to which teachers have been trained to provide education for children with special needs. In some mainstreamed schools, handicapped children spend only part of the school week with their classmates and receive supplementary training from a specialist teacher at other times. Such 'remedial education' may be provided for an individual child or for a group of children. Given the variety of arrangements, it is difficult to locate any two studies which can be said to have examined the same implementation of mainstreaming.

Any evaluation of mainstreaming needs to assess many different variables in order to provide an adequate overall picture of the effects. Academic attainment is clearly a key variable, but many other effects may be implicated in the complex cost–benefit equation, including non-academic skills development, self-confidence and self-esteem, anxiety levels, aspirations, the quality of peer relationships and the attitudes of non-handicapped peers to those who are intellectually less able.

Faced with all these complexities and variations, it is not surprising that there is as yet no clear-cut answer to the major question of whether mainstreaming is generally beneficial for handicapped children. Most of the relevant studies have examined just one type of mainstreamed arrangement, comparison groups are highly varied and the variables examined in different studies diverge considerably.

Rule et al. (1987) evaluated the impact of three years of mainstreamed daycare (between the ages of three years and five years) on handicapped children. Although these children made significant gains on educational and developmental tests over the three years, their progress did not differ from that of similar children who had not attended the mainstreamed programme. Both groups of children performed similarly on standardized tests and there was no difference in their social skills as rated by parents and teachers, or in the extent of their interaction with non-handicapped peers in a free play situation.

In a study which focused on the social adaptation of mainstreamed handicapped children, Taylor et al. (1987) found that many of these children were rejected by their non-handicapped classmates and that they were often very anxious in the classroom situation. Their teachers judged the handicapped pupils as socially anxious and as less cooperative than most of the other children in the class.

There are various ways in which potential difficulties arising from mainstreaming might be overcome. For example, the threat of a handicapped child being exposed to recurrent failure and ridicule might be reduced if the competitiveness which is normally part of the classroom ethos were to be replaced with a spirit of cooperation. Miller (1989) reviewed studies of the use of cooperative learning as a way of promoting the social and cognitive development of mainstreamed handicapped children, and concluded that those who worked in a cooperative atmosphere with other children formed more friendships and were accepted more by their non-handicapped peers than those who worked in a competitive atmosphere. Such children also performed better academically than handicapped peers who remained in highly competitive classes.

deliberately avoid this kind of contact because they feel that membership of such a group would accentuate, rather than diminish, the impact of the handicap on their lives.

◀Prevention▶▶▶

In the early 1970s, a panel of experts in the USA set a national goal of reducing the incidence (that is, the number of new cases) of mental retardation by 50 per cent before the year 2000 (President's Panel on Mental Retardation, 1972). Such a target is now widely regarded as unrealistic for a variety of reasons, most of which are social, political and economic rather than scientific or medical. Nevertheless, there have been many important developments in the field of prevention in recent years. In considering the issues involved we need to differentiate between the prevention of cases of pathological handicap and the prevention of cases of familial handicap.

The prevention of familial mental handicap

Because intellectual ability is determined to a substantial degree by genetic constitution, there is a tendency for children born to people of low intelligence to have a low IQ themselves. Thus the number of cases of familial mental handicap could be reduced by ensuring that people who are intellectually disabled, and those who have a low level of intelligence within the normal range, are given every opportunity to avoid unwanted pregnancies. This might be achieved by taking special care to educate such people about methods of contraception and ensuring the availability of contraceptives.

More radical interventions, involving sterilization, abortion and sex segregation, clearly raise major ethical issues. Some extremists have argued strongly for eugenic intervention. If reproductive patterns were controlled, as in animal breeding programmes, they argue, then the 'quality' of 'the stock' would improve. If intelligent people were encouraged to have more children and strict limits were placed on the reproduction of people with low IQ scores, then the general intellectual capacity of the population would increase and the proportion of people with learning difficulties would decline. Most people, however, object vehemently to any suggestion of a social engineering strategy for limiting the reproductive freedom of any individual or group of people. Any scheme that compelled one section of the community to limit its reproduction would be regarded as totally unacceptable and would be seen as a major infringement of basic human rights.

In recent years, media attention has focused on a number of legal cases concerning the sterilization of young women with moderate learning disabilities. All of these cases have involved women who were sexually active. Some had had a number of previous conceptions, some had been distressed by the pregnancy and had undergone a number of abortions, and in all cases it was considered that the woman would be incapable of looking after a child herself. For various reasons it was judged that no suitable form of reversible contraception was available, and the legal issue concerned the question of whether the woman should be sterilized.

A number of psychological questions are raised by such cases. Does the woman understand what would be involved in the surgical procedure? Does she understand the effects of sterilization? Does she appreciate her legal rights in the matter? Many important legal and ethical issues also arise, including those concerning whether people with various degrees of intellectual impairment can give informed consent to surgery, whether the person's own wishes and preferences are paramount and whether other people (especially the woman's parents) have any rights in the matter. Some commentators have suggested that the decision about whether or not sterilization is performed should by made jointly by the person herself, members of her family, her physician and a specially constituted ethics committee (Elkins and Anderson, 1992).

The risk that a child born to one or two learning disabled parents will also have some degree of intellectual impairment is relatively high, not only because genetic factors influence intellectual potential, but also because environmental aspects may limit the degree to which the child is able to develop his or her potential. Parents can often be helped to provide a stimulating environment for the child, and the provision of additional educational opportunities in the early years may be effective in preventing a child from becoming intellectually impaired. Enrolment in special compensatory schemes such as 'Head Start' has been shown to help many environmentally disadvantaged children to achieve more of their intellectual potential, and the effects of such schemes appear to be long-lasting (see Box 9.4). On the other hand, there are cases in which a child cannot be provided with adequate stimulation and care within the family, and the alternatives of foster care or adoption may need to be considered.

The prevention of pathological handicap

It is possible to prevent some forms of pathologically based mental handicap, either by preventing or treating the relevant pathology or, if the initial level of impairment is relatively mild, by providing compensatory education. Various strategies can be used to prevent pathological handicap at the pre-fertilization, pre-natal, perinatal or post-natal stages.

Pre-fertilization   There is sometimes an awareness that a couple may be at a particularly high risk of conceiving a child with a specific genetic or chromosomal abnormality, either because a previous conception resulted in such an abnormality or because the family history points to this possibility. In such cases genetic investigation and genetic counselling may be useful in assessing the level of risk and helping a couple to make plans. Genetic counselling usually involves at least two or three meetings between the couple and the genetic counsellor (often a doctor who specializes in genetic medicine). Some couples who learn that they are at relatively high risk of producing a child with a major genetic defect will decide to remain childless. Others will try to

Box 9.4
Compensatory Education Schemes

Whether learning disabilities are familial or have a pathological basis, the child's early years may provide a special 'window of opportunity' for intervention. Children are more likely to realize their intellectual potential if they are exposed to a stimulating environment, and a number of programmes have been devised to promote the cognitive, emotional and social development of young children. Infant stimulation programmes instruct parents about normal development, and teach them ways of enhancing cognitive growth. Such programmes also encourage parents to take pride in their child and to express interest and warmth (McGuire and Earls, 1991).

In 1965, the United States government provided funding for Head Start, a compensatory education scheme targetted mainly on 2–5-year-old children from lower social class and ethnic backgrounds. Since 1973 the project has also been required by law to accept severely handicapped children (Zigler and Styfco, 1989). Children take part in a wide range of structured activities, most of which combine instruction with play, and their parents are also encouraged to become closely involved. Nearly half a million American children participate in the programme every year, and similar Head Start schemes have now been introduced in a number of other countries. Head Start aims to improve not only children's intellectual development, but also their health and self-esteem. Medical and dental care is provided for the children, and health education is provided for the families. In addition, the social service needs of the families are assessed, and close contact is maintained between Head Start professionals and those from other helping agencies.

Although several early evaluations of the project were somewhat disappointing, the cumulative evidence clearly indicates that Head Start does produce significant positive changes in children's intellectual performance, at least in the short term. The effects then tend to fade somewhat (to 'wash out') as children progress through the school years. Although there is a centrally devised Head Start 'curriculum', and standard materials are used, the project is implemented somewhat differently in different areas, and some implementations may be significantly more effective than others.

More intensive and more highly resourced programmes have been shown to produce significant increases in measured IQ and to reduce the likelihood that a child will be placed in a special education class (Lazar and Darlington, 1982). One key feature which appears to increase the effectiveness of such programmes is the active involvement of parents. Indeed, some projects place a major emphasis on training parents in how to provide a richly stimulating environment for the child (Darlington, 1986). There is evidence of several long-lasting benefits of the best and most comprehensive of the programmes, including reductions in rates of teenage pregnancy and delinquency (Haskins, 1989).

When intensive programmes are not available, intellectual development may be promoted by providing children with stimulating play materials and encouraging them to interact with adults and other children. In some areas, special toy libraries and playgroups have been established so that handicapped children, including those from poor homes, may have an opportunity to explore an extensive range of games and playthings and to interact with children of a similar age. The provision of optimal stimulation and enhanced educational resources in the early years can provide considerable benefits to all children, including those who have a learning disability (Clarke and Clarke, 1985).

conceive but then rely on the results of antenatal tests before deciding whether or not the pregnancy will proceed to term.

One other 'pre-fertilization' method of avoiding giving birth to a child with a learning disability is to ensure that all women of child-bearing age have been vaccinated against rubella (German measles).

Pre-natal While nothing can be done following conception to change the genetic or chromosomal make-up of the developing foetus, it is at least possible to diagnose many defects at an early stage in the pregnancy. Antenatal testing techniques are under constant development. Since the 1960s it has been possible to map the chromosomal make-up of the developing foetus (a process known as karyotyping). Various foetal metabolic disorders and infections can also be diagnosed, and recent technical advances allow an increasing number of problems to be recognized at an early stage in the pregnancy. Furthermore, a range of antenatal tests have become more widely available, and ultrasound foetal monitoring techniques are now used routinely to detect abnormal rates of growth and gross malformations such as spina bifida (see Box 9.1 for further information on antenatal testing).

If it becomes apparent that the foetus is malformed, or that there is a serious chromosomal abnormality, the couple facing the prospect of giving birth to a child with a serious disabling condition may opt for a therapeutic abortion, although this decision is usually taken with immense regret and sorrow. In some cases, however, legal restrictions mean that there is no prospect of terminating the pregnancy, and in other cases the couple's religious or personal beliefs mean that they will decide to let the pregnancy proceed.

In some cases, a mental handicap results from poor maternal health during pregnancy. It is necessary, for the woman's own health and the health of her child, that the highest standards of maternal self-care and professional care are maintained throughout the pregnancy. To help to ensure normal foetal development, the pregnant woman needs to be carefully monitored for any signs of anaemia, hypertension or diabetes, all of which can affect the baby's growth. A pregnant woman also needs to be wary about exposing herself to toxins and infections. Public education campaigns in many countries alert pregnant women to the dangers of smoking, drinking alcohol and using non-prescribed drugs.

Perinatal When birth is imminent, uterine activity and the foetal heart rate can be monitored for signs of foetal distress, and if the results give cause for concern then the baby may need to be delivered by Caesarean section. Strenuous efforts must be made during the birth process to ensure that adequate oxygen continues to reach the baby's brain. Oxygen deprivation, which may occur as the result of partial strangulation by the umbilical cord, can lead to cerebral palsy and mental handicap, and in some cases a forceps delivery will result in excessive pressure being exerted on the skull.

Immediately following the birth a number of disorders and abnormalities may be detected, and in some cases immediate medical or surgical treatment will reduce the risk of handicap. Tests of the baby's blood and urine are now routinely undertaken some days after birth to investigate the possibility of PKU and various other metabolic abnormalities. If problems are detected, effective preventive action can often be taken.

Post-natal Improvements in paediatric care have helped to reduce the risk that a baby or infant will become mentally handicapped as a result of an infection or poisoning. Conditions such as bacterial meningitis, for example, are now more readily recognized and more effectively treated than in the past. The risk that a baby or young child will ingest a toxic substance has also been reduced as public health authorities, manufacturers and parents have become increasingly aware of the hazards associated with lead-based paints and other poisons. Considerable controversy still surrounds the issue of atmospheric lead. Some authorities maintain that the lead pollution levels found in many major cities produce a small but significant reduction in children's IQ scores, while other authorities strenuously deny this. For many years the argument has continued (Dietrich et al., 1993). Meanwhile, there has been a substantial reduction in the use of lead – particularly in fuel – with a resulting decrease in atmospheric levels.

Health promotion strategies, scientific and medical developments and improvements in the delivery of health care over the past twenty or thirty years has helped to bring about significant reductions in the number of children born with a pathological mental handicap. At the same time, medical advances have made it possible to prolong the lives of many mentally handicapped children and adults.

◀Conclusions▶▶▶

Mental handicap is generally present from birth and continues throughout the person's lifetime. There are many pathological causes, including chromosomal and metabolic abnormalities, gross neurological malformations, infection during pregnancy or in infancy, the presence of toxins (including alcohol) during foetal development and trauma at birth. However, in most cases of mild handicap, the condition derives from familial (mainly genetic) sources.

A number of explanations have been put forward to account for the psychological deficits associated with mental handicap. These mostly focus on various aspects of information processing, and raise the question of whether differences in cognitive functioning between mentally handicapped people and others are qualitative or quantitative. Many learning disabled people suffer from physical disorders, and as a group they are at relatively high risk of developing psychiatric disorders, both in childhood and in adulthood. In addition, many mentally handicapped people display challenging behaviours. They are also particularly vulnerable to both physical and sexual abuse.

Although there is no 'cure' for mental handicap, there is much that can be done to help. In some cases it may be possible to arrest an underlying pathology. Early training programmes may be used to ensure that the child develops his or her full cognitive potential. And it is possible in almost all cases to assist in the development of social and self-care skills. Caring for a mentally handicapped person can be highly stressful, both for professionals and for family members. There is some evidence that some parents and siblings of people with learning difficulties become distressed by the burden of care, but many cope well. People who are moderately or severely handicapped will need special support throughout their lifetime, and those who are profoundly handicapped are likely to need constant nursing care. However, many of those who are only mildly handicapped manage to live an independent life as adults. Many find employment, get married and have children, although some then find it difficult to cope as parents. It is crucial that a variety of residential facilities should be provided so that, whatever his or her level of handicap, each person is able to live in the least restrictive environment.

Measures that can be used to prevent pathological handicap include vaccination against rubella, the use of genetic tests at the embryonic stage of development, improved techniques used at birth to ensure a continuous supply of oxygen to the infant's brain and measures to prevent infection or poisoning of the infant in the months after birth. Much has been achieved in prevention over recent years.

◀Further Reading▶ ▶ ▶

Clarke, A.M., Clarke, A.D.B. and Berg, J.B. (eds) (1985) *Mental Deficiency: the Changing Outlook*, 4th edn. London: Methuen.

This book provides detailed reviews of many key areas within the field, including characteristics, causes, prevention and amelioration. Through its several editions this book has been a standard handbook for psychologists who work with mentally handicapped people.

Zigler, E. and Hodapp, R. (1986) *Understanding Mental Retardation*. Cambridge: Cambridge University Press.

This book provides a critical and learned account of many relevant issues, and describes the results of many years of research by a group of psychologists from Yale University who have long advocated a developmental psychological approach to understanding mental retardation.

Byrne, E.A., Cunningham, C.C. and Sloper, P. (1988) *Families and their Children with Down's Syndrome: One Feature in Common*. London: Routledge.

A detailed account of the impact of a handicapped child on the family, based on a major study conducted in Manchester, England.

Remington, B. (ed.) (1991) *The Challenge of Severe Mental Handicap: a Behaviour Analytic Approach*. Chichester: Wiley.

Contributions illustrate the applications of behaviour analytic thinking (closely associated with the work of B. F. Skinner) to the functional analysis and intervention for challenging behaviours. There is a particular emphasis on the application of behavioural approaches to problems of communication and language in people with severe mental handicap.

Zarkowska, E. and Clements, J. (1994) *Problem Behaviour and People with Severe Learning Disabilities: The S.T.A.R.* London: Chapman & Hall.

A practical guide for professionals, this book introduces the use of behavioural programmes for dealing with 'challenging behaviours' and also provides a useful discussion of ethical issues relating to such programmes.

Hall, J. (1996) *Social Devaluation and Special Education: the Right to Full Mainstream Inclusion and an Honest Statement.* London: Routledge.

An educational psychologist argues for mainstreaming (or 'inclusive education') for all special children, whatever the nature or degree of their disability. Challenges the medical model of disability in favour of the social model and the principle of normalization.

◄Discussion Points►► ►

1   Discuss the issues involved in choosing between various terms, including 'mental handicap', 'mental retardation' and 'learning difficulties', to describe the condition of people who have broad intellectual deficits and difficulties in adaptive functioning.
2   What are the causes of learning disability?
3   Consider the potential problems and benefits (for the child, the family and peers) of a moderately mentally handicapped child being educated in a school with non-handicapped children. How might a teacher seek to increase the benefits and overcome the difficulties that might arise from such mainstreaming?
4   Attempt to explain *either* why a relatively high proportion of people with learning difficulties engage in highly disturbed behaviour ('challenging behaviours') *or* why a relatively high proportion of people with learning difficulties develop various forms of psychiatric disorder.
5   Write an essay: 'The prevention of mental handicap'. Consider a broad range of possible prevention strategies, and include a discussion of relevant ethical issues.
6   How far is it possible to enhance the cognitive and social skills of mentally handicapped people?

References

Abbott, D.W. and Mitchell, J.E. 1993: Antidepressants vs. psychotherapy in the treatment of bulimia nervosa. *Psychopharmacology Bulletin*, 29, 115–19.

Abel, G.G. and Rouleau, J.L. 1990: The nature and extent of sexual assault. In W.L. Marshall, D.R. Laws and H.E. Barbaree (eds), *Handbook of Sexual Assault: Issues, Theories and Treatment of the Offender*. New York: Plenum.

Abel, G.G., Osborn, C.A., Anthony, D. and Gardos, P. 1992: Current treatments of paraphiliacs. *Annual Review of Sex Research*, 3, 255–90.

Abramson, L.Y., Seligman M.E.P. and Teasdale, J. 1978: Learned helplessness in humans: critique and reformulation. *Journal of Abnormal Psychology*, 87, 49–74.

Advisory Centre for Education 1990: *ACE Special Education Handbook: The Law on Children with Special Needs*. London: Advisory Centre for Education.

Affonso, D.D. and Domino, G. 1984: Postpartum depression: a review. *Birth Issues in Perinatal Care and Education*, 11, 231–5.

Agras, W.S., Rossiter, E.M., Arnow, B. and Schneider, J.A. 1992: Pharmacologic and cognitive–behavioral treatment for bulimia nervosa: a controlled comparison. *American Journal of Psychiatry*, 149, 82–7.

Allen, D. and Lowe, K. 1995: Providing intensive community support to people with learning disabilities and challenging behaviour: a preliminary analysis of outcomes and costs. *Journal of Intellectual Disability Research*, 39, 67–82.

Allen, M.G. 1976: Twin studies of affective illness. *Archives of General Psychiatry*, 33, 1476–8.

Alloy, L.B. and Abramson, L.Y. 1979: Judgment of contingency in depressed and nondepressed students: sadder but wiser? *Journal of Experimental Psychology: General*, 108, 441–85.

Amaducci, L., Falcini, M. and Lippi, A. 1992: Descriptive epidemiology and risk factors for Alzheimer's disease. *Acta Neurologica Scandinavica*, 85 (suppl.), 21–5.

American Association on Mental Retardation (AAMR) 1992: *Mental Retardation: Definition, Classification and Systems of Supports*, 9th edn. Washington, DC: AAMR.

American Psychiatric Association 1952: *Diagnostic and Statistical Manual of Mental Disorders*. Washington, DC: APA.

American Psychiatric Association 1968: *Diagnostic and Statistical Manual of Mental Disorders*, 2nd edn. Washington, DC: APA.

American Psychiatric Association 1980: *Diagnostic and Statistical Manual of Mental Disorders*, 3rd edn. Washington, DC: APA.

American Psychiatric Association 1987: *Diagnostic and Statistical Manual of Mental Disorders*, 3rd edn, revised. Washington, DC: APA.

American Psychiatric Association 1994: *Diagnostic and Statistical Manual of Mental Disorders*, 4th edn. Washington, DC: APA.

Andersen, A.E. 1983: Anorexia nervosa and bulimia: a spectrum of eating disorders. *Journal of Adolescent Health Care*, 4, 15–21.

Andersen, A.E. 1985: *Practical Comprehensive Treatment of Anorexia Nervosa and Bulimia*. London: Edward Arnold.

Andrews, G., Stewart, G., Allen, R. and Henderson, A.S. 1990: The genetics of six neurotic disorders: a twin study. *Journal of Affective Disorders*, 19, 23–9.

Bagenholm, A. and Gillberg, C. 1991: Psychosocial effects on siblings of children with autism and mental retardation: a population-based study. *Journal of Mental Deficiency Research*, 35, 291–307.

Bakan, R., Birmingham, C.L., Aeberhardt, L. and Goldner, E.M. 1993: Dietary zinc intake of vegetarian and nonvegetarian patients with anorexia nervosa. *Journal of Eating Disorders*, 13, 229–33.

Baker, A.W. and Duncan, S.P. 1985: Child sexual abuse: a study of prevalence in Great Britain. *Child Abuse and Neglect*, 9, 457–67.

Baker, C.D. 1993: A cognitive–behavioural model for the formulation and treatment of sexual dysfunction. In J.M. Ussher and C.D. Baker (eds), *Psychological Perspectives on Sexual Problems: New Directions in Theory and Practice*. London: Routledge.

Baker, C.D. and de Silva, P. 1988: The relationship between male sexual dysfunction and belief in Zilbergeld's myths: an empirical investigation. *Sexual and Marital Therapy*, 3, 229–38.

Balter, M.B., Manheimer, D.I., Mellinger, G.D. and Uhlenhuth, E.H. 1984: A cross-national comparison of anti-anxiety/sedative drug use. *Current Medical Research and Opinion*, 8 (suppl. 4), 5–20.

Bancroft, J. 1984: Hormones and human sexual behaviour. *Journal of Sex and Marital Therapy*, 10, 3–22.

Bancroft, J. 1993: Sexual disorders. In R.E. Kendall and A.K. Zealey (eds), *Companion to Psychiatric Studies*, 5th edn. Edinburgh: Churchill Livingstone.

Bandura, A. 1977: Self efficacy: toward a unifying theory of behavioral change. *Psychological Review*, 84, 191–215.

Barker, M. and Beech, A. 1993: Sex offender treatment programmes: a critical look at the cognitive behavioural approach. *Issues in Criminological and Legal Psychology*, 19, 37–42.

Barlow, D., Mavissakalian, M. and Hay, L. 1981: Couples' treatment of agoraphobia: changes in marital satisfaction. *Behaviour Research and Therapy*, 19, 245–55.

Barlow, D.H. 1988: *Anxiety and Its Disorders: the Nature and Treatment of Anxiety and Panic*. New York: Guilford.

Barlow, D.H. 1992: Cognitive–behavioral approaches to panic disorder and social phobia. *Bulletin of the Menninger Clinic*, 56, 14–28.

Barlow, D.H. and Craske, M.G. 1988: The phenomenology of panic. In S. Rachman and J.D. Maser (eds), *Panic: Psychological Perspectives*. Hillsdale, NJ: Lawrence Erlbaum Associates.

Barlow, D.H., Leitenberg, H. and Agras, W.S. 1969: Experimental control of sexual deviation through manipulation of the noxious scene in covert sensitization. *Journal of Abnormal Psychology*, 74, 597–601.

Barlow, D.H., Reynolds, E.J. and Agras, W.S. 1973: Gender identity change in a transsexual. *Archives of General Psychiatry*, 29, 569–76.

Barrowclough, C. and Fleming, I. 1986: *Goal Planning with Elderly People: Making Plans to Meet Individual Needs.* Manchester: Manchester University Press.

Bartus, R.T. 1990: Drugs to treat age-related neurodegenerative problems: the final frontier of medical science? *Journal of the American Geriatrics Society*, 38, 680–95.

Bateson, G., Jackson, D.D., Haley, J. and Weakland, J. 1956: Toward a theory of schizophrenia. *Behavioural Science*, 1, 251–64.

Baumeister, A.A. and Baumeister, A.A. 1989: Mental Retardation. In C.G. Last and M. Hersen (eds), *Handbook of Child Psychiatric Diagnosis.* New York: Wiley.

Baxter, L.R., Phelps, M.E. and Mazziotta, J.C. 1987: Local cerebral glucose metabolic rates in obsessive–compulsive disorder: a comparison with rates in unipolar depression and in normal controls. *Archives of General Psychiatry*, 44, 211–18.

Beach, F. (ed.) 1977: *Human Sexuality in Four Perspectives.* Baltimore: Johns Hopkins Press.

Beach, S.R.H. and O'Leary, K.D. 1986: The treatment of depression occurring in the context of marital discord. *Behavior Therapy*, 17, 43–9.

Bean, P. and Mounser, P. 1993: *Discharged from Mental Hospitals.* Basingstoke: Macmillan (in association with MIND).

Beck, A.T. 1967: *Depression: Clinical, Experimental and Theoretical Aspects.* New York: Harper and Row.

Beck, A.T. 1988: Cognitive approaches to panic disorder: theory and therapy. In S. Rachman and J.D. Maser (eds), *Panic: Psychological Perspectives.* Hillsdale, NJ: Lawrence Erlbaum Associates.

Beck, A.T. and Emery, G. 1985: *Anxiety Disorders and Phobias: a Cognitive Perspective.* New York: Basic Books.

Beck, A.T. and Emery, G.D. 1977: *Cognitive Therapy of Substance Abuse.* Philadelphia, PA: Center for Cognitive Therapy.

Becker, J.V. and Skinner, L.J. 1983: Assessment and treatment of rape-related sexual dysfunctions. *The Clinical Psychologist*, 36, 102–5.

Bell, A.P., Weinberg, M.S. and Hammersmith, S.K. 1981: *Sexual Preference: Its Development in Men and Women.* Bloomington, IN: Indiana University Press.

Belsher, G. and Costello, C.G. 1988: Relapse after recovery from unipolar depression: a critical review. *Psychological Bulletin*, 104, 84–96.

Bennun, I. 1988: Involving spouses and families in the treatment of adult psychological problems. In F.N. Watts (ed.), *New Developments on Clinical Psychology: Volume II.* Chichester: Wiley.

Benton, D. and Cook, R. 1991: Vitamin and mineral supplements improve the intelligence scores and concentration of six-year old children. *Personality and Individual Differences*, 12, 1151–8.

Biernacki, P. 1986: *Pathways from Heroin Addiction: Recovery without Treatment.* Philadelphia, PA: Temple University Press.

Birchwood, M. 1992: Early intervention in schizophrenia: theoretical background and clinical strategies. *British Journal of Clinical Psychology*, 31, 257–78.

Birchwood, M., Hallett, S. and Preston, M. 1988: *Schizophrenia: an Integrated Approach to Research and Treatment.* London: Longman.

Birchwood, M., Smith, J., Macmillan, F., Hogg, B., Prasad, R., Harvey, C. and Bering, S. 1989: Predicting relapse in schizophrenia; the development and implementation of an early signs monitoring system using patients and families as observers. *Psychological Medicine*, 19, 649–56.

Blackburn, I.M. 1988: Psychological processes in depression. In E. Miller and P.J. Cooper (eds), *Adult Abnormal Psychology*. London: Churchill Livingstone.

Blair, C.D. and Lanyon, R.I. 1981: Exhibitionism: etiology and treatment. *Psychological Bulletin*, 89, 439–63.

Blanchard, R. and Hucker, S.J. 1991: Age, transvestism, bondage, and concurrent paraphilic activities in 117 fatal cases of autoerotic asphyxia. *British Journal of Psychiatry*, 159, 371–7.

Blanchard, R., Steiner, B.W., Clemmensen, L.H. and Dickey, R. 1989: Prediction of regrets in postoperative transsexuals. *Canadian Journal of Psychiatry*, 34, 43–5.

Bloom, B.L., Asher, S.R. and White, S.W. 1979: Marital disruption as a stressor. *Psychological Bulletin*, 85, 867–94.

Borkovec, T.D. 1994: The nature, functions and origins of worry. In G. Davey and F. Tallis (eds), *Worrying: Perspectives on Theory, Assessment and Treatment*. Chichester: Wiley.

Borkovec, T.D. and Costello, E. 1993: Efficacy of applied relaxation and cognitive–behavioral therapy in the treatment of generalized anxiety disorder. *Journal of Consulting and Clinical Psychology*, 61, 611–19.

Botvin, G.J. and Wills, T.A. 1985: Personal and social skills training: cognitive–behavioural approaches to substance abuse prevention. In C.S. Bell and R. Battjes (eds), *Prevention Research: Deterring Drug Abuse among Children and Adolescents* (NIDA Research Monograph 63). Washington, DC: US Government Printing Office.

Bower, G.H. 1981: Mood and memory. *American Psychologist*, 36, 129–48.

Bowlby, J. 1980: *Attachment and Loss. Volume 3: Loss, Sadness and Depression*. New York: Basic Books.

Boyd, J.H., Rae, D.S., Thompson, J.W. and Burns, B.J. 1990: Phobia: prevalence and risk factors. *Social Psychiatry and Psychiatric Epidemiology*, 25, 314–23.

Bradford, J.M. and Pawlak, A. 1993: Double blind placebo crossover study of cyproterone acetate in the treatment of the paraphilias. *Archives of Sexual Behavior*, 22, 383–402.

Bradley, B., Phillips, G., Green, L. and Gossop, M. 1990: Circumstances surrounding the initial relapse to opiate use following detoxification. *British Journal of Psychiatry*, 254, 354–9.

Broadbent, D.E. 1958: *Perception and Communication*. Oxford: Pergamon.

Bromley, J. and Emerson, E. 1995: Beliefs and emotional reactions of care staff working with people with challenging behaviour. *Journal of Intellectual Disability Research*, 39, 341–52.

Brooks, N.D. 1991: The head-injured family. *Journal of Clinical and Experimental Neuropsychology*, 13, 155–88.

Brooks, N.D. and McKinlay, W.W. 1983: Personality and behavioural change after severe blunt head injury: a relatives' view. *Journal of Neurology, Neurosurgery and Psychiatry*, 46, 336–44.

Brooks, N.D., Campsie, L., Symington, C., Beattie, A. and McKinlay, W.W. 1986: The five-year outcome of severe blunt head injury: a relatives' view. *Journal of Neurology, Neurosurgery and Psychiatry*, 49, 764–70.

Broverman, I.K., Broverman, D.M., Clarkson, F.E., Rosenkrantz, P.S. and Vogel, S.R. 1970: Sex-role stereotypes and clinical judgments of mental health. *Journal of Consulting and Clinical Psychology*, 34, 1–7.

Brown, G.W. and Birley, J.L.T. 1968: Crisis and life change at the onset of schizophrenia. *Journal of Health and Social Behaviour*, 9, 203–24.

Brown, G.W. and Harris. T.O. 1978: *Social Origins of Depression*. London: Tavistock.

Brown, G.W., Birley, J.L.T. and Wing, J.K. 1972: The influence of family life on the course of schizophrenic disorders: a replication. *British Journal of Psychiatry*, 121, 241–58.

Bruch, H. 1962: Perceptual and cognitive disturbances in anorexia nervosa. *Psychosomatic Medicine*, 24, 187–94.

Bruch, H. 1978: *The Golden Cage*. Cambridge, MA: Harvard University Press.

Bruch, M.A. 1989: Familial and developmental antecedents of social phobia: issues and findings. *Clinical Psychology Review*, 9, 37–47.

Bruch, M.A. and Heimberg, R.G. 1994: Differences in perceptions of parental and personal characteristics between generalized and nongeneralized social phobics. *Journal of Anxiety Disorders*, 8, 155–68.

Buckhalt, J.A., Halpin, G., Noel, R. and Meadows, M. 1992: Relationship of drug use to involvement in school, home, and community activities: results of a large survey of adolescents. *Psychological Reports*, 70, 139–46.

Bulik, C., Beidel, D.C., Duchmann, E. and Weltzin, T.E. 1992a: Comparative psychopathology of women with bulimia nervosa and obsessive–compulsive disorder. *Comprehensive Psychiatry*, 33, 262–8.

Bulik, C.M., Sullivan, P.F., Epstein, L.H. and McKee, M. 1992b: Drug use in women with anorexia and bulimia nervosa. *International Journal of Eating Disorders*, 11, 213–25.

Bushman, B.J. and Cooper, H.M. 1990: Effects of alcohol on human aggression: an integrative research review. *Psychological Bulletin*, 107, 341–54.

Butler, G., Cullington, A., Hibbert, G., Klimes, I. and Gelder, M. 1987: Anxiety management for persistent generalised anxiety. *British Journal of Psychiatry*, 151, 535–42.

Butler, G., Fennell, M., Robson, P. and Gelder, M. 1991: Comparison of behavior therapy and cognitive behavior therapy in the treatment of generalized anxiety disorder. *Journal of Consulting and Clinical Psychology*, 59, 167–75.

Byrne, E.A., Cunningham, C.C. and Sloper, P. 1988: *Families and their Children with Down's Syndrome: One Feature in Common*. London: Routledge.

Caffey, E.M., Diamond, L.S. and Frank, T.V. 1964: Discontinuation or reduction of chemotherapy in chronic schizophrenics. *Journal of Chronic Diseases*, 17, 347–58.

Carey, G. and Gottesman, I.I. 1981: Twin and family studies of anxiety, phobic and compulsive disorders. In D.F. Klein and J.G. Rabkin (eds), *Anxiety: New Research and Changing Concepts*. New York: Raven Press.

Cargan, L. and Melko, M. 1982: *Singles: Myths and Realities*. Beverly Hills, CA: Sage.

Caro, I., Miralles, A. and Rippere, V. 1983: What's the thing to do when you're feeling depressed: a cross-cultural replication. *Behaviour Research and Therapy*, 21, 477–83.

Carr, A. 1974: Compulsive neurosis: a review of the literature. *Psychological Bulletin*, 81, 311–18.

Carr, J. 1994: Long-term outcome for people with Down's syndrome. *Journal of Child Psychology and Psychiatry*, 35, 425–39.

Charney, E.A. and Weissman, M.M. 1988: Epidemiology of depressive illness. In: J.J. Mann (ed.), *The Depressive Illness Series. Volume I: Phenomenology of Depressive Illness*. New York: Human Sciences Press.

Clark, D.M. 1986: A cognitive approach to panic. *Behaviour Research and Therapy*, 24, 461–70.

Clark, D.M. 1988: A cognitive model of panic attacks. In S. Rachman and J.D. Maser (eds), *Panic: Psychological Perspectives*. Hillsdale, NJ: Lawrence Erlbaum Associates.

Clark, D.M. and Hemsley, D.R. 1982: The effects of hyperventilation: individual variability and its relation to personality. *Journal of Behaviour Therapy and Experimental Psychiatry*, 13, 41–7.

Clark, D.M. and Teasdale, J.D. 1982: Diurnal variation in clinical depression and accessibility of memories of positive and negative experiences. *Journal of Abnormal Psychology*, 91, 87–95.

Clarke, A.M. and Clarke, A.D.B. 1985: Lifespan development and psychosocial intervention. In A.M. Clarke, A.D.B. Clarke and J.M. Berg (eds), *Mental Deficiency: the Changing Outlook*, 4th edn. London: Methuen.

Cobb, J., Mathews, A.M., Childs-Clarke, A. and Blowers, C. 1984: The spouse as co-therapist in the treatment of agoraphobia. *British Journal of Psychiatry*, 144, 282–7.

Coger, R.W. and Serafetinides, E.A. 1990: Schizophrenia, corpus callosum, and interhemispheric communication: a review. *Psychiatry Research*, 34, 163–84.

Cohen, S. and Wills, T.A. 1985: Stress, social support and the buffering hypothesis. *Psychological Bulletin*, 98, 310–57.

Cole, M. and Dryden, W. (eds) 1988: *Sex Therapy in Britain*. Milton Keynes: Open University Press.

Coleman, P.G. 1986: *The Aging Process and the Role of Reminiscence*. Chichester: Wiley.

Collacott, R.A., Cooper, S.A. and McGrother, C. 1992: Differential rates of psychiatric disorder in adults with Down's syndrome compared with other mentally handicapped adults. *British Journal of Psychiatry*, 161, 675–9.

Collins, A.M. and Loftus, E.M. 1975: A spreading activation theory of semantic processing. *Psychological Review*, 82, 407–28.

Conboy-Hill, S. and Waitman, A. 1992: *Psychotherapy and Mental Handicap*. London: Sage Publications.

Cooper, J.E., Kendell, R.E., Gurland, B.J., Sharpe, L., Copeland, J.R.M. and Simon, R. 1972: *Psychiatric Diagnosis in New York and London* (Maudsley Monograph). Oxford: Oxford University Press.

Cooper, P.J. and Fairburn, C.G. 1983: Binge-eating and self-induced vomiting in the community. *British Journal of Psychiatry*, 142, 139–44.

Cooper, P.J. 1985: Eating disorders. In: F.N. Watts (ed.), *New Developments in Clinical Psychology*. Leicester: BPS/Chichester: Wiley.

Cooper, P.J. and Fairburn, C.G. 1993: Confusion over the core psychopathology of bulimia nervosa. *International Journal of Eating Disorders*, 13, 385–9.

Coyne, J.C. 1976: Depression and the response of others. *Journal of Abnormal Psychology*, 85, 186–93.

Coyne, J.C. 1982: A critique of cognitions as causal entities with particular reference to depression. *Cognitive Therapy and Research*, 6, 3–13.

Coyne, J.C. 1984: Strategic therapy with manic-depressed persons: agenda, themes and intervention. *Journal of Marital and Family Therapy*, 10, 53–62.

Crisp, A.H. 1980: *Anorexia Nervosa: Let Me Be*. London: Academic.

Crisp, A.H., Callender, J.S., Halek, C. and Hsu, L.G. 1992: Long-term mortality in anorexia nervosa: a 20-year follow-up of the St George's and Aberdeen cohorts. *British Journal of Psychiatry*, 161, 104–7.

Crisp, A.H., Norton, K., Gowers, S. and Halek, C. 1991: A controlled study of the effect of therapies aimed at adolescent and family psychopathology in anorexia nervosa. *British Journal of Psychiatry*, 159, 325–33.

Crowe, R.R. 1990: Panic disorder: genetic considerations. *Journal of Psychiatric Research*, 24, 129–34.

Cummings, C., Gordon, J.R. and Marlatt, G.A. 1980: Relapse: strategies of prevention and prediction. In: W.R. Miller (ed.), *The Addictive Behaviours*. Oxford: Pergamon.

Cummings, J.L. and Victoroff, J.I. 1990: Noncognitive neuropsychiatric syndromes in Alzheimer's disease. *Neuropsychiatry, Neuropsychology, and Behavioral Neurology*, 3, 140–58.

Dare, C., Eisler, I., Colahan, M., Crowther, C., Senior, R. and Asen, E. 1995: The listening heart and the chi square: clinical and empirical perceptions in the family therapy of anorexia nervosa. *Journal of Family Therapy*, 17, 31–57.

Darlington, R.B. 1986: Longterm effects of preschool programs. In: U. Neisser (ed.), *The School Achievement of Minority Children*. Hillsdale, NJ: Erlbaum.

Dauncey, K., Giggs, J., Baker, K. and Harrison, G. 1993: Schizophrenia in Nottingham: lifelong residential mobility of a cohort. *British Journal of Psychiatry*, 163, 613–19.

Davidson, J.R., Hughes, D.L., George, L.K. and Blazer, D.G. 1993: The epidemiology of social phobia: findings from the Duke Epidemiological Catchment Area Study. *Psychological Medicine*, 23, 709–18.

Davies, M. 1988: Sex therapy with people with a physical disability. In: M. Cole and W. Dryden (eds), *Sex Therapy in Britain*. Milton Keynes: Open University Press.

Davis, J.M., Schaffer, C.B., Killian, G.A., Kinard, C. and Chan, C. 1980: Important issues in the drug treatment of schizophrenia. *Schizophrenia Bulletin*, 6, 70–87.

Davis, K.L., Kahn, R.S., Ko, G. and Davidson, M. 1991: Dopamine in schizophrenia: a review and reconceptualization. *American Journal of Psychiatry*, 148, 1474–86.

de Silva, P., Rachman, S.J. and Seligman, M.E.P. 1977: Prepared phobias and obsessions: therapeutic outcome. *Behaviour Research and Therapy*, 15, 65–78.

Deary, I.J. and Whalley, L.J. 1988: Recent research on the causes of Alzheimer's disease. *British Medical Journal*, 297, 807–8.

DeGroot, J.M., Kennedy, S., Rodin, G. and McVey, G. 1992: Correlates of sexual abuse in women with anorexia nervosa and bulimia nervosa. *Canadian Journal of Psychiatry*, 37, 516–18.

DeLisi, L.E., Mirsky, A.F., Buchsbaum, M.S., van Kammen, D.P., Berman, K.F., Phelps, B.H., Karoum, F., Ko, G.N., Korpi, E.R. et al. 1984: The Genain quadruplets 25 years later: a diagnostic and biochemical follow-up. *Psychiatric Research*, 13, 59–76.

Demchak, M. 1990: Response prompting and fading methods: a review. *American Journal on Mental Retardation*, 94, 603–15.

Department of Health 1990: *Health and Personal Social Services Statistics for England: 1990 Edition*. London: Her Majesty's Stationery Office.

Des Jarlais, D.C., Friedman, S.R., Casriel, C. and Kott, A. 1987: AIDS and preventing initiation into intravenous drug use. *Psychology and Health*, 1, 179–94.

Dewey, D. and Hunsley, J. 1990: The effects of marital adjustment and spouse involvement on the behavioral treatment of agoraphobia: a meta-analytic review. *Anxiety Research*, 2, 69–83.

Dielman, T.E., Butchart, A.T., Shope, J.T. and Miller, M. 1991: Environmental correlates of adolescent substance use and misuse: implications for prevention programs. Special issue: environmental factors in substance misuse and its treatment. *International Journal of the Addictions*, 25(7A–8A), 855–80.

Dietrich, K.M., Berger, O.G., Succop, P.A. and Hammond, P.B. 1993: The developmental consequences of low to moderate prenatal and postnatal lead exposure: intellectual attainment in the Cincinatti Lead Study Cohort following school entry. *Neurotoxicology and Teratology*, 15, 37–44.

Dobson, K. and Franche, R.L. 1989: A conceptual and empirical review of the depressive realism hypothesis. Special issue: clinical depression. *Canadian Journal of Behavioural Science*, 21, 419–33.

Dobson, K.S. 1989: A meta-analysis of the efficacy of cognitive therapy for depression. *Journal of Consulting and Clinical Psychology*, 57, 414–19.

Dodge, E., Hodes, M., Eisler, I. and Dare, C. 1995: Family therapy for bulimia nervosa in adolescents: an exploratory study. *Journal of Family Therapy*, 17, 59–78.

Dolan, B. 1991: Cross-cultural aspects of anorexia nervosa and bulimia: a review. *International Journal of Eating Disorders*, 10, 67–79.

Dossetor, D.R. and Nicol, A.R. 1989: Dilemmas of adolescents with developmental retardation: a review. *Journal of Adolescence*, 12, 167–85.

Dowdney, L. and Skuse, D. 1993: Parenting provided by adults with mental retardation. *Journal of Child Psychology and Psychiatry*, 34, 25–47.

Durgin, C.J. 1989: Techniques for families to increase their involvement in the rehabilitation process. *Cognitive Rehabilitation*, 7, 22–5.

Durham, R.C., Murphy, T., Allan, T., Richard, K., Treliving, L.R. and Fenton, G.W. 1994: Cognitive therapy, analytic psychotherapy and anxiety management training for generalised anxiety disorder. *British Journal of Psychiatry*, 165, 315–323.

Eagles, J. 1991: Is schizophrenia disappearing? *British Journal of Psychiatry*, 158, 834–5.

Eaton, W.W. 1991: Update of the epidemiology of schizophrenia. *Epidemiologic Reviews*, 13, 320–8.

Eber, M. 1980: Primary transsexualism: a critique of a theory. *Bulletin of the Menninger Clinic*, 46, 168–82.

Edelmann, R.J. 1992: *Anxiety: Theory, Research and Intervention in Clinical and Health Psychology*. Chichester: Wiley.

Eiser, R. 1978: Discrepancy, dissonance and the 'dissonant' smoker. *International Journal of Addiction*, 13, 1295–305.

Elkin, I., Shea, M. T., Watkins, J.T., Imber, S.D., Sotsky, S.M., Collins, J.F., Glass, D.R., Pilkonis, P.A., Leber, W.R., Kocherty, J.P., Fiester, S.J. and Parloff, M.B. 1989: National Institute of Mental Health treatment of depression collaborative research program. *Archives of General Psychiatry*, 46, 971–82.

Elkins, T.E. and Anderson, H.F. 1992: Sterilization of persons with mental retardation. *Journal of the Association for Persons with Severe Handicaps*, 17, 19–26.

Ellis, A. 1962: *Reason and Emotion in Psychotherapy*. New York: Lyle Stuart.

Ellis, A. and Whitely, J.M. (eds) 1979: *Theoretical and Empirical Foundations of Rational Emotive Therapy*. New York: Springer.

Ellis, E.M. 1985: A review of empirical rape research: victim reactions and response to treatment. *Clinical Psychology Review*, 3, 473–90.

Ellis, N.R. and Dulaney, C.L. 1991: Further evidence for cognitive inertia of persons with mental retardation. *American Journal on Mental Retardation*, 95, 613–21.

Emmelkamp, P.M.G. 1982: *Phobic and Obsessive–Compulsive Disorders: Theory, Research and Practice*. New York: Plenum.

Emmelkamp, P.M.G., Bouman, T.K. and Scholing, A. 1992: *Anxiety Disorders: a Practitioner's Guide*. Chichester: Wiley.

Emmelkamp, P.M.G., Brilman, E., Kuipers, H. and Mersch, P. 1986: The treatment of agoraphobia: a comparison of self-instructional training, rational-emotive therapy and exposure *in vivo*. *Behavior Modification*, 10, 37–53.

Emmelkamp, P.M.G., Mersch, P.P.A. and Vissia, E. 1985a: The external validity of analogue outcome research: evaluation of cognitive and behavioral interventions. *Behaviour Research and Therapy*, 23, 83–6.

Emmelkamp, P.M.G., Mersch, P.P.A., Vissia, E. and van der Helm, M. 1985b: Social phobia: a comparative evaluation of cognitive and behavioral interventions. *Behaviour Research and Therapy*, 23, 365–9.

Engel, G. 1980: The clinical application of the biopsychosocial model. *American Journal of Psychiatry*, 137, 535–44.

Eysenck, H.J. 1985: *The Decline and Fall of the Freudian Empire*. Harmondsworth: Penguin.

Fairbank, J.A. and Nicholson, R.A. 1987: Theoretical and empirical issues in the treatment of post-traumatic stress disorder: evaluating outcome with a behavioral code. *Journal of Clinical Psychology*, 43, 44–55.

Fairbank, J.A., Gross, R.T. and Keane, T.M. 1983: Treatment of posttraumatic stress disorder: evaluation of outcome with a behavioral code. *Behavior Modification*, 7, 557–68.

Fairburn, C.G. 1985: Cognitive behavioral treatment for bulimia. In D.M. Garfinkel and P.M. Garfinkel (eds), *Handbook of Psychotherapy for Anorexia Nervosa and Bulimia*. New York: Guilford Press.

Fairburn, C.G. 1993: Eating disorders. In: R.E. Kendall and A.K. Zealley (eds), *Companion to Psychiatric Studies*, 5th edn. Edinburgh: Churchill Livingstone.

Fairburn, C.G. and Beglin, S.J. 1990: Studies in the epidemiology of bulimia nervosa. *American Journal of Psychiatry*, 147, 401–8.

Fairburn, C.G. and Cooper, P.J. 1984: Binge-eating, self-induced vomiting and laxative abuse: a community study. *Psychological Medicine*, 14, 401–10.

Fairburn, C.G. and Hay, P.J. 1992: The treatment of bulimia nervosa. Special section: eating disorders. *Annals of Medicine*, 24, 297–302.

Fairburn, C.G., Cooper, P.J., Kirk, J. and O'Connor, M. 1985: The significance of the neurotic symptoms of bulimia nervosa. Conference on Anorexia Nervosa and Related Disorders (1984, Swansea, Wales). *Journal of Psychiatric Research*, 19, 135–40.

Fairburn, C.G., Jones, R., Peveler, R.C. and Hope, R.A. 1993: Psychotherapy and bulimia nervosa: longer-term effects of interpersonal psychotherapy, behavior therapy, and cognitive behavior therapy. *Archives of General Psychiatry*, 50, 419–28.

Fairweather, G.W., Sanders, D.H., Maynard, H. and Cressler, D.L. 1969: *Community Life for the Mentally Ill: an Alternative to Institutional Care*. San Francisco: Jossey-Bass.

Favazza, A.R. and Conterio, K. 1989: Female habitual self-mutilators. *Acta Psychiatrica Scandinavica*, 79, 283–9.

Fedoroff, J.P. and Fedoroff, I.C. 1992: Buspirone and paraphilic sexual behavior. Special issue: Sex offender treatment, psychological and medical approaches. *Journal of Offender Rehabilitation*, 18, 89–108.

Fedoroff, J.P., Wisner Carlson, R., Dean, S. and Berlin, F.S. 1992: Medroxy-progesterone acetate in the treatment of paraphilic sexual disorders: rate of relapse in paraphilic men treated in long-term group psychotherapy with or without medroxy-progesterone acetate. Special Issue: Sex offender treatment, psychological and medical approaches. *Journal of Offender Rehabilitation*, 18, 109–23.

Fenwick, P. 1987: Epilepsy and psychiatric disorders. In A. Hopkins (ed.), *Epilepsy*. London: Chapman & Hall.

Ferretti, R.P., Cavalier, A.R., Murphy, M.J. and Murphy, R. 1993: The self-management of skills by persons with mental retardation. *Research in Developmental Disabilities*, 14, 189–205.

Ferris, S.H. 1992: Diagnosis by specialists: psychological testing. *Acta Neurologica Scandinavica*, 85, 32–5.

Ferster, C.B. 1973: A functional analysis of depression. *American Psychologist*, 28, 857–70.

Figley, C.R. 1988: A five-phase treatment of post-traumatic stress disorder in families. *Journal of Traumatic Stress*, 1, 127–41.

Flor-Henry, P. 1976: Lateralized temporal limbic dysfunction and psychopathology. *Annals of the New York Academy of Science*, 280, 777–97.

Flor-Henry, P., Lang, R.A., Koles, Z.J. and Frenzel, R.R. 1991: Quantitative EEG studies of pedophilia. Special issue: IX International Symposium,

Neurophysiological correlates of psychopathological conditions. *International Journal of Psychophysiology*, 10, 253–8.

Foa, E.B. 1979: Failure in treating obsessive-compulsives. *Behaviour Research and Therapy*, 16, 391–9.

Foa, E.B. and Kozak, M.J. 1986: Emotional processing of fear: exposure to corrective information. *Psychological Bulletin*, 99, 20–35.

Foa, E.B. and Rothbaum, B.O. (1992) Post-traumatic stress disorder: clinical features and treatment. In: R. DeV. Peters, R.J. McMahon and V.L. Quinsey (eds), *Aggression and Violence Throughout the Lifespan*. New York: Sage.

Foa, E.B., Rothbaum, B.O., Riggs, D. and Murdock, T. 1991: Treatment of post-traumatic stress disorder in rape victims: a comparison between cognitive behavioral procedures and counseling. *Journal of Consulting and Clinical Psychology*, 59, 715–23.

Foa, E.B., Zimberg, R. and Rothbaum, B.O. 1992: Uncontrollability and unpredictability in post-traumatic stress disorder: an animal model. *Psychological Bulletin*, 112, 218–38.

Forness, S.R. and Kavale, K.A. 1993: Strategies to improve basic learning and memory deficits in mental retardation: a meta-analysis of experimental studies. *Education and Training in Mental Retardation*, 28, 99–110.

Forsyth, A.J., Farquhar, D., Gemmell, M., Shewen, D. and Davies, J.B. 1993: *Drug and Alcohol Dependency*, 32, 277–80.

Fortuny, L.A.I., Briggs, M., Newcombe, F., Ratcliffe, G. and Thomas, C. 1980: Measuring the duration of post-traumatic amnesia. *Journal of Neurology, Neurosurgery and Psychiatry*, 43, 377–9.

Frank, E. and Stewart, B.D. 1984: Depressive symptoms in rape victims. *Journal of Affective Disorders*, 1, 269–77.

Franko, D.L. 1993: The use of a group meal in the brief group therapy of bulimia nervosa. *International Journal of Group Psychotherapy*, 43, 237–42.

Freeman, C. 1992: Day patient treatment for anorexia nervosa. *British Review of Bulimia and Anorexia Nervosa*, 6, 3–8.

Freud, S. 1917: Mourning and melancholia. In: J. Rickman (ed.), *A General Selection from the Works of Sigmund Freud*. Garden City, NY: Doubleday (1957).

Friedman, A.S. 1975: Interaction of drug therapy with marital therapy in depressive patients. *Archives of General Psychiatry*, 32, 617–37.

Frith, C.D. 1979: Consciousness, information processing and schizophrenia. *British Journal of Psychiatry*, 134, 225–35.

Fromm-Reichman, F. 1948: Notes on the development of treatment of schizophrenics by psychoanalytic psychotherapy. *Psychiatry*, 11, 263–73.

Frude, N.J. 1991: *Understanding Family Problems: a Psychological Analysis*. Chichester: Wiley.

Fuchs, C.Z. and Rehm, L.P. 1977: A self-control behaviour therapy program for depression. *Journal of Consulting and Clinical Psychology*, 45, 206–15.

Fyer, A.J. 1993: Heritability of social anxiety: a brief review. *Journal of Clinical Psychiatry*, 54, 10–12.

Gallup and Wrangler 1992: *The Youth Report*. London: Gallup.

Garety, P.A. 1985: Delusions: problems in definition and measurement. *British Journal of Medical Psychology*, 58, 25–34.

Garfinkel, P.E. and Garner, D.M. 1982: *Anorexia Nervosa: a Multidimensional Perspective*. Now York: Brunner Mazel.

Gath, A. 1978: *Down's Syndrome and the Family: the Early Years*. London: Academic Press.

Gath, A. and Gumley, D. 1986: Behaviour problems in retarded children with special reference to Down's syndrome. *British Journal of Psychiatry*, 149, 156–61.

Gelder, M.G. 1989: Panic disorder: fact or fiction? *Psychological Medicine*, 19, 277–83.

Gelles, R.J. 1987: *The Violent Home*, updated edition. Beverly, Hills, CA: Sage.

Gilhooly, M. 1984: The impact of caregiving on caregivers: factors associated with the psychological well-being of people supporting a dementing relative in the community. *British Journal of Medical Psychology*, 57, 35–44.

Godlewski, J. 1988: Transsexualism and anatomic sex ratio reversal in Poland. *Archives of Sexual Behavior*, 17, 547–8.

Goldberg, E.M. and Morrison, S.L. 1963: Schizophrenia and social class. *British Journal of Psychiatry*, 109, 785–802.

Golden, C.J. 1978: *Diagnosis and Rehabilitation in Clinical Neuropsychology*. Springfield, IL: Charles C. Thomas.

Goldfried, M.R. and Davison, G.C. 1976: *Clinical Behavior Therapy*. New York: Holt, Rinehart and Winston.

Goldstein, A. and Chambless, D. 1978: A reanalysis of agoraphobia. *Behavior Therapy*, 9, 47–59.

Goldstein, M.J. and Strachan, A.M. 1987: The family and schizophrenia. In T. Jacob (ed.), *Family Interaction and Psychopathology: Theories, Methods and Findings*. New York: Plenum.

Gosselin, C.C. and Wilson, G.D. 1980: *Sexual Variations: Fetishism, Transvestism and Sadomasochism*. London: Faber & Faber.

Gossop, M. 1987: *Living with Drugs*. Aldershot: Wildwood Smith.

Gossop, M., Green, L., Phillips, G. and Bradley, B. 1990: Factors predicting outcome among opiate addicts after treatment. *British Journal of Clinical Psychology*, 29, 209–16.

Gotlib, I.A. and Colby, C.A. 1987: *Treatment for Depression: an Interpersonal Systems Approach*. Oxford: Pergamon Press.

Gottesman, I.I. 1991: *Schizophrenia Genesis: the Origins of Madness*. New York: Freeman.

Gottesman, I.I. and Bertelsen. A. 1989: Confirming unexpressed genotypes for schizophrenia: risks in the offspring of Fischer's Danish identical and fraternal discordant twins. *Archives of General Psychiatry*, 46, 867–72.

Gottesman, I.I. and Shields, J. 1972: *Schizophrenia and Genetics*. New York: Academic Press.

Graham, J.W., Johnson, C.A., Hansen, W.B., Flay, B.R. and Gee, M. 1990: Drug use prevention programs, gender and ethnicity: Evaluation of three seventh-grade Project SMART cohorts. *Preventive Medicine*, 19, 305–13.

Graves, R.B., Openshaw, D.K. and Adams, G.R. 1992: Adolescent sex offenders and social skills training. *International Journal of Offender Therapy and Comparative Criminology*, 36, 139–53.

Grayson, J.B., Foa, E.B. and Steketee, G. 1985: Obsessive–compulsive disorder. In M. Hersen and A.S. Bellack (eds), *Handbook of Clinical Behavior Therapy*. New York: Plenum Publishing.

Greenberg, M. 1987: Ideational components of distress in panic disorder. Doctoral dissertation, quoted in Beck (1988).

Greist, J.H. 1992: An integrated approach to treatment of obsessive compulsive disorder. *Journal of Clinical Psychiatry*, 53, 38–41.

Grinspoon, L., Ewalt, J. and Shader, R.I. 1968: Psychotherapy and pharmacotherapy in chronic schizophrenia. *American Journal of Psychiatry*, 124, 67–75.

Grisset, N.I. and Norvell, N.K. 1992: Perceived social support, social skills, and quality of relationships in bulimic women. *Journal of Consulting and Clinical Psychology*, 60, 293–9.

Groveman, A.M. and Brown, E.W. 1985: Family therapy with closed head injured patients. *Family Systems Medicine*, 3, 440–6.

Habermas, T. 1992: Possible effects of the popular and medical recognition of bulimia nervosa. *British Journal of Medical Psychology*, 65, 59–66.

Hagnell, O., Lanke, J., Rorsman, B. and Ojesjo, L. 1982: Are we entering an age of melancholy? Depressive illnesses in a prospective epidemiological study over 25 years: the Lundby Study, Sweden. *Psychological Medicine*, 12, 279–89.

Halmi, K.A., Falk, J.R. and Schwartz, E. 1981: Binge-eating and vomiting: a survey of a college population. *Psychological Medicine*, 11, 697–706.

Hamer, D.H., Hu, S., Magnuson, V.L. and Hu, N. 1993: A linkage between DNA markers on the X chromosome and male sexual orientation. *Science*, 261, 321–7.

Hanson, M.J. 1981: Down's syndrome children: characteristics and intervention research. In M. Lewis and L.A. Rosenblum (eds), *The Uncommon Child*. New York: Plenum.

Haracz, J.L. 1982: The dopamine hypothesis: an overview of studies with schizophrenic patients. *Schizophrenia Bulletin*, 8, 438–69.

Harlow, J.M. 1868: Recovery from the passage of an iron bar through the head. *Publication of the Massachusetts Medical Society*, 2, 327–31.

Haskins, R. 1989: Beyond metaphor: the efficacy of early childhood education. *American Psychologist*, 44, 274–82.

Hastings, R.P. and Remington, B. 1994: Staff behaviour and its implications for people with learning disabilities and challenging behaviours. *British Journal of Clinical Psychology*, 33, 423–38.

Hawkins, R.C. and Clement, P.F. 1980: Development and construct validation of a self-report measure of binge eating tendencies. *Addictive Behaviors*, 5, 219–26.

Hawton, K.E. 1985: *Sex Therapy: a Practical Guide*. Oxford: Oxford University Press.

Hayward, P., Wardle, J. and Higgitt, A. 1989: Benzodiazepine research: current findings and practical consequences. *British Journal of Clinical Psychology*, 28, 307–27.

Hedderly, R. and Jennings, K. 1987: *Extending and Developing Portage*. Windsor: National Foundation for Educational Research.

Heimberg, R.G., Salzman, D.G., Holt, C.S. and Blendell, K.A. 1993: Cognitive–behavioral group treatment for social phobia: effectiveness at five-year followup. *Cognitive Therapy and Research*, 17, 325–39.

Helmerson, P. 1983: *Family Interaction and Communication in Psychopathology: an Evaluation of Recent Perspectives*. London: Academic Press.

Hemsley, D.R. 1988: Psychological models of schizophrenia. In E. Miller and A. Cooper (eds), *Adult Abnormal Psychology*. London: Livingstone.

Henderson, A.S. 1986: Epidemiology of mental illness. In H. Häfner, G. Moschel and N. Sartorius (eds), *Mental Health in the Elderly: a Review of the Present State of Research*. Berlin: Springer.

Herz, M.I. and Melville, C. 1980: Relapse in schizophrenia. *American Journal of Psychiatry*, 137, 801–12.

Heston, L.L. 1966: Psychiatric disorders in foster home reared children of schizophrenic mothers. *British Journal of Psychiatry*, 112, 819–25.

Hibbert, G.A. 1984a: Hypertension as a cause of panic attacks. *British Medical Journal*, 288, 263–4.

Hibbert, G.A. 1984b: Ideational components of anxiety: their origin and content. *British Journal of Psychiatry*, 144, 618–24.

Higgitt, A., Golombok, S., Fonagy, P. and Lader, M. 1987: Group treatment of benzodiazepine dependence. *British Journal of Addictions*, 82, 517–32.

Hile, M.G. and Vatterott, M.K. 1991: Two decades of treatment for self-injurious biting in individuals with mental retardation or developmental disabilities: a treatment focused review of the literature. *Journal of Development and Physical Disabilities*, 3, 81–113.

Hill, A.J. 1993: Pre-adolescent dieting: implications for eating disorders. *International Review of Psychiatry*, 5, 87–99.

Hiroto, D.S. and Seligman, M.E.P. 1975: Generality of learned helplessness in man. *Journal of Personality and Social Psychology*, 31, 311–27.

Hirst, W. 1982: The amnesic syndrome: descriptions and explanations. *Psychological Bulletin*, 91, 435–60.

Hodes, M. 1993: Anorexia nervosa and bulimia nervosa in children. *International Review of Psychiatry*, 5, 101–8.

Hodgson, R. 1988: Alcohol and drug dependence. In E. Miller and P.J. Cooper (eds), *Adult Abnormal Psychology*. Edinburgh: Churchill Livingstone.

Hodgson, R.J. 1982: Behavioural psychotherapy for compulsions and addictions. In J.R. Eiser (ed.), *Social Psychology and Behavioural Medicine*. Chichester and New York: Wiley.

Hoehn-Saric, R. and McLeod, D.R. 1988: The peripheral nervous system: its role in normal and pathological anxiety. *Psychiatric Clinics of North America*, 11, 375–86.

Hoek, H.W. 1993: Review of the epidemiological studies of eating disorders. *International Review of Psychiatry*, 5, 61–74.

Hogarty, G.E., Anderson, C.M., Reiss, D.J., Kornblith, S.J., Greenwald, D.P., Javna, C.D. and Madonia, M.J. 1986: Family psychoeducation, social skills training and maintenance chemotherapy in the aftercare treatment of schizophrenia: I. One-year effects of a controlled study on relapse and expressed emotion. *Archives of General Psychiatry*, 43, 633–42.

Holden, U.P. and Woods, R.T. 1988: *Reality Orientation: Psychological Approaches to the 'Confused' Elderly*, 2nd edn. Edinburgh: Churchill Livingstone.

Holland, A., Sicotte, N. and Treasure, J. 1988: Anorexia nervosa – evidence for a genetic basis. *Journal of Psychosomatic Research*, 32, 549–54.

Hollon, S.D. and Beck, A.T. 1979: Cognitive therapy in depression. In P.C. Kendall and S.D. Hollon (eds), *Cognitive–behavioural Interventions: Theory, Research and Procedures*. New York: Academic Press.

Hooley, J.M. and Teasdale, J.D. 1989: Predictors of relapse in unipolar depressives: expressed emotion, marital distress, and perceived criticism. *Journal of Abnormal Psychology*, 98, 229–35.

Hopkins, J., Marcus, M., Campbell, S.B. 1984: Postpartum depression: a critical review. *Psychological Bulletin*, 95, 498–515.

Hopkins, R.E. 1993: An evaluation of social skills groups for sex offenders. *Issues in Criminological and Legal Psychology*, 19, 52–9.

Hops, H., Biglan, A., Sherman, L., Arthur, J., Friedman, L. and Osteen, V. 1987: Home observations of family interactions of depressed women. *Journal of Consulting and Clinical Psychology*, 55, 341–6.

Horne, R.L., Pettinati, H.M., Sugerman, A. and Varga, I. 1985: Comparing bilateral to unilateral electroconvulsive therapy in a randomized trial with EEG monitoring. *Archives of General Psychiatry*, 42, 1087–92.

Horowitz, M. 1979: Psychological response to serious life events. In V. Hamilton and D.M. Warburton (eds), *Human Stress and Cognition: an Information Processing Approach*. Chichester: Wiley.

Horowitz, M. 1986: *Stress Response Syndromes*, 2nd edn. Northvale, NJ: Jason Aronson.

Hotaling, G.T. and Sugarman, D.B. 1986: An analysis of risk markers in husband to wife violence: the current state of knowledge. *Violence and Victims*, 1, 101–24.

Hunter, J.A. and Goodwin, D.W. 1992: The clinical utility of satiation therapy with juvenile sexual offenders: variations and efficacy. *Annals of Sex Research*, 5, 71–80.

Huntington's Disease Collaborative Research Group 1993: A novel gene containing a trinucleotide repeat that is expanded and unstable on Huntington's disease chromosomes. *Cell*, 72, 971–83.

ISDD 1992: *National Audit of Drug Misuse in Britain*. London: Institute for the Study of Drug Dependence.

ISDD 1996: *National Audit of Drug Misuse in Britain*. London: Institute for the Study of Drug Dependence.

Iversen, L.L. 1982: Biochemical and pharmacological studies: the dopamine hypothesis. In J.K. Wing (ed.), *Schizophrenia: towards a New Synthesis*. London: Academic Press.

Jacobs, S. and Myers, J. 1976: Recent life events and acute schizophrenia psychosis: a controlled study. *Journal of Nervous and Mental Disease*, 162, 75–87.

Janicak, P.G., Davis, J.M., Gibbons, R.D., Ericksen, S., Chang, S. and Gallagher, P. 1985: Efficacy of ECT: a meta-analysis. *American Journal of Psychiatry*, 142, 297–302.

Janoff-Bulman, R. 1985: The aftermath of victimization: rebuilding shattered assumptions. In C.R. Figley (ed.), *Trauma and Its Wake*. New York: Brunner/Mazel.

Janoun, L., Oppenheimer, C. and Gelder, M. 1982: A self-help treatment manual for anxiety state patients. *Behavior Therapy*, 13, 103–11.

Janowsky, D.S., El-Yousef, M.K., Davis, J.M. and Serkerke, H.J. 1972: A cholinergic–adrenergic hypothesis of mania and depression. *Lancet*, ii, 632–5.

Jehu, D. 1988: *Beyond Sexual Abuse: Therapy with Women Who Were Childhood Victims*. Chichester: Wiley.

Jenike, M., Hyman, S. and Baer, L. 1990: A controlled trial of fluvoxamine for obsessive compulsive disorder: implications for a serotogenic theory. *American Journal of Psychiatry*, 147, 1209–15.

Jennett, B., Snoes, J., Bond, M.R. and Brooks, N.D. 1981: Disability and severe head injury: observations on the use of the Glasgow Outcome Scale: *Journal of Neurology, Neurosurgery and Psychiatry*, 44, 285–93.

Jones, M. 1952: *Social Psychiatry: a study of Therapeutic Communities*. Tavistock: London.

Jones, R.S. 1991: Stereotypy: challenging behaviour or adaptive response. *Scandinavian Journal of Behaviour Therapy*, 20, 25–40.

Jones, R.S. and Baker, L.J. 1990: Differential reinforcement and challenging behaviour: a critical review of the DRI schedule. *Behavioural Psychotherapy*, 18, 35–47.

Joseph, S., Yule, W., Williams, R. and Andrews, B. 1993: Crisis support in the aftermath of disaster: a longitudinal perspective. *British Journal of Clinical Psychology*, 32, 177–85.

Judd, L.L. 1994: Social phobia: a clinical overview. *Journal of Clinical Psychiatry*, 55, 5–9.

Kahn, J., Coyne, J.C. and Margolin, G. 1985: Depression and marital conflict: the social construction of despair. *Journal of Social and Personal Relationships*, 2, 447–62.

Kail, R. 1992: General slowing of information-processing by persons with mental retardation. *American Journal on Mental Retardation*, 97, 333–41.

Kane, J., Honigfeld, G., Singer, J., Meltzer, H. and the Clorazil Collaborative Study Group 1988: Clozapine for the treatment-resistant schizophrenia. *Archives of General Psychiatry*, 45, 789–96.

Kaner, A., Bulik, C.M. and Sullivan, P.F. 1993: Abuse in adult relationships of bulimic women. *Journal of Interpersonal Violence*, 8, 52–63.

Kaplan, H.S. 1974: *The New Sex Therapy*. New York: Brunner/Mazel.

Kaplan, H.S. 1990: The combined use of sex therapy and intrapenile injections in the treatment of impotence. *Journal of Sex and Marital Therapy*, 16, 195–207.

Kay, D.W. 1989: Genetics, Alzheimer's disease and senile dementia. *British Journal of Psychiatry*, 154, 311–20.

Kaye, W.H., Rubinow, D., Gwirtsman, H.E. and George, D.T. 1988: CSF somatostatin in anorexia nervosa and bulimia: relationship to the hypothalamic pituitary–adrenal cortical axis. *Psychoneuroendocrinology*, 13, 265–72.

Kaye, W.H., Weltzin, T.E. and Hsu, L.G. 1993: Relationship between anorexia nervosa and obsessive and compulsive behaviors. *Psychiatric Annals*, 23, 365–73.

Keane, T.M., Fairbank, J.A., Caddell, J.M. and Zimering, R.T. 1989: Implosive (flooding) therapy reduces symptoms of PTSD in Vietnam combat veterans. *Behavior Therapy*, 20, 245–60.

Keane, T.M., Zimering, R.T. and Caddell, J.M. 1985: A behavioral formulation of post-traumatic stress disorder in Vietnam veterans. *The Behavior Therapist*, 8, 9–12.

Keller, M.B., Herzog, D.B., Lavori, P.W. and Bradburn, I.S. 1992: The naturalistic history of bulimia nervosa: extraordinarily high rates of chronicity, relapse, recurrence, and psychosocial morbidity. *International Journal of Eating Disorders*, 12, 1–9.

Kendler, K.S., MacLean, C., Neale, M., and Kessler, R.C. 1991: The genetic epidemiology of bulimia nervosa. *American Journal of Psychiatry*, 148, 1627–37.

Kendler, K.S., Neale, M.C., Kessler, R.C. and Heath, A.C. 1992: Major depression and generalized anxiety disorder: same genes, (partly) different environments? *Archives of General Psychiatry*, 49, 716–22.

Kennedy, P.G.E. 1988: Neurological complications of human immunodeficiency virus infection. *Postgraduate Medical Journal*, 64, 180–7.

Kennerly, H. and Gath, D. 1986: Maternity blues reassessed. *Psychiatric Developments*, 1, 1–17.

Kety, S.S., Rosenthal, D., Wender, P.H. and Schulsinger, F. 1968: The types and prevalence of mental illness in the biological and adoptive families of adopted schizophrenics. In D. Rosenthal and S.S. Kety (eds), *The Transmission of Schizophrenia*. Elmsford, NY: Pergamon.

Kiernan, C., Reeves, D. and Alborz, A. 1995: The use of anti-psychotic drugs with adults with learning disabilities and challenging behaviour. *Journal of Intellectual Disability Research*, 39, 263–74.

Kilpatrick, D.G. and Amick, A.A. 1985: Rape trauma. In M. Hersen and C.G. Last (eds), *Behavioral Therapy Casebook*. New York: Springer.

Kilpatrick, D.G., Saunders, B.E., Veronen, L.J., Best, C.L. and Von, J.M. 1987: Criminal victimization: lifetime prevalence, reporting to police, and psychological impact. *Crime and Delinquency*, 33, 479–89.

Kilpatrick, D.G., Veronen, L.J. and Resick, P.A. 1982: Psychological sequelae to rape: assessment and treatment strategies. In D.M. Dolays and R.L. Meredith (eds), *Behavioral Medicine: Assessment and Treatment Strategies*. New York: Plenum.

King, D.J. and Cooper, S.J. 1989: Viruses, immunity and mental disorder. *British Journal of Psychiatry*, 154, 1–7.

Kinsey, A.C., Pomeroy, W.B., Martin, C.E. and Gebhard, P.H. 1948: *Sexual Behavior in the Human Male*. New York: W.B. Saunders and Co.

Kinsey, A.C., Pomeroy, W.B., Martin, C.E. and Gebhard, P.H. 1953: *Sexual Behavior in the Human Female*. New York: W.B. Saunders and Co.

Klerman, G.L. and Schechter, G. 1982: Drugs and psychotherapy. In E.S. Paykel (ed.), *Handbook of Affective Disorders*. New York: Guilford Press.

Klerman, G.L., Weissman, M.N., Rounsaville, B.J. and Cheveron, E.S. 1984: *Interpersonal Psychotherapy of Depression*. New York: Basic Books.

Knight, J.G. 1982: Dopamine-receptor-stimulating antibodies: a possible cause of schizophrenia. *Lancet*, ii, 1073–6.

Knight, R.A. 1984: Converging models of cognitive deficit in schizophrenia. In W.D. Spaulding and J.K. Cole (eds), *Theories of Schizophrenia and Psychosis*. London: University of Nebraska Press.

Koller, H., Richardson, S.A. and Katz, M. 1988: Marriages in a young adult mentally retarded population. *Journal of Mental Deficiency Research*, 17, 193–216.

Kozlowski, B.W. 1992: Megavitamin treatment of mental retardation in children: a review of effects on behavior and cognition. *Journal of Child and Adolescent Psychopharmacology*, 2, 307–20.

Krantz, S. and Hammen, S.L. 1979: Assessment of cognitive bias in depression. *Journal of Abnormal Psychology*, 88, 611–19.

Kreipe, R.E., Churchill, B.H. and Strauss, J. 1989: Long term outcome in adolescents with anorexia nervosa. *American Journal of Diseases in Childhood*, 143, 1322–7.

Kuiper, B. and Cohen-Kettenis, P. 1988: Sex reassignment surgery: a study of 141 Dutch transsexuals. *Archives of Sexual Behavior*, 17, 429–57.

Lacey, J.H. 1983: Bulimia nervosa, binge-eating and psychogenic vomiting: a controlled treatment study and long-term outcome. *British Medical Journal*, 286, 1609–13.

Lacey, J.H. 1992: Homogamy: the relationships and sexual partners of normal-weight bulimic women. *British Journal of Psychiatry*, 161, 638–42.

Lacey, J.H. 1993: Self-damaging and addictive behaviour in bulimia nervosa: a catchment area study. *British Journal of Psychiatry*, 163, 190–4.

Lamb, M.E. 1983: Fathers of exceptional children. In M. Seligman (ed.), *The Family with a Handicapped Child: Understanding and Treatment*. New York: Grune and Stratton.

Lang, R.A. 1993: Neuropsychological deficits in sexual offenders: implications for treatment. Special issue: Paraphilias. *Sexual and Marital Therapy*, 8, 181–200.

Lask, B. and Bryant Waugh, R. 1992: Early-onset anorexia nervosa and related eating disorders. *Journal of Child Psychology and Psychiatry and Allied Disciplines*, 33, 281–300.

Lask, B. and Fosson, A. 1989: *Childhood Illness: the Psychosomatic Approach – Children Talking with Their Bodies*. Chichester: Wiley.

Laws, D.R. and Marshall, W.L. 1991: Masturbatory reconditioning with sexual deviates: an evaluative review. *Advances in Behaviour Research and Therapy*, 13, 13–25.

Lawton, M.P. and Bordy, E.M. 1969: Assessment of older people: Self-maintaining and instrumental activities of daily living. *Gerontologist*, 9, 179–86.

Lazar, I. and Darlington, R.B. 1982: Lasting effects of early education. *Monographs of the Society for Research in Child Development*, 47(2/3).

Leff, J. 1992: Schizophrenia and similar conditions. *International Journal of Mental Health*, 21, 25–40.

Leff, J.P. 1976: Schizophrenia and sensitivity to the family environment. *Schizophrenia Bulletin*, 2, 566–74.

Leff, J.P., Kuipers, L., Berkowitz, R., Eberlein-Vries, R. and Sturgeon, D. 1982: A controlled trial of social intervention of schizophrenic patients. *British Journal of Psychiatry*, 141, 121–34.

Leiblum, S. and Rosen, R.C. 1988: *Sexual Desire Disorders*. New York: Guilford.

LeVay, S. 1993: *Genes that Are Designed to Turn You on: the Sexual Brain*. Cambridge, MA: MIT Press.

Levine, P. 1988: 'Bulimic' couples: dynamics and treatment. *Family Therapy Collections*, 25, 89–104.

Lewinsohn, P.M. 1974: Clinical and theoretical aspects of depression. In K.S. Calhoun, H.E. Adams and K.M. Mitchell (eds), *Innovative Treatment Methods in*

Psychopathology. Chichester: Wiley.

Lewinsohn, P.M., Mischel, W., Chaplin, W. and Barton, R. 1980: Social competence and depression: the role of illusory self-perceptions. *Journal of Abnormal Psychology*, 89, 203–12.

Lewy, A.J., Sack, L., Miller, S. and Hoban, T.M. 1987: Antidepressant and circadian phase-shifting effects of light. *Science*, 235, 352–4.

Lezak, M.D. 1982: Coping with head injury in the family. In G. Broe and R. Tate (eds), *Proceedings of the Fifth Annual Brain Impairment Conference*. Sydney: Postgraduate Committee in Medicine.

Liberman, R.P., Mueser, K.T. and Wallace, C.J. 1986: Social skills training for schizophrenic individuals at risk for relapse. *American Journal of Psychiatry*, 143, 523–6.

Lindemalm, G., Korlin, and Undenberg, N. 1986: Long-term follow-up of 'sex change' in 13 male-to-female transsexuals. *Archives of Sexual Behaviour*, 15, 182–210.

LoPiccolo, J. and Friedman, J.M. 1988: Broad spectrum treatment of low sexual desire: integration of cognitive, behavioral and systemic therapy. In S. Leiblum and R.C. Rosen (eds), *Sexual Desire Disorders*. New York: Guilford.

Lothstein, L.M. 1987: Theories of transsexualism. In E.E Shelp (ed.), *Sexuality and Medicine, Volume I*. Dordrecht, Netherlands: Reidel.

Lowe, K. and Felce, D. 1995: The definition of challenging behaviour in practice. *British Journal of Learning Disabilities*, 23, 118–23.

MacAndrew, C. and Edgerton, R.B. 1969: *Drunken Comportment: a Social Explanation*. London: Nelson.

McCann, U.D. and Ricaurte, G.A. 1991: Lasting neuropsychiatric sequelae of (±) methylenedioxymethamphetamine ('ecstasy') in recreational users. *Journal of Clinical Psychopharmacology*, 11, 302–5.

McCormack, B. 1991: Sexual abuse and learning difficulties. *British Medical Journal*, 303, 143–4.

McGhie, A. and Chapman, J.S. 1961: Disorders of attention and perception in early schizophrenia. *British Journal of Medical Psychology*, 34, 103–16.

Maguire, G.P., Lee, E.G., Bevington, D.J., Kuchemann, C.S., Crabtree, R.J. and Cornell, C.E. 1978: Psychiatric problems in the first year after mastectomy. *British Medical Journal*, i, 963–5.

McGuire, J. and Earls, F. 1991: Prevention of psychiatric disorders in early childhood. *Journal of Child Psychology and Psychiatry*, 32, 129–52.

McGuire, P.K. 1994: Diversity of psychopathology associated with use of 3,4-methylenedioxymethamphetamine ('Ecstasy'). *British Journal of Psychiatry*, 165, 391–5.

McGuire, R.J., Carlisle, J.M. and Young, B.G. 1965: Sexual deviations as conditioned behaviour: a hypothesis. *Behaviour Research and Therapy*, 2, 185–90.

McKinlay, W.W. and Hickox, A. 1988: How can families help in the rehabilitation of the head injured? *Journal of Head Trauma Rehabilitation*, 3, 64–72.

McKinney, B. and Peterson, R.A. 1987: Predictors of stress in parents of developmentally disabled children. *Journal of Pediatric Psychology*, 12, 133–50.

McNeil, T.F. and Kaij, L. 1978: Obstetric factors in the development of schizophrenia: complications in the births of preschizophrenics and in reproduction by schizophrenic patients. In L.C. Wynne, R.L. Cromwell and S. Matthysse (eds), *The Nature of Schizophrenia: New Approaches to Research and Treatment*. New York: Wiley.

Malin, N. 1983: *Group Homes for Mentally Handicapped People*. London: Her Majesty's Stationery Office.

Mansell, J. 1994: Challenging behaviour: the prospect for change. A keynote review. *British Journal of Learning Disabilities*, 22, 2–5.

Marchetti, A.G. and McCartney, J.R. 1990: Abuse of persons with mental retardation: characteristics of the abused, the abusers, and the informers. *Mental Retardation*, 28, 367–71.

Marks, I.M. 1969: *Fears and Phobias*. London: Heinemann.

Marks, I.M. 1987: *Fears, Phobias and Rituals*. New York: Oxford University Press.

Marlatt, G.A. 1978: Craving for alcohol, loss of control and relapse: a cognitive–behavioral analysis. In P. Nathan, G.A. Marlatt and T. Loberty (eds), *Alcoholism: New Directions in Behavioral Research and Treatment*. New York: Plenum.

Marlatt, G.A. 1982: Relapse prevention: a self-control programme for the treatment of addictive behaviors. In R.B. Stuart (ed.), *Adherence, Compliance and Generalization in Behavioral Medicine*. New York: Brunner/Mazel.

Marlatt, G.A. and Gordon, J.R. 1985: *Relapse Prevention: Maintenance Strategies in the Treatment of Addictive Behaviors*. New York: Guilford Press.

Marlatt, G.A. and Rosenow, D. 1980: Cognitive processes in alcohol use: expectancy and balanced placebo design. In N. Mello (ed.), *Advances in Substance Abuse: Behavioral and Biological Research*. Greenwich, CT: JAI Press.

Marshall, W.L. 1979: Satiation therapy: a procedure for reducing deviant sexual arousal. *Journal of Applied Behavior Analysis*, 12, 377–89.

Marshall, W.L. 1988: An appraisal of expectancies, safety signals and the treatment of panic disorder patients. In S. Rachman and J.D. Maser (eds), *Panic: Psychological Perspectives*. Hillsdale, NJ: Lawrence Erlbaum Associates.

Marshall, W.L. 1989: Intimacy, loneliness and sexual offenders. *Behaviour Research and Therapy*, 27, 491–503.

Marshall, W.L. 1993: The treatment of sex offenders: what does the outcome data tell us? A reply to Quinsey, Harris, Rice, and Lalumiere. *Journal of Interpersonal Violence*, 8, 524–30.

Marshall, W.L. and Pithers, W.D. 1994: A reconsideration of treatment outcome with sex offenders. Special issue: the assessment and treatment of sex offenders. *Criminal Justice and Behavior*, 21, 10–27.

Mason, J.W., Kosten, T.R., Southwick, S.M. and Giller, E.L. 1990: The use of psychoendocrine strategies in post-traumatic stress disorder. *Journal of Applied Social Psychology*, 20, 1822–46.

Masters, W.H. and Johnson, V.E. 1966: *Human Sexual Response*. Boston: Little, Brown.

Masters, W.H. and Johnson, V.E. 1970: *Human Sexual Inadequacy*. Boston: Little, Brown.

Mathews, A.M. and MacLeod, C. 1986: Discrimination of threat cues without awareness in anxiety states. *Journal of Abnormal Psychology*, 95, 131–8.

Mathews, A.M., Gelder, M.G. and Johnston, D.W. 1981: *Agoraphobia: Nature and Treatment*. London: Tavistock.

Mattick, R.P., Andrews, G., Hadzi Pavlovic, D. and Christensen, H. 1990: Treatment of panic and agoraphobia: an integrative review. *Journal of Nervous and Mental Disease*, 178, 567–76.

Mattick, R.P., Peters, L. and Clark, J.C. 1989: Exposure and cognitive restructuring for social phobia. *Behavior Therapy*, 20, 3–23.

May, R. 1950: *The Meaning of Anxiety*. New York: Ronald Press.

Meakin, C.J. 1992: Screening for depression in the medically ill. *British Journal of Psychiatry*, 160, 212–16.

Meera, R., Abdalla, M., Smee, C. and Fallon, C. 1994: Evaluation of a community facility for people with learning disabilities and behaviour disorder (challenging behaviour). *British Journal of Learning Disabilities*, 22, 11–17.

Mendlewicz, J., Papdimitriou, G. and Wilmotte, J. 1993: Family study of panic disorder: comparison with generalized anxiety disorder, major depression and normal subjects. *Psychiatric Genetics*, 3, 73–8.

Mersch, P.P.A., Emmelkamp, P.M.G., Bogels, S.M. and van der Sleen, J. 1989: Social phobia: individual response patterns and the effects of behavioural and cognitive interventions. *Behaviour Research and Therapy*, 27, 421–34.

Meyers, A., Mercatoris, M. and Sirota, A. 1976: Case study: use of covert self-instruction for the elimination of psychotic speech. *Journal of Consulting and Clinical Psychology*, 44, 480–2.

Miller, D.A., McCluskey Fawcett, K. and Irving, L.M. 1993: The relationship between childhood sexual abuse and subsequent onset of bulimia nervosa. *Child Abuse and Neglect*, 17, 305–14.

Miller, E. 1984: *Recovery and Management of Neuropsychological Impairments*. Chichester: Wiley.

Miller, E. 1989: Language impairment in Alzheimer type dementia. *Clinical Psychology Review*, 9, 181–95.

Miller, K.A. 1989: Enhancing early childhood mainstreaming through cooperative learning: a brief literature review. *Child Study Journal*, 19, 285–92.

Minuchin, S., Rosman, B. and Baker, L. 1978: *Psychosomatic Families: Anorexia Nervosa in Context*. Cambridge, MA: Harvard University Press.

Mohr, D.C. and Beutler, L.E. 1990: Erectile dysfunction: a review of diagnostic and treatment procedures. *Clinical Psychology Review*, 10, 123–50.

Money, J. 1987: Treatment guidelines: antiandrogen and counseling of paraphilic sex offenders. *Journal of Sex and Marital Therapy*, 13, 219–23.

Money, J. 1990: Forensic sexology – paraphilic serial rape (biastophilia) and lust murder (erotophonophilia). *American Journal of Psychotherapy*, 44, 26–36.

Morgan, S.R. 1987: *Abuse and Neglect of Handicapped Children*. Boston: Little Brown.

Morris, L.W., Morris, R.G. and Britton, P.G. 1988: The relationship between marital intimacy, perceived strain and depression in spouse caregivers of dementia sufferers. *British Journal of Medical Psychology*, 61, 231–6.

Mowrer, O.H. 1939: Stimulus response theory of anxiety. *Psychological Review*, 46, 553–65.

Mowrer, O.H. 1947: On the dual nature of learning – a reinterpretation of 'conditioning' and 'problem-solving'. *Harvard Educational Review*, 17, 102–48.

Mowrer, O.H. 1960: *Learning Theory and Behavior*. New York: Wiley.

Murphy, E. 1991: *After the Asylums*. London: Faber & Faber.

Muscettola, G., Potter, W.Z., Pickar, D. and Goodwin, F. 1984: Urinary 3-methoxy-4-hydroxyphenylglycol and affective disorders. *Archives of General Psychiatry*, 41, 337–42.

Musson, R.F. and Alloy, L.B. 1988: Depression and self-directed attention. In L.B. Alloy (ed.), *Cognitive Processes in Depression*. New York: Guilford Press.

Neidigh, L. 1991: Implications of a relapse prevention model for the treatment of sexual offenders. *Journal of Addictions and Offender Counseling*, 11, 42–50.

Nettlebeck, T. and Lally, M. 1979: Age, intelligence and inspection time. *Journal of Mental Deficiency*, 83, 398–401.

Newman, S.C. and Bland, R.C. 1994: Life events and the 1-year prevalence of major depressive episode, generalized anxiety disorder, and panic disorder in a community sample. *Comprehensive Psychiatry*, 35, 76–82.

Nicholson, P. 1993: Public values and private beliefs: why do women refer themselves for sex therapy? In J.M. Ussher and C.D. Baker (eds), *Psychological Perspectives on Sexual Problems: New Directions in Theory and Practice*. London: Routledge.

Nihira, K., Foster, R., Shellhaas, M. and Leland, H. 1974: *AAMD Adaptive Behavior Scale (1975 R5 Revision)*. Washington, DC: American Association on Mental

Deficiency (later the American Association on Mental Retardation).

Nijinsky, R. (ed.) 1966: *The Diary of Vaslav Nijinsky*. London: Panther.

Nolen-Hoeksema, S. 1987: Sex differences in unipolar depression: evidence and theory. *Psychological Bulletin*, 101, 259–82.

Nolen-Hoeksema, S. 1991: Responses to depression and their effects on the duration of depressive episodes. *Journal of Abnormal Psychology*, 100, 569–82.

Norre, J. and Vandereycken, W. 1991: The limits of out-patient treatment for bulimic disorders. *British Review of Bulimia and Anorexia Nervosa*, 5, 55–63.

Norton, G.R. and Jehu, D. 1984: The role of anxiety in sexual dysfunctions: a review. *Archives of Sexual Behaviour*, 13, 165–83.

Norton, G.R., Dorward, J. and Cox, B.J. 1986: Factors associated with panic attacks in nonclinical subjects. *Behavior Therapy*, 17, 239–52.

Noshirvani, H.F., Kasvikis, Y., Marks, I.M. and Tsakiris, F. 1991: Gender-divergent aetiological factors in obsessive–compulsive disorder. *British Journal of Psychiatry*, 158, 260–3.

Nurnberger, J.I. and Gershon, E.S. 1982: Genetics. In: E.S. Paykel (ed.), *Handbook of Affective Disorders*. New York: Guilford Press.

O'Sullivan, G. and Marks, I. 1991: Follow-up studies of behavioral treatment of phobic and obsessive compulsive neuroses. *Psychiatric Annals*, 21, 368–73.

Ohman, A. 1986: Face the beast and fear the face: animal and social fears as prototypes for evaluating analyses of emotion. *Psychophysiology*, 23, 123–45.

Ohman, A., Erixon, G. and Lofberg, I. 1975: Phobias and preparedness: phobic versus neutral pictures as conditioned stimuli for human autonomic responses. *Journal of Abnormal Psychology*, 84, 41–5.

Oliver, C. and Holland, A.J. 1986: Down's syndrome and Alzheimer's disease: a review. *Psychological Medicine*, 16, 307–22.

Oppenheimer, R., Howells, K., Palmer, R.L. and Chaloner, D.A. 1985: Adverse sexual experience in childhood and clinical eating disorders: a preliminary description. *Journal of Psychiatric Research*, 19, 357–61.

Owen, F., Cross, A.J., Crow, T.J., Longden, A., Poulter, M. and Riley, G.J. 1978: Increased dopamine receptor sensitivity in schizophrenia. *Lancet*, ii, 223–6.

Palazzoli, M.S. 1974: *Self-starvation: from the Intrapsychic to the Transpersonal Approach to Anorexia Nervosa*. London: Chaucer Books.

Palazzoli, M.S., Cirillo, S., Selvini, M. and Sorrentino, A.M. 1988: *Family Games: General Models of Psychic Processes in the Family*. London: Karnac Books.

Palfai, T. and Jankiewicz, H. 1991: *Drugs and Human Behavior*. Dubuque, IA: Wm C. Brown.

Parker, G. and Hadzi-Pavlovic, D. 1990: Expressed emotion as a predictor of schizophrenic relapse: an analysis of aggregated data. *Psychological Medicine*, 20, 961–5.

Pattie, A.H. and Gilleard, C.J. 1979: *Manual of the Clifton Assessment Procedures for the Elderly (CAPE)*. Sevenoaks: Hodder & Stoughton.

Paykel, E.S. 1974: Recent life events and clinical depression. In: E.G. Gunderson and R.H. Rahe (eds), *Life Stress and Illness*. Springfield, IL: Thomas.

Pearlson, G.D., Kirn, W.S., Kubos, K.L., Moberg, P.J., Jarayam, G., Bascom, M.J., Chase, G.A., Goldfinger, A.D. and Tune, L.A. 1989: Ventricle–brain ratio, computed tomographic density and brain area in 50 schizophrenics. *Archives of General Psychiatry*, 46, 690–7.

Peck, D.F. and Plant, M.A. 1986: Unemployment and illegal drug use: concordant evidence from a prospective study and from national trends. *British Medical Journal*, 293, 929–32.

Peniston, E.G. 1986: EMG biofeedback-assisted desensitization treatment for Vietnam combat veterans' post-traumatic stress disorder. *Clinical Biofeedback and Health*, 9, 35–41.

Perlmutter, R.A. 1990: Psychopharmacology of attachment: effects of successful agoraphobia treatment on marital relationships. *Family Systems Medicine*, 8, 279–84.

Peterson, C. and Seligman, M. 1984: Causal explanations as a risk factor for depression: theory and evidence. *Psychological Review*, 91, 347–74.

Pope, H.G. and Hudson, J.I. 1992: Is childhood sexual abuse a risk factor for bulimia nervosa? *American Journal of Psychiatry*, 149, 455–63.

Powell, J., Gray, J. and Bradley, B. 1993: Subjective craving for opiates: Evaluation of a cue exposure protocol for use with detoxified opiate addicts. *British Journal of Clinical Psychology*, 32, 39–53.

President's Panel on Mental Retardation 1972: *National Action to Combat Mental Retardation*. Washington, DC: United States Government Printing Office.

Prigatano, G.P. 1987: Personality and psychosocial consequences after brain injury. In M.J. Meier, A.L. Benton and L. Diller (eds), *Neuropsychological Rehabilitation*. Edinburgh: Churchill Livingstone.

Prochaska, J.O. and DiClemente, C. 1984: *The Transtheoretical Approach: Crossing Traditional Boundaries in Therapies*. Homewood, IL: Dow Jones/Irwin.

Pugh, G. 1981: *Parents as Partners*. London: National Children's Bureau.

Quine, L. and Pahl, J. 1985: Examining the causes of stress in families with severely mentally handicapped children. *British Journal of Social Work*, 15, 501–17.

Quinsey, V.L., Harris, G.T., Rice, M.E. and Lalumiere, M.L. 1993: Assessing the treatment efficacy in outcome studies of sex offenders. *Journal of Interpersonal Violence*, 8, 512–23.

Rabkin, J.G. 1980: Stressful life events and schizophrenia: a review of the research literature. *Psychological Bulletin*, 87, 408–25.

Rachman, S. and Hodgson, R.J. 1968: Experimentally-induced 'sexual fetishism': replication and development. *Psychological Record*, 18, 25–7.

Rachman, S.J. 1977: The conditioning theory of fear acquisition: a critical examination. *Behaviour Research and Therapy*, 15, 375–88.

Rachman, S.J. 1984: Agoraphobia: a safety-signal perspective. *Behaviour Research and Therapy*, 22, 59–70.

Rachman, S.J. 1988: Panics and their consequences: a review and prospect. In S. Rachman and J.D. Maser (eds), *Panic: Psychological Perspectives*. Hillsdale, NJ: Lawrence Erlbaum Associates.

Rachman, S.J. 1993: Obsessions, responsibility and guilt. *Behaviour Research and Therapy*, 31, 149–54.

Rachman, S.J. and Hodgson, R.J. 1980: *Obsessions and Compulsions*. Englewood Cliffs, NJ: Prentice Hall.

Rapoport, J.L. 1989: *The Boy Who Couldn't Stop Washing: the Experience and Treatment of Obsessive–compulsive Disorder*. New York: E.P. Dutton.

Rapoport, S.I., Pettigrew, K.D. and Schapiro, M.B. 1991: Discordance and concordance of dementia of the Alzheimer type (DAT) in monozygotic twins indicate heritable and sporadic forms of Alzheimer's disease. *Neurology*, 41, 1549–53.

Raps, C.S., Petersen, C., Reinhard, K.E. Abramson, L.Y. and Seligman, M.E.P. 1982: Attributional style among depressed patients. *Journal of Abnormal Psychology*, 91, 102–8.

Rau, J.H. and Green, R.S. 1975: Compulsive eating: a neuropsychologic approach to certain eating disorders. *Comprehensive Psychiatry*, 16, 223–31.

RBL 1989: *Anti-misuse of Drugs Campaign Evaluation: Report of Findings of Stages I–VII*. RS 2452. RBL.

Reveley, D.A. 1985: CT scans and schizophrenia. *British Journal of Psychiatry*, 146, 367–71.

Rholes, W.S., Riskind, J.H. and Lane, J.W. 1987: Emotional states and memory biases: Effects of cognitive priming on mood. *Journal of Personality and Social Psychology*, 52, 91–9.

Riley, A.J. 1988: Drugs and the treatment of sexual dysfunction. In M. Cole and W. Dryden (eds), *Sex Therapy in Britain*. Milton Keynes: Open University Press.

Rippere, V. and Williams, R. 1985: *Wounded Healers: Mental Health Workers' Experiences of Depression*. Chichester: Wiley.

Rist, F. and Wazl, H. 1983: Self-assessment of relapse risk and assertiveness in relation to treatment outcome of female alcoholics. *Addictive Behaviours*, 8, 121–7.

Roberts, G.W. 1991: Schizophrenia: a neuropathological perspective. *British Journal of Psychiatry*, 158, 8–17.

Robins, L., Helzer, J., Weissman, M., Ovaschel, H., Gruenberg, E., Burke, J. and Reiger, D. 1984: Lifetime prevalence of specific psychiatric disorders in three sites. *Archives of General Psychiatry*, 41, 949–58.

Robins, L.M. 1978: The interaction of setting and pre-dispositions in explaining novel behavior: drug initiations before, in and after Vietnam. In: D.B. Kandel (ed.), *Longitudinal Research in Drug Use*. New York: Halstead.

Robinson, L.A., Berman, J.S. and Neimeyer, R.A. 1989: Psychotherapy for the treatment of depression: a comprehensive review of controlled outcome research. *Psychological Bulletin*, 108, 30–49.

Roche, L. 1984: *Glutton for Punishment*. London: Pan.

Rogers, C.R. 1961: *On Becoming a Person: a Therapist's View of Psychotherapy*. Boston: Houghton Mifflin.

Rosenhan, D.L. 1973: On being sane in insane places. *Science*, 179, 250–8.

Rosenhan, D.L. 1975: The contextual nature of psychiatric diagnosis. *Journal of Abnormal Psychology*, 84, 442–52.

Rosenhan, D.L. and Seligman, M.E.P. 1989: *Abnormal Psychology*, 2nd edn. New York: Norton.

Rosenthal, D. (ed.) 1963: *The Genain Quadruplets*. New York: Basic Books.

Rosenthal, N.E., Sack, D.A., Gillin, J.C., Lewy, A.J., Goodwin, F.K., Davenport, Y., Mueller, P.S., Newsome, D.A. and Weher, T.A. 1984: Seasonal affective disorder. *Archives of General Psychiatry*, 41, 72–80.

Ross, J.L. 1977: Anorexia nervosa: an overview. *Bulletin of the Menninger Clinic*, 41, 418–36.

Ross, M.W. and Need, J.A. 1989: Effects of adequacy of gender reassignment surgery on psychological adjustment: a follow-up of fourteen male-to-female patients. *Archives of Sexual Behavior*, 18, 145–53.

Rule, S., Stowitschek, J.J., Innocenti, M. and Striefel, S. 1987: The Social Integration Program: an analysis of the effects of mainstreaming handicapped children into day care centers. *Education and Treatment of Children*, 10, 175–92.

Russell, G. 1979: Bulimia nervosa: an ominous variant of anorexia nervosa. *Psychological Medicine*, 9, 429–48.

Rutter, M., Graham, P. and Birch, H.G. 1970: *A Neuropsychiatric Study of Childhood*. Clinics in Developmental Medicine no. 35/36. London: Heinemann.

Ryan N.D. 1989: Major depression. In: C.G. Last and M. Hersen (eds), *Handbook of Child Psychiatric Diagnosis*. New York: Wiley.

Ryan, N.D., Puig-Antich, J., Ambrosini, P., Rabinovich, H., Robinson, D., Nelson, B., Iyengar, S. and Twomey, J. 1987: The clinical picture of major depression in children and adolescents. *Archives of General Psychiatry*, 44, 854–61.

Sacks, O. 1985: *The Man Who Mistook His Wife for a Hat*. London: Duckworth.

Salkovskis, P.M. 1985: Obsessional–compulsive problems: a cognitive-behavioural analysis. *Behaviour Research and Therapy*, 23, 571–83.

Sanders, D. 1985: *The Woman Book of Love and Sex*. London: Sphere.

Sanders, T. and Bazalgette, P. 1993: *You Don't Have to Diet*. London: Bantam.

Sanderson, W.C. and Barlow, D.H. 1990: A description of patients with DSM-III Revised generalized anxiety disorder. *Journal of Mental and Nervous Disease*, 178, 588–91.

Sartorius, N., Jablensky, A., Korten, A., Ernberg, G., Anker, M., Cooper, J.E. and Day, R. 1986: Early manifestations and first-contact incidence of schizophrenia in different cultures. *Psychological Medicine*, 16, 909–28.

Schleifer, S.J., Keller, S.E., Meyerson, A.T., Raskin, M.J., Davis, K.L. and Stein, M. 1984: Lymphocyte function in major depressive disorder. *Archives of General Psychiatry*, 41, 484–6.

Schmidt, U., Tiller, J. and Treasure, J. 1993: Psychosocial factors in the origins of bulimia nervosa. *International Review of Psychiatry*, 5, 51–9.

Schoenthaler, S.J., Amos, S.P., Eysenck, H.J., Peritz, E. and Yudkin, J. 1991: Controlled trial of vitamin-mineral supplementation effects on intelligence and performance. *Personality and Individual Differences*, 12, 351–62.

Schuster, C.R. and Kilbey, M.M. 1992: Prevention of drug abuse. In J.M. Last and R.B. Wallace (eds), *Public Health and Preventive Medicine*, 13th edn. Norwalk, CT: Appleton and Lange.

Schwartz, R.C., Barrett, M.J. and Saba, G. 1985: Family therapy for bulimia. In D.M. Garner and P.E. Garfinkel (eds), *Handbook of Psychotherapy for Anorexia Nervosa and Bulimia*. New York: Guilford.

Schwarz, N. and Clore, G.L. 1983: Mood, misattribution, and judgements of well-being: informative and directive function of affective states. *Journal of Personality and Social Psychology*, 45, 513–23.

Seagull, E.A.W. and Scheurer, S.L. 1986: Neglected and abused children of mentally retarded parents. *Child Abuse and Neglect*, 10, 493–500.

Seidman, L.J. 1983: Schizophrenia and brain dysfunction: an integration of recent neurodiagnostic findings. *Psychological Bulletin*, 94, 195–238.

Seligman, M.E.P. 1975: *Helplessness: On Depression, Development and Death*. San Francisco: Freeman.

Sham, P.C., Maclean, C.J. and Kendler, K. 1993: Risk of schizophrenia and age differences with older siblings: evidence of a maternal viral hypothesis? *British Journal of Psychiatry*, 163, 627–33.

Shapiro, F. 1995: *Eye Movement Desensitization and Reprocessing: Basic Principles, Protocols and Procedures*. New York: Guilford.

Sharp, C.W. and Freeman, C.P. 1993: The medical complications of anorexia nervosa. *British Journal of Psychiatry*, 162, 452–62.

Shearer, M.S. and Shearer, D.E. 1972: The Portage Project: a model for early childhood education. *Exceptional Children*, 39, 210–17.

Shedler, J. and Block, J. (1990) Adolescent drug use and psychological health: a longitudinal inquiry. *American Psychologist*, 45, 612–30.

Sher, K., Frost, R., Kushner, M., Crews, T. and Alexander, J. 1989: Memory deficits in compulsive checkers: replication and extension in a clinical sample. *Behaviour Research and Therapy*, 27, 65–9.

Sherrington, R., Brynjolfsson, J., Petersson, H., Potter, M., Dudleston, K., Barraclough, B., Wasmuth, J., Dobbs, M. and Gurling, H. 1988: Localization of a susceptibility locus for schizophrenia on chromosome 5. *Nature*, 336, 164–7.

Silver, S.M., Brooks, A. and Obenchain, J. 1995: Eye movement desensitization and reprocessing treatment of Vietnam war veterans with PTSD: comparative effects with biofeedback and relaxation training. *Journal of Traumatic Stress*, 8, 337–42.

Silverton, L. and Mednick, S. 1984: Class drift and schizophrenia. *Acta Psychiatrica Scandanavica*, 70, 304–9.

Sinason, V. 1989: Uncovering and responding to sexual abuse in psychotherapeutic settings. In H. Brown and A. Craft (eds), *Thinking the Unthinkable: Papers on Sexual Abuse and People with Learning Difficulties*. London: Family Planning Association.

Skinner, B.F. 1953: *Science and Human Behavior*. New York: Macmillan.

Slade, P. and Brodie, D. 1994: Body-image distortion and eating disorder: a reconceptualization based on recent literature. *European Eating Disorders Review*, 2, 32–46.

Smith, J. and Birchwood, M. 1987: Specific and non-specific effects of educational intervention with families living with a schizophrenic relative. *British Journal of Psychiatry*, 150, 649.

Smith, J., Birchwood, M. and Haddrell, A. 1992: Informing people with schizophrenia about their illness: the effect of residual symptoms. *Journal of Mental Health*, 1, 61–70.

Smith, M. 1986: Recent work on low level lead exposure and its impact on behavior, intelligence and learning: a review. *Journal of the American Academy of Child Psychiatry*, 24, 24–32.

Solowij, N., Hall, W. and Lee, N. 1992: A profile of 'Ecstasy' users and their experience with the drug. *British Journal of Addiction*, 87, 1161–72.

Sparrow, S.S., Balla, D.A. and Cicchetti, D.V. 1985: *The Vineland Adaptive Behavior Scale*. Circle Pines, NM: American Guidance Service.

Spitzer, R.L., Skodol, A.E., Gibbon, M. and Williams, J.B.W. 1981: *DSM Casebook*. Washington, DC: American Psychiatric Association.

Steele, C.M. and Josephs, R.A. 1990: Alcohol myopia: its prized and dangerous effects. *American Psychologist*, 45, 921–33.

Stein, J.A., Newcomb, M.D. and Bentler, P.M. 1987: An 8-year study of multiple influences on drug use and drug use consequences. *Journal of Personality and Social Psychology*, 53, 1094–105.

Sternberg, S. 1975: Memory scanning: new findings and current controversies. *Quarterly Journal of Experimental Psychology*, 27, 1–32.

Stimson, G.V., Oppenheimer, E. and Thorley, A. 1978: Seven-year follow-up of heroin addicts: drug use and outcome. *British Medical Journal*, 1, 1190–2.

Stoller, R.J. 1968: *Sex and Gender: On the Development of Masculinity and Femininity*. London: The Hogarth Press and the Institute of Psychoanalysis.

Stone, E.A. 1975: Stress and catecholamines. In A.J. Friedhoff (ed.), *Catecholamines and Behavior*. New York: Plenum.

Studd, J.W.W. and Thom, M.H. 1981: Ovarian failure and ageing. *Clinics in Endocrinology and Metabolism*, 10, 89–113.

Sullivan, P.M. and Scanlan, J.M. 1990: Psychotherapy with handicapped sexually abused children. Special issue: Sexual abuse. *Developmental Disabilities Bulletin*, 18, 21–34.

Sutton, S. 1987: Social-psychological approaches to understanding addictive behaviours: attitude–behaviour and decision-making models. *British Journal of Addiction*, 82, 355–70.

Sweeney, P.O., Anderson, K. and Bailey, S. 1986: Attributional style in depression: a meta-analytic review. *Journal of Personality and Social Psychology*, 50, 974–91.

Tallis, F. 1995: *Obsessive Compulsive Disorder: a Cognitive and Neuropsychological Perspective*. Chichester: Wiley.

Tarrier, N. and Main, C.J. 1986: Applied relaxation training for generalised anxiety and panic attacks: the efficacy of a learnt coping strategy on subjective reports. *British Journal of Psychiatry*, 149, 330–6.

Taylor, A.R., Asher, S.R. and Williams, G.A. 1987: The social adaptation of mainstreamed mildly retarded children. *Child Development*, 58, 1321–34.

Taylor, C.B. and Arnow, B. 1988: *The Nature and Treatment of Anxiety Disorders*. New York: Free Press.

Taylor, S. 1989: *Positive Illusions: Creative Self-deception and the Healthy Mind*. New York: Basic Books.

Teasdale, J.D. 1983: Negative thinking in depression: cause, effect or reciprocal relationship? *Advances in Behaviour Research and Therapy*, 5, 3–25.

Teichman, Y. and Teichman, M. 1990: Interpersonal view of depression: Review and integration. *Journal of Family Psychology*, 3, 349–67.

Tennant, C.C. 1985: Stress and schizophrenia: a review. *Integrative Psychiatry*, 3, 248–61.

Tharinger, D., Horton, C.B. and Millea, A.S. 1990: Sexual abuse and exploitation of children and adults with mental handicap and other handicaps. *Child Abuse and Neglect*, 14, 301–12.

Thompson, J.A., Charlton, P.F.C., Kerry, R., Lee, D. and Turner, S.W. 1995: An open trial of exposure therapy based on deconditioning for post-traumatic stress disorder. *British Journal of Clinical Psychology*, 34, 407–16.

Thorpe, G. and Burns, I. 1983: *The Agoraphobic Syndrome*. Chichester: Wiley.

Tienari, P., Sorri, A., Lahti, I., Naarala, M.N., Wahlberg, E., Moring, J., Pohjola, J. and Wynne, L.C. 1987: Genetic and psychosocial factors in schizophrenia: the Finnish adoptive family study. *Schizophrenia Bulletin*, 13, 477–84.

Toufexis, A. 1988: Why mothers kill their babies. *Time*, 20 June, 81–2.

Tough, S.C., Butt, J.C. and Sanders, G.L. 1994: Autoerotic asphyxial deaths: Analysis of nineteen fatalities in Alberta, 1978 to 1989. *Canadian Journal of Psychiatry*, 39, 157–60.

Trepper, T.S. and Barrett, M.J. 1989: *Systemic Treatment of Incest: a Therapeutic Handbook*. New York: Brunner/Mazel.

Trower, P. and Turland, D. 1984: Social phobia. In: S. Turner (ed.), *Behavioral Theories and Treatment of Anxieties*. New York: Plenum.

Turner, R.J. and Wagenfield, M.O. 1967: Occupational mobility and schizophrenia: an assessment of the social causation and social selection hypothesis. *American Sociological Review*, 32, 104–13.

Tyerman, A. and Humphrey, M. 1988: Personal and social rehabilitation after severe head injury. In F.N. Watts (eds), *New Developments in Clinical Psychology: Volume Two*. Chichester: BPS/Wiley.

Tyler, A., Morris, M., Lazarou, L., Meredith, L., Myring, J. and Harper, P.S. 1992: Presymptomatic testing for Huntington's disease in Wales 1987–1990. *British Journal of Psychiatry*, 161, 481–8.

Tyrer, P., Murphy, S., Oates, G. and Kingdon, D. 1984: Psychological treatment for benzodiazepine dependence. *British Medical Journal*, 288, 1101–2.

Uhde, T.W., Roy-Byrne, P.P., Vittone, B.J., Boulenger, J.P. and Post, A.M. 1985: Phenomenology and neurobiology of panic disorder. In A.H. Tuma and J.D. Maser (eds), *Anxiety and Anxiety Disorders*. Hillside, NJ: Erlbaum.

Ullman, L.P. and Krasner, L. 1975: *A Psychological Approach to Abnormal Behaviour*, 2nd edn. Englewood Cliffs, NJ: Prentice Hall.

Ussher, J.M. 1993: The construction of female sexual problems: regulating sex, regulating women. In: J.M. Ussher and C.D. Baker (eds), *Psychological*

Perspectives on Sexual Problems: New Directions in Theory and Practice. London: Routledge.

Van Bilson, H.P.J.G. 1986: Heroin addiction: morals revisited. *Journal of Substance Abuse Treatment,* 3, 279–84.

van Oppen, P. and Arntz, A. 1994: Cognitive therapy for obsessive compulsive disorder. *Behaviour Research and Therapy,* 32, 79–87.

Vaughn, C.E. and Leff, J.P. 1976: The influence of family and social factors on the course of psychiatric patients. *British Journal of Psychiatry,* 129, 125–37.

Veale, D. 1993: Classification and treatment of obsessional slowness. *British Journal of Psychiatry,* 162, 198–203.

ver Ellen, P. and van Kammen, D.P. 1990: The biological findings in post-traumatic stress disorder: a review. Special issue: Traumatic stress. New perspectives in theory, measurement, and research: II. Research findings. *Journal of Applied Social Psychology,* 20, 1789–821.

Vicari, S., Albertini, G. and Caltagirone, C. 1992: Cognitive profiles in adolescents with mental retardation. *Journal of Intellectual Disability Research,* 36, 415–23.

Waddington, J.L. 1989: Sight and insight: Brain dopamine receptor occupancy by neuroleptics visualised in living schizophrenic patients by positron emission tomography. *British Journal of Psychiatry,* 154, 433–6.

Wade, D.T., Hewer, R.L., Skilbeck, C.E. and David, R.M. 1986: *Stroke: a Critical Approach to Diagnosis, Treatment and Management.* London: Chapman & Hall.

Waller, G. 1991: Sexual abuse as a factor in eating disorders. *British Journal of Psychiatry,* 159, 664–71.

Waller, G. 1992: Sexual abuse and the severity of bulimic symptoms. *British Journal of Psychiatry,* 161, 90–3.

Warburton, D.M. 1992: Nicotine as a cognitive enhancer. *Progress in Neuro-Psychopharmacology and Biological Psychiatry,* 16, 181–91.

Wardle, J. 1994: Disorders of eating and weight: treatment. In: S.J.E. Lindsay and G.E. Powell (eds), *The Handbook of Clinical Adult Psychology.* London: Routledge.

Wardle, J. and Marsland, L. 1990: Adolescent concerns about weight and eating: a social-developmental perspective. *Journal of Psychosomatic Research,* 34, 377–91.

Warren, R. and Zgourides, G.D. 1991: *Anxiety Disorders: a Rational–Emotive Perspective.* New York: Pergamon Press.

Warrington, E.K. and Weiskrantz, L. 1972: An analysis of long-term and short-term memory defects in man. In J.A. Deutsch (ed.), *The Psychological Basis of Memory.* New York: Academic Press.

Watson, J.B. and Rayner, R. 1920: Conditioned emotional reactions. *Journal of Experimental Psychology,* 3, 1–14.

Watson, L.S. and Uzell, R. 1981: *Handbook of Behavior Modification with the Mentally Retarded.* New York: Plenum.

Watts, F. and Bennett, D.H. (eds) 1983: *Theory and Practice in Psychiatric Rehabilitation.* Chichester: Wiley.

Weatherall, D. 1983: *The New Genetics and Clinical Practice.* Oxford: Nuffield Provincial Hospitals Trust.

Weiss, J.M., Glazer, H.I. and Pohoresky, L.A. 1976: Coping behaviour and neurochemical change in rats: an alternative explanation for the original 'learned helplessness' experiments. In G. Serban and A. King (eds), *Animal Models in Human Psychobiology.* New York: Plenum.

Weiss, J.M., Stone, E.A. and Harrell, N. 1970: Coping behaviour and brain norepinephrine level in rats. *Journal of Comparative and Physiological Psychology,* 72, 153–60.

Weissman, M., Prusoff, B.A., DiMascio, A., Neu, C., Goklaney, M. and Klerman, G.L. 1979: The efficacy of drugs and psychotherapy in the treatment of acute depressive episodes. *American Journal of Psychiatry*, 136, 555–8.

Wellings, K., Field, J., Johnson, A.M. and Wadsworth, J. 1994: *Sexual Behaviour in Britain: the National Survey of Sexual Attitudes and Lifestyles.* Harmondsworth: Penguin.

Werler, M.M., Pober, B.R. and Holmes, L.B. 1985: Smoking and pregnancy. *Teratology*, 32, 473–81.

Whitman, B.Y. and Accardo, P. 1990: *When a Parent Is Mentally Retarded.* Baltimore: Paul H. Brookes.

Williams, J.M.G. 1992: *The Psychological Treatment of Depression: a Guide to the Theory and Practice of Cognitive Behaviour Therapy*, 2nd edn. London: Routledge.

Winters, K.C. and Neale, J.M. 1985: Mania and low self-esteem. *Journal of Abnormal Psychology*, 94, 282–90.

Woodman, C.L. 1993: The genetics of panic disorder and generalized anxiety disorder. *Annals of Clinical Psychiatry*, 5, 231–9.

World Health Organization 1973: *Report of the International Pilot Study of Schizophrenia: Volume 1.* Geneva: World Health Organization.

World Health Organization 1992: *Tenth Revision of the International Classification of Diseases.* Geneva: WHO.

Zarkowska, E. and Clements, J. 1988: *Problem Behaviour in People with Severe Learning Difficulties: a Practical Guide to a Constructional Approach.* London: Croom Helm.

Zeaman, D. and House, B.J. 1979: A review of attention theory. In N.R. Ellis (ed.), *Handbook of Mental Deficiency: Psychological Theory and Research.* Hillsdale, NJ: Lawrence Erlbaum Associates.

Zigler, E. and Styfco, S.J. (eds) 1989: *Head Start and Beyond: National Plan for Extended Childhood Intervention.* New Haven, CT: Yale University Press.

Zigler, E.F. and Hodapp, R.M. 1986: *Understanding Mental Retardation.* Cambridge: Cambridge University Press.

Author Index

Subject Index